THE INDIAN CHILD WELFARE ACT HANDBOOK

A Legal Guide to the Custody and Adoption of Native American Children

FOURTH EDITION

KELLY GAINES-STONER AND JACK F. TROPE

AMERICAN BAR ASSOCIATION
Family Law Section

Cover design by Mary Anne Kulchawik/ABA Design

Printed in the United States of America.

29 28 27 26 25   5 4 3 2 1

A catalog record for this book is available from the Library of Congress.

Discounts are available for books ordered in bulk. Special consideration is given to state bars, CLE programs, and other bar-related organizations. Inquire at Book Publishing, ABA Publishing, American Bar Association, 321 N. Clark Street, Chicago, Illinois 60654-7598.

www.shopABA.org

Contents

Introduction to the Fourth Edition

Since the third edition of this Indian Child Welfare Act (ICWA) handbook was published, there have been some significant legal developments. We believe these developments have significantly strengthened the ICWA and have led to an increased focus on the ICWA as an essential tool to protect Indian children, families, and tribes.

On the judicial front, the U.S. Supreme Court upheld the constitutionality of the ICWA in the case of *Haaland v. Brackeen.* While the Court did not completely close the door to future challenges, the Court's ruling clearly upheld the right of Congress to enact the ICWA and override state family law when Indian children and families are involved. One of the striking aspects of the case was the strong support from states urging the court to uphold the constitutionality of the ICWA, notwithstanding that the state of Texas was one of the plaintiffs in the case. Twenty-three states and Washington, D.C., filed an amicus curiae brief supporting the ICWA, while only two states filed a brief in support of Texas.

On the legislative front, an increasing number of states have enacted state ICWAs. As of the publication of this book, there are now 18 states that have enacted comprehensive state ICWA legislation. The purpose of these laws has been to enhance the visibility of ICWA within the state, particularly for attorneys and judges, to include provisions that are more protective than the federal standards or which clarify federal law, and to incorporate some of the federal regulations directly into statute.

During the seven years since the third edition was printed, there have also been hundreds of new cases. These are the first cases decided since the promulgation of ICWA regulations in 2016 and many state courts have had to reconsider whether their preexisting case law needs to be tweaked or reconsidered based upon the new regulatory requirements.

Hopefully, this evidence of increasing state support for and focus upon the ICWA and its requirements will translate into enhanced compliance with ICWA and better outcomes for families and children. This is vitally important, as we still see serious shortcomings in terms of the implementation of the act. Although there has been progress from the removal rates that existed prior to the enactment of the ICWA (as well as the 90 percent placement of children in non-Native homes that was occurring prior to 1978), the removal rate for Indian children is still three times that of non-Native children and a majority of children who are removed are still placed in non-Native homes. One positive development in the larger child welfare system has been an increased emphasis on placing children with relatives, including federal subsidies for relative guardianships. This is consistent with what the ICWA has always prioritized. Indeed, national child welfare organizations have called the ICWA the gold standard of child welfare that should be applied to all children. This is because the ICWA prioritizes keeping children with parents whenever possible, provides a preference with placing children with relatives when they cannot safely stay with a parent, and also emphasizes continuing contact between that child and the child's culture and community regardless of whether the child stays with his or her parents or whether a relative can be located.

It is also critical to reinforce the critical role that tribes play in making ICWA work and the unique interest that tribes have in their children and families. Studies indicate that early tribal involvement in state court proceedings increases reunification of children with their parents and shortens the time required for reunification and tribes can play a vital role in identifying extended family members and connecting children and families with culturally appropriate services and supports. Keeping children connected with their tribal communities is also vitally important for the health and well-being of those communities and consistent with the principles of tribal sovereignty, which is an essential component of the ICWA.

We urge that the ICWA's gold standard be applied consistently and vigorously, with a sense of cultural humility, and with a recognition and deep appreciation for the critical role that tribes play in making ICWA work. If this approach is followed, we believe that not only will compliance with the ICWA improve but also, most importantly, the well-being of Indian children and families will be better protected and maximized. We hope that the information in this handbook will be a tool for those seeking these vitally important outcomes.

About the Authors

Kelly Gaines-Stoner serves as TLPI's victim advocacy legal specialist. She graduated from the University of Oklahoma College of Law in 1988. Kelly has taught at the North Dakota School of Law and Oklahoma City University School of Law (OKCU), where she taught American Indian/tribal law, Indian Child Welfare Act, and domestic violence–related classes. She directed the University of North Dakota Native American Law Project, which served clients of the Spirit Lake Reservation with a caseload that targeted Indian child custody cases and domestic violence and sexual assault cases. At OKCU, Kelly directed the Native American Legal Resource Center, where she supervised law students prosecuting domestic violence, sexual assault, and stalking cases, providing representation in Indian Child Welfare Act cases and for victims of domestic violence and sexual assault in civil matters and in criminal cases regarding victims' rights. She also taught doctrinal courses in American Indian law, tribal law, and the Indian Child Welfare Act.

Kelly helped to launch Oklahoma's only tribal coalition against domestic violence, sexual assault, and stalking: the Native Alliance Against Violence. She also supervised a project in partnership with the Apache Tribe of Oklahoma that established a SAFE unit at a local hospital, recruited SANEs, and targeted community education on domestic violence and sexual assault.

Kelly currently serves as a special justice in the Mandan Hidatsa and Arikara Supreme Court. In 2011, Kelly was appointed as a judge for the Seminole Nation of Oklahoma and served in that position for eight years. Kelly has testified before the U.S. Indian Affairs Committee regarding victimization issues in Indian country. She is a frequent lecturer and commission member for the American Bar Association's Commission on Domestic Violence and for the Office on Violence Against Women's national technical assistance providers on domestic violence issues in Indian country.

Jack F. Trope is currently an independent legal consultant working primarily with tribes and Indian organizations. He also serves as an associate justice on the High Court of the Upper Mattaponi Tribe. He formerly worked as a senior director for Public Policy and National Partnerships in the Indian Child Welfare Program at Casey Family Programs. In this role, he focused upon national, state, tribal, and local initiatives aimed at promoting compliance with the Indian Child Welfare Act, increasing tribal access to the Title IV-E Foster Care and Adoption Assistance Program and the Family First Prevention Services Act, and improving child welfare outcomes for children and families in state and tribal systems through training and systems improvement. Previously, Jack served as the executive director of the Association on American Indian Affairs (AAIA) for more than 13 years (and as staff attorney earlier in his career), where he worked on a variety of legal and policy matters, with a heavy emphasis on issues related to youth and the protection and preservation of Native American Indian tribal cultures, particularly the protection of sacred places and the repatriation of human remains and cultural items to Indian tribes. He has also served as director of the Albuquerque-based Western Area Office for the Save the Children Federation, was a partner with the law firm of Sant'Angelo & Trope, an assistant counsel to two New

Jersey governors, and clerked for a New Jersey Supreme Court Justice. He is a graduate of Rutgers College and Harvard Law School. Jack has worked on Indian child welfare matters since 1985, including litigation; amicus briefs in a number of cases including ICWA cases decided by the United States Supreme Court; training for tribal, state, and local judges, attorneys, social workers, and government leaders; and advocacy involving both the legislative and executive branches of government. He has also written extensively about child welfare issues pertaining to Indian children and families over the years, addressing issues such as ICWA and tribal access to Title IV-E.

Acknowledgments

We would like to thank and recognize Judge B.J. Jones who was the sole author of the first edition of The Indian Child Welfare Act Handbook and primary author of the second edition and Mark Tilden who was a co-author of the second and third editions of this book. This fourth edition of the book builds upon Judge Jones's groundbreaking work in the first two editions, and even more than 25 years after the first edition was printed, many of his observations remain cogent and relevant and are included in this edition almost verbatim. Similarly, much of what Mark contributed is still a critical part of this fourth edition. We hope that our effort has risen to the standards that they set.

We would also like to thank Jeffrey Salyards and his colleagues working under the auspices of the American Bar Association for their support and Hannah Ditzenberger of the National Council of State Legislatures for preparing the list of state laws pertaining to Indian children and families and permitting us to include this information in Appendix D. Likewise, we want to thank the Native American Rights Fund for allowing us to use their draft pleadings, which have also been included in Appendix F. Finally, and most importantly, we want to thank all of those who work every day to implement the letter and spirit of the ICWA to protect and enhance the well-being of Indian children and families, and the integrity of tribal nations and communities.

The Indian Child Welfare Act and Its Foundations

1

Let us put our minds together and see what kind of life we can build for our children.
—Sitting Bull, Hunkpapa Sioux[1]

In 1978 the U.S. Congress heeded the call of the great Lakota leader Sitting Bull by passing the Indian Child Welfare Act of 1978, Public Law No. 95-608, 92 Stat. 3069 (Nov. 8, 1978), commonly known as the ICWA (text set out in Appendix A of this handbook). Codified at 25 U.S.C. §§ 1901–1963, the law has had a substantial impact on the practices and procedures of state juvenile courts, state social services agencies, and private adoption agencies in this country.[2] The goal of the law was to change the practices of state entities that had tended to remove an inordinately large number of Native American[3] children from their homes without a full appreciation of traditional Native American child-rearing practices.[4]

The ICWA states its purpose as follows:

> The Congress hereby declares that it is the policy of this Nation to protect the best interest of Indian children and to promote the stability and security of Indian tribes and families by the establishment of minimum federal standards for the removal of Indian children from their families and the placement of such children in foster or adoptive homes which will reflect the unique values of Indian culture, and by providing for assistance to Indian tribes in the operation of child and family programs.[5]

Displacement of Indian Children

State Involvement

Before 1978, Congress noted that the wholesale removal of Native American children from their families and tribes by state social services agencies and courts was common.[6] Surveys by the Association on American Indian Affairs found that in states with large Native American populations an incredible 25 to 35 percent of all Native American children had been removed from their homes and placed in foster or adoptive homes at one time in their lives.[7] In Minnesota, for example, one of every four Native American children under the age of one was adopted, usually by a non-Native American family.[8] In South Dakota, the number of Native American children in foster care was, per capita, 16 times greater than the rate for other children.[9] In Washington, the adoption rate for Native American children was 19 times greater than the rate for other children.[10] What makes these statistics even more sobering is that in many of these states the overwhelming majority of Native Americans resided on reservations where ostensibly the state courts and welfare agencies had no authority to order the removal of Native American children.

Federal Involvement

The displacement of Indian children was even more of a national outrage because of the federal government's complicity in carrying out the destruction of Native American families. A recent Department of Interior investigative report found that between 1819 and 1969, the federal government funded 417 boarding school institutions across 37 states or territories and 973 children died while attending these schools.[11] Attendance at these schools was sometimes coerced, and in many of these boarding schools, children were punished for speaking their Native languages or practicing their religious beliefs.[12] In others, children were sent so far away from their birth communities that contact between them and their families was impractical.[13]

Grounds for Removal

Native American children were rarely removed because of physical abuse; instead, their families were routinely judged unfit by non-Native American social workers and judges because of alleged neglect or emotional mistreatment.[14] A common ground for removal was that the natural parent had left the child with an extended relative for a prolonged period of time.[15] To the non-Native American social worker ignorant of the traditional ways of child-rearing such behavior was unacceptable under Euro-American traditions.[16] To Native American families, however, such methods of raising children were common, because the notion of extended family included not only those in the nuclear family and blood relations but also those related by marriage or by some other traditional bond.[17]

Another commonly cited ground for removal was the abuse of alcohol.[18] Although alcoholism was, and remains, a problem among Native American families, studies demonstrated that the number of Native American children removed from their homes because of this malady was disproportionate compared to other families afflicted by the disease.[19]

Removal Without Due Process

Compounding the removal problem, in many states Native American children were taken from their families without a modicum of due process.[20] Many of the children were removed from families dependent on the federal and state governments for financial support.[21] Congress documented instances of state welfare agencies pressuring Native American families into signing away custody of their children to the state under threat of the termination of welfare benefits.[22] State welfare departments often controlled the everyday lives of Native American people, and endearing oneself to non-Native American social workers was critical to financial survival.[23]

The process provided in state courts was no more beneficial than the practices of state social services agencies. In most states, parents were provided with neither counsel nor interpreters, even if they spoke only their Native tongues; instead, parents relied on the same social workers who were seeking to displace the children.[24] Non-Native American social workers, ignorant of the ways and traditions of the very people they worked with, were the "experts" who advised the courts that the abject poverty many Native American families struggled to confront prevented the families from properly parenting their children.[25] Courts rarely received the expert testimony of Native people who could familiarize state judges with traditional child-rearing practices.[26] The result was often the judicial countenance of abusive practices of state welfare agencies.[27] As stated at 25 U.S.C. § 1901(5), Congress specifically found that "the States, exercising their recognized jurisdiction over Indian child custody proceedings through administrative and judicial bodies, have often failed to recognize the essential tribal relations of Indian people and the cultural and social standards prevailing in Indian communities and families."[28]

Placement of Indian Children Away from Their Families and Communities and Outside of Their Cultures

In addition to the flawed process by which Native American children were dislodged from their homes, the fate of the children after removal gave Congress pause.[29] In 1969, a survey of 16 states revealed that approximately 85 percent of Native American children in foster homes were living in non-Native homes.[30] Some 90 percent of nonrelative adoptions of Native children involved non-Native Americans adopting Native children.[31] This led to the alienation of many Native American children from their unique cultural values and mores, a trend that would have continued unabated without intervention by Congress. Psychological and sociological studies have suggested that Native American children brought up in non-Native homes often suffer from a variety of adjustment disorders once they discover their unique ancestral and cultural identity.[32] These children have a foothold in the dominant society's world, but eventually long to discover their Indigenous roots.[33] This longing can result in maladaptive behavior by them, contributing little to either the dominant society or the Native traditions.[34]

Federal Policy Behind ICWA

By 1978, preserving the unique nature of Native traditions and values was more important to Congress than promoting the assimilation of Native people into the dominant Euro-American culture.[35] Although this congressional objective has been subject to unpredictable shifts since the turn of the century,[36] an understanding of it as a motivation behind the ICWA is key to understanding certain provisions of the act. Congress clearly felt that maintaining Native American children in homes that reflect the children's unique Native cultures and values would be in their "best interest."[37]

During the same period the ICWA was enacted, the federal government was promoting Native American self-determination through a series of legislative enactments, including the ICWA.[38] At one of the hearings that led to the enactment of the ICWA, Chief Calvin Isaac of the Mississippi Band of Choctaw Indians and representative of the National Tribal Chairmen's Association spoke of the destructive effect of the "massive removal of their children" on tribal survival and tribal sovereignty.

> Culturally, the chances of Indian survival are significantly reduced if our children, the only real means for the transmission of the tribal heritage, are to be raised in non-Indian homes and denied exposure to the ways of their People. Furthermore, these practices seriously undercut the tribes' ability to continue as self-governing communities. Probably in no area is it more important that tribal sovereignty be respected than in an area as socially and culturally determinative as family relationships.[39]

Although concerns about involuntary removals by state agencies were a major impetus for the ICWA, it is clear that "voluntary" adoptions of Indian children were likewise of concern to Congress based upon the evidence it considered. Congress recognized that children could be lost through this mechanism, and that there was a great demand for Indian children for adoption and evidence that adoption agencies only rarely utilized Indian families for placement.[40]

Overview of Provisions of the ICWA

There are both procedural and substantive provisions of the ICWA. Both are designed to accomplish three primary objectives: (1) to eliminate the need to remove Indian children from their families, both nuclear and extended, particularly when based upon cultural bias and ignorance, and to provide services to keep them together whenever possible; (2) to ensure that Indian children that need to be removed for their own protection are placed with their extended families, or alternatively in foster and adoptive homes that reflect their unique cultures and backgrounds; and (3) to encourage tribal court adjudication of child custody proceedings involving Indian children.

The ICWA applies to state court "child custody proceedings" involving "Indian children."[41] A child custody proceeding under the ICWA is defined as a foster care placement, termination of parental rights proceeding, preadoptive placement, or adoptive placement of an Indian child.[42] The ICWA does not apply to custody disputes between parents if custody is to be awarded to one of the parents, either as part of a divorce or nondivorce proceeding, nor does it apply to delinquency proceedings involving Indian children who commit acts that would be criminal if committed by an adult.[43] It is important to note that the child custody proceeding need not involve some state action, such as the removal of an Indian child by a state or county child protection entity, in order for the ICWA to apply.[44] The ICWA applies to private placements and adoptions as well as those initiated by state and county agencies.[45]

An "Indian child" is defined under the federal law as an unmarried child under 18 who is a member of a federally recognized Indian tribe or is eligible for membership in a federally recognized tribe and the biological child of a member of an Indian tribe.[46] The ICWA recognizes the inherent sovereign right of Indian tribes to determine their own membership and a state court must defer to a tribal determination of membership.[47] In any child custody proceeding in state court where a party believes or has reason to know that the child involved is an Indian child, there is an affirmative obligation on the part of all parties, and their attorneys, to report such to the court so that notice may be given to the Indian child's tribe.[48] A few states have carved out an exception to application of the act to certain Indian children, commonly referred to as the

Existing Indian Family Exception, and held that the act's purposes to prevent the breakup of Indian families are not met by applying the act to an otherwise qualified Indian child who has not lived with an Indian family or with an Indian family with few or no ties to an Indian tribe.[49] The language of the act does not support such an exception, U.S. Supreme Court cases have at least implicitly rejected such a limitation, and the ICWA regulations reject this interpretation of the ICWA.[50] Most states rejected this limitation even before the regulations were issued,[51] and in other instances state legislatures have taken action to repeal the judicially created exception.[52]

The procedural requirements of the ICWA are contained generally at 25 U.S.C. §§ 1911 and 1912. Section 1911 distinguishes between the jurisdiction of state and tribal courts in child custody proceedings involving Indian children.[53] The exclusive jurisdiction of Indian tribal courts over child custody proceedings involving Indian children resident or domiciled on Indian reservations is recognized, as is exclusive jurisdiction over children who are wards of tribal courts.[54] This rule applies in all states, except to the extent that Pub. Law 83-280 (P.L. 280) has been interpreted to provide states with concurrent jurisdiction along with tribal courts over child custody proceedings involving Indian children resident or domiciled on an Indian reservation.[55] For Indian children domiciled off reservations, state courts can exercise jurisdiction over child custody proceedings, but the exercise of that jurisdiction is subject to a transfer of jurisdiction to the tribal court of the Indian child's tribe.[56] In general, the ICWA favors a transfer of jurisdiction of a child custody proceeding involving an Indian child to a tribal court unless certain findings are made by the state court judge.[57] The parent of an Indian child can always veto a transfer to a tribal court and the tribal court can decline a transfer of jurisdiction to its court.[58] Although tribal jurisdiction is preferred, it is not unusual for an Indian tribe to not transfer jurisdiction over the majority of child custody proceedings involving its children, often because the tribe lacks the resources to provide for its children that state and county agencies can access.[59]

Notice is a vital component of the ICWA. The act requires any party to an involuntary child custody proceeding involving an Indian child to give notice to the child's parents, Indian custodian (if one exists), and to the Indian child's tribe of the commencement of the proceeding.[60] Notice is triggered when a court or agency has reason to know that a child is an Indian child and any tribe with possible affiliation must be given notice.[61] There is a division of opinion between courts as to whether failure to serve proper notice is a jurisdictional defect that spoils the proceedings.[62] In many cases, more than one tribe must be given notice because of differing or uncertain tribal affiliations among the parents.[63] If a party cannot determine with which tribe the child is affiliated, notice may be given to the Bureau of Indian Affairs (BIA), which is then charged with the responsibility to help identify relevant tribes.[64]

Other procedural requirements of the ICWA govern the weight of the evidence and type of evidence necessary to sustain an involuntary foster care placement or involuntary termination of parental rights.[65] In order to achieve an involuntary placement of an Indian child outside of his or her home, the party seeking removal must establish by clear and convincing evidence, supported by the testimony of a qualified expert witness, that the child would suffer severe emotional or physical harm if left in the child's home.[66] The moving party must also establish that active remedial and rehabilitative services were offered to the family in an attempt to avoid removal.[67] To sustain a termination of parental rights, the court must find beyond a reasonable doubt that the child would suffer severe emotional or physical harm.[68] The requirement that a qualified expert witness's testimony support removal or termination is an attempt by Congress to ensure that a person with specific knowledge of Indian child-rearing practices testifies to the cultural propriety of removal or termination.[69] The need to demonstrate that active remedial and rehabilitative services are provided to Indian families is similar to the reasonable efforts requirement found elsewhere in federal law,[70] although most courts have concluded that the active efforts requirement places a stronger obligation upon agencies than the reasonable efforts requirement.[71] In that regard, the recently adopted regulations include requirements that appear to exceed the reasonable efforts requirement[72] and, unlike the reasonable efforts requirement in general federal child welfare law, the ICWA does not include an aggravated circumstances exception.[73]

Indian parents and custodians are also entitled to the appointment of counsel in ICWA cases.[74] If a state would otherwise not appoint counsel in a particular matter, but does so because of the mandate of the ICWA, that state can apply to the BIA for reimbursement for the expenses of court-appointed counsel.[75]

The ICWA recognizes that Indian tribes have unique rights that must be preserved in litigation regarding the placement of their children.[76] To protect these rights, the act explicitly gives an Indian tribe the right to intervene at any stage of a foster care or termination of parental proceeding and also vests in the tribe the right to request a transfer of the proceeding to a tribal court.[77] Tribes are also given additional time to prepare for litigation after notice is provided and they also have a fairly unlimited right of discovery in ICWA cases.[78] Lastly, Indian tribes are given an independent right to discover the placement location of their tribal members and are also given the right to collaterally challenge actions taken by state courts and entities in violation of the ICWA.[79]

Some of the most important substantive provisions of the ICWA are found in the placement preference provisions contained at 25 U.S.C. § 1915. These provisions are designed to ensure that Indian children who are removed from their homes are placed with their relatives and, if that is not possible, then they should be placed in homes that reflect their unique cultures.[80] There are separate placement preference provisions governing foster care and adoptive placement preferences.[81] Both recognize that Indian tribes should have the right to alter the placement preferences by enacting their own preferences for placement of their children.[82] Absent that, state courts are directed in the case of foster care to place Indian children first with their extended families (which in the case of a child of both Indian and non-Indian parents would include the non-Indian family members), second with a home licensed by the tribe, third with an Indian foster home approved by a nontribal agency, and fourth with a tribally operated or approved facility.[83] The child must also be placed within reasonable proximity to his or her home, taking into account the child's special needs.[84] In the case of adoption, the first placement preference is again extended family, followed by members of the child's tribe and other Indian families.[85] Only when good cause is present should a child be placed outside of the preferences.[86] Despite this mandate of the ICWA, many Indian children continue to be placed with non-Indian foster and adoptive families, partially due to the failure of some states to recruit sufficient Indian foster and adoptive families.[87]

Post-ICWA Legislative and Regulatory Developments

Congressional Activity

Although Congress has never seen fit to amend the language of the ICWA since its passage in 1978, there have been unsuccessful efforts to amend the ICWA. In 1988, Senator Dan Evans (D-WA) introduced a bill that would have addressed some of the court decisions that interpreted the ICWA in a manner that supporters of the ICWA believed were contrary to the legislative intent.[88] In 1995, Representative Deborah Pryce (R-OH), in response to a California case involving an Ohio couple seeking to adopt Indian twins,[89] sought to amend the ICWA to exclude any Indian child, member or not, whose parents did not have sufficient political, cultural, or economic ties to the tribe.[90] The bill passed the House of Representatives after a contentious battle on the House floor,[91] which then gave rise to an alternative consensus bill developed by tribal leaders and adoption attorneys that was sponsored by Senator John McCain (R-AZ). That bill would have, inter alia, amended the act to impose deadlines for tribes to intervene and object to voluntary adoption proceedings, while at the same time vesting tribes with the explicit right to notice in voluntary proceedings.[92] The McCain bill passed the Senate[93] and neither bill was ultimately enacted. For a number of years thereafter, the last time in 2003, bills similar to the McCain bill were introduced, the most recent iterations by Representative Don Young (R-AK).[94] None of those bills moved out of committee.

There have been only two legislative enactments specifically mentioning the ICWA since it was enacted (excluding appropriations bills that have included ICWA grants authorized by Title II of the ICWA). Title IV-B of the Social Security Act, which provides child welfare funding to states and tribes, was amended in 1994 to require state Title IV-B plans that are reviewed by the Department of Health and Human Services (HHS) "to contain a description, developed after consultation with tribal organizations (as defined in section 5304 of title 25) in the State, of the specific measures taken by the State to comply with the ICWA [25 U.S.C. 1901 et seq.]," a requirement that was expanded by recent 2024 amendments.[95] In addition, the 118th Congress recently enacted legislation to strengthen the role of HHS in terms of the implementation of ICWA by state agencies.[96] This new law requires HHS to collect data from states regarding cases where ICWA is applied and to provide technical assistance (with guidance from the BIA) to states and tribes implementing ICWA.[97]

Finally, it is worth mentioning that in 2005, after conducting a two-year study at the request of House Majority Leader Tom DeLay of Texas, the U.S. Government Accountability Office (GAO) issued a report concerning the implementation of the ICWA in the states. The GAO report examined (1) the factors that influence placement decisions for Indian children; (2) the extent to which delays, if any, have occurred in the foster or adoptive placement of children subject to the ICWA due to issues related to the implementation of the ICWA and how any such delays have affected children's experiences in care; and (3) the federal government's role in overseeing implementation of ICWA by the states.[98] The GAO surveyed child welfare officials in all 50 states and the District of Columbia regarding their implementation of the ICWA and their views on the ICWA's provisions.[99]

The GAO found that data collected from four states that could identify children subject to the ICWA showed "no consistent differences when comparing the length of time they spent in foster care compared to Caucasian or other minority children who exited foster care."[100] It also found, inter alia, that information received by the Administration for Children and Families (ACF) from its Child and Family Services Reviews (CFSRs) supplied insufficient and sporadic information on ICWA implementation efforts within the states. In ten out of 51 child and family service review reports, mostly from states without significant populations of Native Americans, there was no discussion of ICWA implementation within the state.[101] Further, the GAO found that many state welfare agencies expressed concerns that its agents did not have adequate training or guidance in implementing the ICWA's provisions. In its final significant finding, 32 states had concerns with regard to ICWA implementation within their states.[102] The report recommended, first, that the Secretary of HHS direct the ACF to review ICWA implementation information from its CFSRs and require states to incorporate improvements on ICWA implementation in their program improvement plans, and, second, that ACF use the information on ICWA implementation to "target guidance and assistance to states in addressing any identified issues."[103] These recommendations were addressed, in part, in the law recently passed in 2024.

Executive Branch Activity

Shortly after the enactment of the ICWA, the U.S. Department of the Interior issued regulations pertaining to notice in involuntary proceedings, payment for appointed counsel, and ICWA grants.[104] It also issued guidelines in 1979 addressing how certain provisions of the act should be interpreted and implemented.[105] The guidelines were nonbinding and advisory.[106]

In February 2015, the Department of the Interior issued a revised set of guidelines.[107] Its stated purpose was to promote uniformity of the law and to address interpretative and implementation issues that had arisen during the 35 years since the original guidelines were issued.[108] The guidelines were much more comprehensive than the 1979 guidelines.[109] These guidelines have since been superseded by another set of guidelines issued in December 2016 that are tied to new regulations promulgated by the Department of the Interior.[110]

Over the years, courts have often cited the guidelines to support their decisions on certain issues,[111] but courts have also occasionally rejected the guidelines on a given issue finding that they were not binding and contrary to that court's interpretation of the law.[112]

In June 2016, the department took the most significant action in terms of compliance with and interpretation of the ICWA by issuing binding regulations that took effect on December 12, 2016 for any proceedings commenced after that date, including any subsequent proceedings (but not pending proceedings) in existing cases involving the custody or placement of an Indian child.[113] The regulations are based upon the authorization in the ICWA for the Secretary to "promulgate such rules and regulations as may be necessary to carry out the provisions of the Act."[114] We have incorporated the requirements of the regulations into our analysis of the ICWA.

Another significant executive branch activity involved HHS. In 2016, HHS revised the requirements for the Adoption and Foster Care Analysis and Reporting System (AFCARS), data that must be submitted by all states and tribes that operate Title IV-E, to include a number of data elements specific to the requirements of the ICWA and the new ICWA regulations, including information about whether the state had reason to know the child is Indian, the child was determined to be a member or eligible for membership in an Indian tribe, the ICWA was applied, the Indian tribe was notified, the case was transferred to tribal court, active efforts to prevent the breakup of the family took place, ICWA standards of proof for a foster care placement or termination of parental rights were applied, and the placement preferences were followed.[115] In 2020, this requirement was modified to eliminate some of the data elements included in the 2016 rule, although more ICWA-related data elements were included in that rule as compared to the pre-2016 rules;[116] but in 2024 requirements similar to the 2016 requirements were approved.[117] The 2024 changes will not need to be implemented until October 1, 2028.[118]

"Best Interest" of Indian Children

A significant reason that the ICWA exists is because it is in the best interest of tribal children to be raised by their families and extended families, whenever possible, and to be strongly connected to their tribal communities and cultures. These principles have been recognized as the "gold standard" of child welfare practice by national child welfare organizations that should be applied to all children.[119]

The Department of Interior recognized these principles in the commentary to the new regulations. It noted that it

> finds compelling the views of child-welfare specialists who opine that "the cornerstone of an effective child-welfare system is the presumption that children are best served by supporting and encouraging their relationship with fit birth parents who are interested in raising them and are able to do so safely . . . [a]mong the most important components of a sound child-welfare system is the requirement for agencies responsible for children's well-being to be vigilant in striving to keep children in their families; to remove them only when necessary to protect them from serious harm; and to work diligently to assist families with overcoming obstacles to children's safe return."[120]

In fact, there have been many recent studies documenting the trauma of removing children from their parents unnecessarily.[121]

Similarly, in terms of the preferred placement of children with relatives when a parent is unable to care for a child, the department quoted national standards and research supporting the conclusion that for all children, "[a]n appropriate relative who is willing to provide care is almost always a preferable caretaker to a nonrelative."[122] In fact, federal child welfare law pertaining to all children has now adopted this concept.[123] Research has shown that kinship care placements are more stable than placements in non-kin care and result in fewer behavioral problems and mental health disorders and better child well-being.[124]

Finally, the department also noted that seeking placements within a child's community is also a principle applicable to all children.[125] Community placements help to provide some stability to a child that has been removed from parents and can keep the child connected to a network of caring adults.[126]

Thus, the principles that are central to the ICWA are not only mainstream but broadly supported by the child welfare community and the underlying research.

Despite this recognition of the universal applicability of ICWA concepts, these policy objectives have sometimes clashed with the theory of the "best interest of the child" that has often been utilized by social workers and courts alike. The genesis for this divergent idea of best interest is most popularly derived from a work by Joseph Goldstein, Anna Freud, and Albert J. Solnit in their often-cited book *Beyond the Best Interest of the Child*. The theory emphasizes the importance of a child's psychological bonding with at least one adult who is perceived by that child as his or her psychological parent.[127] The book essentially speaks of the need for a psychological parent in universal terms—not acknowledging in general the importance of ties with the biological family and the child's culture and community. More specifically, the book does not address the cultural diversity of the American population and the essential extended family and tribal relations of Native American people.

Indeed, attachment theory (which is the underlying basis for the bonding/attachment criteria used by courts) is based squarely on Euro-American cultural norms. The viability of its application outside that context, particularly in the context of Indigenous cultures, has been questioned by a number of researchers and social scientists.[128] The regulations reflect these ideas, in part, by providing that good cause may not be based "solely on ordinary bonding or attachment that flowed from time spent in a non-preferred placement made in violation of ICWA,"[129] and noting in the commentary to the regulations that "concepts of bonding and attachment can have serious limitations in court determinations . . . are based on Western or Euro-American cultural norms and may have little application outside that context."[130] Nonetheless, the potential for conflict between the psychological parent theory and the

ICWA has created consternation in certain state courts where the goals of the ICWA have been perceived as counterproductive to promoting the best interest of the child.[131]

In addition to being based upon sound child welfare principles, however, the ICWA is also a realization that Native Americans have unique practices and traditions regarding child-rearing that are not susceptible to judgment using a non-Indian barometer. Although generalizations are difficult because of the diversity of Native people who flourished in North America before the arrival of Europeans, there seem to be certain characteristics shared by most North American tribes.

First, Native Americans were tribal people whose existence as individuals depended on the survival of the "whole" to which they belonged.[132] This type of holistic thinking was impressed upon Indian children at an early stage, both through the social structure[133] and through the oral storytelling tradition.[134] Indian children were raised by their families within the context of a larger clan, often related either by blood or marriage, whose responsibilities extended to all children in the clan and not just lineal descendants. In many tribal cultures, family extends to grandparents, siblings, aunts and uncles, and even to elders, clan members, significant friends, and the broader community. Although many children were raised outside of the nuclear family, it was the ultimate loss for a child to be cast out of the collective group.[135] Thus, if a parent or set of parents is not able to properly care for a child, it is usually believed that removing the child to a place outside the family or tribal community will do more harm than good because it alienates the child from his or her culture. From a tribal perspective, if parents need to be removed from their parenting roles, the preferred alternative is to allow the broader network of family and community to care for and raise the child in a safe and culturally rich way.

Second, within the collective group, children were taught unwritten rules regarding their relations with almost everyone in the group. These rules were not enforced through corporal punishment but instead through storytelling sometimes involving animals and the earth.[136] To many Native Americans, both the animals and the earth were larger models of their own existence, and the habits of animals were often used as models for human behavior.

This knowledge of the role people played in social order was passed along to future generations primarily through the oral storytelling tradition, and not through any formal educational process. Thus, the removal of a child from the tribe or clan severely curtailed that child's ability to foster an understanding of appropriate roles and behavior within his or her respective tribal culture.

For these reasons, there has been considerable misunderstanding in the non-Indian community of Indian child-rearing practices. It is not uncommon for a grandparent[137] to raise an Indian child even when the natural parents are quite fit to do so. Such a practice is not an indication of parental neglect but, rather, a fulfillment of the grandparents' obligation to the extended family, which, if defied, may result in a rift in the extended family.

Congress did not adopt the standard espoused in *Beyond the Best Interest of the Child* when it enacted the ICWA. Indeed, that standard is not consistent with how child welfare experts view the best interests of all children today. Thus, as the legislative history professes and as stated explicitly in the guidelines, proper implementation of the act itself serves the best interest of the Native American child.[138] In this way, Congress believed that the act would best protect Indian children and families and eliminate the many subjective applications of the best interest standard to Native American children that had led to the perilous situation that existed before 1978.[139]

Indian Law as a Foundation for the ICWA

Under what authority did Congress intervene in this area of law traditionally left to the states? An examination of the answer requires some historical background on the area of Indian law.

Indian tribes are sovereign entities whose existences predate the ratification of the U.S. Constitution.[140] The Supreme Court long ago recognized tribes as "domestic dependent nations" with a unique relationship to the federal government.[141] The sovereignty of Indian tribes is subject to the paramount authority of the federal government over the affairs of tribes.[142] However, the federal government can exercise that paramount, or plenary, authority only if the exercise of that authority is consistent with certain obligations the government has toward Indian tribes.[143]

Those obligations, characterized by the Supreme Court as the obligations a guardian has toward a ward, have often been referred to as a trust responsibility.[144] That responsibility has been described as the duty of one nation toward "a nation claiming and receiving the protection of one more powerful, not that of individuals abandoning their national character and submitting as subjects to the laws of a master."[145] The obligations of the United States toward Indian tribes are primarily borne out of treaties entered into by the parties, as well as federal laws enacted for the benefit of Indian tribes.[146]

This relationship between Indian tribes and the federal government is a "political" relationship between two nations, not a relationship based on the racial classification of Native Americans. The Supreme Court has recognized that Congress can treat Native Americans differently from other racially distinct groups and not run afoul of traditional equal protection notions because of the unique relationship between the tribes and the government.[147]

Congress has the exclusive authority to regulate the affairs of Indian tribes through the provision in the U.S. Constitution (the Indian Commerce Clause) that grants the federal government the exclusive authority to regulate "commerce with Indian tribes."[148] This grant of authority is broad and expansive and is generally limited only by the constraints of the Bill of Rights. One product of this broad grant of authority to Congress is that, as a general principle, states are preempted from exercising any authority over Indian tribes if that exercise of authority clashes with federal authority, although state actions in furtherance of the trust relationship (as opposed to actions seeking to limit tribal sovereignty) have been upheld.[149]

Indian nations have long been recognized as retaining the inherent authority to regulate domestic relations among their members.[150] Even before the enactment of ICWA, the courts had acknowledged that Indian tribes had the power to regulate marriage among tribal members,[151] adoption of Native American children,[152] divorce and property distribution among Native Americans,[153] and the rights and privileges of children.[154] In many ways, therefore, the ICWA is simply a realization and codification of the legal landscape that existed before its passage. The ICWA reaffirms the continuing authority of Indian tribes over their members who reside within reservation boundaries.

In other ways, however, ICWA represents an extension of congressional authority to enact remedial legislation for Native American people. Before the ICWA, it was a generally recognized tenet of the law that once a Native American ventured off a reservation and into state territory his or her actions would be governed by state law,[155] although there have been prior exceptions.[156] This was especially true in the area of domestic relations, an area traditionally governed by the police powers of the state.[157]

Finally, it is worth noting that evolving international law supports the emphasis on the importance of the connection between Indigenous tribal communities and their children that is incorporated in the ICWA. In particular, both the United Nations Declaration on the Rights of Indigenous Peoples (UNDRIP)[158] and the American Declaration on the Rights of Indigenous Peoples (OAS American Declaration)[159] have provisions that apply to areas covered by the ICWA.

The UNDRIP recognizes the shared responsibilities of Indigenous families and communities for the upbringing, training, education, and well-being of their children and that Indigenous peoples have the right to belong to an Indigenous community or nation, and strongly proscribes the forcible removal of the children of an Indigenous group to another group.[160] The OAS American Declaration provides that "indigenous people have the right to preserve, maintain and promote their own family systems"; requires states to "recognize, respect, and protect" Indigenous forms of family (particularly extended family); and particularly notes that in considering the best interests of children "in matters related to custody, adoption [and] severance of family ties," the right of the child to enjoy his or her own culture, religion, and language must be taken into account and that in so doing states must "look to the indigenous laws of the peoples concerned and shall consider their points of view, rights and interests. . . ."[161]

United States Supreme Court Cases

In the almost 40 years since the ICWA was enacted, the U.S. Supreme Court has accepted three ICWA cases. These cases have been important in shaping state court decisions interpreting the

ICWA and the regulations implementing the ICWA, as well as confirming the authority of Congress to enact ICWA under the Constitution.

In 1988, the Court decided *Mississippi Band of Choctaw Indians v. Holyfield*.[162] The case involved an attempted adoption in state court of twins born off of the reservation to parents whose permanent residence was on the Choctaw reservation. The Court held that the tribal court had exclusive jurisdiction over the adoption based upon the provision in the ICWA (which was consistent with pre-ICWA case law) recognizing exclusive tribal jurisdiction over children resident or domiciled on the reservation.[163] In so doing, it rejected the state court's unusual interpretation of the concept of domicile and the stated desire of the parents to place their children for adoption in state court and instead adopted a federal law definition based upon generally understood principles of domicile as established by federal and state courts.[164]

Its explanation for this holding has provided the legal underpinning for many subsequent state court ICWA decisions and the regulations. The key elements were as follows:

- The ICWA was based on the perception of Congress that states were partly responsible for the problems that the ICWA sought to address and thus Congress intended to "curtail state authority."[165]
- Congress intended "a uniform federal law of domicile for the ICWA."[166]
- The ICWA's provisions are designed to protect not only the interests of individual Indian children and families but also of the tribes themselves, and the tribe "has an interest in the child which is distinct from but on a parity with the interest of the parents."[167]

- "Congress' concern over the placement of Indian children in non-Indian homes was based in part on evidence of the detrimental impact on the children of . . . placements outside their culture" and that Congress subjected such placements to the ICWA even in the case of voluntary adoptions "because of concerns going beyond the wishes of individual parents."[168]

In 2013, the Court decided *Adoptive Couple v. Baby Girl.*[169] The case involved an attempted adoption of a Cherokee girl by non-Indians over the objection of the Cherokee father. The Court held that because the father had never had either legal or physical custody of the child prior to the adoption proceeding, the termination of parental rights provision in § 1912 of the ICWA did not apply to him.[170] In addition, because of his lack of prior custody and a conclusion by the court that he had abandoned his child (father had no contact with his daughter during the first four months of her life), the requirement in the law that active efforts be provided to prevent the breakup of the Indian family did not apply to him either.[171] As a result, it reversed the application of these sections of the ICWA by the state court to the father and remanded for further proceedings under state law.[172]

Some of the most significant elements of the decision were as follows:

- The Court concluded that its holding in the case was consistent with the "primary" purpose of the ICWA to prevent the "removal" of Indian children from their families and that the ICWA's intent was not to "create" parental rights for unwed fathers where they would not otherwise exist.[173]
- The Court found that the state court ruling would have placed vulnerable, potentially adoptable, Indian children at a "disadvantage" and would raise "equal protection" concerns.[174]

- The Court indicated that the placement preferences are not triggered in a private adoption proceeding until someone within the preferences formally indicates a willingness to adopt the child.[175]
- Although given an opportunity to do so, the court did not adopt the Existing Indian Family Exception (EIFE). Rather, it referenced the *Holyfield* court for the proposition that the ICWA applied because the case involved an Indian child in a child custody proceeding (although certain sections did not apply to the father) and did not dispute the dissent's recitation of sections of the act that would continue to apply to noncustodial parents (and tribes) even after its decision.[176]
- In a concurring opinion, Justice Stephen Breyer (one of the justices in the 5–4 majority) expressed his opinion that the Court had "decided no more than is necessary" and gave a number of examples where he thought the provisions in question would be applied to a noncustodial father.[177] He did not address the potential inconsistencies between his opinion and the majority opinion (which he joined). His opinion raises the issue as to whether the *Baby Girl* case should have broad application beyond the type of factual circumstances that were present in that case.

Ten years later, it appears that the impact of this case has been limited. While a few courts have declined to apply § 1912 protections to noncustodial fathers who have had limited contact with their children, particularly in Montana, at least one court has followed the suggestion in Justice Breyer's concurrence that the case be read narrowly.[178] In reality, it appears that (outside of Montana) the *Baby Girl* case is seldom raised in ICWA cases and the act is routinely applied in its entirety whenever there is an Indian child in a child custody proceeding.

The third case decided by the Supreme Court is *Haaland v. Brackeen*, which addressed constitutional issues related to the ICWA. That case is addressed in full later in the chapter.

Constitutional Challenges to ICWA

Predictably, there have been constitutional challenges to the ICWA by parties claiming that the act is unconstitutional. All of the cases brought during the first decade and a half after the ICWA was enacted upheld the constitutionality of the act, including cases from Maine,[179] South Dakota,[180] Arizona,[181] Michigan,[182] Oklahoma,[183] and Oregon.[184] In those cases, the courts held that, as long as a rational basis existed for Congress to legislate as it did, the authority of Congress extended to the legislative purpose achieved by the ICWA. In upholding the constitutionality of the ICWA, these courts referred to the Indian Commerce Clause of the U.S. Constitution as a justification for congressional action in the arena of the welfare of Native American children. The courts also rejected constitutional challenges premised on the 14th Amendment Equal Protection Clause brought by non-Indians asserting that the different standard for termination of parental rights was an illegitimate race-based distinction.[185]

A few limited challenges to ICWA's constitutionality were successful. Specifically, courts in two judicial districts in California refused to apply the ICWA to children who were never fully integrated into Indian families (one version of the Existing Indian Family Exception [EIFE]), a ruling which they held was necessary to preserve the constitutionality of the ICWA. Thus, in *In re Bridget R.*,[186] a California Court of Appeals court held that the application of the ICWA in a case in which, according to the court, neither the child nor either parent maintained any significant social, cultural, or political relationship with the tribe would be unconstitutional on several grounds including the Equal Protection and Due Process Clauses in the Fifth and 14th Amendments, and the Tenth Amendment to the U.S. Constitution. Another judicial district in California reached a similar conclusion,[187] but the California Courts of Appeals in four other districts disagreed with this analysis, as has a subsequent decision by the same judicial district that decided *Bridget R.*[188] Courts in other states have also continued to find the act to be constitutional.[189] Chapter 2 of this book contains a thorough analysis of recent developments involving the EIFE to ICWA, a judicially created exception that some state courts have adopted to avoid the application of the ICWA to any child who has not been reared in an "Indian family."

Most recently, three lawsuits were filed in federal court challenging the constitutionality of the ICWA, as well as the regulations or the now-superseded 2015 guidelines.[190] Two of these cases were ultimately dismissed, one on the merits and the other based upon procedural infirmities.[191] The third case, the aforementioned *Haaland v. Brackeen*, resolved many of the constitutional claims that have been raised, but not all of them. Given the importance of the case, the next section provides a detailed analysis of the background of the case and the legal analysis by the Court.

Haaland v. Brackeen[192]

The constitutional challenge in *Haaland v. Brackeen* was initiated by a lawsuit filed in federal court in the Northern District of Texas by foster/adoptive parents, a biological parent, and the states of Texas, Louisiana, and Indiana. (By the time that the case made it to the Supreme Court, only the state of Texas was still a party.)

The primary constitutional issues raised were:

- ICWA exceeds the authority of Congress provided by the Indian Commerce Clause.
- ICWA is a race-based law that violates the Equal Protection Clause.
- ICWA commandeers state agencies and courts to enforce federal law in violation of the Tenth Amendment, which protects states' rights.
- ICWA improperly delegates authority to tribes to change the placement preferences.[193]

In a 7–2 opinion (Justices Alito and Thomas dissenting) the Supreme Court rejected all of the challengers' arguments, some on the merits and some on procedural grounds.

Specifically, the Court held that Congress had the authority to enact the ICWA based upon the Indian Commerce Clause, Treaty Clause, the Constitution, and the trust relationship between Indian people and tribes and the federal government. It found that Congress's power to legislate in the area of federal Indian law is "plenary and exclusive" and includes authority over family law when Indians are involved.[194]

Secondly, it held that the law did not impermissibly commandeer state agencies. The Court's analysis focused largely on the active efforts requirement in the law. Since the active efforts requirement applies to any party (and in fact has been applied to private parties as well as state agencies), the Court held that it does not violate the principles of anti-commandeering.[195]

Finally, the Court decided the equal protection issue on procedural grounds, not substantive grounds.[196] It ruled that none of the parties had standing to raise this claim.

In terms of the foster and adoptive parents, the Court found that they could not show that the injury they claimed to have suffered was likely to be fixed by a judgment from the Court because it is state courts that make these decisions and state agencies that carry out the court-ordered placements.[197] Neither the state courts nor the state agencies were parties to the case.

In terms of Texas, the court ruled that the state could not make an equal protection claim on behalf of its citizens and that it had not suffered a direct injury.[198] Of note, particularly in connection with Texas's claims of economic injury, the court emphasized that the state's costs were not "fairly traceable" to the placement preferences, implicitly dismissing the broader equal protection arguments against the statute that would have caused the state to incur the costs that it asserted as one of the bases for its standing.[199] Justice Kavanaugh's concurring opinion, stating his view that the equal protection issue was serious, also focused solely upon the impact of the placement preferences in child welfare cases and did not reference any of the broader equal protection claims.[200]

Finally, it should be mentioned that Justice Gorsuch wrote a powerful concurring opinion (joined in part by Justices Sotomayor and Jackson) laying out the history of the separation of Native families by government actors and emphasizing the importance of tribal sovereignty.[201]

State ICWAs

States have undertaken legislative initiatives to clarify and expand upon the ICWA's requirements. To date, 39 states have enacted some legislative provisions relating to the ICWA.[202] (These provisions are listed in Appendix D.) In fact, 18 states have enacted fairly comprehensive statutes that cover a wide range of the issues covered by the ICWA.[203]

The ICWA specifically provides that where state law provides a higher standard of protection to the rights of the parent or Indian custodian than the ICWA, then the state law applies,[204] and the 2016 ICWA guidelines specifically recognize that some state ICWAs establish protections "beyond the minimum federal standards," noting that in such circumstances the more protective state law would apply.[205] Thus, there are no cases that have found state ICWAs to be beyond the authority of the states to enact in general, although there are cases that have found that specific provisions in state statutes that diminished parental rights were unconstitutional[206] and an Iowa state court case found that a provision in that state's ICWA defining Indian child to include children not eligible for tribal membership was unconstitutional.[207]

In general, the comprehensive state ICWAs seek to clarify or expand upon the protections of the federal law. In addition, a number of the more recent enactments have taken portions of the ICWA regulations and incorporated them into state law. Although a full analysis of state ICWAs is beyond the scope of this handbook, the following are some examples of provisions in state ICWAs that seek to go beyond what is in the federal law itself.

Modifications to ICWA definitions:

- Extended family. Iowa and Nebraska add clan and band members and any cousin; New Mexico adds godparents.[208]
- Indian child. Minnesota and Michigan cover all children who are eligible for membership in the tribe regardless of whether a parent is a member.[209]

Additional definitions:

- Best interests of the child. Washington has a definition that includes preventing unnecessary removal and recognizing the value to the child of a political, cultural, social, and spiritual relationship with the tribal community.[210]

- Tribal customary adoption. Washington includes a definition clarifying that adoptions can take place without Termination of Parental Rights (TPR).[211]
- Imminent physical damage or harm. Minnesota includes a definition of this term, which is applicable to emergency removals.[212]

Notice:

- Nebraska requires notice to tribes in voluntary proceedings and when an Indian family is offered in-home services.[213]

Intervention and transfer:

- Minnesota clarifies that the right to intervene and transfer applies to all child custody proceedings.[214]
- California and Oregon incorporate ICWA regulations specifying what a court may not consider as good cause to deny transfer when a petition to transfer is made.[215]
- Iowa sets affirmative criteria for what constitutes good cause to deny transfer, limited to tribal declination, lack of jurisdiction, parental objection or forum non conveniens.[216]

Active efforts:

- Michigan incorporates examples in ICWA regulations into the statute.[217]
- Minnesota specifies that active efforts are more than reasonable efforts.[218]
- Wisconsin includes a list of eight activities and services that must be provided for the active efforts standard to be met.[219]
- Nebraska requires active efforts when there is a voluntary placement, or in-home services are being provided, and the

Indian child's tribe has the right to participate in or consult with the state agency regarding the provision of voluntary services.[220]

Standards for removal:

- North Dakota incorporates the requirement from the ICWA regulations requiring that a causal connection between the parent's behavior and harm to the child be shown.[221]

Emergency removals:

- Iowa requires formal notice of an emergency removal to the tribe within three days.[222]
- North Dakota requires that Indian children be placed within placement preferences in an emergency placement unless emergency conditions necessitate placement outside of the placement preferences.[223]

Tribal-state agreements:

- Oregon and New Mexico require good faith efforts by the state to enter into ICWA agreements with tribes.[224]
- Minnesota authorizes agreements between tribes and counties.[225]

Placement preferences—additional preferences:

- North Dakota and Colorado add additional preferences before other Indian families—including an Indian family with whom the child has a relationship or a tribe that is culturally similar or linguistically connected with the Indian child's tribe.[226]
- Iowa, Nebraska, and Washington add a final preference for a non-Indian family that is committed to participation in cultural and ceremonial events/child's relationship with the tribe and family visitation.[227]

Placement preferences—additional requirements:

- Minnesota defers to the Indian child's tribe on the suitability of a placement.[228]
- New Mexico and Colorado require a cultural compact (if requested by the tribe) in an adoption decree.[229]
- Oklahoma applies the placement preferences to pre-adjudicatory placements.[230]

Placement preferences—good cause:

- Minnesota incorporates the good cause provisions in the ICWA regulations and specifies that the child-placing agency must testify that a diligent search has been conducted.[231]

State-recognized tribes:

- New York extends the coverage of ICWA provisions to state-recognized tribes.[232]

Thus, practitioners need to be aware of their own state statutes (as well as any applicable court rules) when handling child custody proceedings involving Indian children.

This chapter has reviewed the legislative purpose behind the enactment of the ICWA and provided an overview of its provisions, as well as information about Supreme Court cases and state ICWAs. The chapters that follow will discuss the ICWA with a greater degree of specificity. The practitioner should always keep the objectives of Congress in mind while reviewing specific provisions of the act, with an eye toward how the specific provisions achieve the stated objective of Congress to further the best interest of Native American children and protect the integrity and future of Indian tribes.

Endnotes

1. Sitting Bull apparently made this statement upon his return from exile in Canada, when it was becoming apparent that the nomadic lifestyle of his Hunkpapa people was being proscribed by the white settlers. *See* ROBERT M. UTLEY, THE LANCE AND THE SHIELD: THE LIFE AND TIMES OF SITTING BULL (Henry Holt and Company 1993).
2. The need for a working knowledge of the ICWA is perhaps best exemplified by an Alaska decision, Doe v. Hughes, 838 P.2d 804 (Alaska 1992), wherein the Alaska Supreme Court held that a law firm had committed malpractice by not obtaining the consent of the natural mother of an Indian child conceived by artificial insemination in a private adoption in violation of the ICWA.
3. In this book, the terms "Native American," "Native," and "Indian" will be used interchangeably.
4. *See, e.g.,* Donna J. Goldsmith, *Individual v. Collective Rights: The Indian Child Welfare Act*, 13 HARV. WOMEN'S L.J. 1 (1990); Rennard Strickland, *Indian Law and the Miner's Canary: The Signs of Poison Gas*, 39 CLEV. ST. L. REV. 483 (1991).
5. 25 U.S.C. § 1902.
6. There are several documents evidencing the legislative history behind the ICWA: the House Report, H.R. REP. NO. 1386, 95th Cong., 2d Sess. (1978), *reprinted in* 1978 U.S. CODE CONG. & AD. NEWS 7530 [hereinafter House Report]; the Senate Report, S. Rep. No. 597, 95th Cong., 1st Sess. (1977); two Senate hearings, *Problems That American Indian Families Face in Raising Their Children and How These Problems are Affected by Federal Action or Inaction: Hearings Before the Subcomm. on Indian Affairs, S. Comm. on Interior and Insular Affairs*, 93rd Cong., 2d Sess. (Aug. 4, 1974) [hereinafter 1974 Senate Hearing], and *Indian Child Welfare Act of 1977: Hearing on S. 1214 Before the S. Select Committee on Indian Affairs*, 95th Cong. 1st Sess. [hereinafter 1977 Senate Hearing]; a House of Representatives hearing, *Hearings on S. 1214 Before the Subcomm. on Indian Affairs and Public Lands of the House Comm. on Interior and Insular Affairs*, 95th Cong., 2d

Sess. (1978) [hereinafter House Hearing] and floor statements captured in the Congressional Record. 123 Cong. Rec. 21042–21044, 37223–37226 (1977), and 123 Cong. Rec. 38101–38112 (1978).

7. *See* House Report, *supra* note 6, at 9.
8. *Id.*
9. *Id.*
10. *Id.*
11. Dep't of the Interior, Bureau of Indian Affairs, Federal Indian Boarding School Initiative, https://www.bia.gov/service/federal-indian-boarding-school-initiative (last visited Aug. 10, 2025). The boarding schools and removal by state agencies were not the only methods by which Indian children were removed from their families and communities. From 1958 to 1967, the BIA and Child Welfare League of America (CWLA) worked together to actively promote the adoption of Indian children to non-Indian families across the country, resulting in 395 adoptions during that period. *See The Indian Adoption Project—1958 through 1967—Report of Its Accomplishments, Evaluation and Recommendations for Adoption Services to Indian Children*, at 1, 6, and 8, Child Welfare League of America Papers, Box 16, Folder 2, Social Welfare History Archives, University of Minnesota. The executive director of CWLA later apologized for the involvement of his organization. *See, e.g.*, Judith Graham, *Adoption Apology too Late for Indians*, Chi. Trib. (May 7, 2001), https://www.chicagotribune.com/2001/05/07/adoption-apology-too-late-for-indians/.
12. House Report, *supra* note 6, at 9.
13. *Id.*
14. *Id.* at 10.
15. *Id.*
16. *Id.*
17. *Id.*
18. *Id.*
19. *Id.* Some Native American children of alcoholic mothers suffer from fetal alcohol spectrum disorder. Such a condition potentially may lead to growth deficiencies, mental retardation, and learning and behavioral problems.

See MICHAEL DORRIS, THE BROKEN CORD (HarperCollins 1989); ANN STREISSGURTH, A MANUAL ON ADOLESCENTS AND ADULTS WITH FETAL ALCOHOL SYNDROME WITH SPECIAL REFERENCE TO AMERICAN INDIANS (Indian HEALTH SERVICES 1988). This problem was the subject of a television movie, *The Broken Cord*, based on the book of the same title.

20. House Report, *supra* note 6, at 11.
21. *Id.*
22. *Id.* The House cited to a South Dakota entrapment case where parents signed away custody of their children under duress and that relinquishment was later used as evidence of abandonment.
23. *Id.*
24. *Id.*
25. *Id.*
26. *Id.*
27. *Id.*
28. 25 U.S.C. § 1901(5).
29. House Report, *supra* note 6, at 9.
30. *Id.*
31. *Id.* The 90 percent figure was derived from statistics out of the state of Minnesota, which Congress noted was one of the few states to keep detailed statistics. Congress believed, however, that Minnesota's statistics were representative of other states.
32. Gaylene J. McCartney, *The American Indian Child Welfare Crisis: Cultural Genocide or First Amendment Preservation*, 7 COLUM. HUM. RTS. L. REV. 529 (1975); Irving N. Berlin, *Anglo Adoptions of Native Americans: Repercussions in Adolescence*, 17 AM. ACAD. CHILD PSYCH. 387–88 (1978); Joseph Westermeyer, *The Apple Syndrome in Minnesota: A Complication of Racial-Ethnic Discontinuity*, 10 J. OPERATIONAL PSYCH., 134–40 (1979).
33. *Id.*
34. There has been surprisingly little empirical data addressing the impact of the removal of Indian children from their culture and their placement in the non-Indian, Euro-American culture, especially in light of the fact that Congress believed the problem was so serious that it threatened the existence

of an entire culture. Much of what Congress relied on was anecdotal and statistical information and the inferences drawn from that. There are studies that suggest that the problems confronting Indian children who grow up in the non-Indian world are serious. *See* Berlin, *supra* note 32; Irving N. Berlin, *Suicide Among Native American Adolescents: An Overview*, 17 SUICIDE & LIFE THREATENING BEHAV. 218–32 (1987); Damien McShane, *An Analysis of Mental Health Research with American Indian Youth*, special issue, 11 J. ADOLESCENCE 87–116 (1988). Indian adoptees have written about the challenges which they faced and the healing that has taken place once reunited with the Native community. *See, e.g.*, SANDY WHITE HAWK, A CHILD OF THE INDIAN RACE: A STORY OF RETURN (St. Paul: Minnesota Historical Society Press 2022). There are also studies that generally pertain to transracial adoptions and the effect on minority children, which are clearly apposite to the plight of Indian children. *See* Kim Forde-Mazrui, *Black Identity and Child Placement: The Best Interests of Black and Biracial Children*, 92 MICH. L. REV. 925 (1994); Timothy P. Glynn, *The Role of Race in Adoption Proceedings: A Constitutional Critique of the Minnesota Preference Statute*, 77 MINN. L. REV. 925 (1993); Jo Beth Eubanks, *Transracial Adoption in Texas: Should the Best Interests Standard Be Color-Blind?*, 24 ST. MARY'S L.J. 1225 (1993).

35. *See, e.g.*, Indian Self-Determination Act, 25 U.S.C. §§ 450 *et seq.*

36. *See* FELIX S. COHEN, HANDBOOK OF FEDERAL INDIAN LAW 127–206 (Michie, Bobbs-Merrill 1982 ed.). Federal policy has shifted from a desire to assimilate Indians into the mainstream American society, as exemplified by the era of allotment from 1871 to 1928 and termination from 1943 to 1961, to a desire to maintain tribal independence and sovereignty, as exemplified by the enactment of the Indian Reorganization Act, 25 U.S.C. §§ 461 *et seq.*, in 1934 and the period of self-determination of which the enactment of the ICWA is an extension.

37. *See In re* Adoption of M.T.S., 489 N.W.2d 285 (Minn. App. 1992) (court holds that it is presumptively in the best interest of an Indian child to be placed with Indian grandmother rather than with non-Indian foster parents for adoption because of child's need to be raised in his culture).

38. *See* Indian Self-Determination Act, *supra* note 35.
39. 1977 Senate Hearing, *supra* note 6, at 193.
40. 123 Cong. Rec. 21043 (1977); *see also, e.g.*, 1977 Senate Hearing, *supra* note 6, at 271, 359 (statements of Don Milligan, Washington Department of Social and Health Services; and Virgil Cook, Colville Business Council); 1974 Senate Hearing, *supra* note 6, at 61 (statement of Dr. Carl Mindell).
41. 25 U.S.C. § 1903(1), (4).
42. *Id.* § 1903(1)(i–iv).
43. *Id.* § 1903(1)(iv). *See* Application of Defender, 435 N.W.2d 717 (S.D. 1989) and *In re* Custody of Sengstock, 165 Wis. 2d 86, 477 N.W.2d 310 (Wis. App. 1991) (ICWA does not apply to disputes between parents); *see also* State in Interest of T.D.C., 748 P.2d 201 (Utah App. 1988) and *In re* Enrique Q., 137 Cal. App. 4th 728 (Cal. App. 5th Dist. 2006) (ICWA not applicable to delinquency proceedings).
44. *See* 25 U.S.C. § 1903(1) defining the four types of child custody proceedings covered by ICWA, none of which require the "child custody proceeding" to be commenced by a state or county agency.
45. *See* 25 U.S.C. § 1903(1)(iv); *see also* S.S. v. Stephanie H., 241 Ariz. 419, 388 P.3d 569 (Ariz. Ct. App. 2017), *cert. denied* 538 U.S. 959 (2017); *In re* N.B., 199 P.3d 16 (Colo. App. 2007), *cert. denied* 2008 WL 757927 (2008).
46. *See* 25 U.S.C. § 1903(4).
47. 25 C.F.R. § 23.108; *see also In re* Adoption of Riffle, 922 P.2d 510 (Mont. 1996) (tribal determination on membership is conclusive); *In re* Welfare of S.N.R., 617 N.W.2d 77 (Minn. Ct. App. 2000) (court holds that tribal determination of membership is conclusive and cannot be collaterally challenged).
48. 25 U.S.C. § 1912(a). As discussed later in this book, notice is not mandatory in voluntary proceedings under federal law presently, although some states mandate notice in such cases, the 2016 regulations require contacting the tribe if necessary to determine Indian status, 25 C.F.R. § 23.124(b), and the guidelines recommend notice in all voluntary cases. BIA Guidelines for Implementing the Indian Child Welfare Act § I.3 (Dec. 2016).
49. *In re* Alexandria Y., 45 Cal. App. 4th 1483, 53 Cal. Rptr. 2d 679 (Cal. App. 4th Dist. 1996); Rye v. Weasel, 934 S.W.2d 257 (Ky. 1996).

50. Mississippi Band of Choctaw Indians v. Holyfield, 490 U.S. 30, 42 (1988); Adoptive Couple v. Baby Girl, 133 S. Ct. 2552, 2556 n.1 (2013).
51. *See* Chapter 2, note 108.
52. *See* Cal. Welf. & Inst. Code § 224(C) (2014); Iowa Code § 232B.5 (1999); Minn. Stat. § 260.771 (2010); Okla. Stat. tit. 10, § 40.1 (2010); Wash. Rev. Code § 13.34.040(3) (2011); Wis. Stat. § 938.028(3)(A) (2011).
53. 25 U.S.C. § 1911(a) grants Indian tribal courts exclusive jurisdiction over child custody proceedings involving Indian children domiciled on Indian reservations (broadly defined in 25 U.S.C. § 1903(10)), except where jurisdiction may otherwise be vested in state courts (see discussion on P.L. 280 contained in Chapter 3 of this book), and where an Indian child is a ward of the tribal court. 25 U.S.C. § 1911(b), on the other hand, permits state courts to exercise jurisdiction over child custody proceedings involving Indian children off Indian reservations, but requires the state court to transfer the case to the tribal court unless a parent objects, the tribal court declines the case, or "good cause," discussed in Chapter 3 of this book, is found by the state court judge.
54. *See* 25 U.S.C. § 1911(a).
55. *See* Chapter 3, note 18.
56. *See* 25 U.S.C. § 1911(b).
57. *See Holyfield*, 490 U.S. 30 (referred to tribal court jurisdiction over off-reservation child custody proceedings as "presumptive").
58. 25 U.S.C. § 1911(b); *see In re* Appeal of Maricopa Cnty. Juv. Action No. JD-6982, 922 P.2d 319 (Ariz. App. 1996) (parent entitled to veto transfer of child custody proceeding to tribal court).
59. For example, unlike states, tribes are not eligible for direct funding under Title XX of the Social Security Act (42 U.S.C. § 1397). See Chapter 7 for more information on funding.
60. *See* 25 U.S.C. § 1912(a).
61. *In re* A.U., 141 Cal. App. 4th 326 (2006) (failure of state agency to give notice to several tribes after mother and relatives self-identified as Indian violates notice provisions of the ICWA). For a discussion of what factors trigger the notice requirement, see the section titled When Notice Is Required in Chapter 4.

62. *Compare In re* H.D., 729 P.2d 1234 (Kan. App. 1986) (failure to give tribe notice of termination proceeding renders the proceeding null and void) *with In re* Veronica G., 157 Cal. App. 4th 179, 68 Cal. Rptr. 3d 465 (2007) (failure of notice is not jurisdictional and court may remand for compliance with the ICWA notice requirement and for an ICWA-compliant hearing if the ICWA is found to be applicable without invalidating existing court orders).
63. People *ex rel.* DSS in Interest of C.H., 510 N.W.2d 119 (S.D. 1993). See Chapter 4 for more information on notice.
64. *See* Chapter 4, section titled Type of Notice Required.
65. *See* 25 U.S.C. § 1912(b)–(f).
66. *Id.* § 1912(e).
67. *Id.* § 1912(d).
68. *Id.* § 1912(f).
69. *See* People in Interest of M.H., 691 N.W.2d 622 (S.D. 2005).
70. 42 U.S.C. § 671(a)(15).
71. *See, e.g., In re* P.S.E., 816 N.W.2d 110 (S.D. 2012).
72. 25 C.F.R. § 23.2.
73. *Compare* 25 U.S.C. § 1912(d) with 42 U.S.C. § 671(a)(15). For a more thorough discussion of this issue, see the discussion on active efforts in Chapter 4.
74. *See* 25 U.S.C. § 1912(b).
75. *Id.* Most states provide appointed legal counsel for indigent parents in child custody proceedings, but this section may be more relevant when legal counsel is appointed for an Indian custodian.
76. These rights are recognized in numerous sections regarding tribal rights including right to notice, 25 U.S.C. § 1912(a); right to intervene as a matter of right, 25 U.S.C. § 1911(c); right to petition for transfer of jurisdiction, 25 U.S.C. § 1911(b); and the right to alter the placement preferences in the ICWA, 25 U.S.C. § 1915(c).
77. *See* 25 U.S.C. § 1911 (b), (c).
78. The law grants Indian tribes a right to request an additional 20 days to prepare for foster care or termination of parental rights proceedings, 25

U.S.C. § 1912(a), and the right to review all documents upon which a state court has made a determination of placement. *See* 25 U.S.C. § 1912(c).

79. *See* 25 U.S.C. § 1915(e) for the right of tribes to discover the placement of their children and 25 U.S.C. § 1914 for the rights of tribes to collaterally challenge violations of the ICWA.
80. *See* 25 U.S.C. § 1915. In *Mississippi Band of Choctaw Indians v. Holyfield*, the Supreme Court indicated that the "most important substantive requirements imposed upon state courts" are the placement preferences expressed in § 1915 of the ICWA.
81. 25 U.S.C. § 1915(a) (adoptive placement preferences) and (b) (foster care placement preferences).
82. *Id.* § 1915(c).
83. *Id.* § 1915(b).
84. *Id.*
85. *Id.* § 1915(a).
86. *Id.* § 1915(a), (b).
87. *See, e.g.*, Analysis by Casey Family Programs using the 2020 Adoption and Foster Care Analysis and Reporting System (AFCARS) data made available by the National Data Archive on Child Abuse and Neglect Data (NDACAN) at Cornell University, https://www.casey.org/media/ICWA-data.pdf (indicating that 55 percent of Native children were placed in nonrelative, non-Native homes in 2020); Rose M. Kreider, *Interracial Adoptive Families and Their Children: 2008*, *in* National Council for Adoption Factbook V 109 (2011) (reporting that in 2008 more Indian children in adoptive placements lived in non-Indian adoptive homes than Indian adoptive homes).
88. S. 1976, 100th Cong. (1987).
89. *In re* Bridget R., 49 Cal. Rptr. 2d 507 (Cal. App. 1996).
90. *See* H.R. Rep. No. 542, 104th Cong., 2d Sess. (1996).
91. 142 Cong. Rec. H4807 (May 10, 1996).
92. *See* S. 569 & H.R. 1082, 105th Cong. (1997); *Indian Child Welfare Joint Hearing*, 105th Cong., 1st Sess., 1997 WL 11234052 (explaining that tribal representatives met with adoption attorneys and child welfare specialists to develop proposals that addressed concerns of multiple constituencies).

93. 142 Cong. Rec. S11455–11456 (Sep. 26, 1996).
94. H.R. 2644, 107th Cong. (2001); H.R. 4733, 107th Cong. (2002); Marcia Yablon, *The Indian Child Welfare Act Amendments of 2003*, 38 Fam. L.Q. 689, 695 (2005).
95. 42 U.S.C. § 622(b)(9); see Chapter 7, footnote 9 for the text of the recent amendments to this section.
96. Pub. Law No. 118-258, § 107.
97. *Id.*
98. U.S. Gov't Accountability Off., GAO-05-290, Report to Congressional Requesters, Indian Child Welfare Act: Existing Information on Implementation Issues Could Be Used to Target Guidance and Assistance to States 2 (2005).
99. *Id.*
100. *Id.* at 4.
101. *Id.* at 5.
102. *Id.*
103. *Id.*
104. 25 C.F.R. Part 23.
105. 44 Fed. Reg. 67584 (Nov. 26, 1979).
106. *Id.*
107. 80 Fed. Reg. 10146 (Feb. 25, 2015).
108. *Id.*
109. *Compare* 2015 guidelines at 80 Fed. Reg. 10146 *et seq. with* the 1979 guidelines at 44 Fed. Reg. 67584 *et seq.*
110. The 2016 guidelines can be found at https://www.bia.gov/sites/default/files/dup/assets/bia/ois/pdf/idc2-056831.pdf.
111. *See, e.g., In re* J.J.C., 302 S.W.3d 896 (Tex. App. 2009); *In re* Maricopa Cnty. Juv. Action No. JS-8287, 171 Ariz. 404, 828 P.2d 1245 (Ct. App. 1991), *rev. denied* (1992).
112. *See, e.g., In re* J.S., 315 P.3d 1030 (Okla. App. 2013).
113. *Id.*
114. 25 U.S.C. § 1952.

115. 45 C.F.R. Part 1355 was adopted on December 14, 2016, to take effect on October 1, 2019. Department of Health and Human Services, Administration for Children and Families, Adoption and Foster Care Analysis and Reporting System (Dec. 14, 2016), 81 Fed. Reg. 90524.
116. 85 Fed. Reg. 28410 (May 20, 2020).
117. 89 Fed. Reg. 96569 (Dec. 5, 2024).
118. *Id.*
119. *See* brief filed on behalf of Casey Family Programs and 26 other child welfare and adoption organizations in *Haaland v. Brackeen*, https://turtletalk.blog/wp-content/uploads/2022/08/cfpamicus.pdf.
120. 81 Fed. Reg. at 38813.
121. *See, e.g.*, Amy M. Salazar et al., *Trauma Exposure and PTSD Among Older Adolescents in Foster Care*, 48 Soc. Psych. & Psych. Epidemiology 545, 547, 550 (2013); Delilah Bruskas, *Children in Foster Care: A Vulnerable Population at Risk*, 21 J. Child & Adolescent Psych. Nursing 70–77 (2008); Robert Racusin et al., *Psychosocial Treatment of Children in Foster Care: A Review*, 41 Cmty. Health J. 199–221 (2005); Judith Silver et al., *Starting Young: Improving the Health and Developmental Outcomes of Infants and Toddlers in the Child Welfare System*, 78 Child Welfare 148–65 (1999).
122. 81 Fed. Reg. at 38838.
123. 42 U.S.C. § 671(a)(19).
124. *See, e.g.*, Annie E. Casey Foundation, Variations in the Use of Kinship Diversion Among Child Welfare Agencies 8 (2019); Marc A. Winokur et al., Cochrane Database Sys. Rev., Kinship Care for the Safety, Permanency, and Well Being of Children Removed from the Home for Maltreatment (2014).
125. 81 Fed. Reg. at 38838.
126. *See, e.g.*, Casey Family Programs, Child and Family Services Practice Model 10 (Mar. 2021), https://www.casey.org/media/101-Practice-Model-1.pdf; Sixto Cancel, *I Will Never Forget That I Could Have Lived with People Who Loved Me*, N.Y. Times (Sep. 16, 2021); Richard A. Perry, *Relative*

Preference, Emotional Attachments, and the Best Interest of the Child in Need of Assistance, 50 U. BALT. L.F. 83, 93 (2020) (placement with fictive kin can lessen trauma).

127. JOSEPH GOLDSTEIN, ANNA FREUD & ALBERT J. SOLNIT, BEYOND THE BEST INTEREST OF THE CHILD 53 (New York: Free Press 1973).

128. CARA FLANAGAN, EARLY SOCIALISATION: SOCIABILITY AND ATTACHMENT (Psychology Press 1999); JOHN W. BERRY ET AL., CROSS-CULTURAL PSYCHOLOGY: RESEARCH AND APPLICATIONS (Cambridge Univ. Press 1992); Fred Rothbaum et al., *Attachment and Culture: Security in the United States and Japan*, 55 AM. PSYCH. 1093–104 (2000); Annemarie Huiberts et al., *Connectedness with Parents and Behavioural Autonomy Among Dutch and Moroccan Adolescents*, 29 ETHNIC & RACIAL STUDIES 315 (2006); Chia-Chih D. Wang & Brent S. Mallinckrodt, *Differences Between Taiwanese and US Cultural Beliefs About Ideal Adult Attachment*, 53 J. COUNSELING PSYCH. 192 (2006); Maureen E. Kenny et al., *Self-Image and Parental Attachment Among Late Adolescents in Belize*, 5 J. ADOLESCENCE 649 (2005); Raymond Neckoway et al., *Is Attachment Theory Consistent with Aboriginal Parenting Realities?*, 3 FIRST PEOPLES CHILD & FAM. REV. 65 (2007); Soo See Yeo, *Bonding and Attachment of Australian Aboriginal Children*, 12 CHILD ABUSE REV. 292 (2003).

129. 25 C.F.R. § 23.132(e); *see also* In the Interest of A.R., 310 P.3d 1007 (Colo. Ct. App. 2012) (attachment to foster parents is not an adequate reason to deviate from the placement preferences).

130. Dep't of the Interior, Bureau of Indian Affairs, Final Rule Indian Child Welfare Act Proceedings, 81 Fed. Reg. 38778, 38830, 38846 (June 14, 2016).

131. An example of this is a case from Montana, *Matter of T.S.*, 801 P.2d 77 (Mont. 1990), where a guardian ad litem for an Indian child questioned whether the ICWA does further the best interests of Indian children. *See also In re* Baby Girl A., 230 Cal. App. 3d 1611, 282 Cal. Rptr. 105 (Cal. App. 4 Dist. 1991) (tribe allowed to intervene in voluntary adoption proceeding by Indian mother raised by non-Indian adoptive parents, but court strongly suggests that the rights of the mother to keep child out of Indian home more important than cultural attachment to child's Native family).

132. *See generally* JOHN F. BRYDE, MODERN INDIAN PSYCHOLOGY (Institute of Indian Studies, University of South Dakota 1971).
133. An excellent discussion of traditional Lakota (Sioux) child-rearing practices can be gleaned through reading the novel *Waterlily* by Ella Cara Deloria, published in 1990 by the University of Nebraska Press. The novel, set in the mid-1800s when the Lakota culture was flourishing, details a Lakota woman's life from birth to old age.
134. *See* MICHAEL J. CADUTO & JOSEPH BRUCHAC, KEEPERS OF THE ANIMALS: NATIVE AMERICAN STORIES AND WILDLIFE ACTIVITIES FOR CHILDREN (Fulcrum Publishing 1991).
135. *See* Deloria, *supra* note 133, at 20.
136. One of the greatest Lakota storytellers was Fools Crow, who had the ability to enthrall young children with his stories about animals and traditional values. *See* THOMAS MAILS, FOOLS CROW: WISDOM AND POWER (Council Oak Books 1991).
137. A "grandparent" is not necessarily a lineal ancestor of an Indian child, but in many Indian societies great-aunts and great-uncles as well as cousins are considered grandparents. *See* Gray v. Pann, 513 N.W.2d 154 (Mich. App. 1994) (grandmother of Indian child brings action to obtain custody of child against father).
138. *See* House Report, *supra* note 6, at 19, where the House stated that compliance with the ICWA is "in the best interest of an Indian child"; *see also* BIA GUIDELINES, *supra* note 48, § M.1.
139. House Report, *supra* note 6, at 19, quoting a U.S. Supreme Court case noting that judges may find it difficult using the "vague" best interest standard "to avoid decisions resting on subjective values."
140. *See* Cherokee Nation v. Georgia, 30 U.S. (5 Pet.) 1 (1831).
141. *Id.* at 17.
142. United States v. Wheeler, 435 U.S. 313 (1978).
143. For example, the United States cannot exercise its plenary power in a manner that results in a taking of property without just compensation, *see United States v. Sioux Nation*, 100 S. Ct. 2716 (1980), or in a manner that violates the Due Process Clause in the Fifth Amendment, *Delaware Tribal Bus. Comm. v. Weeks,* 430 U.S. 73 (1977).

144. *See* Cherokee Nation v. Georgia, 30 U.S. (5 Pet.) 1, 15 (1831); United States v. Mitchell, 463 U.S. 206 (1980).
145. Worcester v. Georgia, 31 U.S. (6 Pet.) 515, 555 (1832).
146. *See, e.g.*, Seminole Nation v. United States, 316 U.S. 286 (1942).
147. *See* Morton v. Mancari, 417 U.S. 535 (1974).
148. U.S. CONST., art. I, § 8, cl. 3.
149. *See* Williams v. Lee, 358 U.S. 217 (1959).
150. *See, e.g.*, Fisher v. District Ct., 424 U.S. 382 (1976) (exclusive authority to grant on-reservation adoption); No Fire v. United States, 164 U.S. 657 (1897) (authority to grant marriage license); Conroy v. Conroy, 575 F.2d 175 (8th Cir. 1978) (authority to divide marital property). This recognition is consistent with the evolving international norms pertaining to Indigenous peoples reflected in the recently adopted United Nations Declaration on the Rights of Indigenous Peoples.
151. Carney v. Chapman, 247 U.S. 102 (1918).
152. *Fisher*, 424 U.S. 382.
153. *Conroy*, 575 F.2d 175.
154. *See, e.g.*, Heart v. Ellenbecker, 689 F. Supp. 989 (D.S.D. 1988).
155. *See, e.g.*, Mescalero Apache Tribe v. Jones, 411 U.S. 145 (1973).
156. *See, e.g.*, United States v. Holliday, 70 U.S. 407, 418 (1866) and United States v. Nice, 241 U.S. 591 (1916) (cases upholding laws regulating liquor sales to Indians, whether located on or off the reservation); Washington v. Fishing Vessel Ass'n, 443 U.S. 658, 673 n.20 (1979) (recognizing off-reservation fishing rights of treaty Indians); Peyote Way Church v. Thornburgh, 922 F.2d 1210 (5th Cir. 1991) (upholding a regulation exempting religious ceremonial use of peyote by traditional Indian practitioners, whether on or off reservation [a regulation that has now become federal law, 42 U.S.C. § 1996a]).
157. Popovici v. Agler, 280 U.S. 379 (1930).
158. The text of the UNDRIP can be found at https://www.un.org/development/desa/indigenouspeoples/wp-content/uploads/sites/19/2018/11/UNDRIP_E_web.pdf. The UNDRIP was approved by the U.N. General Assembly in 2007. Originally, the United States was one of four countries that voted against the

Declaration. In 2010, President Obama announced that the United States would lend its support to the document, although it released a document that included "interpretations" as to the meaning of certain provisions of the document. *See* https://2009-2017.state.gov/s/srgia/154553.htm.

159. The text of the OAS American Declaration can be found at http://www.narf.org/wordpress/wp-content/uploads/2015/09/2016oas-declaration-indigenous-people.pdf. It was adopted by the Organization of American States in 2016.
160. UNDRIP Statements of Intent, art. 7, para. 2, and art. 9.
161. OAS American Declaration, art. XVII.
162. 490 U.S. 30 (1988).
163. *Id.* at 42, 51–54.
164. *Id.* at 46–48.
165. *Id.* at 44–45 & n.17.
166. *Id.* at 45–47.
167. *Id.* at 52 quoting *In re* Adoption of Halloway, 732 P.2d 962, 969–70 (1986).
168. *Id.* at 49–50.
169. 570 U.S. 637, 133 S. Ct. 2552 (2013).
170. *Id.* at 2562.
171. *Id.* at 2564.
172. *Id.* at 2565.
173. *Id.* at 2561, 2563.
174. *Id.* at 2565.
175. *Id.* at 2564. The exact meaning of this phrase has given rise to litigation and differing opinions on what it means for someone to indicate formally that they would like to adopt a specific child. *See* Native Village of Tununak v. State, Dep't of Health & Soc. Servs. (*Tununak II*), 334 P.3d 165 (Alaska 2014) (holding that because the grandmother did not file an adoption petition or any formal court document she had not formally sought to adopt her granddaughter and the preferences were inapplicable); *id.* (Winfree, J. dissenting) (grandmother indicating willingness to adopt during the pendency of the foster care proceeding sufficient to trigger preferences). *See also* Alaska Stat. § 47.1.112 (defining what constitutes a proxy for filing

an adoption petition). The recent case of *Haaland v. Brackeen*, 599 U.S. 255, 143 S. Ct. 1609 (2023) also addressed this issue in a slightly different context. In its analysis of the Tenth Amendment commandeering issue, it noted that the agency did not have the responsibility to find a preferred placement—that it was up to "the tribe or other objecting party to produce a higher-ranked placement." 143 S. Ct., at 1635.

176. *Id.* at 2557 & n.1. *See* Jack Trope & Adrian Smith, *The Continued Protection of Indian Children and Families After* Adoptive Couple v. Baby Girl: *What the Case Means and How to Respond*, Am. Indian L.R. 434, 463–66 (Spring 2014); *see also In re* G.V., 2016 Okla. Civ. App. 6 (2015) (finding that although active efforts were not required to be provided to the father in the case before the court, other provisions in the ICWA that protect the tribe's interest would still be applicable).
177. *Id.* at 2571.
178. See discussion at pages 153–155, 163, and 166.
179. *In re* Marcus S., 638 A.2d 1158 (Me. 1994).
180. *In re* D.L.L. & C.L.L., 291 N.W.2d 278 (S.D. 1980).
181. *In re* Appeal of Pima Cnty. Juv. Action, S-903, 635 P.2d 187 (Ariz. Ct. App. 1981), *cert. denied*, 455 U.S. 1007 (1982).
182. *In re* Miller, 182 Mich. App. 70, 451 N.W.2d 576 (1990) (non-Indian parent's challenge to the ICWA on ground that it gave Indian parents preferential treatment denied).
183. *In re* Two Babies (Okla. Dist. Ct. #JF 79-1121, 1980).
184. State *ex rel.* CSD v. Graves, 848 P.2d 133 (Or. App. 1993); *see also* Angus v. Joseph, 60 Or. App. 546 (Or. Ct. App. 1982).
185. *See In re* Interest of Phoenix L., 270 Neb. 870, 708 N.W.2d 786 (2006); Knight v. State, 1998 Okla. App. 118, 964 P.2d 241.
186. *In re* Bridget R., 49 Cal. Rptr. 2d 507 (Cal. App. 1996).
187. *In re* Alexandria Y., 45 Cal. App. 4th 1483, 53 Cal. Rptr. 2d 679 (Cal. App. 4th Dist. 1996).
188. *See In re* Alicia S., 65 Cal. App. 4th 79, 76 Cal. Rptr. 2d 121 (Cal. App. 1998); *In re* Adoption of Hannah S., 142 Cal. App. 4th 988 (Cal. App.

2006); *In re* Adoption of Lindsay C., 229 Cal. App. 3d 404, 280 Cal. Rptr. 194 (Cal. App. 1991); *In re* Vincent M., 150 Cal. App. 4th 1247 (2007). The case from the same judicial district that rejected the holding in the *Bridget R.* case was *In re* Alexandria P., 45 Cal. App. 4th 1483, 53 Cal. Rptr. 2d 679 (Cal. App. 4th Dist. 1996).

189. *See, e.g., In re* Baby Boy C., 805 N.Y.S.2d 313 (App. Div., 2015); *In re* Beach, 246 P.3d 845 (Wash. Ct. App. 2011).
190. Nat'l Council for Adoption v. Jewell, Case No. 1:15-cv-675-GBL-MSN (E.D. Va. 2015); A.D. v. Washburn, Case No. CV-15-1259-PHX-NVW (D. Ariz. 2015); Brackeen v. Zinke, Case No. 4:17-cv-00868-O (N.D. Tex. 2017).
191. In *Nat'l Council for Adoption v. Jewell*, 156 F. Supp. 3d 727 (E.D. Va. 2015), the trial court dismissed all claims and granted summary judgment for the defendants. The case was later dismissed by consent of the parties. In *A.D. v. Washburn*, 2017 WL 1019685 (D. Ariz. 2017), the trial court found that there was no genuine case or controversy before the court. On appeal, the case was ultimately dismissed as moot. A.D. v. Tahsuda, 739 Fed. Appx. 823 (9th Cir. 2018).
192. 599 U.S. 255, 143 S. Ct. 1609 (2023).
193. *Id.* at 1626.
194. *Id.* at 1627–31.
195. *Id.* at 1631–34.
196. *Id.* at 1638.
197. *Id.* at 1638–40.
198. *Id.* at 1640–41.
199. *Id.*
200. *Id.* at 1661–62. Post-*Brackeen*, at least one case challenging the constitutionality of the placement preferences has been brought based upon an equal protection claim, although thus far the plaintiffs have been unsuccessful. *In re* Welfare of Children of L.K. and A.S., 9 N.W.3d 174 (Minn. Ct. App. 2024) (appeal pending before the Minnesota Supreme Court).
201. *Id.* at 1641–61.
202. See Appendix D.

203. These states are California, Colorado, Connecticut, Iowa, Maine, Michigan, Minnesota, Montana, Nebraska, Nevada, New Mexico, North Carolina, North Dakota, Oklahoma, Oregon, Washington, Wisconsin, and Wyoming. In some cases, these statutes are stand-alone comprehensive statutes and in other cases the provisions are scattered through the provisions in state law that deal with child welfare more generally. Appendix D contains a list of the applicable state provisions compiled by the National Conference of State Legislatures, reprinted with their permission. It is anticipated that more states will adopt state ICWAs in the next few years.

204. 25 U.S.C. § 1921.

205. BIA GUIDELINES, *supra* note 48, § A.1.

206. A.J.B. v. Mont. Eighteen Jud. Dist. Ct., 411 Mont. 201, 523 P.3d 519 (2023) (state law which denied Indian parent the right to request an emergency protective service hearing unconstitutional); *In re* N.V., 744 N.W.2d 634 (Iowa 2008) (provision that placed limitations on a parent's ability to seek a placement that would deviate from the ICWA's placement preferences unconstitutional).

207. *In re* A.W., 741 N.W.2d 793, 812 (Iowa 2007). Another provision in Iowa's state ICWA that did not allow for a child to challenge transfer based upon the child's best interest was found to be unconstitutional in *In re* L.R. & S.G., 779 N.W.2d 481 (Iowa Ct. App. 2009), but this case was overruled by *In re* T.F., 972 N.W.2d. 1 (Iowa 2022).

208. IOWA CODE ANN. § 232B.3(a); NEB. REV. STAT. § 43-1503(5); N.M. STAT. ANN. § 32A-28-2(F).

209. MICH. COMP. LAWS ANN. § 712B.3(k); MINN. STAT. ANN. § 260.755(8).

210. WASH. REV. CODE § 13.38.040(2).

211. *Id.* § 13.38.040(16). Of note, some states have fairly elaborate code sections on Traditional Cultural Adoption. *See, e.g.*, CAL. WELF. & INST. CODE § 366.24.

212. MINN. STAT. ANN. § 260.755(6a).

213. NEB. CODE § 43-1506(3).

214. MINN. STAT. ANN. § 260.755(6a).

215. *Id.* § 260.771(2a).

216. Cal. Welf. & Inst. Code § 305.5; Or. Rev. Stat. § 419B.630(4)(d).
217. Mich. Comp. Laws Ann. § 712B.3(a).
218. Minn. Stat. Ann. § 260.755(1a)(b).
219. Wis. Stat. § 48.028(g).
220. Neb. Code § 43-1506(4) and (5).
221. N.D. Cent. Code § 27-20.2-15(3).
222. Iowa Code Ann. § 232B.6(2).
223. N.D. Cent. Code § 27-19.1.05(3).
224. Or. Rev. Stat. § 419B.624; N.M. Stat. Ann. § 32A-28-8.
225. Minn. Stat. Ann. § 260.7745.
226. Colo. Rev. Stat. § 19-1.2-120(1)(d), (2)(B); N.D. Cent. Code § 27-19.1.05(1)(c).
227. Iowa Code Ann. § 232B.9(1)(e); Neb. Rev. Stat. § 43-1508(1)(d), (2)(e); Wash. Rev. Code § 13.38.180(2)(f).
228. Minn. Stat. Ann. § 260.773(5).
229. Colo. Rev. Stat. § 19-1.2-120(5); N.M. Stat. Ann. § 32A-28-23.
230. Okla. Stat. Ann. tit. 10, § 40.6
231. Minn. Stat. Ann. § 260.773(10).
232. N.Y. Soc. Serv. § 39; N.Y. Comp. Codes R. & Regs. tit. 18, § 431.18; *see also In re* Dupree M., 171 A.D.3d 752 (N.Y. Ct. App. 2019).

2 Applicability of the ICWA

There are two predicates necessary for the Indian Child Welfare Act (ICWA) to apply in a child custody case in state court.[1] Statutory ICWA definitions are crucial to the analysis.[2] The first predicate is whether the case is a child custody proceeding. The ICWA defines a child custody proceeding to include foster care placements, termination of parental rights, preadoptive placements, and adoptive placements as those terms are uniquely defined in the act. The second predicate includes whether the child involved in the child custody proceeding is an Indian child as defined in the act.

This chapter will identify the parameters of an ICWA child custody proceeding and explore whether a child is an Indian child for ICWA purposes. The chapter also illuminates what types of cases fall outside the parameters of the ICWA and concludes with the current status of a highly questionable judicially created exception to the ICWA known as the Existing Indian Family Exception (EIFE). The substantive protections and procedural requirements for each type of ICWA custody proceeding are fully addressed in Chapters 4 and 5.

The Types of Child Custody Proceedings Covered by the ICWA

The ICWA defines a child custody proceeding to include foster care placements, terminations of parental rights, and preadoptive and adoptive placements, both voluntary and involuntary. Note that emergency proceedings are not encompassed in the definition of a child custody proceeding; nonetheless, the ICWA statutory language and the ICWA regulations address emergency proceedings, recognizing the need might arise for states to remove Indian children to prevent imminent physical damage or harm to the child.[3] More information regarding emergency proceedings involving an Indian child is addressed in Chapter 4.

Foster Care Placement

The ICWA defines a "foster care placement" as any action removing an Indian child from a parent or Indian custodian for temporary placement in a foster home or institution or the home of a guardian or conservator where the parent or Indian custodian cannot have the child returned upon demand, but where parental rights have not been terminated.[4] A foster care placement requires an act of removing an Indian child from either a parent or Indian custodian. The ICWA defines a "parent" to include any biological parent or parents of an Indian child or any Indian person who has lawfully adopted an Indian child, including adoptions under tribal law or custom, but does not include an unwed father where paternity has not been acknowledged or established.[5] A "parent" encompasses paternity determined by tribal acknowledgment, tribal adoptions, tribal laws, and tribal customs, as well as state law.[6] The term "Indian custodian" includes any Indian person who has legal custody of an Indian child under tribal law or custom or under state law or to whom temporary physical care, custody, and control has been transferred by the parent of such child.[7] An Indian person may demonstrate that he or she is an Indian custodian by looking to tribal law, tribal custom, or state law.[8]

The ICWA applies to both voluntary and involuntary foster care placements of an Indian child.[9] A voluntary placement is a placement made with the consent of a biological parent or Indian custodian. Section 1913 of the statute specifies the formalities for consent and withdrawal of consent to a foster care placement.[10] Note that ICWA does not include a placement where the parent or Indian custodian can regain custody of the child upon demand.[11] The regulations clarify that "upon demand" means that the parent can have the child returned upon a mere verbal request, without any express or implied formalities or contingencies.[12] This exclusion ensures that parents and courts are not burdened every time a parent is desirous of temporarily placing a child, but the regulations and guidelines are clear-cut that any time a court is invoked, or formal action required, the ICWA would apply.

Thus, the ICWA would apply in voluntary proceedings where an Indian parent or Indian custodian voluntarily places his or her child with a state social services agency or private agency on a temporary basis according to a state court custody order, since the parent/Indian custodian cannot have the child returned upon verbal request.[13] It is also important to note that if a parent or Indian custodian consents to a foster care placement because of threats by an agency that a child will otherwise be removed if parental consent is not forthcoming, that is considered an involuntary proceeding under the act, not a voluntary proceeding.[14]

The application of the ICWA to involuntary foster care proceedings is straightforward. The ICWA applies to the involuntary removal of the Indian child from a parent or Indian custodian.[15] The ICWA also applies to involuntary guardianships or conservatorships.[16] The ICWA is activated[17] if the *possible result* of a proceeding includes a foster care placement or termination of parental rights, even if the actual decision at the proceeding is to leave the child in the home.[18] The act applies even if the outcomes ultimately do not materialize.[19] ICWA will also apply to proceedings involving status offenses if any part of the proceeding results in the need for out-of-home placement of the child, including a foster care, termination of parental rights, preadoptive or adoptive placement.[20]

Termination of Parental Rights Proceedings

The ICWA defines "termination of parental rights" to mean any action resulting in the termination of the parent–child relationship.[21] As with the foster care placement segment already mentioned, it is critical to determine whether the termination of parental rights is a voluntary proceeding or an involuntary proceeding, as the ICWA has specific statutory language and substantive and due process protections based upon that distinction.[22] Although the ICWA does not prohibit the practice of allowing Indian parents to voluntarily terminate their parental rights, the ICWA does place stringent requirements on the procedures for termination including a provision that sets forth that any consent given prior to, or within ten days after, birth of the Indian child shall not be valid.[23] The act applies to private terminations of parental rights,[24] including any proceeding in which the termination of parental rights is a potential disposition.[25] This includes stepparent adoptions.[26]

Preadoptive Placements

The ICWA states that a "preadoptive placement" means the temporary placement of an Indian child in a foster home or institution after the termination of parental rights, but prior to or in lieu of adoptive placement.[27] While the ICWA pertains to a preadoptive placement as a child custody proceeding, the distinction between a preadoptive placement and a termination of parental rights proceeding or foster care placement may be important for jurisdictional purposes because of the specific language in the ICWA intervention and transfer sections, which reference foster care placements and termination of parental rights proceedings and not specifically preadoptive or adoptive placements.[28] As a result, a recent Arizona case held that a tribe may not obtain a transfer from state court to tribal court of a preadoptive or adoptive placement pursuant to the ICWA, although it opined that transfer might occur under other authorities.[29] Preadoptive placements include any long-term foster care placement, provided the parental rights of both of the natural parents have been terminated. In *In re Guardianship of A.K.*,[30] the Arizona Court of Appeals found that a permanent guardianship petition filed after parental rights have been terminated is also a preadoptive placement under ICWA.

Most of the ICWA provisions germane to preadoptive placements pertain to where Indian children should be placed and not to any particular procedural formalities a state court must satisfy to effectuate a preadoptive placement. The ICWA placement preference provisions are addressed in Chapter 5.

Adoptive Placements

The ICWA defines adoptive placements as "the permanent placement of an Indian child for adoption, including any action resulting in a final decree of adoption."[31] This definition covers adoptions arranged by state social services agencies as well as private adoption agencies.[32] It also encompasses stepparent adoptions. It is difficult to reconcile the adoptive placement preference provisions with the stepparent adoption scenario, especially when the custodial parent is non-Indian, although the request of a parent may be grounds for deviating from the placement preferences.[33]

The ICWA strongly suggests that the provisions of the ICWA continue to apply up to the point of a final adoption decree being rendered by a state court and not only up to the point where an adoptive placement is effected. This may be important in certain cases when an Indian tribe or relatives of an Indian family become aware of an Indian child being placed for adoption after the placement is accomplished.[34] The ICWA clearly permits these parties to advance the goals of the act even though the placement has already been effected. Indeed, the ICWA even applies to certain matters that arise after a final decree of adoption has taken place, as one provision allows certain parties collaterally to attack a final decree of adoption,[35] and yet another provision allows a parent to petition for the return of an adopted Indian child if the adoption is vacated.[36] ICWA guidelines clarify that termination of parental rights is not required prior to adoption by stating that adoptions that do not involve a termination of parental rights are still included within the ICWA's definition of a "child custody proceeding" as either a foster care placement or an adoptive placement because the statutory language of the ICWA does not require a termination of parental rights prior to adoption.[37]

Indian Child

The ICWA applies to the types of child custody proceedings previously discussed that involve an Indian child.[38] The ICWA definition of "Indian child" includes any unmarried person who is under the age of 18 and is either a member of an Indian tribe or is eligible for membership in an Indian tribe and is the biological child of a member of an Indian tribe.[39] An Indian tribe is defined as any Indian tribe, band, nation, or other organized group or community of Indians recognized as eligible for services provided to Indians by the U.S. Bureau of Indian Affairs because of their status as Indians, including any Alaska Native village.[40] A federally recognized Indian tribe meets this criteria.

Tribal membership is based on the child's political ties to a federally recognized Indian tribe, either by virtue of the child's own citizenship in the tribe or through a biological parent's citizenship and the child's eligibility for citizenship.[41] The terms "citizen" and "citizenship" are used in the ICWA regulations because these terms are synonymous with "member" and "membership" as determined by tribal governments.[42] Congressional power to act for these children's protection is grounded in the political tie to the federally recognized tribe through parental citizenship and the child's own eligibility.[43] This is consistent with other contexts in which the citizenship of a parent is relevant to the child's political affiliation to that sovereign.[44]

Not all Indian tribes are federally recognized.[45] Certain tribes are recognized by the states in which they are located.[46] Other tribes were federally recognized at one time but had their status as federally recognized tribes terminated in the 1950s when Congress terminated several tribes during a period of assimilation, specifically providing that federal law applicable to Indians would no longer apply to those tribes. Many of these tribes are seeking to have their federally recognized status restored; and other tribes who are not federally recognized can seek recognition through the federal acknowledgment process or through legislation. Thus, new tribes are sometimes added to the list of federally recognized tribes. Therefore, it is important to make proper inquiry with the Department of the Interior to determine whether a particular tribe is eligible for federal services. The Secretary of the Interior annually publishes a list of Indian tribes eligible for federal services and programs. The link to the website that contains the list is included in Appendix E.

Membership in a federally recognized tribe should not be equated necessarily with enrollment with the tribe. Enrollment with a tribe is the most common method for tribes to compile a list of tribal members, but it certainly is not the exclusive manner of citizenship recognition.[47] Each tribe may have its own method of determining its membership and different types of membership, and therefore a tribe needs to be consulted in any case where it appears that a child may have some affiliation with that tribe.[48] The definition of Indian child would seem to preclude ICWA coverage where a non-Indian child has been adopted by an Indian family; however, if the particular tribe allows that particular child to become a member by tribal law, tribal practice, or custom and tradition, then ICWA would apply.[49]

The determination by a tribe of whether a child is a member, whether a child is eligible for membership, or whether a biological parent is a member is solely within the jurisdiction and authority of the tribe.[50] The state court may not substitute its own determination regarding a child's membership in a tribe, a child's eligibility for membership in a tribe, or a parent's membership in a tribe.[51] The Department of the Interior is not authorized to make a determination that a child is not a member or eligible for membership with a tribe.[52] The best way to obviate the need to establish that a child is an Indian child under the ICWA is to have the relevant tribe declare that the child is either a member or eligible for membership and the biological child of a member of a federally recognized tribe. Note that the adult member does, in fact, have the final say on the adult member's relationship with the tribe, as it may be possible for tribal membership to be renounced.[53] Where a tribe cannot or does not make a determination of membership or eligibility after multiple attempts to obtain this information from the tribe, a state court may make the determination of whether the child is an Indian child for the purposes of the application of the ICWA based upon all of the evidence before it.[54] In such a case, the burden of proof would be on the person seeking the application of the ICWA.[55]

The ICWA regulations indicate that state courts must ask each participant in an emergency, voluntary or involuntary, child custody proceeding whether the participant knows or has reason to know that the child is an Indian child.[56] The inquiry should be made at the commencement of the proceeding, and all responses should be on the record. To provide the court with information it needs, the state agency or other party seeking placement should ask the child, parents, and extended family which tribe they may be affiliated with and obtain genealogical information.[57] State courts must instruct the parties to inform the court if they subsequently receive information that provides reason to know the child is an Indian child.[58] A new inquiry must be made in every case involving the child[59] and it has been held that a court may order that a new inquiry be made at the TPR stage even where the child was found not to be an Indian child at the initial foster care hearing.[60] A conditional remand to the lower court for further inquiry to determine whether the ICWA should have been applied is a common remedy utilized by courts on appeal when the initial inquiry has been deemed to be inadequate.[61]

State courts that have reason to know a child is an Indian child must treat the child as an Indian child and apply the ICWA to that child, unless and until it is determined on the record that the child does not meet the definition of an Indian child.[62] In addition to circumstances where the court has specifically been provided with information relevant to the determination of whether the child is an Indian child, a state court also has reason to know that a child is an Indian child if the court is informed that the domicile or residence of the child, the child's parent, or the child's Indian custodian is on a reservation or in an Alaska Native village.[63] The location of the parent, Indian custodian, or child does not create a presumption that the child is an Indian child if that provision is triggered; rather, such domicile or residence is a factor that requires further investigation because it gives the court "reason to know" that the child is an Indian child. See Chapter 4 for a more detailed discussion of the case law interpreting "reason to know."

The regulations require that the party seeking placement for an Indian child exercise due diligence in reaching out to tribes in which the child may be a member or eligible for membership.[64] If only the ancestral group is known, each of the tribes in that ancestral group should be contacted.[65] Written notice is required and informal contact (telephone, email) is recommended; conversations should be documented.[66] It is recommended that a request for verification include the following:

- Genograms or ancestry/family charts for both parents
- All known names of both parents
- Current and former addresses of parents and extended family
- Birthdates, place of birth (and death) of both parents
- All known tribal affiliation for anyone on the ancestry/family charts
- Domicile/resident addresses[67]

As noted earlier, it is only after multiple inquiries have been made to the tribe, without response, that a court should decide whether a child is an Indian child based upon the information available to it.[68]

If a child or the child's parent(s) resides on a tribe's reservation, the party seeking the placement must contact that tribe to find out if the child is a citizen or the child's parent is a citizen and the child is eligible for citizenship and the tribe would normally have exclusive jurisdiction over the proceeding. In addition to reservations, the provision highlights Alaska Native villages because Alaska is home to approximately one-half of the federally recognized Indian tribes, but there is only a single reservation. Thus, it is similarly required to contact the tribe associated with the Alaska Native village where the child or parents reside.[69] The ICWA regulations provide guidance to state courts if a case arises wherein an Indian child is eligible for membership in more than one tribe.[70]

In certain cases, it will not become apparent that a child custody proceeding involves an Indian child until the proceeding is in the advanced stages of a case. This has created inequities in cases where tribes mistakenly assert that a child is not a member and then, on further inquiry, determine that the original determination was erroneous. Most courts that have dealt with the issue have held that the late discovery will not vitiate the proceedings up to that point but that the ICWA would have to be adhered to in future proceedings.[71] However, if the court or any officer of the court, including guardians ad litem and lawyers in the case, was aware of certain circumstances, more adequately set out in the guidelines, that would put the court on notice that an Indian child is involved, the proceedings may be invalidated.[72] A few courts have held that the failure of a party or tribe to invoke the ICWA early in the proceedings may constitute a waiver of the argument against ICWA's application later in the proceedings.[73] These courts appear to be in the minority, however, as most courts have held that the late invocation of the ICWA requires the trial court to make the determination at the point the issue is raised.[74]

It is critical to note that if the ICWA applies at the commencement of a proceeding, it will not cease to apply simply because the child reaches age 18 during the pendency of the proceeding.[75] Where state and/or federal law provides for a child custody proceeding to extend beyond an Indian child's 18th birthday, the ICWA would not stop applying to the proceeding simply because of the child's age. This is to ensure that a set of laws applies consistently throughout a proceeding, and to discourage strategic behavior or delays in ICWA compliance in circumstances where a child's 18th birthday is near. The ICWA requires the Indian child need be under the age of 18 only at the commencement of the proceeding for the ICWA to apply.

Proceedings Not Covered by the ICWA

Tribal Court Proceedings

The ICWA does not apply to child custody proceedings involving Indian children that take place in tribal court.[76] A tribal court is defined as "a court with jurisdiction over child custody proceedings and which is either a Court of Indian Offenses, a court established and operated under the code or custom of an Indian tribe or any other administrative body of a tribe, which is vested with authority of child custody proceedings."[77] The ICWA only applies to child custody proceedings involving Indian children in state courts.[78] One of the central reasons for the ICWA was that state courts had often failed to recognize the essential tribal relations of Indian people and the cultural and social standards prevailing in Indian communities.[79]

Voluntary Placements

The ICWA will not apply to a voluntary placement that either parent, both parents, or the Indian custodian has, of his or her or their free will, without a threat of removal by a state agency, chosen for the Indian child and that does not operate to prohibit the child's parent or Indian custodian from regaining custody of the child upon demand without any formalities or contingencies.[80] The key concepts are that the placement was at the parent(s) or Indian custodian's free will and the child will be returned upon the parent(s) or Indian custodian's verbal request without condition. For example, a parent or Indian custodian could voluntarily place an Indian child with a relative or trusted adult while seeking medical care or when traveling for long periods of time. The test for a voluntary placement is whether the parent can regain the child with only a verbal request.

Divorce Proceedings

The ICWA does not apply to child custody disputes arising between the natural parents of a child married or unmarried—even if the child is Indian.[81] This is true even if the child's parents are both Indian, if neither one is Indian, or if one is Indian and the other is not.[82] As discussed in more detail later, the ICWA does apply to private disputes between parents and nonparents as part of guardianship proceedings or other legal proceedings, or to any case where any party seeks to place the Indian child in a temporary placement other than the alternate parent or Indian custodian.[83]

Delinquency Proceedings

ICWA does not apply to delinquency proceedings although the ICWA will apply if an Indian child is placed in foster care or another out-of-home placement as a result of a status offense.[84] A status offense is defined as offenses that would not be considered criminal if committed by an adult; they are acts prohibited only because of a person's status as a minor (for example, truancy, incorrigibility, possession of alcohol).[85]

In practice, there are different ways in which this general rule might be applied. If, for example, a state court were to attempt to terminate the parental rights of a parent over an Indian child because of delinquent acts committed by that child, the ICWA would govern the termination proceeding, though not the adjudication of delinquency. Similarly, if the gravamen of the delinquency petition were acts of truancy (a status offense) instead of criminal behavior, the ICWA would govern the adjudication of delinquency as well as disposition. In addition, if the underlying basis for the removal of the Indian child involves parental inability to adequately exercise custodial responsibilities and not the criminal behavior in which he or she engaged, the ICWA would appear to apply.[86]

In the majority of cases, however, when an Indian child commits a delinquent act neither his or her placement nor the proceedings whereby he or she is adjudicated delinquent are governed by the ICWA. One troubling area regarding dispositional placements due to delinquent behavior, however, that may implicate the ICWA is the tendency of some state corrections/probation officials to keep children in out-of-home placements, initiated because of delinquent acts, because of determinations by state corrections officials that the child's home would not be an appropriate placement for a child on probation. Although there is scarcity of case law on this subject, it would appear that if the out-of-home placement is continued due solely to a determination that the Indian child's home is inappropriate for the return of the child, the ICWA notice provisions and burdens of proof, discussed herein, apply.[87]

First Nations/Canada

Note that tribes encompassed in ICWA's definition of Indian tribe do not include Canadian tribes, even if those tribes can show a historical and genealogical relationship to tribes of the United States. One court has noted an exception to this general rule that the ICWA does not apply to Canadian First Nations children when it held that, notwithstanding the apparent inapplicability of the ICWA to the procedural requirements of a state court case, the provision of the ICWA governing the release of adoptive records to a person's tribe applied to a Canadian native.[88] Of note, if a U.S. tribe recognizes Canadian Indians from related tribes as members of the U.S. tribe, then presumably the ICWA would apply in that instance.

Judicially Created Exceptions

Intrafamilial Disputes

One question that arose shortly after the act was passed was whether it applied to intrafamilial custody disputes. Although the

ICWA and the ICWA regulations exclude custody disputes between parents, the act can apply to other types of intrafamily disputes, assuming that such disputes otherwise meet the statutory and regulatory definitions, because the ICWA makes only two exceptions to application of the act in child custody proceedings involving an Indian child, neither of which are for intrafamily disputes.[89] Thus, while there was some early case law that held that the ICWA did not apply to custody disputes between a parent and a nonparent, it now appears well settled that ICWA applies in such circumstances.[90] This is consistent with the ICWA regulations, which state that if an intrafamily dispute meets the definition of a child custody proceeding and involves an Indian child, the provisions of the ICWA apply.[91] An example where the act would be triggered in an intrafamilial dispute arises where a nonparent applies to a court for the guardianship of a minor Indian child against the wishes of a parent.[92] In addition, the act also applies if a custodial parent attempts to terminate the parental rights of the noncustodial parent for purposes of commencing a stepparent adoption or otherwise.[93]

Existing Indian Family Exception

Although most states have rejected the doctrine, some state courts have adopted an exception to the application of the ICWA that has become known as the Existing Indian Family Exception (EIFE) based on the state courts' interpretation of the ICWA's intent. These courts have held that the provisions of the ICWA are inapposite in a child custody proceeding in which an Indian child is not being removed from an Indian family or an Indian cultural setting equivalent to an Indian family. Early cases adopting this exception routinely involved non-Indian parents attempting to terminate the parental rights of Indian parents where the Indian parents and the family had little or no contact with the child. More recent variations of the exception have included the state court weighing the tribal contacts of the Indian child and parents to determine whether an Indian family exists.

Relying on the legislative history behind the enactment of the ICWA, these state courts that have embraced the EIFE have held that the act should not apply unless the child is being removed from an existing Indian family or from a family where the child was exposed to Indian culture. The EIFE effectively shifts the focus from the ICWA's application in child custody proceedings involving an Indian child to a state court's conclusion of whether the child is being removed from an Indian family as that term is defined by state courts. It is a shift that clearly undermines congressional intent to correct the pernicious effects of applying state laws and non-Indian standards to Indian child custody proceedings.

The earliest decision to sanction the EIFE was in *Baby Boy L.*,[94] wherein the Kansas Supreme Court refused to follow the dictates of ICWA when a non-Indian mother petitioned to terminate the parental rights of an incarcerated Indian father. The court held that its application of ICWA to that factual situation would not serve the purposes articulated by congress. Many state courts quickly followed suit, including courts of South Dakota,[95] Indiana,[96] Missouri,[97] Oklahoma,[98] and Mississippi.[99]

The U.S. Supreme Court granted certiorari in the Mississippi case, albeit for a different issue, and appeared to have laid the EIFE to rest in *Mississippi Band of Choctaw Indians v. Holyfield*.[100] In that case, the court examined a situation where a reservation-domiciled Indian couple placed their twins with a non-Indian family residing off the reservation for adoption. The adoption was permitted by the state court despite the Indian tribe's contention that the state court lacked jurisdiction under the provision of the ICWA, which vested the Indian tribal court with exclusive jurisdiction over child custody proceedings involving reservation-domiciled Indian children. The Mississippi Supreme Court affirmed the adoption, holding that ICWA did not apply because the children had never resided with an Indian family and were not domiciled on the reservation, all facts determined by the state court. The U.S. Supreme Court rejected the Mississippi Supreme Court's conclusion that the children were not domiciled on the reservation and reversed the state adoption order, sending the case back to the tribal court. In so doing, the court strongly suggested that the EIFE adopted by the Mississippi Supreme Court and others to the application of ICWA was doctrinally flawed. A number of state courts reversed their position on the EIFE post-*Holyfield*, including the state that originated the doctrine—Kansas.[101]

In *Adoptive Couple v. Baby Girl*,[102] a sharply divided U.S. Supreme Court narrowed the application of three provisions of the ICWA in the adoption case of a Cherokee girl by non-Indians over the objection of the Cherokee father based upon the fact that the father never had physical or legal custody of the child and had in the opinion of the court "abandoned" the child prior to birth. In so doing, the Court utilized some of the language that can be found in EIFE cases, namely that there was no Indian family relationship that would be discontinued by the termination of the Indian parent's rights since the father had never had legal or physical custody of the child. Although given an opportunity to do so, however, the Court did not explicitly adopt the EIFE. Instead, the Court referenced the *Holyfield* decision for the proposition that the ICWA applied because the case involved an Indian child in a child custody proceeding as defined by the ICWA, although certain sections did not apply to the father since the father had not had legal or physical custody of the child. See Chapter 1 for further discussion of both the *Mississippi Band of Choctaw Indians* and *Adoptive Couple v. Baby Girl* U.S. Supreme Court cases.

Flash forward to the ICWA regulations of 2016 that directly prohibit states from applying the criteria utilized by courts that had adopted the EIFE. The regulations found that the ICWA includes no provision for a state court to determine the applicability of the

ICWA based on an Indian child's or parent's social, cultural, or geographic ties to the tribe.[103] The Department of Interior further concluded that reliance on the EIFE frustrates the ICWA's purpose to curtail state authorities from making child custody determinations based on misconceptions of Indian family life and encroaches on the power of tribes to define their own rules of membership.[104] Further repudiating the EIFE, the ICWA regulations prohibit state courts from considering factors such as the participation of the parents or the Indian child in tribal cultural, social, religious, or political activities; the relationship between the Indian child and his or her parents; whether the parent ever had custody of the child; or the Indian child's blood quantum.[105] The regulations are consistent with the overwhelming trend in state courts prior to the issuance of the regulations.

Indeed, no court has adopted the EIFE since the regulations, and at least one state that had adopted the EIFE appears to be reconsidering.[106] In *Delaware Tribe of Indians v. Nowicki-Eldridge*,[107] the West Virginia Supreme Court analyzed the history of the EIFE. It determined that although the exception was adopted and applied in approximately 20 states in the 1980s and 1990s, in recent years all but seven jurisdictions presented with the exception have either repudiated or rejected the EIFE.[108]

The West Virginia court found the analysis in *Thompson v. Fairfax County Department of Family Services*[109] especially persuasive as to why the EIFE exception must be rejected. The *Thompson* court noted:

> We decline to recognize the [EIF] Exception for a number of reasons. First, the plain text of the statute does not recognize the application of this exception. There is no threshold requirement in the Act that the child must have been born into or must be living with an existing Indian family, or that the child must have some particular type of relationship with the tribe or his or her Indian

> heritage. Because Congress has clearly delineated the nature of the relationship between an Indian child and tribe necessary to trigger application of the Act, judicial insertion of an additional criterion for applicability is plainly beyond the intent of Congress and must be rejected.

This chapter has explored the type of state court child custody proceedings to which the ICWA applies, whether a child is an Indian child, the types of cases that the ICWA does not apply to, and the highly questionable application of the judicially created EIFE. The chapters that follow discuss in more detail the jurisdictional, procedural, and substantive provisions of the ICWA.

Endnotes

1. 25 C.F.R. § 23.103.
2. 25 U.S.C. § 1903.
3. 25 U.S.C. § 1922; Dep't of the Interior, Bureau of Indian Affairs, Indian Child Welfare Proceedings (2016), 81 Fed. Reg. 38793, 38872.
4. 25 U.S.C. § 1903(1)(i); In Jude M. v. DHSS, 394 P.3d 543 (Alaska 2017), the court found that a long-term guardianship where parental rights have not been terminated is considered a foster care placement and not a de facto termination of parental rights.
5. 25 U.S.C. § 1903(9).
6. In the Commentary to the regulations, the Department of Interior noted that state courts may be required to provide full faith and credit to a tribe's determination that a father has acknowledged or established paternity. Dep't of the Interior, Bureau of Indian Affairs, Indian Child Welfare Proceedings, 81 Fed. Reg. 38796 (2016). Such determinations may be based upon a tribe's organic documents such as tribal constitutions and tribal codes, as well as tribal custom and tradition. *But cf.* Adoptive Couple v. Baby Girl, 570 U.S. 637, 133 S. Ct. 2552 (2013) (holding that because the Indian father in

the case never had either legal or physical custody of the child prior to the adoption proceeding, the unwed father was not entitled to certain ICWA protections, including § 1912(f) applicable to termination of parental rights of a parent). For a deeper discussion of this case, see Chapter 1 and for a deeper discussion of the meaning of the term "parent," particularly in the context of unwed fathers, see Chapter 3.

7. 25 U.S.C. § 1903(6). For a deeper discussion of the meaning of Indian custodian, see Chapter 3.
8. 25 C.F.R. § 23.2; *see also* In the Best Interest of M.R.P. C., 794 N.W.2d 373 (Minn. Ct. App. 2011) (holding that the paternal grandparents were entitled to an evidentiary hearing to prove their de facto custodian status in an ICWA case).
9. 25 C.F.R. § 23.103(a)(1)(i), (ii).
10. 25 U.S.C. § 1913.
11. 25 C.F.R. § 23.103(b)(4).
12. *Id.*; BIA Guidelines for Implementing the Indian Child Welfare Act § L.20 (Dec. 2016). (The final rule clarifies that "upon demand" means that custody can be regained by a verbal request, and "without any formalities or contingencies." Examples of formalities or contingencies are formal court proceedings, the signing of agreements, and the repayment of the child's expenses).
13. 25 C.F.R. § 23.2.
14. *Id.* (definition of "involuntary proceeding"); *see also In re* J.M., 218 P.3d 1213 (Mont. 2009) (consent to temporary legal custody after involuntary proceeding had commenced did not transform case into voluntary proceeding); *In re* Welfare of MG, 201 P.3d 354 (Wash. App. 2009) (consent to a dependency order in an involuntary proceeding does not make the proceeding voluntary).
15. 25 C.F.R. § 23.103; *see also id.* § 23.2 (Involuntary proceeding means a child custody proceeding in which the parent does not consent of his or her free will to the foster care, preadoptive or adoptive placement, or termination of parental rights or in which the parent consents to the foster

care, preadoptive, or adoptive placement or termination of parental rights under threat of removal of the child by a state court or agency.).

16. 25 U.S.C. § 1903 ((1) 'child custody proceeding' shall mean and include— . . . (a) foster-care placement which shall mean any action removing an Indian child from his or her parent or Indian custodian for temporary placement in a foster home or institution or the home of a guardian or conservator where the parent or Indian custodian cannot have the child returned upon demand, but where parental rights have not been terminated.").
17. 25 U.S.C. § 1903(1).
18. *See* State *Ex rel.* Juvenile Dept. v. Cook, 744 P.2d 596 (Or. Ct. App. 1987) (holding the ICWA applies even if the result of the dependency petition is not the removal of the child from the parent's home). *See also* 25 C.F.R. § 23.3 (A proceeding in which the parent agrees to an out-of-home placement of the child under threat that the child will be otherwise removed is not "voluntary.").
19. 25 C.F.R. § 23.2; Dep't of the Interior, Bureau of Indian Affairs, Indian Child Welfare Proceedings, 81 Fed. Reg. 38793, 38799 (2016) (a "child custody proceeding" is "an activity that may culminate in foster care placement, a preadoptive placement, an adoptive placement, or termination of parental rights . . . the ICWA requirements would apply to an action that may result in one of the placement outcomes, even if it ultimately does not. For example, the ICWA would apply to an action where a court was considering a foster care placement of a child but ultimately decided to return the child to the parent(s). Thus, even though the action did not result in a foster care placement, it may have culminated in such a placement and, therefore, should be considered a 'child custody proceeding' under the statute.").
20. 25 C.F.R. § 23.103(1)(iii).
21. 25 U.S.C. § 1903(1)(ii).
22. *Id.* §§ 1912, 1913.
23. *Id.* § 1913(a). *See also* discussion in Chapter 4.
24. 25 C.F.R. § 23.103.

25. *Id.* § 23.103(a).
26. *See In re* the Petition of M.G., 465 P.3d 120 (Colo. Ct. App., Div. IV, 2020) (ICWA applies to stepparent adoptions even when the child remains with the biological parent); and *In re* Adoption of T.A.W., 186 Wash. 2d 828, 849, 383 P.3d 492 (Wash. S. Ct. 2016) (ICWA applies to stepparent adoptions).
27. 25 U.S.C. § 1903(1)(iii).
28. *Id.* § 1911(b).
29. Gila River Indian Cmty. v. Dep't of Child Safety, 242 Ariz. 277, 395 P.3d 286 (Ariz. 2017) (holding that the ICWA does not mandate transfer of a preadoptive or adoptive placement to the tribe, but also does not preclude a tribe from requesting the transfer to tribal court of a preadoptive or adoptive placement under other authority); *see also In re* Guardianship of A.K., 557 P.3d 770 (Ct. App. Ariz., Div. 1 2024) ("it may be appropriate to transfer preadoptive and adoptive proceedings involving children residing outside of a reservation to tribal jurisdiction in particular circumstances" but declining to identify criteria).
30. 557 P.3d 770 (Ct. App. Ariz., Div. 1 2024).
31. 25 U.S.C. § 1903(1)(iv).
32. *See* Adoptive Couple v. Baby Girl, 570 U.S. 637, 133 S. Ct. 2252 (2013) (holding a private adoption is covered by the ICWA, but that any parties seeking custody of or adoption of an Indian child must formally indicate a willingness to adopt to be considered as an adoptive placement).
33. The adoption placement preference provisions address the placement of an Indian child when neither parent is able to care for the child. The placement preferences do not conform well to the stepparent adoption scenario where the minor child remains with one of the parents after adoption. However, at least one court has held that a state court is still bound to apply the placement preferences even in a stepparent adoption. *In re* Adoption of Lindsay C., 229 Cal. App. 3d 404, 280 Cal. Rptr. 194 (Cal. App. 1991); *see also* 25 C.F.R. § 23.132(c)(1) (The request by one parent may be grounds to find good cause to deviate from the placement preferences if the parent has reviewed the options that would comply with the placement preferences.).

34. 25 U.S.C. § 1913(d); *id.* § 1916(a). *See In re* Petition of Phillip A.C. v. Tlingit & Haida Tribes of Alaska, 122 Nev. 1284, 149 P.3d 51 (Nev. S.Ct. 2006) (holding that the district court had authority to set aside adoption for failure to adhere to ICWA's consent requirements and that the tribe had standing to contest the adoption of the Indian child). *See also In re* J.R.S., 690 P.2d 10 (Alaska 1984) (intervention by tribe in post-termination adoption proceeding involving Indian child was necessary to preserve tribe's interest in its child member).
35. 25 U.S.C. §§ 1914, 1916(a).
36. *Id.* § 1916(a).
37. BIA GUIDELINES, *supra* note 12, § L.3; By contrast, many state laws do require that before a court may make a child available for adoption, it must terminate the parental rights of the biological parents. *See, e.g., In re* the Adoption of B.B., 2017 UT 59, 417 P.3d 1 (2017).
38. 25 U.S.C. § 1903(4).
39. *Id.* In *Native Vill. of Chignik v. State of Alaska*, 518 P.3d 708 (Alaska 2022), the court held that the child must be eligible for and the parent a member of the same tribe. The statutory language does not make that explicit linkage, however, and it is possible that other courts will reach a different conclusion. Where a child is eligible, but the parent is not a member, then a court may find that the child is not an Indian child. *See In re* the Petition of M.G., 465 P.3d 120 (Colo. Ct. App., Div. IV, 2020) (holding that the child was not an Indian child although eligible for enrollment in Comanche Nation since mom was not enrolled and testified she had no tribal affiliation); *In re* Adoption of C.D., 751 N.W.2d 236 (S. Ct. N.D. 2008) (holding that notwithstanding evidence of Native American heritage, child was not an "Indian child" under ICWA, absent evidence of mother's current membership in a federally recognized Indian tribe). However, some state ICWAs have eliminated the requirement that the parent be a member if the child is eligible. See discussion of state ICWAs in Chapter 1
40. 25 U.S.C. § 1903(8). The Alaska Native Claims Settlement Act (ANCSA) referenced in this section was an attempt by Congress to settle the land

rights of Alaska Natives and to set up regional corporations that would then select for their use some of the lands set aside by Congress for the use of Native corporations. However, the ICWA includes all Alaska Natives, including those from Native villages, as well as resident and nonresident members of the regional corporations set up by ANCSA.

41. 25 C.F.R. § 23.2.
42. Dep't of the Interior, Bureau of Indian Affairs, Indian Child Welfare Proceedings, 81 Fed. Reg. 38795 (2016).
43. *Id.*
44. *See* 8 U.S.C. §§ 1401, 1431 (providing for U.S. citizenship for persons born outside of the United States when one or both parents are citizens and certain other conditions are met).
45. 25 U.S.C. § 1903(8) (Indian tribe means any Indian tribe, band, nation, or other organized group or community of Indians recognized as eligible for the services provided to Indians by the Secretary because of their status as Indians, including any Alaska Native village as defined in § 1602(c) of title 43); 25 C.F.R. Part 83 (regulations providing standards for tribes seeking federal recognition); *see also* N.C. GEN. STAT. ch. 71A (state recognition of a number of tribes located in North Carolina who are not recognized by the federal government).
46. Generally, ICWA has been interpreted to apply only to federally recognized tribes, but there have been exceptions to this rule. *See In re* M.B., E.B., & B.B., 204 P.3d 1242 (Mont. 2009) (applying the ICWA to a state-recognized tribe in Montana); *cf. In re* Dupree M., 171 A.D.3d 752 (N.Y. Ct. App. 2019); (ICWA applied to the Unkechaug Indian Nation, even though the nation was not federally recognized, since a state statute applied ICWA to state-recognized tribes and the state of New York recognized Unkechaug as an Indian tribe).
47. United States v. Broncheau, 597 F.2d 1260, 1263 (9th Cir. 1979); Nelson v. Hunter, 132 Or. App. 361, 888 P.2d 124 (1995) (court, after concluding that person can be member of a tribe without being enrolled, determined that mother of Indian children was not Indian under the ICWA because she could not prove "membership"). *But cf. In re* Manuel C. v. Amber S. & Red Lake Band of Chippewa Indians, 314 Neb. 91, 988 N.W.2d 520 (S. Ct. Neb.

2023) (where mother had begun the enrollment process, but not completed it, and the children were eligible for membership, the court found that the children were not yet Indian children [although they might become Indian children in the future], even though the tribe indicated that it considered the mother and children to be members of the tribe for ICWA purposes.). Where enrollment is the tribal mechanism for making the child a member, at least one court has opined that while an agency is not required by the statute to enroll a child in the tribe when the child is eligible, it would be a best practice. People in Interest of K.C. & L.C., 487 P.3d 263 (Colo. 2021).

48. *See In re* N.C.H., 311 Or. App. 102, 489 P.3d 139 (Ct. App. Or. 2021) (holding that a child was an Indian child when the Karuk Tribe testified that although the child was not a fully enrolled member because his blood quantum was too low, he was nonetheless was eligible for a descendancy membership, which allows him to "maintain a connection with all our tribal members or all of our tribal people" and receive a "very minimal amount of support services."). *See also In re* A.A. v. GG et al., 88 Cal. App. 5th 393 (Ct. App., 4th Dist., Div. 2, 2023). In this case, the children could not be enrolled with the Jemez Pueblo due to low blood quantum, but they were eligible for naturalization with the tribe and could receive health benefits but not federal funds. The paperwork for naturalization was sent to mom but was never completed and no objection was made to the court's finding these were not Indian children. It was unclear from the record whether the tribe would have considered these children to be members of the tribe for the purposes of ICWA if naturalized.

49. *In re* Dependency & Neglect of A.L., 442 N.W.2d 233 (S.D. 1989) (Although the children were the biological child of Caucasian parents, they were also enrolled tribal members and thus, based upon the full faith and credit clause, it was held that ICWA applied to all three children and tribe had concurrent jurisdiction in these proceedings.).

50. 25 C.F.R. § 23.108; *see* Santa Clara Pueblo v. Martinez, 436 U.S. 49 (1978); Richmond v. Native Vill. of Selawik, 2023 WL 3764599 (unpublished); *In re* Welfare of S.N.R., 617 N.W.2d 77 (Minn. Ct. App. 2000); *In re* Adoption of Riffle, 922 P.2d 510 (Mont. 1996); *In re* Dependency of A.L.W., 32 P.3d 297 (Wash. Ct. App. 2001) (holding tribal determinations of membership

conclusive). *See also In re* Morris, 491 Mich. 81, 815 N.W.2d 62 (S. Ct. Mich. 2012) (holding that the definition of Indian child requires a determination of tribal membership or eligibility for tribal membership, and it is well established that only the Indian tribe can determine its membership); *but see In re* Manuel C. v. Amber S. & Red Lake Band of Chippewa Indians, 314 Neb. 91, 988 N.W.2d 520 (S. Ct. Neb. 2023) (where mother had begun the enrollment process, but not completed it, and the children were eligible for membership, the court found that the children were not yet Indian children [although they might become Indian children in the future], even though the tribe indicated that it considered the mother and children to be members of the tribe for ICWA purposes).

51. 25 C.F.R. § 23.108; *cf. In re* L.D., 414 P.3d 768 (Mont. 2018) (where there is reason to know, the court cannot rely on parent's stipulation but must seek conclusive tribal determination regarding the child's membership status and eligibility).
52. 25 C.F.R. § 23.11; 81 Fed. Reg. 38807 (June 14, 2016).
53. Dep't of the Interior, Bureau of Indian Affairs, Indian Child Welfare Proceedings, 81 Fed. Reg. 38807 (2016); *see* Means v. Navajo Nation, 432 F.3d 924, 934 n.68 (9th Cir. 2005) ("The authorities suggest that members of Indian tribes can renounce their membership."); Thompson v. Cnty. of Franklin, 180 F.R.D. 216, 225 (N.D.N.Y. 1998) (giving effect to individual's unequivocal renunciation of tribal membership); *see* FORT PECK COMPREHENSIVE CODE OF JUSTICE TITLE 4, ENROLLMENT § 217A(b) (1989) ("Any adult member of the Assiniboine and/or Sioux Tribes may apply for relinquishment of their respective tribal enrollment, at any time."); *but see In re* M.K.T., 368 P.3d 771 (Okla. 2016) (holding that the state did not meet its burden to show the father relinquished his membership in tribe or that such relinquishment could alter the Indian status of the child.).
54. BIA GUIDELINES, *supra* note 12, § B.7; *In re* A.G., 109 P.3d 756 (Mont. 2005) (trial court had affirmative obligation to determine whether children were Indian despite fact that tribe did not conclusively demonstrate eligibility).
55. See footnote 35 in Chapter 4.

56. 25 C.F.R. § 23.107.
57. BIA GUIDELINES, *supra* note 12, § B.1.
58. 25 C.F.R. § 23.107 (b) (if there is reason to know the child is an Indian child, but the court does not have sufficient evidence to determine that the child is or is not an "Indian child," the court must confirm, by way of a report, declaration, or testimony included in the record, that the agency or other party used due diligence to identify and work with all of the tribes of which there is reason to know the child may be a member or eligible for membership to verify whether the child is in fact a member or a biological parent is a member and the child is eligible for membership).
59. In the Interest of A.D. & Tr. D., 2017 COA 61, 413 P.3d 290 (Colo. Ct. App. 2017) (trial court cannot find the child is not an Indian child based upon a finding in an earlier case as it is required that the Department make inquiry in each new child custody proceeding).
60. *In re* A.J.J., 975 N.W.2d 130 (Minn. Ct. App. 2022).
61. *See, e.g., In re* Dezi C., 553 P.3d 829, 324 Cal. Rptr. 3d 275 (Cal. Sup. Ct. 2024).
62. 25 C.F.R. § 23.107 (b)(2). *See also* 25 C.F.R. § 23.107(c) (listing circumstances where a court has reason to know); *In re* L.A.G., 393 Mont. 146, 429 P.3d 629 (2018), *reh'g. denied* (finding reversible error for trial court violation of the ICWA when trial court terminated mother's parental rights before having conclusive determination of children's status in Indian tribe where mother had announced affiliation with a federally recognized tribe and indicated children were eligible for enrollment); *In re* H.S., 2016 Ill. App. (1st) 161589 (6th Div. 2016) (holding that the court had reason to know that the children might be Indian children, thereby triggering the ICWA). See generally discussion of "reason to know" in Chapter 4, section titled When Notice Is Required.
63. 25 C.F.R. § 23.107; Dep't of the Interior, Bureau of Indian Affairs, Indian Child Welfare Proceedings, 81 Fed. Reg. 38803, 38870 (2016) "Reservation" is defined in 25 U.S.C. § 1903(10).
64. 25 C.F.R. § 23.107(b)(1).
65. BIA GUIDELINES, *supra* note 12, § B.4.

66. BIA GUIDELINES, *supra* note 12, § B.6.
67. BIA GUIDELINES, *supra* note 12, § B.6.
68. BIA GUIDELINES, *supra* note 12, § B.6.
69. Dep't of the Interior, Bureau of Indian Affairs, Indian Child Welfare Proceedings, 81 Fed. Reg. 33805 (2016).
70. 25 C.F.R. § 23.109 states that "(a) If the Indian child is a member or eligible for membership in only one Tribe, that Tribe must be designated as the Indian child's Tribe. (b) If the Indian child meets the definition of 'Indian child' through more than one Tribe, deference should be given to the Tribe in which the Indian child is already a member, unless otherwise agreed to by the Tribes. (c) If an Indian child meets the definition of "Indian child" through more than one Tribe because the child is a member in more than one Tribe or the child is not a member of but is eligible for membership in more than one Tribe, the court must provide the opportunity in any involuntary child-custody proceeding for the Tribes to determine which should be designated as the Indian child's Tribe. (1) If the Tribes reach an agreement, the agreed-upon Tribe should be designated as the Indian child's Tribe. (2) If the Tribes are unable to reach an agreement, the State court designates, for the purposes of the ICWA, the Indian Tribe with which the Indian child has the more significant contacts as the Indian child's Tribe, taking into consideration: (i) Preference of the parents for membership of the child; (ii) Length of past domicile or residence on or near the reservation of each Tribe; (iii) Tribal membership of the child's custodial parent or Indian custodian; and (iv) Interest asserted by each Tribe in the child-custody proceeding; (v) Whether there has been a previous adjudication with respect to the child by a court of one of the Tribes; and (vi) Self-identification by the child, if the child is of sufficient age and capacity to meaningfully self-identify. (3) A determination of the Indian child's Tribe for purposes of the ICWA and the Regulations in this subpart do not constitute a determination for any other purpose.").
71. *See, e.g.*, Adoption of Kenten H. v. Mark J. & Sharon J., 272 Neb. 846, 864 N.W.2d 242 (Neb. 2007) (rejecting the biological mother's claim that prior orders entered in the case should be invalidated on the ground of noncompliance with notice provisions of ICWA, but requiring that the provisions

of ICWA and NICWA apply prospectively from the date Indian child status was established on the record); *In re* Welfare of B.W., 454 N.W.2d 437 (Minn. App. 1990).

72. *In re* Desiree, 83 Cal. App. 4th 460 (Ct. App., 5th Dist. 2000) (*modified on denial of reh'g* 2000) (failure to provide necessary notice rendered actions taken in violation of the ICWA invalid and required remand); *see also In re* Kahlen W., 285 Cal. Rptr. 507 (Cal. App. 5th Dist. 1991) and *In re* J.L.M., 451 N.W.2d 377 (Neb. 1990).
73. *In re* S.B., 130. Cal. App. 4th 1148 (2005) (where Mother failed to object to the failure of the court to apply ICWA at earlier stages of the proceeding, even though she was aware of her Native ancestry, she forfeited her right to later raise ICWA at the permanency phase of the proceeding).
74. *In re* Isaiah, 1 Cal. 5th 1, 203 Cal. Rptr. 3d 633, 373 P.3d 444 (2016) (Even though mother failed to timely appeal from the ICWA finding in the juvenile court's dispositional order, she is not foreclosed from raising the issue on appeal from the order terminating her parental rights because the juvenile court had a continuing duty to inquire whether Isaiah was an Indian child in all dependency proceedings, including a proceeding to terminate parental rights.); *In re* D.S., 46 Cal. App. 5th 1041, 259 Cal. Rptr. 3d 903 (Ct. App., 4th Dist., Div. 1 Cal. 2020) (the Court of Appeals exercised its discretion to consider mother's argument that county health and human services agency's ICWA inquiry into whether child was an Indian child was inadequate, even though mother raised this argument for the first time in her reply brief on appeal, as the agency had fully briefed the issue of ICWA compliance in its respondent's brief, and Indian tribes had an interest in ascertaining whether child was an Indian child); *but see In re* T.D., 890 So. 2d 473 (Fla. App. 2004) (mother's assertion of Indian ancestry at closing argument during termination hearing not sufficient to invoke the ICWA, but court cautioned the state to do a better job of determining ICWA applicability early in proceedings).
75. 25 C.F.R. § 23.103(d).
76. *Id.* § 23.103(b); 81 Fed. Reg. 38868 (July 2016). However, ICWA would apply in tribal courts if tribal law mandates that ICWA apply in the respective tribal court.

77. 25 U.S.C. § 1903(12).
78. *Id.* § 1903(1); *see* 23 C.F.R. § 23.103(a)(1) (The ICWA does not require state action to be invoked as the ICWA also applies to private placements and adoptions where the biological parents or Indian custodian cannot have the child returned upon demand.).
79. 25 U.S.C. § 1901(4).
80. 25 C.F.R. § 23.103; BIA Guidelines, *supra* note 12, § L.20. Note that the issue of whether the placement was of the parents' own free will and whether the parents can have the child back upon demand should be thoroughly vetted. *See* 81 Fed. Reg. 38866 (June 2016).
81. 25 U.S.C. § 1903 (1); 25 C.F.R. § 23.103 (b)(3); *In re* Marriage of Baisley, 749 P.2d 446 (Colo. App. 1987); Malatarre v. Malatarre, 293 N.W.2d 139 (N.D. 1980); *see also In re* Defender, 435 N.W.2d 717, 139 (S.D. 1989); *In re* Custody of Sengstock, 477 N.W.2d 310 (Wis. Ct. App. 1991) (both cases held that the ICWA does not apply to a custody dispute between the unwed parents of an Indian child).
82. The ICWA does not distinguish between the parents of an Indian child based upon whether that parent is an Indian under the law. 25 U.S.C. § 1903(9).
83. 25 U.S.C. § 1903(1). *See also, e.g., In re* Guardianship of Eliza W., 304 Neb. 995, 938 N.W.2d 307 (2020) (case in which a maternal grandmother sought to establish a guardianship for an Indian child over the objection of her daughter is governed by ICWA and NICWA); *In re* Jennifer A., 103 Cal. App. 4th 692, 700, 127 Cal. Rptr. 2d 54 (2002) (finding that the ICWA requirements applied because the "issue of possible foster-care placement was squarely before the juvenile court," even though the child was eventually placed with the noncustodial father).
84. 25 U.S.C. § 1903(1); 25 C.F.R. § 23.103(1)(iii).
85. 25 C.F.R. § 23.2.
86. *See generally* T. Gonzalez, *Reclaiming the Promise of the Indian Child Welfare Act: A Study of State Incorporation and Adoption of Legal Protection for Indian Status Offenders*, 41 N. Mex. L. Rev. 131 (2012); *see also In re* Ramon N., 789 N.W. 272 (Neb. 2010) (applying the ICWA to a curfew violation, which resulted in an out-of-home placement); In Interest of B.B.,

500 N.W.2d 9 (Iowa 1993) (The ICWA applies to a proceeding in which a mentally retarded Indian child was declared minor in need of assistance.).

87. 25 C.F.R. § 23.103(b); 81 Fed. Reg. 38801 (June 2016) (The ICWA applies to any status offense proceeding that results in a placement of the Indian child because of the status offense.).
88. *In re* Adoption of Linda J.W., 682 N.Y.S.2d 565 (N.Y. Fam. Ct. 1998) (although members of tribes outside the United States are not included in the ICWA, members of Canadian tribes under the Jay Treaty may have rights under the ICWA).
89. 25 U.S.C. § 1903(1) (The ICWA does not apply to the custody disputes between parents or to delinquency proceedings.).
90. *In re* L.R. J., C.M.J. & C.S.J. et al., 411 Mont. 149, 523 P.3d 22 (Mont. 2023) (holding ICWA applies to internal family dispute when parent's voluntary placement of Indian child with relative does not allow parent to regain custody of child upon demand); Rice v. McDonald, 390 P.3d 1133 (Alaska 2017) (ICWA applies to case where maternal relative seeking to remove child from paternal relative's custody); Starr v. George, 175 P.3d 50 (Alaska 2008) (holding ICWA divorce exception, which excepts from ICWA provisions custody awards to one parent in a divorce proceeding, did not extend to custody disputes between grandparents); *In re* Custody of A.K.H., 502 N.W.2d 790, 794 (Minn. Ct. App. 1993) (holding placement of child with grandmother would be placement in home of "guardian or conservator," within meaning of ICWA, entitling Indian tribe to intervene in custody dispute; and intrafamily custody disputes were not excluded from ICWA).
91. Dep't of the Interior, Bureau of Indian Affairs, Indian Child Welfare Proceedings, 81 Fed. Reg. 38800 (2016); BIA GUIDELINES, *supra* note 12, § B.2. The statute and final rule exclude custody disputes between parents, but can apply to other types of intrafamily disputes, assuming that such disputes otherwise meet the statutory and regulatory definitions. The ICWA can apply to other types of intrafamily disputes because the statute makes only two exceptions, neither of which are for intrafamily disputes other than parental custody disputes. *See also* 25 U.S.C. § 1903(1) (The ICWA

exclusions only apply to custody disputes between parents or to delinquency proceedings involved activities that would be crimes if committed by an adult.).

92. A number of cases have held that the provisions of the ICWA apply to proceedings wherein a nonparent is seeking placement of the child with her or him. *See, e.g., In re* Guardianship of Eliza W., 304 Neb. 995, 938 N.W.2d 307 (2020) (ICWA applies in case where grandmother seeking a guardianship over the objection of the mother); *In re* Ashley Elizabeth R., 863 P.2d 451 (N.M. App. 1993) (placement of an Indian child with a non-Indian paternal great-aunt is a foster care placement covered by the ICWA); *In re* Custody of A.K.H., 502 N.W.2d 790 (Minn. Ct. App. 1993) (Indian tribe allowed to intervene in a custody dispute between a grandparent and a parent as the ICWA applied); *see also* A.B.M. v. M.H. & A.H., 651 P.2d 1170 (Alaska 1982); *In re* Custody of S.B.R., 719 P.2d 154 (Wash. App. 1986).
93. *See In re* N.B., 199 P.3d 16 (Colo. App. 2007), *cert. denied*, 2008 WL 757927 (2008); *In re* Adoption of R.L.A., 147 P.3d 306 (Okla. Civ. App. 2006) (holding application of mother and stepfather for adoption of Indian child without father's consent was not exempted from ICWA by "Indian family exception," as exception had been explicitly rejected by Oklahoma Supreme Court); *In re* Adoption of T.A.W., 383 P.3d 492 (Wash. 2016) (holding that ICWA and WICWA applied to stepparent adoption cases); S.S. v. Stephanie H., 241 Ariz. 419, 388 P.3d 569 (Ariz. Ct. App. 2017) (applying ICWA where father sought to terminate mother's parental rights).
94. 643 P.2d 168 (Kan. 1982), *overruled by In re* A.J.S., A Minor Child, 204 P.3d 543 (Kan. 2009).
95. Claymore v. Serr, 405 N.W.2d 650 (S.D. 1987), *overruled by In re* Adoption of Baade, 462 N.W.2d 485 (S.D. 1990).
96. *In re* Adoption of T.R.M., 525 N.E.2d 298 (Ind. 1988). *T.R.M.* was criticized but not overruled in *In re D.S.,* 577 N.E.2d 572 (Ind. 1991).
97. *In re* S.A.M., 703 S.W.2d 603 (Mo. Ct. App. 1986).
98. *In re* Baby Boy D., 742 P.2d 1059 (Okla. 1985), *overruled by In re* Baby Boy L., 103 P.3d 1099 (Okla. 2004).

99. *In re* B.B., 511 So. 2d 918 (Miss. 1987), *rev'd sub nom.* Mississippi Band of Choctaw Indians v. Holyfield, 490 U.S. 30 (1989).
100. 490 U.S. 30 (1988).
101. *In re* A.J.S., A Minor Child, 204 P.3d 543 (Kan. 2009); *see also, e.g.*, preceding footnotes 94, 95, 98, and 99.
102. Adoptive Couple v. Baby Girl, 570 U.S. 637, 133 S. Ct. 2252 (2013).
103. 25 C.F.R. § 23.103(c).
104. Dep't of the Interior, Bureau of Indian Affairs, Indian Child Welfare Proceedings, 81 Fed. Reg. 38782 (2016).
105. 23 C.F.R. § 23.103(4)(c).
106. *See In re* Epik W., 2024 WL 4602720 (Ct. App. Tenn. 2024).
107. Delaware Tribe of Indians v. Nowicki-Eldridge, 888 S.E.2d 866 (S. Ct. W. Va. 2023).
108. Those jurisdictions appearing to still consider the EIFE include only six states (Alabama, Indiana, Kentucky, Missouri, Nevada, and Tennessee) and a single appellate district in California. *See In re* Adoption of T.R.M., 525 N.E.2d 298 (Ind. 1988); Rye v. Weasel, 934 S.W.2d 257 (Ky. 1996); C.E.H. v. L.M.W., 837 S.W.2d 947 (Mo. Ct. App. 1992); *In re* N.J., 125 Nev. 835, 221 P.3d 1255 (2009); *In re* Morgan, No. 02A01-9608-CH-00206, 1997 WL 716880 (Tenn. Ct. App. Nov. 19, 1997); *In re* Alexandria Y., 45 Cal. App. 4th 1483, 53 Cal. Rptr. 2d 679 (1996); *but see In re* Epik W., 2024 WL 4602720 (Ct. App. Tenn. 2024) (in remanding the case, the appellate court noted that both the Department and the Tribe rejected application of the EIFE, based upon the fact that the federal regulations "foreclose reliance" on it). Cases refusing to apply the EIFE include *In re* Baby Boy C., 27 A.D.3d 34 (S. Ct., App. Div., 1st Dept. N.Y. 2005); *In re* Adoption of T.N.F., 781 P.2d 973, 977 (Alaska 1989); *In re* N.B., 199 P.3d 16 (Colo. App. 2007), *cert. denied*, 2008 WL 757927 (2008); *In re* Adoption of Baade, 462 N.W.2d 485, 489–90 (S.D. 1990); *In re* Alexandria P., 176 Cal. Rptr. 3d 468, 484–86 (Cal. Ct. App. 2014); J.W. v. R.J., 951 P.2d 1206 (Alaska 1998); Michael J. Jr. v. Michael J. Sr., 7 P.3d 960 (Ariz. Ct. App. 2000); *In re* Baby Boy Doe, 849 P.2d 925 (Idaho 1993); *In re* S.S., 657 N.E.2d 935

(Ill. 1995); *In re* R.E.K.F., 698 N.W.2d 147 (Iowa 2005); *In re* Elliott, 554 N.W.2d 32 (Mich. Ct. App. 1996); *In re* Adoption of Riffle, 922 P.2d 510 (Mont. 1996); *In re* Child of Indian Heritage, 543 A.2d 925 (N.J. 1988); *In re* Baby Boy C., 805 N.Y.S.2d 313 (N.Y. App. Div. 2005); *In re* A.D.L., 612 S.E.2d 639 (N.C. Ct. App. 2005); *In re* A.B., 663 N.W.2d 625 (N.D. 2003); *In re* Baby Boy L., 103 P.3d 1099 (Okla. 2004); Quinn v. Walters, 881 P.2d 795 (Or. Ct. App. 1994); *In re* W.D.H., 43 S.W.3d 30 (Tex. App. 2001); *In re* D.A.C., 933 P.2d 993 (Utah Ct. App. 1997); and Thompson v. Fairfax Cnty. Dep't of Fam. Servs, 747 S.E.2d 838 (Va. Ct. App. 2013).

109. *Thompson*, 747 S.E.2d at 847.

Jurisdictional Provisions of the ICWA

3

This chapter will discuss the jurisdictional provisions in the ICWA and issues related to transfer jurisdiction. The Supreme Court noted in *Mississippi Band of Choctaw Indians v. Holyfield*[1] that the jurisdictional provisions of the Indian Child Welfare Act (ICWA) are at the very heart of the law.[2] These provisions are designed to maximize the opportunity for tribal court judges who, in most cases, are more knowledgeable than state court judges about Indian child-rearing traditions and customs to determine the fate of Indian children.[3] As a result, and consistent with long-standing principles of tribal sovereignty, the ICWA recognizes that tribal courts have exclusive jurisdiction over child custody proceedings "when an Indian child resides or is domiciled within the jurisdiction of such tribe. . . ."[4]

When a child custody proceeding arises outside of the jurisdiction of a tribe (i.e., in a state court's jurisdiction), the ICWA provides that the proceeding shall be transferred to the tribal court absent declination by the tribal court, objection by a parent, or upon a showing of good cause to the contrary.[5] This transfer jurisdiction of a tribal court was referred to by the Supreme Court as the tribal court's "presumptive" jurisdiction.[6]

Of note, the Uniform Child Custody Jurisdiction Enforcement Act (UCCJEA)[7] may also be relevant to issues of jurisdiction in a child custody case when the Indian child is not domiciled in Indian country or a ward of the tribal court. While a deep dive into the potential interplay between the ICWA and UCCJEA is beyond the scope of this book, practitioners would be well-advised to be familiar with a relevant state's UCCJEA provisions.

The ICWA also allows states and tribes to enter into agreements allocating jurisdiction, which has engendered much positive development in the area of cooperative agreements between tribes and states.[8]

Exclusive Jurisdiction

The ICWA confirms that a tribal court exercises exclusive jurisdiction over any child custody proceeding involving an Indian child residing or domiciled within the reservation,[9] except when jurisdiction is otherwise vested in the state under existing federal law.[10] The tribal court also retains exclusive jurisdiction over any Indian child who remains a "ward" of the tribal court, notwithstanding the child's residence or domicile, but note that courts are split regarding whether exclusive tribal jurisdiction requires the child to be domiciled on the reservation at the time the tribal court issues the ward order.[11]

The exclusive jurisdiction provisions of the ICWA apply to all Indian children within a tribal court's jurisdiction, regardless of whether a child who is the subject of a custody proceeding is a member of the tribe that is exercising jurisdiction, provided the exercise of jurisdiction is consistent with the particular tribe's organic laws.[12] Although federal court decisions proscribe tribal criminal jurisdiction over nonmember Indians,[13] there is no similar prohibition against tribal jurisdiction in the civil context. In effect, Congress has expressly confirmed that Indian tribes have exclusive jurisdiction over all Indian children residing or domiciled on a reservation, much the same way Congress vested tribal courts with criminal jurisdiction over all Indians after the *Duro v. Reina* decision.[14]

The reference to an existing federal law exception in the exclusive jurisdiction section is nonspecific. Pub. Law 83-280 (P.L. 280) was enacted by Congress in the early 1950s to allow states to fill what Congress believed was a vacuum in the enforcement of misdemeanor criminal laws on Indian reservations.[15] The law vested five states with mandatory civil and criminal jurisdiction over reservations in those states (Alaska became the sixth mandatory state when it was admitted to the Union in 1959) and permitted other states to unilaterally extend their jurisdiction over Indian country within their borders.[16] Although P.L. 280 does not strip tribes of their inherent jurisdiction and right to exercise both civil and criminal jurisdiction, it did lead to a withdrawal of federal support for tribal justice systems in those states. This withdrawal was particularly acute in both Alaska and California. In both cases, many tribes simply do not have access to the resources available to tribes in other states for law enforcement or tribal courts, although this is changing.

In the civil context, the U.S. Supreme Court has held that states and tribes in P.L. 280 states have concurrent civil jurisdiction over issues involving civil prohibitory conduct, while tribes maintain exclusive jurisdiction over civil regulatory conduct.[17] Notwithstanding these cases, however, a few courts have held that states have concurrent jurisdiction over on-reservation child welfare cases.[18] Another issue involves P.L. 280's intersection with the ICWA, particularly the provision in the ICWA requiring tribes subject to P.L. 280 to petition the Secretary of the Interior to "reassume jurisdiction" over the child welfare matters covered in the ICWA. However, courts have found that since P.L. 280 is not a divestiture statute, tribes continue to have inherent jurisdiction over their members, and that this provision of the ICWA refers to reassuming exclusive jurisdiction over on-reservation child welfare matters.[19] As such, under the ICWA, state courts must grant full faith and credit to tribal court orders.[20] Practitioners should acquaint themselves with the law of the state in which they work if that state is a P.L. 280 state.

Domicile on Reservation

If an Indian child is domiciled[21] on or resides[22] on an Indian reservation, the tribal court, with a few exceptions, has exclusive jurisdiction over a child custody proceeding involving that child.[23] The only exceptions to this rule are P.L. 280, just discussed, and a section in the ICWA that gives state officials and courts the authority to remove an Indian child temporarily and place him or her in an emergency foster home in a situation where the child is temporarily off the reservation.[24] In that circumstance, the state must immediately notify tribal officials so that they may take appropriate action.[25] The definition of "reservation" under the ICWA is a broad one.[26] The definition refers to a criminal statute, the Major Crimes Act, which broadly defines "Indian country" as (1) any territory located within the exterior boundaries of an Indian reservation, including fee-owned land; (2) any dependent Indian community; and (3) any Indian allotment and the rights of way running through them.[27] There are hundreds of law review articles, treatises, and cases discussing what constitutes "Indian country" under the Major Crimes Act.[28] This handbook cannot possibly detail every nuance and interpretation of this definition. In brief, there are certain reservations in this country that have been diminished or disestablished.[29] This means that these reservations have lost part of their land base because of certain congressional enactments in which

Congress purchased surplus lands for non-Indians to homestead out of the original land set aside for tribes by treaty or congressional enactment.[30] Some may not even have exterior boundaries defining their reservation.[31]

Certain Indian communities located on land held in trust for the tribe or individual Indians are still located in those areas that were taken from the tribes by congressional enactment.[32] These communities are called dependent Indian communities because they retain much similarity to the communities located within the exterior boundaries of the reservation. Other lands, called allotments, were parceled out to individual Indians by Congress out of the original tribally owned land base in an effort to break up reservations and assimilate Indians into the dominant white society.[33] Many of these allotments are located outside of the exterior boundaries of reservations but are nonetheless considered part of Indian country for jurisdictional purposes. The best way to determine whether a particular area is Indian country is to confer with the U.S. Department of the Interior or individual tribes about the status of the land ownership in the area.[34] Other reservations retain their land base as set out in the individual treaty or congressional enactment setting up that reservation.[35] For those reservations, any land that lies within the exterior boundaries of the reservation is Indian country, even if the land is held by non-Indians in fee simple.[36]

In *Holyfield*, the U.S. Supreme Court dealt with the definition of "domicile" contained in the exclusive jurisdiction provisions of the ICWA.[37] In that case, the Mississippi Supreme Court held that Indian twins born outside of the reservation borders to an Indian mother domiciled on the reservation were not "domiciled" on the reservation for purposes of the exclusive jurisdiction provisions of the ICWA.[38] The Supreme Court reversed this determination.[39] *Holyfield* held that a state court, in determining the domicile of an Indian child, should look to generally accepted federal and common-law concepts of domicile.[40] The court distinguished between residence and domicile in concluding that a person's domicile need not necessarily be his or her residence, especially with respect to minor children who usually assume the domicile of their natural parents.[41]

Importantly, the *Holyfield* court noted that state courts should not interpret "domicile" in a manner that frustrates the congressional intent behind the enactment of the ICWA.[42] Therefore, because the ICWA expresses an intent to allow tribal courts to exercise exclusive jurisdiction over Indian children domiciled on the reservation, it would be violative of that intent to allow natural parents to circumvent a tribe's rights to exercise its jurisdiction by placing children off the reservation shortly after birth. The Supreme Court therefore adopted a broad definition of domicile, one that maximizes a tribal court's opportunity to exercise its authority in the ICWA cases.[43]

Holyfield teaches that a tribal court's jurisdiction is not preempted by a natural parent arranging to have a child off the reservation or by placing that child for adoption off reservation shortly after birth.[44] Although some may criticize this principle as violative of the natural parents' rights to determine the destiny of their child, the issue is who decides the case, not what the decision is. Congress clearly weighed the tribe's interests in preserving tribal culture and values and its ability to make decisions that reflect the social and cultural values in the community where the parents are resident or domiciled against the rights of natural parents to dictate a particular placement. This balancing of tribal interests, the child's interest, and parental rights is evident throughout the ICWA and is discussed more thoroughly in the section on transfer of jurisdiction

Holyfield did resolve a simmering dispute among state courts on the issue of domicile in cases where the natural parent made a concerted effort to avoid tribal court jurisdiction. A good rule of thumb is that any child custody proceeding involving an infant, including adoption, should commence in the tribal court if the mother of the child resided on the reservation immediately preceding the birth.[45] One should also consult the regulations, which aim to provide a complete explanation of how to determine domicile for an adult. The regulations clarify that the domicile for an Indian child whose parents are not married is the domicile of the Indian child's custodial parent.[46]

Tribal Court Wardship

A second basis for exclusive tribal court jurisdiction is when the Indian child is a ward of the tribal court.[47] "Ward" is not defined under the ICWA and there is very little guidance in the legislative history or the regulations as to its import. In *Holyfield*, the Supreme Court, without defining the term, stated that it means that tribal courts exercise exclusive jurisdiction over "wards . . . regardless of domicile."[48] The most commonly accepted understanding of wardship is when a tribal court, or a tribal governing council,[49] has exercised legitimate jurisdiction over an Indian child in a child custody proceeding and continues to exercise that jurisdiction, a state court's exercise of jurisdiction is precluded, except on an emergency basis.[50]

The wardship provision covers the situation in which a tribal court is exercising its proper jurisdiction over an Indian child when that child is placed off the reservation or moves off with his or her parents or other relatives.[51] In that situation, the tribal court clearly has the exclusive authority to continue its jurisdiction over that child.[52]

The cases that create friction are those in which the Indian child is located off the reservation, but the tribal court nonetheless exercises some authority over the child in a child custody proceeding. The language in *Holyfield* stresses that a child need not be domiciled on a reservation for a tribal court to continue to exercise its exclusive jurisdiction.[53] Nonetheless, state courts have been split on this issue.[54] Is a finding that a child is a ward of a tribal court, however, entitled to the same deference as a finding that the child is a member or eligible for membership in the tribe? Clearly, the latter finding is entitled to full faith and credit by the state court under § 1911(d).[55] Full faith and credit is not synonymous with blind allegiance, however, and, as with the federal and constitutional full faith and credit provisions, it appears that a state can make proper inquiry into whether the tribal court's exercise of jurisdiction is consistent with federal law before deferring its otherwise proper jurisdiction to the tribal court.[56] A mere assertion that an Indian child is a ward of a tribal court, without some supporting documentation or intervention by the tribe to assert such a status, may foreclose a claim that a child is a ward.[57]

Transfer Jurisdiction

If an Indian child is the subject of a foster care placement or termination of parental rights proceeding in state court, the state court shall transfer the proceeding to the jurisdiction of the tribe, absent objection by either parent, upon an oral request on the record or written request by either parent, the Indian custodian, or the Indian child's tribe.[58] When a request is made, the state court must ensure the tribal court[59] is promptly notified in writing of the request.[60] And the state court may request a timely response from the tribal court in its notification.[61] Transfer shall not take place if the state court finds good cause not to transfer[62] or the tribal court declines the transfer.[63] Either parent of the child also has the right to veto the transfer of jurisdiction to the tribal court, irrespective of whether that parent had the legal custody of the child prior to the commencement of the proceedings.[64]

The "good cause" provision in § 1911(b) has resulted in considerable litigation, primarily since Congress permitted denials of transfer because of "good cause" and many state and tribal officials can sometimes disagree on what that term means.[65] The Supreme Court in *Holyfield* indicated that Congress believed that transfer should be the rule and not the exception.[66] If one recalls the discussion of the legislative impetus behind the enactment of the ICWA, one of Congress's concerns was that state courts and social services personnel, because of the cultural gap between predominantly non-Indian judges and social workers and Indian families, were perhaps incapable of passing judgment on the fitness of Indian child-rearing practices.[67] The transfer provision was inserted into the ICWA to further the best interest of Indian children by permitting a tribal judge, who optimally would have more knowledge of traditional native child-rearing practices, to assess a family's capability to provide for a child.[68] The denial of a transfer motion, although interlocutory in nature, may be immediately appealable as a "final" order in some jurisdictions.[69]

Under the regulations, it frames the inquiry in terms of what should not be considered when determining if "good cause" exists.[70] The Bureau of Indian Affairs (BIA) explains in the comments that the legislative history shows Congress intended to allow a state court to apply a modified doctrine of forum non conveniens, when appropriate, but believed that the rights of the Indian child, Indian parents or Indian custodian, and tribe could be best protected in tribal court.[71] Thus, Congress intended for limited discretion in determining "good cause,"[72] and the regulations reflect the intent to limit a state court's discretion with its prohibitions.[73]

It is important to note that a "transfer" under the ICWA refers to a transfer of jurisdiction and not necessarily to a physical transfer of a child back to a reservation. This confusion often permeates discussion of transfer and leads to state courts and officials misunderstanding that a tribal judge can consider all of the circumstances in the case in making a decision about where the child should be placed after a transfer is granted. Many tribes, after a transfer of jurisdiction, may choose to leave a child at his or her placement immediately preceding a transfer request and may even request that state officials monitor the placement.[74] Some states and tribes have entered into cooperative agreements addressing this issue as well as others that are subject to resolution by agreement under the provisions of the ICWA.[75]

Proceedings Covered by the Transfer Provisions

The language in the transfer provisions of the ICWA only refers to two types of child custody proceedings: foster care placements and termination of parental rights proceedings.[76] The ICWA does not explain why transfer is not explicitly required in preadoptive and adoptive placements, nor is there much discussion of this apparent discrepancy in the case law. Notwithstanding the lack of statutory authority to transfer, many states do transfer preadoptive and adoptive placement proceedings to tribal courts,[77] primarily because tribes may be in a better position to find an adoptive placement in compliance with the placement preference provisions discussed later in Chapter 5. The guidelines indicate the appropriateness in some circumstances of transferring a preadoptive or adoptive proceeding to a tribal jurisdiction.[78]

Standing to Request Transfer and to Object

Under the ICWA, four separate parties may request a transfer of jurisdiction to tribal court.[79] Either parent, the Indian child's tribe, or an "Indian custodian" may request a transfer. All four of these parties are defined by the ICWA in important ways.[80] Only a natural parent can absolutely veto a transfer of jurisdiction by interjecting an objection.[81]

Definition of "Parent"

"Parent" is defined under the ICWA as any biological parent or parents of an Indian child or any Indian person who has lawfully adopted an Indian child, including adoptions under tribal law or custom.[82] The term excludes unwed fathers whose paternity has not been acknowledged or established, although a putative father may make the acknowledgment during the course of the ICWA proceedings.[83] Most courts, but not all, have held that in order to acknowledge paternity an unwed father need not strictly comply with state laws for establishing paternity or acknowledge paternity in a formal legal setting.[84] A few things are apparent from this definition. The ICWA does not give an Indian parent more rights than a non-Indian parent, except for non-Indian adoptive parents.[85] A natural parent of an Indian child, either Indian or non-Indian, can prevent a transfer of a child custody proceeding to tribal court by objecting to a transfer.[86] Only an Indian adoptive parent has standing, however, to object to a transfer.[87]

The right of a parent to veto absolutely a transfer of jurisdiction to tribal court is one area where Congress recognized the rights of natural parents who are resident or domiciled off reservation to have their case heard in state court, notwithstanding the presumption of tribal jurisdiction.[88] Regardless of how fit a natural parent is, or the severity of charges of abuse or neglect, that parent retains the right to overrule a transfer request. Although some have argued that the right to veto a transfer request even survives the termination of parental rights because the definition of parent under the ICWA refers to biological, not legal, parent, such a right may cease to exist under prevailing state law,[89] and the guidelines agree that a parent whose rights have been terminated should no longer have the right to object.[90] Thus, although one court has affirmed the right of a parent to veto a transfer even after her parental rights had been terminated,[91] this now seems to be in doubt.[92] At least one court has ruled that the right to veto transfer survives the death of the parents, reversing the trial court who had found that it would be "markedly unfair" to those still living to deny transfer based upon the deceased father's objection.[93] It remains to be seen whether other courts will agree with the Illinois trial court or the appellate court on this issue.

The ICWA excludes the unwed father of an illegitimate child from its definition of parent unless the father has either acknowledged the child or has had his paternity judicially established.[94] Therefore, if a putative father has not been adjudicated the father of an Indian child or has not acknowledged the child, either in writing or orally, he has no rights to veto a transfer of jurisdiction to a tribal court.[95] Nor would such a putative father have standing to file a collateral challenge to a child custody decision.[96] This should not be confused with the right of a putative father to notice of proceedings that may lead to the termination of his inchoate rights. As the Supreme Court recognized in *Stanley v. Illinois*,[97] a putative father may still be entitled to notice of any proceedings implicating his rights.[98] At least one court in New Jersey has apparently concluded that the ICWA's definition of "parent" does not require notice to a putative father who only orally acknowledged a child before the child's placement with an adoptive home, although that same court did conclude that the child there was Indian for purposes of application of the ICWA.[99]

Definition of "Indian Custodian"

Another party to a child custody proceeding who may request a transfer to tribal court, but who has no standing to veto a transfer request, is an Indian custodian. "Indian custodian" is defined under the ICWA as any Indian person who has legal custody of an Indian child under tribal law or custom or state law or who has been granted temporary physical care, custody, and control by the natural parent.[100]

The inclusion of an Indian custodian as a person vested with certain rights under the ICWA is an acknowledgment by Congress of the role the extended Indian family plays in the rearing of Indian children. In many instances, for example, the right to request a transfer and to notice of proceedings, the ICWA treats an Indian custodian the same as a natural parent.[101] An Indian custodian is not granted the privileges and procedural protections of the ICWA when the child is removed from the Indian custodian and returned to the natural parent.[102] In that situation, the Indian custodian presumably cannot request a transfer of the proceeding to tribal court. Non-Indian custodians of Indian children do not qualify as Indian custodians under the ICWA even if the person is a blood relation to one of the natural parents. That person, however, does qualify for a relative placement, discussed later in Chapter 5.[103]

An Indian custodian in most circumstances is a relative of the Indian child, but a blood relationship is not a prerequisite to finding a person an Indian custodian.[104] Nor is the fact that a person is a blood relative of the child qualify the person as an Indian custodian.[105] The first type of Indian custodian is one who has been granted "legal" custody under either state or tribal law, including the customs and traditions of the particular tribe.[106] At least two courts have held that an Indian relative foster care placement is not an Indian custodian under the ICWA because the state, in that circumstance, retains the legal custody of the child.[107] Legal custody is not synonymous with the existence of a court order granting custody, however, because the legislative history makes it clear that Congress appreciated that a person could have custody under the traditions and practices of a tribe without having followed the formalities of obtaining a custody order from the tribal court.[108] If a person claims legal custody of a child under the traditions of a particular tribe, consultation with that tribe may be necessary to verify those traditions.[109] If a person has received the custody of a child from the parents, but then proceeds to surrender that custody to a state social services department, the person may have lost the right to claim Indian custodian status.[110]

The second type of Indian custodian is one who has received the custody of the child voluntarily from a natural parent, a not uncommon occurrence among Indian people.[111] In that situation, the ICWA does not seem to require the formalization of the placement arrangement.[112] Nonetheless, a consent to custody or some type of temporary guardianship executed by a natural parent would perhaps eliminate any confusion over the status of an Indian custodian.

Definition of "Indian Child's Tribe"

Lastly, an Indian child's tribe can request a transfer to tribal court.[113] The tribe can also prevent a transfer to the tribal court by declining to exercise jurisdiction over the case on a transfer basis.[114]

In many cases, determining which tribe is the "Indian child's tribe" is not difficult because the child and his or her family only claim affiliation with one tribe. If a child is a member of only one tribe, that tribe is the Indian child's tribe[115] and only that tribe can request a transfer of jurisdiction. However, in a case where the child is a member of more than one tribe, which is rare, or eligible for membership in more than one tribe, the regulations set out some considerations—all of which concern the affinity of the child and the child's parents to a particular tribe—for a state court to follow in determining which tribe is the Indian child's tribe.[116] Only one tribe can be declared the Indian child's tribe, even if substantial contacts between the child and more than one tribe exist.[117] Every tribe that the child claims some affiliation with must be notified of the proceedings, however, to allow each of the tribes some input in the state court decision-making process.[118]

Obviously, the state court needs to make the Indian child's tribe determination before addressing transfer issues. The only circumstance justifying a state court reconsidering its determination of an Indian child's tribe is when the child becomes a member of a different tribe during the pendency of the action, at which time the state court is to consider the tribe where the Indian child is a member as the child's tribe from that point on.[119] Any proceedings that took place before that occurrence will not be vitiated.[120]

Only those tribes that are federally recognized are eligible to be declared an "Indian child's tribe" under the ICWA.[121] The reader is referred to the *Federal Register Notice of Indian Entities Recognized and Eligible to Receive Services from the United States Bureau of Indian Affairs* (89 Fed. Reg. 99899), which is the official listing of all federally recognized tribes in the United States, pursuant to the Federally Recognized Indian Tribe List Act of 1994 (P.L. 103-454, 108 Stat. 4791–4792). It is updated annually and the reader is advised to check for updated lists and contact the BIA contact person listed in the *Federal Register Notice* for any additions and updates to the list, because occasionally the list changes before a new list is published.

The reader is also referred to *Indian Child Welfare Act: Designated Tribal Agents for Service of Notice*, which designates an agent other than a tribal chairman for service of notice of proceedings under the act. The current list is found at https://biamaps.geoplatform.gov/ICWA-Agents-Directory/; also see Appendix E.

Grounds for Denying Transfer Request; Prohibited Considerations

In the absence of good cause to the contrary or a declination by the tribal court, a state court must transfer a child custody proceeding to the tribal court upon an appropriate request by either parent, the Indian custodian, or the Indian child's tribe.[122] The request need not be a conventional written petition but can be made orally on the record.[123]

Protocol would perhaps call for a motion to the tribal court to accept jurisdiction before moving the state court to transfer, but an affirmative acceptance of jurisdiction by the tribal court in advance is not a prerequisite to the state court transferring jurisdiction.[124]

A parent, as that term is defined under the ICWA and the regulations, has the right to veto the transfer of jurisdiction.[125]

The legislative history of the ICWA, in discussing good cause for a state court to deny a transfer request, declared that a state court should apply a "modified doctrine of forum non conveniens, in appropriate cases, to ensure that the rights of the child as an Indian, the Indian parents or custodian, and the rights of the [t]ribe are fully protected."[126]

The burden of proving good cause to deny a transfer of jurisdiction to tribal court is upon the party opposing transfer that good cause exists not to transfer a case, with a "strong trend" toward courts requiring that standard must be established by clear and convincing evidence.[127] There are numerous reported state court decisions discussing transfer issues.[128] Some of the pre-regulations case may no longer be good law as the regulations set forth specific reasons that a state court may not consider in determining good cause, intending clearly to limit a state court's discretion and address some of the cases which the BIA believed were inconsistent with Congress's intent.

The regulations state that in determining whether good cause exists, a state court must not consider:

(1) whether the foster care or termination-of-parental-rights proceeding is at an advanced stage if the Indian child's parent, Indian custodian, or tribe did not receive notice of the child custody proceeding until an advanced stage;
(2) whether there have been prior proceedings involving the Indian child for which no petition to transfer was filed;
(3) whether transfer could affect the placement of the Indian child;
(4) the Indian child's cultural connections with his or her tribe or reservation; or
(5) socioeconomic conditions or any negative perception of tribal or BIA social services or judicial systems.[129]

Proceeding at Advanced Stage When Transfer Request Is Made, No Notice

Prior to the enactment of the regulations, if the state court proceedings were at an advanced stage when the request is made *and* it appeared that the requesting party did not act promptly to request a transfer after receiving notice of the proceedings, the state court could find good cause to deny a transfer request.[130] The regulations do not eliminate entirely advanced stage as a consideration, but they severely circumscribe it.

Until now, courts have differed on the relevant time frame for determining timeliness in transfer requests of termination proceedings, with some courts indicating that the proceedings are commenced when the child/children are initially removed from the parents or guardians, while other courts have looked at when the termination petition was filed without consideration of how long the foster care placement proceeding was pending.[131] The relevant time frame was often dependent upon state law and whether a termination proceeding is a discrete action, separate and apart from a foster care placement proceeding, or whether it is a dispositional alternative in a foster care placement proceeding.

The regulations clarify, however, that for the purpose of notice and determining whether a case is at an advanced stage, a foster care proceeding and termination of parental rights proceeding are to be considered as two separate proceedings.[132] Thus, those cases that have denied transfer of a proceeding based upon a finding that the case was at an advanced stage—even though in such cases the termination of parental rights had just been filed—would appear to be inconsistent with the regulations. There are reasons why a tribe may not initially choose to transfer. For example, some tribes choose not to seek transfer until reunification efforts have failed—often because the state court and agency may be better situated to work with the family to reunify in a given circumstance—but choose to transfer once it is clear that a different permanent home will need to be found for the child.[133] Indeed, the regulations specifically preclude denial of a transfer petition based upon the fact that there were no petitions filed in a previous proceeding.[134]

In addition, the regulations prohibit a state court from considering as good cause whether the proceeding is at an advanced stage if the Indian child's parent, Indian custodian, or tribe did not receive notice of the child custody proceeding until an advanced stage.[135] The case law has generally agreed that if any party to a case who is entitled to notice of the proceedings does not receive adequate and timely notice, this ground cannot be used to defeat that party's transfer request.[136]

If notice was timely received and a particular proceeding before the court has been going on for an extended period, presumably this factor is still open for consideration. In this way, a party is prevented from engaging in forum shopping when it appears that the case is not proceeding in his or her favor in state court.[137]

If a party makes an "untimely" request for transfer but the proceedings are still in the early stages (e.g., pre-adjudication), this would not appear to be a ground to deny a transfer as it would not serve the objectives cited by the drafters of the regulations.[138] Of course, timely requests for transfer (subject to some of the countervailing factors discussed already) can be an efficacious way of achieving the desired results for Indian children and families, and the conscious decision to delay a transfer request could result in a denial of the request.[139] This is especially true in light of the accelerated standards states often apply based upon the Adoption and Safe Families Act emphasis on achieving permanent placements.[140] At least one court has looked to these standards for permanency in determining whether an Indian child custody proceeding was at an advanced stage when a transfer petition was filed.[141]

Whether the Placement of the Child Will Be Affected ("Best Interests of the Child")

The regulations prohibit consideration of whether the transfer will affect the placement of the child.[142] This is a recognition that the question is not where the child is to be placed, but who will make that decision.

The only reference in the ICWA to the "best interest of the child" standard, commonly used in non-Indian child custody proceedings, appears in the section allowing an Indian parent to petition a state court for the return of her or his child if an adoption of that child is set aside.[143] The phrase is conspicuously absent from the section of the law discussing transfer of jurisdiction issues,[144] and that clearly expresses that it would be in the best interest of an Indian child for a tribal judge to decide the child's fate, except in the rare situation.[145]

A close examination of many of the cases that have utilized the best interest standard reveals that many of them involve Indian children who have been in foster homes and bonded with the foster parents.[146] As a result, the state's or guardian ad litem's argument against transfer may revolve around the issue of separation from the foster parents and the psychological impact such a separation would have on the child. A similar argument was made by the adoptive parents of the Indian twins in *Holyfield* in opposition to the tribe's *exclusive* jurisdiction there and in similar cases.[147] The argument was soundly rebuffed by the Supreme Court, which held that the only issue before it was who should make the decision about the placement of an Indian child, not what that decision should be.[148]

This distinction also exists in the transfer of jurisdiction arena and, as recognized in a number of cases, is directly addressed by the prohibition in the regulations against considering whether a placement would be changed.[149] The regulations and the guidelines recognize that the concrete issue in a transfer proceeding is whether the tribal court is in a position to hear all the evidence and make a decision without causing a hardship on the parties and witnesses, not whether the tribal court will make the so-called right decision.[150] Congress found that tribal courts were better equipped than state courts to make decisions regarding the future of Indian children.

It is often difficult for state courts, however, to appreciate this distinction, especially when a tribe seems eager to remove children from homes where the children have resided for a prolonged period of time. It is sometimes assumed that the position of the tribe advanced by the tribal attorney or social worker before the state court will automatically be adopted by the tribal judge—an erroneous assumption that fails to recognize that tribal judges (like state judges) are not bound by the position of the child welfare agency and exercise their own judgment consistent with applicable statutes and codes and in the child's best interest.[151] Many courts have noted the weakness of the logic behind the use of "best interests" and criticized those courts that have adopted the "best interest of the child" standard to deny transfer requests.[152] The regulations do not expressly address "best interest" but provide guidance by referencing in the comments two cases that hold that best interests of the child should not be considered in determining whether good cause exists for the reasons stated therein.[153]

Child Has Had Little Contact with Tribe and Members

The regulations prohibit a state court from considering an Indian child's cultural connections with his or her tribe or reservation as a basis for good cause.[154] If one is mindful of the discussion on the legislative impetus behind the enactment of the ICWA, one of Congress's concerns was that state courts and social services personnel, because of the cultural gap between predominantly non-Indian judges and social workers and Indian families, were ill-equipped to recognize the essential tribal relations of Indian peoples and the cultural and social standards prevailing in Indian communities and families.[155] Thus, to permit state courts to determine the sufficiency of an Indian child's cultural connections with his or her tribe or reservation in evaluating a petition to transfer conflicts with Congress's intent. Remember that either parent may veto a transfer request to the tribal court if he or she believes that it would not be an appropriate forum to adjudicate their case.[156]

Socioeconomic Conditions and Capacity of Tribe

Another ground that clearly cannot be used by the state court to deny a transfer request is a showing that the relevant socioeconomic conditions on the reservation are not conducive to the child leading a healthy lifestyle or that the tribal social services or court system is incapable of handling the case.[157] This prohibition was placed in the regulations to forbid parties from parading out before a state court judge a variety of statistics regarding life expectancy, unemployment, poverty, alcoholism, and other maladies on certain reservations in an effort to convince the judge that no child should suffer the fate of a reservation Indian child. These problems do plague certain reservations in this country, but Congress clearly concluded that Indian families remain the focal point for the conservation of traditional values and cultures that are inimical to many of the problems facing reservation Indians and, indeed, may be the solution to them.[158]

Obviously, if a tribe does not have a tribal court there would be no entity to accept a transfer. The definition of "tribal court" under the ICWA is an expansive one, however, and would include informal, traditional dispute resolution bodies such as a council of elders or tribal leaders.[159] A conventional judicial entity is not mandated in order to receive a transfer of jurisdiction.[160] The definition of tribal court includes any administrative body vested with authority over child custody proceedings.[161]

Child Objects to Transfer

It is interesting to observe how Congress treated the rights of the Indian child in the ICWA. The child has no standing to request a transfer of jurisdiction to the tribal court nor does the child have an absolute right to veto that transfer.[162] Even so, a state court may consider a child's objection to transfer, provided it is not based upon criteria that may not be considered by a court, such as a desire to resist a change in placement.[163]

Inconvenient Forum

The most commonly cited ground for denying a transfer request is when the evidence necessary to decide the case could not be adequately presented in the tribal court without undue hardship to the parties or witnesses.[164] This appears to be the original impetus behind granting state courts the authority to deny transfer requests as it is referred to in the legislative history.[165] There does not appear to be any clearly delineated benchmark in the case law for deciding when transfer would cause undue hardship, as some courts have held that transferring a case hundreds or even thousands of miles away from the location of the state court would not cause hardship,[166] whereas another court has ruled that transferring a case to a tribal court "two hours away" from the state court would.[167]

Tribal courts, in an attempt to foreclose the use of this ground for denying transfer, may wish to convene hearings at a more convenient location to the parties and witnesses or allow participation by other alternative methods.[168] The regulations contemplate this as a possibility, so state courts should not automatically deny a transfer request from a tribe or other party when it appears that travel to the tribal court would be burdensome without examining the possibility of the tribal court adjusting venue or even conducting telephonic or videoconferencing proceedings.[169] When a state court does refuse to transfer a case or opts to transfer a case, the standard for reviewing that decision is most frequently reviewed under an abuse of discretion standard.[170]

Endnotes

1. 490 U.S. 30 (1989).
2. *Id.* at 36.
3. 25 U.S.C. § 1911(a) (exclusive jurisdiction provisions) and *id.* § 1911(b) (transfer jurisdiction provisions).
4. *Id.* § 1911(a).
5. *Id.* § 1911(b).
6. Mississippi Band of Choctaw Indians v. Holyfield, 490 U.S. 30, 36, 109 S. Ct. 1597, 1601–02 (Section 1911(b) . . . creates concurrent[,] but presumptively tribal jurisdiction[,] in the case of children not domiciled on the reservation[.]"). *See also, e.g., In re* J.D.M.C., 739 N.W.2d 796 (S. Ct. S.D. 2007) (holding that if a case originates in state court and the Indian child is not a domiciliary or resident of the reservation, or ward of the tribal court, it creates concurrent jurisdiction between the Indian tribe and the state court).
7. https://www.uniformlaws.org/viewdocument/final-act-34?CommunityKey=4cc1b0be-d6c5-4bc2-b157-16b0baf2c56d (later amended to address international custody orders in 2013). The UCCJEA provides the framework for determining which state has jurisdiction over child custody matters and preventing jurisdictional disputes between states. The text of the UCCJEA has a key provision, if adopted by a particular state, that requires the state to treat tribes as a state when applying the UCCJEA and can be the basis for a state court to recognize a tribal court order based upon full faith and credit. The UCCJEA does not supersede the ICWA, however. *See* Holly C. v. Tohono O'odham Nation, 247 Ariz. 495, 452 P.3d 725 (Ariz. Ct. App. 2019). For more cases on the UCCJEA in the context of tribal courts, see https://turtletalk.blog/2022/08/17/recent-uccjea-cases-involving-tribal-courts/.
8. 25 U.S.C. § 1919; *see* 25 C.F.R. § 23.110; *In re* Parental Rights as to S.M.M.D, 272 P.3d 126 (Nev. 2012) (tribal–state agreement that termination of mother's parental rights would proceed in state district court vested

district court with subject matter jurisdiction to accept mother's voluntary relinquishment of her parental rights); *see also* Doe v. Doe, 349 P.3d 1205 (S. Ct. Idaho 2015). In the S.M.M.D. case, the tribe and the state of Nevada had entered into a verbal "joint decision" to continue with Nevada maintaining jurisdiction and the tribe "being a co-agent and lending support." The Nevada Supreme Court determined that 25 U.S.C. § 1919(a) was meant to be broad, and looking to 25 U.S.C. § 1919(a)'s legislative history, determined the "joint decision" between the tribe and Nevada constituted a case-by-case agreement as contemplated by 25 U.S.C. § 1919(a), and found concurrent jurisdiction between Nevada and the tribe. *See also* SHANNON KELLER O'LOUGHLIN, A SURVEY AND ANALYSIS OF TRIBAL-STATE INDIAN CHILD WELFARE ACT AGREEMENTS (Ass'n on Am. Indian Affairs, 2014), https://www.indian-affairs.org/icwa-state.html.

9. 25 U.S.C. § 1911(a); *Holyfield*, 490 U.S. 30 (finding that a mother who lived on the reservation, but who left the reservation to give birth, was domiciled on the reservation and the tribe had exclusive jurisdiction over the case); *but see In re* S.J.W., 535 P.3d 1235 (S. Ct. Okla. 2023) (holding that a Muscogee (Creek) Indian child domiciled in the Chickasaw Nation's reservation was subject to concurrent state and tribal jurisdiction, as § 1911 refers to territorial jurisdiction but not subject matter jurisdiction). Note that this is the only case that has ruled in this way and, given that the court's reasoning is rather unique and influenced by recent jurisdictional decisions specific to Oklahoma, it is unlikely that other courts will adopt the reasoning in this case.
10. In *Holyfield*, the Supreme Court noted that the language in § 1911(a) excepting its coverage from cases where jurisdiction is otherwise vested in federal or state courts applies to tribes in so-called Pub. Law 280 states where jurisdiction was vested in the state courts pursuant to federal law. *Holyfield*, 490 U.S. at 42 n.16. *See* 28 U.S.C. § 1360. Also, Pub. Law 280 applies to some tribes through land claim settlement and recognition acts. NATIVE AMERICAN RIGHTS FUND, A PRACTICAL GUIDE TO THE INDIAN CHILD WELFARE ACT, at Q12 (2007), https://www.narf.org/nill/documents/icwa/faq/jurisdiction.html#Q12. Of note, some tribes and states have altered the Pub. Law 280

jurisdictional regime through 25 U.S.C. § 1919 agreements and state law. *See supra* note 8.

11. *See* State v. Native Vill. of Tanana, 249 P.3d 734 (Alaska 2011) (tribes have the inherent sovereign right to originate cases involving their children regardless of where they are resident or domiciled); *In re* D.L.L. & C.L.L., 291 N.W.2d 278 (S.D. 1980) (the children were wards of the tribal court prior to the state court action and the reservation residency and domicile of the children was not lost by any supposed abandonment or emancipation on the part of the parent); *but see In re* Guardianship of A.K., 557 P.3d 770 (Ct. App. Ariz., Div. 1 2024) (holding Indian community did not have exclusive jurisdiction over the guardianship proceeding involving child because when the trial court's order adjudicating child a temporary ward of the Indian community's children's court and its protective custody warrant for child was issued, the child was not domiciled or living on the reservation and the state court had established jurisdiction before the tribal court issued the wardship order); *In re* Adoption of K.L.J. and K.P.J., 266 N.C. App. 289, 831 S.E.2d 114 (Ct. App. N.C. 2019) (finding that the ICWA regulations are silent on who should make a finding on whether a child is a ward of the tribal court, and adopting Black's Law definition of "ward," the court held the children were not wards of tribal court despite a tribal court order from Cheyenne River Sioux asserting that the children were wards of the court); *In re* J.D.M.C., 739 N.W.2d 796, 805 (S. Ct. S.D. 2007) (holding the plain language of § 1911(a) and the case law demonstrate the only effective way a wardship order can be used to obtain exclusive jurisdiction is to enter the order while the Indian child is domiciled or resident on the reservation).
12. It should be noted that the ICWA does not govern child custody proceedings in tribal courts. 25 C.F.R. § 23.103(b)(1). Those proceedings are governed by the individual tribe's ordinances and constitution as well as the provisions of the Indian Civil Rights Act, 25 U.S.C. §§ 1301–1303. Therefore, it is possible that under a tribe's law it cannot exercise jurisdiction over a member child from another tribe. *See* Torgerson v. Torgerson, 11 N.W.3d 50 (S. Ct. S.D. 2024) (holding a tribal court's subject matter jurisdiction is

conferred by the tribe's constitution, tribal code, treaties, or decisional law and that a tribal court's jurisdiction may also be limited by express restrictions found within tribal law itself or even, occasionally, by the absence of positive tribal law on point).

13. Oliphant v. Suquamish Tribe, 435 U.S. 191 (1978). *See also* Duro v. Reina, 495 U.S. 676 (1990). In the Violence Against Women Act Amendments, Congress restored inherent tribal criminal jurisdiction over a narrow class of non-Indian defendants. Pub. L. No. 113-4, tit. IX, 127 Stat. 54, 118-26; *see also* 25 U.S.C. § 1304. For more information on Special Tribal Criminal Jurisdiction over non-Indians, please see https://www.home.tlpi.org/vawa2022.
14. *See* 25 U.S.C. § 1301(2).
15. *See* Duro v. Reina, 495 U.S. 676 (U.S. 1990).
16. 18 U.S.C. § 1162. *See also* 25 U.S.C. § 1322. As a result of an amendment to Pub. Law 280 effected by passage of the Indian Civil Rights Act, 25 U.S.C. § 1301, after 1968 tribes must consent to the exercise of state court civil and criminal jurisdiction. *See* Cohen's Handbook of Federal Indian Law § 6.04[3] (LexisNexis 2012).
17. *See* Bryan v. Itasca County, 426 U.S. 373 (1976); California v. Cabazon Band of Mission Indians, 480 U.S. 202 (1987).
18. Doe v. Mann, 415 F.3d 1038 (9th Cir. 2005) (recognizing the concurrent jurisdiction of the state of California, a Pub. Law 280 state, over a child welfare proceeding involving an Indian child resident and domiciled on the reservation); *In re* C.R.H., 29 P.3d 849 (S. Ct. Alaska 2001) (holding that Pub. Law 280 negates a tribe's exclusive jurisdiction under ICWA § 1911(a) and renders state and tribal jurisdiction as concurrent). The exercise of state jurisdiction in Pub. Law 280 states has not been without controversy. The U.S. Supreme Court has interpreted the phrase "civil causes of action" in Pub. Law 280 states as providing states with adjudicatory power over private civil litigation involving American Indians—for example, a lawsuit by an Indian person to enforce a contract—but has not interpreted Pub. Law 280 to allow for the exercise of general state civil regulatory authority over activities taking place on tribal land. *See* Bryan v. Itasca Cnty., 426 U.S.

373, 384–85 (1976); California v. Cabazon Band of Mission Indians, 480 U.S. 205, 208–12 (1987). Based upon this interpretation, at least one state attorney general opinion has been issued that interpreted Pub. Law 280 as giving states concurrent jurisdiction over voluntary proceedings involving reservation residents or domiciliaries, but not involuntary proceedings. 70 *Op Att'y Gen. Wis.* 237 (1981) (holding if the child custody matter involved only private persons, as in voluntary foster care placement, state law could be applied under Pub. Law 280's jurisdictional grant, but it could not be applied to "those proceedings that involve some aspect of the state's regulatory jurisdiction such as involuntary termination of parental rights"). Thus, although *Doe v. Mann* has resolved this issue in favor of concurrent state jurisdiction over child custody proceedings for Pub. Law 280 states that are part of the Ninth Circuit, it is possible that other courts would rule differently if directly faced with the issue.

19. State v. Native Village of Tanana, 249 P.3d 734 (Alaska 2011); 25 U.S.C. § 1918; 25 C.F.R. Part 13.
20. 25 U.S.C. § 1911(d).
21. 25 C.F.R. § 23.2 (definition of domicile), *see also* Mississippi Band of Choctaw Indians v Holyfield, 490 U.S. 30 (1989) (holding that in determining domicile the state court should look to the generally accepted federal and common law concepts of domicile); *In re* Adoption of S.S., 167 Ill. 2d 25, 657 N.E.2d 935 (S. Ct. Ill. 1995) (holding that after the death of the father the domicile of Indian child shifted to that of mother, unless she had aban doned the child); *but cf. In re* Adoption of B.B., 469 P.3d 1093 (Sup. Ct. Utah 2020) (holding the birth mother was not domiciled on an Indian reservation even though she moved back to the reservation shortly after the child's birth because when she moved to Utah she had the intent to stay there and thus became a Utah domiciliary before she gave birth to her child).
22. Merrill v. Altman, 807 N.W.2d 821 (S.D. 2011) (temporary physical presence does not establish residence).
23. 25 U.S.C. § 1911(a).
24. *Id.* § 1922.
25. *See id.* § 1922; 25 C.F.R. § 23.113(d)(3), (9).

26. 25 U.S.C. § 1903(10); 25 C.F.R. § 23.2.
27. 18 U.S.C. § 1151.
28. *See, e.g.*, Rosebud Sioux Tribe v. Kneip, 430 U.S. 584 (1977) (reservation diminished); DeCoteau v. Dist. Ct., 420 U.S. 425 (1975) (reservation disestablished); Solem v. Bartlett, 465 U.S. 463 (1984); South Dakota v. Yankton Sioux Tribe, 522 U.S. 329 (1998), *on remand,* Yankton Sioux Tribe v. Gaffey, 188 F.3d 1010 (8th Cir. 2000); McGirt v. Oklahoma, 591 U.S. 894 (2020) (holding that the state of Oklahoma lacked jurisdiction to prosecute an Indian because, contrary to the position and understanding of the state, the Creek Indian reservation had never been disestablished and the crime took place on the reservation).
29. *See, e.g., DeCoteau*, 420 U.S. 425 (reservation disestablished); Rosebud Sioux Tribe v. Kneip, 430 U.S. 584 (1977) (reservation diminished).
30. *DeCoteau*, 420 U.S. 425.
31. An example is the Sisseton-Wahpeton Tribe in South Dakota, who had their land base diminished by the Supreme Court's decision in *DeCoteau v. District Court*, 420 U.S. 425 (1975).
32. *See* United States v. South Dakota, 665 F.2d 837 (8th Cir. 1981); United States v. Arrieta, 436 F.3d 1246 (10th Cir. 2006).
33. *See* United States v. Stands, 105 F.3d 1565 (8th Cir. 1997).
34. 18 U.S.C. § 1151.
35. Solem v. Bartlett, 465 U.S. 463 (1984).
36. 18 U.S.C. § 1151.
37. 490 U.S. 30 (1989).
38. *In re* B.B., 511 So. 2d 918 (Miss. 1987), *rev'd sub. nom.* Mississippi Band of Choctaw Indians v. Holyfield, 490 U.S. 30 (1989).
39. *Holyfield*, 490 U.S. at 53.
40. *Id.* at 49.
41. *Id.* at 48.
42. *Id.* at 46, 48.
43. *Id.* at 51 n.26. *But see In re* W.L., 260 Mont. 325, 859 P.2d 1019 (1993) (stating state court does not lose the jurisdiction it originally lawfully exercised by the actions of the mother in moving back to the reservation); *In*

re Adoption of B.B., 469 P.3d 1093 (S. Ct. Utah 2020) (even though the mother moved back to the reservation after the child's birth, the court held the birth mother was not domiciled on an Indian reservation because when she moved to Utah while pregnant she had intended to stay there and thus became a Utah domiciliary before she gave birth to her child).

44. *Holyfield*, 490 U.S. at 52.
45. *See In re* Adoption of Halloway, 732 P.2d 962 (Utah 1986) (holding that Navajo mother intended to abandon child when she allowed him to be removed from reservation and to remain with foster parents was sufficiently supported by evidence, but Utah abandonment law, pursuant to which child would have acquired domicile of foster parents and court would have acquired jurisdiction over adoption proceedings, was preempted by federal law providing Indian courts with exclusive jurisdiction over all custody proceedings involving Indian children resident or domiciled on the reservation).
46. 25 C.F.R. § 23.2; *see In re* S.S., 657 N.E.2d 935, 942 (Ill. 1995) (court held that children's domicile shifted to that of mother upon custodial father's death unless mother was found to have abandoned children based upon Illinois law, which would be an issue of fact for the trial court).
47. 25 U.S.C. § 1911(a).
48. Mississippi Band of Choctaw Indians v. Holyfield, 490 U.S. 30, 36 (1989).
49. *See* Owens v. Willick, 690 So. 2d 948 (La. Ct. App. 1997) (in situation where tribal council had previously approved of adoption by a party who then placed child with another family to be adopted, state court found that the child is ward of the tribe and tribe must approve of the placement).
50. *See In re* Parental Placement of M.R.D.B., 787 P.2d 1219 (Mont. 1990), *reh'g denied* (finding tribal court has exclusive jurisdiction over adoption proceeding after mother withdrew consent to adoption and the tribal court had declared the child a ward of the tribal court).
51. 25 U.S.C. § 1911(a).
52. *In re* D.L.L. & C.L.L., 291 N.W.2d 278 (S.D. 1980) (holding that since the children were wards of the tribal court prior to the state court action and the children remained residents and domiciliaries of the reservation, the proper forum for relief was the tribal court).

53. *Holyfield*, 490 U.S. at 49.
54. *See supra* note 11.
55. 25 U.S.C. § 1911(d) requires states to grant full faith and credit to judicial proceedings of tribes making children wards.
56. *See, e.g., In re* Welfare of R.I., 402 N.W.2d 173 (Minn. Ct. App. 1987) (The trial court must give full faith and credit to the wardship orders issued by the Warm Springs Tribe, although it may exercise concurrent jurisdiction over emergency removal.); *but cf. In re* Adoption of K.L.J. & K.P.J., 266 N.C. App. 289, 831 S.E.2d 114 (N.C. Ct. App. 2019) (full faith and credit not appropriate because guardians were not notified of and did not participate in the tribal court proceeding); Starr v. George, 175 P.3d 50 (Alaska 2008) (when paternal grandparents had been granted visitation rights by state court and had filed a petition for custody, failure of tribal court to give notice to paternal grandparents of maternal grandparents adoption petition in tribal court violated due process and precluded recognition of the tribal court order on the basis of full faith and credit).
57. *See In re* Dakota L., 712 N.W.2d 583 (Neb. 2006) (holding Juvenile Court had jurisdiction over Indian children in involuntary foster care placement proceeding, as testimonial evidence was inconclusive as to whether children were currently wards of tribal court, and there was no documentary evidence that demonstrated that children were wards of tribal court).
58. 25 U.S.C. § 1911(b); 25 C.F.R. § 23.115.
59. 25 U.S.C. § 1903(12) (definition of Tribal Court); 25 C.F.R. § 23.2 (same).
60. 25 C.F.R. § 23.116.
61. *Id.*
62. A court is required to conduct an evidentiary hearing on the question of whether good cause exists to deny transfer of a proceeding to a tribe's jurisdiction when such request is challenged, and to make specific factual findings on the issue. See People in Interest of A.O., 896 N.W.2d 652 (S.D. 2017).
63. 25 U.S.C. § 1911(b); 25 C.F.R. § 23.117.
64. *See* 25 C.F.R. § 23.117(a); *In re* Appeal of Maricopa Cnty. Juv. Action No. JD-6982, 922 P.2d 319 (Ariz. Ct. App. 1996) (under ICWA, parent had

absolute veto power over transfer of jurisdiction of proceeding involving Indian child not residing or domiciled within reservation and mother's valid objection to transfer required superior court to retain jurisdiction); *In re* Larissa G., 51 Cal. Rptr. 2d 16 (Ct. App. 1996) (holding that parent of Indian child not domiciled or residing on reservation has veto power over any decision to transfer proceeding for foster care placement or termination of parental rights to tribe's jurisdiction); *In re* A.E., 572 N.W.2d 579 (Iowa 1997) (holding natural father's refusal to consent to transfer of jurisdiction to tribal court in another state foreclosed possibility of such transfer). *But see In re* Andrea Lynn M., 10 P.3d 191 (N.M. Ct. App. 2000) (Mere fact that father of child subject to protections of ICWA objected to transfer of custody proceedings to Navajo Nation Family Court did not demonstrate applicability of ICWA provision permitting either parent to object to transfer to tribal court, where such provision only applied in respect to children domiciled and residing off tribal reservations, and where father, who bore burden of persuasion in opposing transfer, failed to provide evidence of child's domicile.).

65. 25 U.S.C. § 1911(b).
66. Indeed, the Supreme Court called the tribe's jurisdiction over children living outside the reservation boundaries its presumptive jurisdiction. Mississippi Band of Choctaw Indians v. Holyfield, 490 U.S. 30, 36 (1989). *Cf. In re* M.H.C., 381 P.3d 710 (S. Ct. Okla. 2016) (holding ICWA provision allowing transfer of matter from state court to tribal court applied to proceeding to terminate natural mother's parental rights upon mother's enrollment in tribe, even though proceeding was initiated while child was in foster care and while mother was not tribal member).
67. *See* 25 U.S.C. § 1901(5).
68. *Holyfield*, 490 U.S. at 45.
69. *See In re* Brittany C., 693 N.W.2d 592 (Neb. Ct. App. 2005) (permitting appeal from order denying transfer of jurisdiction but affirming the denial of transfer on forum non conveniens grounds using an abuse of discretion appellate standard); People in the Interest of J.L.P., 870 P.2d 1252 (Colo. 1994) (appeal from order denying transfer).

70. 25 C.F.R. § 118.
71. Indian Child Welfare Act Proceedings, 81 Fed. Reg. 38821 (June 14, 2016).
72. *See* H.R. Rep. No. 95-1386, at 21.
73. 25 C.F.R. § 118.
74. Nothing prevents a tribe, under the provisions of the ICWA, from transferring jurisdiction over a child custody proceeding to its court but retaining placement rights with a state or county agency.
75. For more information on tribal–state ICWA agreements, see O'Loughlin, *supra* note 8; State ICWA Developments and Resources—NICWA, https://www.nicwa.org/state-icwa/ (last visited Aug. 15, 2025).
76. 25 U.S.C. § 1911(b).
77. *See In re* Guardianship of A.K., 557 P.3d 770 (Ct. App. Ariz., Div. 1 2024) (holding that § 1911 transfer provision does not apply to preadoptive placements but noting that the provision in ICWA does not prohibit transfers, citing Gila River Indian Cmty. v. Dep't of Child Safety, 242 Ariz. 277, 395 P.3d 286 (Ariz. 2017)); *In re* M.S., 237 P.3d 161 (Okla. 2010) (§ 1911(b) omission of language referring to preadoptive/adoptive placements is not an expression of intent to preclude tribal court jurisdiction when transfer is requested after parental rights are terminated); *see also* In the Interest of L.R.B., S.B.B., and K.B.B., 487 P.3d 1058 (Co. Ct. App. 2019) (Although federal law may not have authorized transfer of a post-termination proceedings, language in the state statute was broader and provided for the transfer of any child custody proceeding.).
78. BIA Guidelines for Implementing the Indian Child Welfare Act § F.2 (Dec. 2016).
79. Either biological parent of the child may request the state court to transfer jurisdiction, or the tribe may do so. Finally, an Indian custodian, if one exists in the particular case, has standing to seek a transfer. 25 U.S.C. § 1911(b).
80. The reader should examine the definitions of these terms closely because in some circumstances a "parent" under state law may differ from the definition of "parent" under the ICWA. For example, because the ICWA defines a "parent" as a biological parent, there are circumstances where a

biological parent whose rights have been terminated under state law may still be considered a "parent" for ICWA purposes.

81. 25 U.S.C. § 1911(b). A parent is absolutely entitled to veto a transfer of jurisdiction by objecting. One court has held that a parent who does not concur in a transfer of jurisdiction nonetheless has acquiesced in transfer by taking the child back to the reservation and placing the child with relatives. *In re* Welfare of R.I., 402 N.W.2d 173 (Minn. Ct. App. 1987).
82. 25 U.S.C. § 1903(9); 25 C.F.R. § 23.2.
83. *See* Noah v. Kelly B., 67 P.3d 359 (Okla. Civ. App. 2003) (holding fact that natural father did not know of mother's pregnancy and subsequent birth of child did not bar him from participating in the ICWA proceeding to challenge a voluntary adoption, since he established his paternity by DNA testing).
84. *See In re* the Adoption of B.B., 2017 UT 59, 417 P.3d 1 (2017) (holding that a federal standard must be applied in determining whether a father acknowledged or established paternity and not the more restrictive state law standard); *see also* Michael J. Jr. v. Michael J. Sr., 7 P.3d 960 (Ariz. Ct. App. 2000) (acknowledgment need not be made in formal legal proceeding); *but see* In the Adoption of Child of Indian Heritage, 543 A.2d 925 (N.J. 1988) (looked to state law to determine whether father had acknowledged or established paternity and noting states may constitutionally deny an unwed father parental status unless and until he manifests an interest in developing a relationship with that child, provided that the qualifications for establishing such rights are not beyond the control of an interested putative father to satisfy); *cf.* Adoptive Couple v. Baby Girl, 570 U.S. 637, 133 S. Ct. 2552 (2013) (declined to address the acknowledgment or establishment issue, instead finding that certain parts of § 1912 did not apply to the father as he never had custody of the child because in the opinion of the court he had abandoned the child).
85. Either parent, Indian or non-Indian, can veto a transfer to tribal court under 25 U.S.C. § 1911(b), but interestingly enough only an Indian adoptive parent can veto a transfer because the definition of parent excludes non-Indian adoptive parents. 25 U.S.C. § 1903(9); 25 C.F.R. § 23.2.
86. *See* definition of "parent" at 25 U.S.C. § 1903(9) and 25 C.F.R. § 23.2.

87. *Id.*
88. A parent need not justify an objection to transfer.
89. Under *Santosky v. Kramer*, the court seems to suggest that once the parental rights of a parent are severed, that parent loses any rights with respect to the child. 455 U.S. 745 (1982). This holding would seem to preclude a parent whose rights have been terminated from objecting to a transfer to tribal court. *See In re* K.D., 630 N.W.2d 492 (S.D. 2001); Carson v. Carson, 13 P.3d 523 (Ct. App. Or. 2000); and BIA GUIDELINES, *supra* note 78, § F.4.
90. BIA GUIDELINES, *supra* note 78, § F.4.
91. *See In re* K.D., 630 N.W.2d 492 (S.D. 2001).
92. *See supra* note 89.
93. *In re* Cal. E., 2023 Ill. App. (4th) 220930 (App. Ct. Ill. 2023) (when foster parents intervened in the proceeding and challenged the transfer of the case to tribal court, the court found that the deaths of the mother and father did not nullify their written objections to the transfer of the child custody proceeding to the tribe).
94. *See supra* note 84.
95. *But see* the discussion in *In re Adoption of Child of Indian Heritage* regarding how a child who is allegedly the natural child of an Indian father whose rights have not been determined is to be treated for purposes of the application of the ICWA. 543 A.2d 925 (N.J. 1988).
96. *See In re* Daniel M., 1 Cal. Rptr. 3d 897 (Ct. App. 2003) (holding alleged father, who did not acknowledge or establish his paternity, lacked standing to claim that juvenile court committed reversible error by not complying with notice requirements of ICWA).
97. 405 U.S. 645 (1972).
98. The court's holding in *Stanley* was modified somewhat in *Michael H. v. Gerald D.*, 491 U.S. 11 (1989), holding that the father of a child conceived by a mother outside her existing marriage did not have a substantive due process right to filiation with the child.
99. *See In re* Adoption of Child of Indian Heritage, 543 A.2d 925, 934 (N.J. 1988).

100. 25 U.S.C. § 1903(6); 25 C.F.R. § 23.2 (the regulation clarifies that whether an individual has legal custody may be determined by looking to either the relevant tribe's law or custom, or to state law).

101. The rights of a "parent" of an Indian child and an "Indian custodian" are the same in almost all respects under the ICWA except an Indian custodian is not granted the right to veto a transfer of jurisdiction under § 1911(b) and since an Indian custodian does not have constitutionally protected rights, arguably the termination of parental rights section would not apply to a case involving an Indian custodian. In addition, the definition of "Indian custodian" contained at § 1903(6) requires the custodian to meet the definition of "Indian" under the ICWA, whereas non-Indian parents can exercise the same rights as Indian parents of an Indian child.

102. 25 U.S.C. § 1916(b) states that the placement preferences and notice provisions of the ICWA do not apply when a child is being returned to a parent or Indian custodian. It is likely, although not clear under the current state of the law, that if a foster care placement proceeding results in a return of custody to the parent and removal of custody from an Indian custodian who received that designation through placement by a state court, that the parent's rights would trump the Indian custodian's rights. Some courts have held that Indian persons cannot receive Indian custodian status by having children placed with them as part of child custody proceedings under the ICWA. *See Rosalind M*, 555 P.3d 505 (S. Ct. AK 2024) (holding foster mother did not have legal custody of Indian child committed to temporary care of Office of Children's Services (OCS), and thus she was not child's "Indian custodian" and did not have right to intervene in child custody proceeding).

103. *Cf.* 25 U.S.C. § 1903(2) and 25 U.S.C. § 1903(6).

104. The only requirement under § 1903(6) is that the Indian person have custody under tribal law or custom, under state law, or has been conveyed the temporary custody by one of the parents of the child. No blood relationship is required.

105. An extended family member is generally a blood relative of the child and several examples of relationships are cited at § 1903(2). However, the fact that the person meets one of those relationship criteria does not render

the person an Indian custodian unless the person meets one of the criteria under § 1903(6); *see also* In the Best Interest of M.R.P.C., 794 N.W.2d 373 (Minn. Ct. App. 2011) (Trial court has an affirmative obligation to inquire into whether the ICWA applied to determination of whether grandparents were child's de facto custodians).

106. 25 U.S.C. § 1903(6); 25 C.F.R. § 23.2.

107. *See* Rosalind M. v. State, Dep't of Fam. & Cmty. Servs., 555 P.3d 505 (S. Ct. Alaska 2024) (holding foster mother did not have legal custody of Indian child committed to temporary care of Office of Children's Services (OCS), and thus she was not child's "Indian custodian" and did not have right to intervene in child custody proceeding); State *ex rel.* Juv. Dep't v. England, 640 P.2d 608 (Or. 1982) (holding aunt, who accepted state funds for her foster care of child, was not an "Indian custodian" within meaning of ICWA so as to be entitled to notice prior to termination of foster care placement).

108. Use of the term "custom" under § 1903(6) strongly suggests that an Indian person may have custodian status without the need to demonstrate "legal custody" through a court order.

109. Some tribes may codify their traditional practices. For example, the Sisseton-Wahpeton Oyate have a traditional "adoption" section in their Tribal Code stipulating that if a child has been voluntarily left with another Indian family for a period of time in excess of two years, there has been an *Ecagwaya*, or traditional adoption. SISSETON-WAHPETON TRIBAL CODE § 38-03-24, https://narf.org/nill/codes/sisseton_wahpeton/index.html.

110. *See In re* J.T., 38 P.3d 245 (Okla. Civ. App. 2002) (holding Indian grandmother who voluntarily surrendered her grandchildren to state DHS lost her right to claim Indian custodian status).

111. Of course, the voluntary placement must be for some sustained period of time and could not be, for example, a situation where the child was left with a babysitter overnight. If, on the other hand, a child is left with an Indian grandmother for extended care, that Indian grandmother could qualify as an Indian custodian under the law.

112. Nothing under § 1903(6) requires that the parent execute a legal document evidencing the placement with the Indian custodian.

113. 25 U.S.C. § 1911(b).
114. *Id.*
115. 25 C.F.R. § 23.109(a).
116. *Id.* § 23.109(c).
117. *Id.*; *but see* Jones v. Lummi Tribal Ct., 2012 WL 6149666 (W.D. Wash. 2012) (tribe may assert jurisdiction over child eligible for membership even where parent is a member of another tribe).
118. 25 C.F.R. § 23.111. *See In re* Junious M., 193 Cal. Rptr. 40 (Ct. App. 1983) (In child custody proceeding in which it appeared that minor may have been an Indian child, trial court erred by not notifying tribe in question and seeking its determination of child's Indian status, which determination would have been conclusive for purpose of deciding whether ICWA was applicable.); In the Interest of C.H., 510 N.W.2d 119 (S.D. 1993); *In re* M.C.P., 571 A.2d 627 (Vt. 1989) (holding state failed to give adequate notice under ICWA to Secretary of Interior and to tribe of which children were possible members so that remand was necessary to allow compliance with notice requirements).
119. 25 C.F.R. § 23.111.
120. In the Interest of C.H., 510 N.W.2d 119 (S.D. 1993) (late discovery that Indian child is involved does not vitiate proceedings, but the ICWA applies from that point on); *but see In re* J.D.B., 584 N.W.2d 577 (Iowa App. 1998) (court holds that failure of tribe to participate in earlier proceedings prevented court from determining children's Indian status).
121. 25 U.S.C. § 1903(8). While the generally accepted interpretation has been that ICWA only applies to federally recognized tribes, at least one case has applied the ICWA to a state-recognized tribe. *In re* M.B., E.B., & B.B., 204 P.3d 1242 (Mont. 2009) (applying the ICWA to a state-recognized tribe in Montana). In addition, one state has applied the ICWA to state-recognized tribes through state law. *See In re* Dupree M., 171 A.D.3d 752 (N.Y. Ct. App. 2019) (ICWA applied to the Unkechaug Indian Nation, even though the nation was not federally recognized, since a state statute applied ICWA to state-recognized tribes and the state of New York recognized Unkechaug as an Indian tribe).
122. 25 U.S.C. § 1911(b); 25 C.F.R. § 23.117.

123. 25 C.F.R. § 23.115. If an oral motion to transfer is made, however, some courts have held that a transfer hearing must be held, preceded by notice to all parties in the proceeding, to permit objections to be aired. Interest of J.L.P., 870 P.2d 1252 (Colo. Ct. App., Div. III 1994) (holding father orally informing juvenile court, less than year after Indian tribe had been notified, that tribe intended to intervene and request transfer of jurisdiction under ICWA in dependency and neglect proceeding involving Indian children living off reservation could be construed as prompt request for transfer of jurisdiction under ICWA in light of Bureau of Indian Affairs (BIA) guidelines stating that request for transfer made orally by parent or tribe of Indian child shall be reduced to writing by court and made part of the record).
124. Although the acceptance of jurisdiction by a tribal court is not a prerequisite for a state court to transfer jurisdiction, it would not be in an Indian child's interest for a state court to transfer a case to the tribal court, potentially ending state or county funding for the child, and to then have the tribe decline the transfer. Some tribes require the party seeking to transfer jurisdiction from a state court to first seek a tribal court order accepting a transfer of jurisdiction, so advocates should be aware of this tribal requirement.
125. 25 U.S.C. § 1911(b); 25 C.F.R. § 23.117(a).
126. H.R. Rep. No. 95-1386, at 21 (1978), *reprinted in* 1978 U.S.C.C.A.N. 7530.
127. *See, e.g., In re* M.E.M., 625 P.2d 1313 (Mont. 1981); People in the Interest of J.L.P., 870 P.2d 1252 (Colo. 1994); BIA Guidelines, *supra* note 78, § F.5 ("recommending that courts follow that 'trend'"). *See also* Interest of T.F., 972 N.W.2d 1 (S. Ct. Iowa 2022) (court held that guardian ad litem objecting to transfer had the "burden of overcoming the Tribe's presumptive jurisdiction," but did not specify the burden of proof); People in Interest of A.O., 896 N.W.2d 652 (S.D. 2017) (mother entitled to evidentiary hearing before motion to transfer can be denied).
128. *See, e.g.,* Interest of E.T., 932 N.W.2d 770 (S. Ct. S.D. 2019) (Where requested, evidentiary hearing was required prior to granting motion to transfer proceeding to tribal court.); *In re* Guardianship of A.K., 557 P.3d 770 (Ct. App. Ariz., Div. 1 2024) (superior court did not abuse its discretion by rejecting permissive intervention by foster parents in child custody proceeding

where they sought intervention in order to oppose transfer of jurisdiction to tribe); *In re* C.R.H., 29 P.3d 849 (Alaska 2001) (court held that Alaska tribes can exercise transfer jurisdiction under 25 U.S.C. § 1911(b)); *In re* Guardianship of J.C.D., 686 N.W.2d 647 (S.D. 2004) (court erred in denying transfer of guardianship petition to tribal court). This includes a number of cases where the transfer request involved cases not explicitly covered by the ICWA. *See, e.g.*, In the Interest of L.R.B., S.B.B., and K.B.B., 487 P.3d 1058 (Colo. Ct. App. 2019) (Although federal law may not have authorized transfer of a post-termination proceedings, language in the state statute was broader and provided for the transfer of any child custody proceeding.); Gila River Indian Cmty. v. Dep't of Child Safety, 242 Ariz. 277, 395 P.3d 286 (Ariz. 2017) (transfer provision does not apply to preadoptive placements but noting that the provision in ICWA does not prohibit transfers).

129. 25 C.F.R. § 23.118(c)

130. *See, e.g.*, *In re* Maricopa Cnty. Juv. Action No. JS-8287, 171 Ariz. 404, 828 P.2d 1245 (Ct. App. 1991), *rev. denied* (1992); *In re* Robert T., 246 Cal. Rptr. 168 (Ct. App. 1988); *In re* Interest of C.W., 479 N.W.2d 105 (Neb. 1991); *In re* Wayne R.N., 757 P.2d 1333 (N.M. Ct. App. 1988); *In re* Laurie R., 760 P.2d 1295 (N.M. Ct. App. 1988); *In re* Dependency & Neglect of A.L., 442 N.W.2d 233 (S.D. 1989).

131. *Compare In re* A.B., 663 N.W.2d 625 (N.D. 2003), *cert. denied sub nom* Hoots v. K.B., 124 S. Ct. 1875 (2004) (holding that a request to transfer a termination proceeding was not untimely, even though foster care placement had been in existence for more than 13 months, because the termination petition had only been pending for a little over one month and was a separate proceeding) *and In re* Interest of Zelena R., 825 N.W.2d 173 (Neb. 2012) (foster care and TPR proceedings are separate for purposes of advanced stage analysis) *with In re* Brandon F., 695 N.W.2d 905 (Wis. 2005) (denying transfer for tribe that waited to transfer jurisdiction until after the termination petition was filed because foster care proceedings had been pending for four years).

132. 25 C.F.R. § 23.2 (definition of child custody proceeding); 25 C.F.R. § 23.118(c)(1); BIA Guidelines, *supra* note 78, § F.5.; *see also* Delaware Tribe of Indians v. Nowicki-Eldridge, 888 S.E.2d 866 (S. Ct. W. Va. 2023)

(Good cause did not exist to deny tribe's motion to transfer termination of parental rights proceedings based on advanced stage of proceedings because although proceedings concerning child had been pending for more than three years, the proceedings involved at least three individual "proceedings" as contemplated by ICWA, namely, termination of mother's parental rights, attempted unification with father, and termination of father's parental rights, and proceeding regarding termination of father's parental rights was not advanced at the time tribe filed the motion to transfer.).

133. *See* BIA Guidelines, *supra* note 78, § F.2; *see* State v. Martina A., 719 N.W.2d 304 (Neb. App. 2006) (tribe intervened but indicated that it did not want to transfer jurisdiction until termination).
134. 25 C.F.R. § 23.118(c)(2).
135. *Id.* § 23.118(c)(1).
136. *See, e.g.*, Guardianship of C.H.S., 394 P.3d 278 (Ct. App. Okla. 2016) (Because guardians of Indian children failed to give tribe proper notice of guardianship action, motion to deny the tribe's motion to transfer the case based upon a claim that the guardianship proceeding was at an advanced stage was denied, even though the tribe's motion was made approximately four years after guardianship was granted, as the delay in filing the motion was beyond tribe's control.); *In re* D.S., 577 N.E.2d 572 (Ind. 1991) (holding that although no request for transfer was made, the lack of notice to tribe and others prevented an option to request transfer).
137. *See generally* BIA Guidelines, *supra* note 78, § F.5; *see also* In the Interest of C.R.W., 962 N.W.2d 730 (S.D. 2021) (when mother moved to transfer the case at the start of the termination hearing and TPR proceeding had been pending for more than six months, transfer petition was denied on the grounds that the proceeding was at an advanced stage).
138. *See* BIA Guidelines, *supra* note 78, § C.1; *cf. In re* Armell, 194 Ill. App. 3d 31 (App. Ct. Ill. 1990) (holding Indian mother was not precluded from consenting to transfer of jurisdiction in neglect and dependency proceeding to tribal court, even though she did not divulge her actual tribal affiliation for two and a half years after institution of proceedings).
139. *See In re* Dependency & Neglect of A.L., 442 N.W.2d 233 (S.D. 1989) (criticizing the lack of involvement from tribe in an ICWA case).

140. *See* Adoption and Safe Families Act, Adoption and Safe Families Act of 1997 (ASFA), Pub. Law No. 105-89, 111 Stat. 2115 (1997). The filing of a petition for termination of parental rights under ASFA is mandatory when the child has been in foster care for 15 out of the 22 preceding months, and when the parent has committed serious abuse upon the child or a sibling or has abandoned the child. *See* 42 U.S.C. § 675(5)(E). The only three exceptions to the rule that the state agency must file when these circumstances are met are when (1) the child is being cared for by a relative; (2) the state has documented a compelling reason that filing a termination petition would not be in the child's best interest; or (3) the situation calls for services to be provided to a non-offending parent and those services have not yet been provided. 42 U.S.C. § 675(E)(i), (ii), and (iii). In addition, ASFA requires that a permanency hearing be held within 12 months (although it does not mandate the outcome of that hearing). 42 U.S.C. § 675(C). ASFA also creates a fiscal incentive scheme for states that encourage adoptive placements of children. 42 U.S.C. § 673b.
141. *See In re* Child of T.T.B., 724 N.W.2d 300, 307 (Minn. 2006) (referencing the Adoption and Safe Families Act, court found good cause to deny transfer of jurisdiction of child protection proceeding to tribal court as proceeding was at advanced stage when motions to transfer were filed by parents and tribe since the initial motion was not made until day on which the permanency trial was initially scheduled).
142. 25 C.F.R. § 23.118(c)(3).
143. *See* 25 U.S.C. § 1916(a).
144. 25 U.S.C. § 1911(b).
145. The U.S. Supreme Court in *Holyfield* referred to the transfer of jurisdiction provisions of the ICWA, 25 U.S.C. § 1911(b), as creating "presumptive jurisdiction over nondomiciliaries" in tribal courts. 490 U.S. 30, at 49.
146. *In re* Maricopa Cnty. Juv. Action No. JS-8287, 171 Ariz. 404, 828 P.2d 1245 (Ct. App. 1991), *rev. denied* (1992) (Trial court did not abuse its discretion in denying Pueblo's petition to transfer parental rights termination proceedings to tribal court since Pueblo had been notified of all proceedings concerning child's dependency, but waited for over two years to petition for transfer, during which time child had bonded to her foster-adoptive family and planning

for child's adoption had begun.); *but cf. In re* Adoption of Halloway, 732 P.2d 962 (Utah 1986) (psychological bonding between foster parents and Indian child is not a sufficient reason to ignore the mandates of the ICWA).

147. A good example of why perhaps the bonding argument is an inappropriate consideration in a transfer of jurisdiction issue is the fate of the twins in *Holyfield*. After remand of that case from the Supreme Court, the case was transferred to the Choctaw tribal court, which held a hearing and determined that the twins should remain with the non-Indian family that was attempting to adopt through state court, as that disposition was in the twins' best interests. This tends to demonstrate that those courts that deny transfers to tribal court because such would be contrary to the best interest of the child fail to appreciate that the tribal court will always attempt to act in the best interest of the child. Solangel Maldonado, *Race, Culture, and Adoption: Lessons from Mississippi Band of Choctaw Indians v. Holyfield*, 17(1) COLUM. J. GENDER & L. (2008).

148. The *Holyfield* court held that "[w]hatever feelings we might have as to where the twins should live, however, it is not for us to decide that question. We have been asked to decide the legal question of *who* should make the custody determination concerning these children—not what the outcome of that determination should be. The law places that decision in the hands of the Choctaw tribal court." *Holyfield*, 490 U.S. at 53.

149. *See, e.g.*, Rosalind M. v. State, Dep't of Fam. & Cmty. Servs., 555 P.3d 505 (S. Ct. Alaska 2024) (superior court was prohibited from considering whether transfer could affect child's placement in deciding the issue of whether to transfer the case and thus could not consider foster parents' best interests argument, which was based squarely on assumption that tribe would change child's placement); Interest of Tavian B., 292 Neb. 804, 874 N.W.2d 456 (2016) (rejecting use of best interest test to find good cause not to transfer noting that the BIA guidelines expressly provide that it is inappropriate for state courts to conduct an independent analysis of the best interests of the Indian child in determining placement preferences and that it makes sense to apply the same rule to transfers since it is presumptively in the best interests of the Indian child to transfer the case to the jurisdiction of

the Indian tribe); Interest of T.F., 972 N.W.2d 1 (S. Ct. Iowa 2022) (In the transfer decision, the best interest of the child has no bearing as it changes the issue to the standard by which the decision is itself is being made, rather than what judicial entity should decide custody, and it negates the concept of "presumptively tribal jurisdiction" over Indian children.).

150. Rosalind M. v. State, Dep't of Fam. & Cmty. Servs., 555 P.3d 505 (S. Ct. Alaska 2024) (The *Rosalind* court referenced the BIA guidelines (§ F.5), which note that state courts "cannot know or accurately predict which placement a Tribal court might consider or ultimately order" and that like state courts, "Tribal courts and agencies seek to protect the welfare of the Indian child and would consider whether the current placement best meets that goal." Thus, it found that a state court's prediction that a tribal court might make a placement decision that it would consider to be ill-advised is not good cause to retain jurisdiction.).

151. *See* BIA Guidelines, *supra* note 78, § F.5.

152. *See* Interest of T.F., 972 N.W. 2d 1 (S. Ct. Iowa 2022) (concluded that the juvenile court erred in considering the best interests of the children on the narrow question of transfer to the tribal court); *In re* Guardianship of J.C.D., 686 N.W.2d 647 (S.D. 2004) (court erred in denying transfer of guardianship petition to tribal court based upon best interest analysis); *In re* Interest of Zelena R., 825 N.W.2d 173 (Neb. 2012) (overruling previous precedent and holding a state court is not permitted to consider best interests of an Indian child in deciding whether there is good cause to deny motion to transfer child custody proceeding to tribal court); Yavapai-Apache Tribe v. Mejia, 906 S.W.2d 152, 169–70 (Tex. Ct. App. 1995) (concluding that applying the best interest of the child standard to transfer would defeat the purpose of ICWA); *In re* Armell, 550 N.E.2d 1060 (Ill. App. Ct. 1990) (Illinois' best interest of the child considerations are inapplicable in determining whether "good cause" exists not to transfer jurisdiction over neglect and dependency proceeding to tribal court).

153. Indian Child Welfare Act Proceedings, 81 Fed. Reg. 38827 (June 14, 2016) citing *In re* Interest of Zelena R., 825 N.W.2d 173 (Neb. 2012) (overruling previous precedent and holding a state court is not permitted to consider

best interests of an Indian child in deciding whether there is good cause to deny motion to transfer child custody proceeding to tribal court); and *In re* A.B., 663 N.W.2d 625, 634 (N.D. 2003) (The best interest of the child is not a consideration for the threshold determination of whether there is good cause not to transfer jurisdiction in termination of parental rights cases to a tribal court.).

154. 25 C.F.R. § 23.118(c)(4).
155. *See* 25 U.S.C. § 1901(5).
156. 25 U.S.C. § 1911(b); 25 C.F.R. § 23.117.
157. 25 C.F.R. § 23.118(c)(5).
158. *See* Frank Pommersheim, *The Reservation as Place: A South Dakota Essay*, 34 S.D. L. REV. 246 (1989).
159. 25 U.S.C. § 1903(12).
160. *Id.* Even a tribal governing body, frequently called a tribal council, could have the authority to exercise jurisdiction over child custody proceedings. This is quite common in states such as Alaska, where formal tribal courts may not exist.
161. *Id.*
162. *See id.* § 1911(b).
163. BIA GUIDELINES, *supra* note 78, § F.4.
164. *In re* Children of Shirley T., 199 A.3d 221 (S. Ct. Me. 2019) (Trial court had "good cause" not to transfer a child protection matter to tribal court in another state where all knowledgeable witnesses and relevant evidence needed to adjudicate the case were in the state of Maine and the tribal court was located approximately 2,000 miles away.); *In re* Navajo Nation, 587 S.W.3d 883 (Ct. App. Tex. 2019) (denying transfer because the evidence necessary to decide the case could not be adequately presented in the tribal court without undue hardship to the parties and the witnesses); *but see* Thompson v. Fairfax Cnty., 747 S.E.2d 838 (Ct. App. Va. 2013) (Transfer of termination of parental rights proceeding involving Indian child to tribal court in North Dakota pursuant to the ICWA would not have caused undue hardship to the parties even though the majority of the witnesses were located in Virginia, where modern technology, audio visual communication, and hearings by telephone allowed the tribal court to hear

evidence without undue hardship.) and *In re* Armell, 550 N.E.2d 1060 (Ill. App. Ct. 1990) (Doctrine of forum non conveniens did not preclude transfer of neglect and dependency proceeding for Indian child, who was temporarily residing in California, to Kansas tribal court as social worker stated by affidavit that it would be no hardship for them to testify before tribal court and copies of all Division of Child Protective Services reports had already been transmitted to tribal court.).

165. H.R. Rep. No. 95-1386, at 21 (1978), *reprinted in* 1978 U.S.C.C.A.N. 7530.

166. *See In re* Armell, 550 N.E.2d 1060 (Ill. App. Ct. 1990) (Doctrine of forum non conveniens did not preclude transfer of neglect and dependency proceeding for Indian child, who was temporarily residing in California, to Kansas tribal court as social worker stated by affidavit that it would be no hardship for them to testify before tribal court and copies of all Division of Child Protective Services reports had already been transmitted to tribal court.).

167. *See In re* Brittany C., 693 N.W.2d 592 (Neb. Ct. App. 2005) (permitting appeal from order denying transfer of jurisdiction but affirming the denial of transfer on forum non conveniens grounds, based upon the fact that the tribal court was "two hours away").

168. 25 C.F.R. § 23.133; *see also In re* Jack C., III, 122 Cal. Rptr. 3d 6 (Cal. App. 2011) (not good cause to deny transfer because tribal court can mitigate the hardship); *In re* A.B., 663 N.W.2d 625 (N.D. 2003) (affirmed lower court rejection of forum non conveniens because tribal court agreed to hold court in an off-reservation city near the litigants).

169. 25 C.F.R. § 23.133.

170. *See* People in Interest of A.O., 896 N.W.2d 652 (S.D. 2017) (Denial of a motion to transfer jurisdiction under the ICWA is reviewed under the abuse of discretion standard.); Thompson v. Fairfax County, 747 S.E.2d 838 (Ct. App. Va. 2013) (The appropriate standard of review for reviewing a decision of whether good cause had been established so as to warrant denial of transfer to tribal court of a termination of parental rights case involving an Indian child is an abuse of discretion.); *but see In re* A.P., 961 P.2d 706 (Kan. App. 1998) (applying a substantial competent evidence test).

Procedural Requirements of the ICWA

4

Once a state court has determined that a proceeding is governed by the Indian Child Welfare Act (ICWA), there are numerous procedural requirements that a court must follow in both voluntary and involuntary proceedings to comport with the ICWA, which is the subject of this chapter. These procedures were enacted to ensure maximum involvement from the Indian child's tribe, as well as to secure the sanctity of the Indian family, by ensuring that the removal of an Indian child from his or her family would be done pursuant to stringent requirements. Some courts have concluded that these procedural requirements are jurisdictional in nature and that failure to adhere to them may invalidate state court proceedings.[1]

The practitioner will note that many of the requirements mandated by the ICWA are similar to procedures states must follow pursuant to Title IV-B and Title IV-E of the Social Security Act.[2] In certain areas, however, the ICWA expands upon the procedural protections afforded parents to require more from a state to remove an Indian child from her or his family, on either a temporary or permanent basis.[3] In a situation where applicable federal or state law provides a higher standard of protection to Indian parents or custodians than the ICWA, that higher standard must be applied.[4] To implement the ICWA, many states have adopted state laws and guidelines that are more stringent than the federal law.[5] In those cases the state law or regulation would apply. Other states, in an apparent response to the ICWA, have amended their dependency and neglect laws to conform to the ICWA, resulting in a higher standard of process and proof required in non-Indian cases as well.[6]

All provisions of Title IV-E of the Social Security Act apply to ICWA cases, even though the ICWA itself does not incorporate these provisions, except where there is a direct conflict between the ICWA and Title IV-E.[7] These include, for example, various criteria related to a periodic review of each foster child's case.[8] The ICWA should be read in pari materia with the provisions of Title IV-E. The procedural protections that are discussed as follows, however, relate specifically to the ICWA. Where appropriate, potential conflicts between and how to synthesize the two laws will be discussed.

Notice Requirements

One of the fundamental underpinnings of the ICWA is the notion that an Indian child's tribe has a distinct interest, separate from a parent's or Indian custodian's, in any proceeding involving the child that must be protected throughout, both because children are the tribe's future and because the tribe has a parens patriae relationship with its children.[9] To protect these interests, the ICWA grants the tribe the right to intervene in the proceedings,[10] as well as the right to request a transfer to tribal court.[11] The exercise of that right is, of course, contingent upon the tribe receiving timely and adequate notice of the proceedings.[12]

Under the ICWA, in any involuntary proceeding where the party initiating the proceeding knows or has reason to know that an Indian child is involved, that party must notify the parent, custodian, and tribe by registered or certified mail, with return receipt requested, of the commencement of the proceedings.[13] Some courts have ruled that the failure to give notice under the act deprives the state court of jurisdiction, although others have developed a practice of remanding the proceedings solely to determine whether notice would result in a finding that the child/children involved are Indian, and disposing of the appeal if that remand does not change the result.[14]

Notice is not specifically required in voluntary proceedings, but the state court must ensure that the party seeking placement has taken all reasonable steps to verify the child's status and this may include contacting the tribe.[15] The commentary to the regulations and the guidelines indicate that states are not precluded from requiring notice in voluntary cases and recommend that tribes receive notice in voluntary cases.[16]

When Notice Is Required

A finding by a state court that a child custody proceeding involves an Indian child is not a prerequisite to the giving of notice to an Indian custodian or tribe under the ICWA.[17] Notice must be given even if doubts remain whether the child is an Indian child.[18] This is so because often only with the input of an Indian tribe will a state court be able to determine whether a child is Indian under the act.[19] Thus, an Indian tribe plays a critical role in the initial determination of the applicability of the ICWA and notice to it is imperative any time the court or any of the parties have reason to know that an Indian child is involved.[20] Some of the factors sufficient to provide an agency or court with reason to know that a child is Indian are set out in the Bureau of Indian Affairs (BIA) regulations. An agency or court has reason to know that a child is an Indian child if any party, agency (or employee thereof), officer of the court or the child provides/has discovered information that the child is Indian or if the domicile or residence of the Indian child is on a reservation or in an Alaska Native village.[21] State courts struggle with the notion that proceedings must halt in order to notify Indian tribes based upon bare assertions of Indian status, however, and some reject the notion that mere self-identification by a parent of a child is sufficient to trigger notice.[22] There is a split on whether "mere suspicion" is enough.[23]

There are a number of different formulations that have been used to describe when notice is required. They range from "virtually any criteria on which tribal membership is based"[24] to "needs only a suggestion of Indian ancestry"[25] to "a low but reasonable probability the child is Indian."[26] Unfortunately, the new regulations have not clarified this issue, as courts have varied in their interpretation of the regulations. Some courts have found that a broad definition of reason to know is required—when a participant indicates that the child has tribal heritage—because this is consistent with tribal sovereignty (the right of tribes to determine membership) and the importance of the early implementation of the ICWA.[27] Other courts focusing on the "reason to know" language (as opposed to "reason to believe") have concluded that "mere assertions" or "suggestions" of ancestry are not enough,[28] even when specific tribes have been identified, although they have recognized that the party who is seeking the out-of-home placement or termination of parental rights has the duty to make adequate inquiries to all applicable tribes about the child's Indian status—which does not require notice but will often involve significant outreach to tribes (see Chapter 2)—and also has the burden of sending the notice once the threshold is met.[29] It is ironic, and most likely unintended, that the new regulations have caused a few courts to raise their threshold for finding that there is reason to know that a child is an Indian child as the Department of Interior specifically "encouraged" state courts and agencies to interpret the reason to know criteria "expansively."[30] Moreover, courts that have adopted a stricter standard have not harmonized that standard with the statutory requirement that agencies notice the Secretary of the Interior[31] (in practice the Bureau of Indian Affairs regional director[32]) when there is reason to know but the tribe cannot be identified—a requirement that presumes you can have reason to know with only a limited amount of information.[33] As one court stated, "the burden . . . of complying with the notice requirement is minimal compared with the potential costs of erroneously failing to send notice. . . ."[34]

In general, the burden of bringing forward sufficient evidence to trigger notice is with the proponent of applying the ICWA.[35] Failure to give notice cannot be justified by a later determination that the child in question is not Indian, as some have attempted to argue.[36] A parent may not waive notice to the tribe,[37] although if a tribe that did not receive legally adequate notice is fully participating in the proceeding this may be viewed as rectifying the deficiency.[38] However, the mere fact that the ICWA was applied does not automatically excuse failure to provide notice to a tribe that may be the Indian child's tribe and the failure of notice may require the case to be remanded for further proceedings.[39]

Many state courts, faced with appellate arguments that improper notice or no notice was provided under the ICWA, have adopted a rule that remand will issue to a trial court to effect proper notice, but if that is done and the lower court determines that the ICWA does not apply, the appellate court will rule on the merits of the underlying appeal without vacating the lower courts' decisions on the merits.[40] These cases are representative of dozens of recent cases where parties have attempted to claim some Indian heritage as a manner of defending against termination proceedings in state courts. A number of courts have allowed appeals to take place on this issue even where the issue was not raised in the lower court.[41] The regulations require that notices and return receipts or proof of service be filed with the court[42] and appellate courts have remanded proceedings to trial courts when there is no evidence in the record that the trial court ever received these documents.[43]

If a child is a member of only one tribe, only that tribe is entitled to notice of the proceedings. However, in many cases the only way to determine where a child is a member is to give notice to every tribe to which the child claims some affiliation.[44] Failure to do so may interfere with the state court's ability to establish where the child is a member or eligible for membership.[45] If tribal affiliation is undetectable, the ICWA permits the state court to notify the U.S. Department of the Interior, which is then charged with helping to identify tribes to contact,[46] but notice to the Department of the Interior is not enough when it is possible to identify a list of tribes with whom the child may be connected.[47] Addresses for the various BIA area offices where notice can be sent are set out in 25 C.F.R. § 23.12. Once a tribe proclaims that a particular child is a member of that tribe, one court has declared, that decision is binding on the state court even if proper and legal notice was not effected upon another tribe claiming an interest.[48] A practitioner should also be aware that certain states have enacted state versions of the ICWA that may trigger notice under state law that must be adhered to prior to the commencement of an action.[49]

The ICWA provision relating to notice unfortunately uses a term that is not defined under the law. The section provides that "in any involuntary proceeding" notice must be provided to the tribe.[50] The regulations address this issue by defining "involuntary" to mean "a child custody proceeding in which the parent does not consent of his or her free will to the foster care, preadoptive, or adoptive placement or termination of parental rights or in which the parent consents to the foster care, preadoptive, or adoptive placement under threat of removal of the child by a state court or agency."[51]

When a proceeding is commenced as a voluntary one, the ICWA does not mandate notice to the tribe in all cases. Most courts that have addressed this issue have held as much.[52] As noted earlier, however, the regulations require that the state court must ensure that the party seeking placement has taken all reasonable steps to verify the child's status, which may include contacting the tribe,[53] and the guidelines indicate that states are not precluded from requiring notice in voluntary proceedings and recommend that tribes receive notice in voluntary proceedings.[54]

The lack of mandatory notice in all voluntary cases highlights the inconsistencies in the statute, particularly the interplay between ICWA notice provisions and the provisions recognizing exclusive tribal jurisdiction over children resident or domiciled on a reservation or the ward of a tribal court, as well as those related to the right of a tribe to intervene in a foster care placement or termination of parental rights proceeding, voluntary or involuntary, discussed later in this chapter. A tribe is entitled to intervene in any foster care placement or termination of parental rights proceeding[55] yet is apparently entitled to mandatory notice only in involuntary proceedings.[56] This, of course, begs the question of how a tribe is to know of a proceeding in which it can intervene if it receives no notice of the proceeding.

This appears to be an instance in which Congress balanced the rights of Indian parents against the interest of the tribe. The failure of a state court to notify a tribe in a voluntary proceeding, however, may lead to more adoptions like the one struck down by the Supreme Court in *Holyfield* where an Indian parent attempted to defeat the tribal court's exclusive jurisdiction by placing the children off the reservation for adoption immediately after birth. If the tribe in *Holyfield* had never found out about the adoption, it appears unlikely that any party would have challenged the state court's jurisdiction there and an illegal adoption would have taken place. Such an adoption, because it is capable of being upset at any time based upon a § 1914 challenge, does not lend stability to the lives of the adopted children and should be avoided. This may be one of the reasons why the Department of the Interior in the guidelines indicated that notice in voluntary proceedings is a recommended practice.[57]

Another anomaly of the statute is that the tribe would also be entitled to request a copy of the record of the placement even if the tribe did not previously receive notice and the parent requested anonymity. This is because the act and implementing regulations require that the state maintain a record of every voluntary or involuntary foster care, preadoptive, and adoptive placement of an Indian child and make that record available within 14 days of a request by the Indian child's tribe.[58]

Type of Notice Required

The ICWA requires service of notice by registered mail or certified mail, return receipt requested, to the parents, Indian custodian, and tribe or, if the tribe cannot be identified, to the Department of the Interior of the appropriate area office of the BIA listed in the regulations.[59] One should also look to state law for proper service of process because many states mandate personal service upon the natural parents when a dependency and neglect action is commenced.[60] A child custody proceeding cannot advance until at least ten days after notice has been effected.[61]

The notice shall include the following:

(1) The name of the child and the child's birthdate and birthplace
(2) The names (including all versions) of parents and other direct lineal ancestors, if known, and their birthdates and birthplaces

(3) The child's tribal affiliation, if known, including each tribe in which the child is a member or may be eligible for membership
(4) A copy of the petition or other document that initiates the action
(5) The name of the petitioner and his or her attorney
(6) A statement informing the parents, Indian custodian, and tribe of their respective rights to intervene at any time
(7) A statement that if the parents or Indian custodian are unable to afford counsel one will be appointed for them
(8) A statement that the parents, Indian custodian, or tribe can have up to 20 additional days to prepare for the proceedings over and above the ten days automatically provided by statute
(9) The location, mailing address, and telephone number of the court and information pertaining to all parties to the proceeding and individuals that have been notified
(10) A statement informing the parents, Indian custodian, or tribe of the right to request a transfer to tribal court
(11) The potential legal consequences on the rights of the parties if the child is adjudicated dependent[62]

A typical notice is included in Appendix F. Failure to follow this format for notice may not invalidate the proceeding, but courts have found the absence of notice[63] or inadequate notices that lacked certain relevant information to be grounds to invalidate lower court orders and to remand cases for further proceedings. Some examples include a notice that (1) had only the names of the children and parents when more information was available,[64] (2) did not show that mother claimed to be an enrolled member living on the reservation receiving tribal services,[65] (3) did not provide information about a grandmother or extended family involved with the agency or in the proceeding,[66] (4) did not provide places of birth for mother and children,[67] (5) did not provide information about key ancestors,[68] and (6) did not indicate that the tribe had the right to intervene.[69] A de minimis error, however, is generally not grounds to overturn a lower court decision.[70] A number of courts have required that notices be filed with the court so that the court is able to review the sufficiency of the notice.[71] That requirement is now included in the regulations,[72] and courts have used the lack of documentation to hold that notice was not provided to the tribe.[73]

If the state court discovers during the pendency of an action that an Indian child is involved, notice shall be required, but the proceedings up to that point will not be rendered null and void.[74] At least one court has held, however, that if a new child is born to the parents during the pendency of a child custody proceeding, that child can be added to the proceeding without the necessity of serving a new and discrete notice, but this has not been uniformly accepted and is probably inconsistent with the new regulations.[75] It is also important to note that both the ICWA and the regulations require that notice be sent when the nature of the proceeding changes (e.g., moves from a foster care placement proceeding to a termination of parental rights proceeding), even if the tribe has failed to intervene in the proceedings up to that point.[76]

Right to Intervene

The ICWA grants to the parents, Indian custodian, and tribe the unqualified right to intervene at any stage of a foster care placement or termination of parental rights proceeding, even when the case is on appeal.[77] The right to intervene is not limited to involuntary cases, but applies to all foster care placement and termination of parental rights proceedings.[78] As with the right to request a transfer of jurisdiction, the language of the section of the statute addressing intervention does not include preadoptive and adoptive placements even though the tribe may have important information regarding the availability of appropriate relative or Indian adoptive homes. Some courts, however, have ruled that the right of an Indian custodian, tribe, or even family member to intervene[79] may derive from the general principles regarding rights of intervention and not necessarily from the ICWA itself.[80] That type of intervention seems to be permissive in nature, whereas the ICWA clearly grants to certain parties the right to mandatory intervention. Intervention in preadoptive and adoptive placement proceedings would therefore likely be governed by the permissive intervention rules of the particular state court. Intervention by a foster or prospective adoptive family alleging that it meets the placement preference criteria is also governed by the permissive intervention rules and is not necessarily granted as a matter of right.[81]

Many states have enacted procedural rules, as a response to the Adoption and Safe Families Act (ASFA), that require notification to foster care providers in child custody proceedings and gives those foster care providers the right to be heard in review hearings and other dispositional hearings.[82] This should not be confused with the right of intervention, however, which renders the person a party to the case. The right to notice would also presumably apply to cases involving Indian children.[83]

Only the Indian child's tribe is entitled to intervene as a matter of right.[84] Several courts, however, have permitted more than one tribe to participate in ICWA proceedings.[85] Other states have resisted efforts by tribes where children are not members or eligible for membership to participate in permanency hearings.[86]

There is no timeliness requirement for intervention in a proceeding.[87] Also, there is no requirement that the intervention be sought by a licensed attorney representing the tribe.[88] Many tribes do not have the resources to hire private counsel in every state in which an ICWA case may arise. As a result, many times they send social services representatives or even tribal judges to advocate the tribe's interests.[89] Recognizing this, some courts have held and the BIA guidelines encourage state courts to permit tribal representatives to appear before the court regardless of whether they are attorneys or, if they are attorneys, regardless of whether they are admitted in the state where the proceeding is taking place.[90] The request to intervene may also be rudimentary, and because of the absolute nature of that right under ICWA, even oral requests should be routinely granted. Regardless, the tribe is entitled to participate as a full party, as opposed to having a limited right to intervention,[91] or a mere right to testify.[92]

Once a tribe intervenes, it becomes a party to the case and is entitled to receive service of all motions and pleadings from that point forward.[93] It is also entitled, along with the parents or Indian custodian, to examine all relevant documents filed with the court on which a decision in the case may be based.[94] A decision permitting an Indian tribe to intervene in a case governed by the ICWA is not generally considered a final order subject to immediate appeal, although a denial of a motion to intervene would be appealable.[95]

Right to Counsel

The ICWA mandates that the state court appoint counsel for an indigent parent or Indian custodian in a "removal, placement, or termination proceeding."[96] If there is no state law mandating appointment of counsel, the state court can apply to the Department of the Interior for reimbursement of court-appointed lawyer's fees in an ICWA case.[97] The ICWA also allows a state court to appoint a lawyer for the Indian child but does not make that appointment mandatory.[98]

The right to counsel attaches in both proceedings initiated by the state and those initiated by private parties, such as in stepparent adoption proceedings and intrafamily disputes.[99] The right to counsel also seems to extend to preadoptive and adoptive placement proceedings and not simply to foster care placement and termination proceedings.[100] The right to counsel attaches at all stages of the child custody proceeding and discharge of an attorney for part of a proceeding can be grounds for reversal.[101]

As a result of *Santosky v. Kramer*,[102] many states already provide for the appointment of counsel in foster care and termination proceedings, but few mandate the appointment of counsel in purely private disputes, such as adoption proceedings where the state is not involved or in a guardianship matter where a private individual is seeking guardianship over an Indian child.[103] The ICWA guarantees counsel in those types of proceedings, although it is unclear whether parents and custodians are being adequately apprised of that right. It is equally unclear how many states have attempted to seek reimbursement from the Department of the Interior for fees paid to court-appointed lawyers in ICWA cases.[104] At least one state court has ruled that the ICWA requires a local government to pay for private counsel, even where that government does not generally provide counsel for indigent parents.[105]

The procedure for a state court to follow in obtaining reimbursement from the Department of the Interior for court-appointed lawyers' fees in ICWA cases is set out in 25 C.F.R. § 23.13, and § 23.11 lists the addresses of the BIA area offices to which the requests can be sent.[106] It should be noted that one of the criteria for denying reimbursement is that no money is available for payment of the expenses.[107] The Department of the Interior's solicitor's office has opined that even if no funding for state court lawyer reimbursement exists at the area office level, the monies should be paid out of a reserve account held at the national level.[108]

The appointment of counsel for the Indian child is purely discretionary with the state court judge,[109] although state law may mandate the appointment of counsel.[110] The BIA reimbursement regulations seem to imply that a state may apply to the BIA for reimbursement of lawyers' fees paid to a guardian ad litem, provided that state law does not mandate an appointment. This appears to be somewhat inconsistent with the use of discretionary, rather than precatory, language in the ICWA section discussing the appointment of counsel.[111]

Of note, a recent decision from the Kansas Court of Appeals confirms that inadequate representation by counsel may be grounds to overturn a termination of parental rights.[112] This is indicative of the importance of the right to counsel as part of the ICWA's panoply of rights.

Standards of Proof

A party attempting to effect a foster care placement of an Indian child or a termination of the parental rights or the custodial rights of an Indian custodian, be it a state social services entity or a private party, must satisfy the standards of proof established by the ICWA—specifically a showing, including testimony by qualified expert witnesses, that continued custody of the child by the parent or Indian custodian is likely to result in serious emotional or physical damage to the child—by clear and convincing evidence in the case of a foster care placement, beyond a reasonable doubt in the case of termination of parental rights (TPR).[113] These standards of proof are unique to child custody proceedings involving Indian children, although in some instances they share similarities to the requirements set out in Title IV-E of the Social Security Act.[114] Once again, the petitioner should remember that the requirements in the ICWA are not exclusive of requirements set out by state or federal law and applicable to child custody proceedings but instead are inclusive of those other requirements unless they are inconsistent with the ICWA.[115]

Emergency Placements

A child may be removed from the custody of a parent or Indian custodian only to prevent imminent physical harm or damage to the child.[116] This provision applies to any emergency removal of an Indian child by a state authority, official, or agency, regardless of the child's residence or domicile,[117] including ex parte requests to remove a child from a parent.[118] The removal or placement must be terminated when it is no longer necessary to prevent imminent physical damage or harm to the child.[119] If the state agency believes that continuing supervision or removal of the child is necessary once the immediate emergency has ended, it has the right to file a petition in regard to the child (assuming the child is not subject to the exclusive jurisdiction of the tribe) that would be subject to the legal requirements described in the foster care placement section that follows.[120]

The regulations emphasize that the state court has the obligation to promptly hold a hearing on the removal and has a continuing obligation to determine whether the potential damage or harm is still present.[121] The regulations specify a number of elements that should be included in a petition for an emergency court order, including what steps have been taken to notice the tribe.[122] Emergency proceedings should normally not continue for more than 30 days.[123]

In general, there is no requirement that a qualified expert witness (QEW) testify or that a finding of active efforts be made at a hearing on an emergency placement,[124] although one court has ruled that an active efforts finding is required under a state ICWA law.[125] Formal notice to the tribe prior to an emergency proceeding is also not required, although it is considered to be a recommended practice to take all practical steps to contact the tribe, and the regulations require agencies to include in its petition for a court order authorizing an emergency removal the steps taken to provide notice to the parents, Indian custodian, and the Indian child's tribe about the emergency proceeding.[126]

Foster Care Placements

A party seeking to accomplish a foster care placement of an Indian child must establish (1) that active efforts have been made to provide remedial and rehabilitative services designed to prevent the breakup of the Indian family, which have been unsuccessful;[127] and (2) by clear and convincing evidence, supported by the testimony of qualified expert witnesses, that the continued custody of the child by the parent or Indian custodian is likely to result in serious emotional or physical damage to the child.[128]

Indian custodians are treated the same as parents in involuntary child custody proceedings under the ICWA, with the exception that they lack the right to veto a transfer of jurisdiction to tribal court.[129] Therefore, if a person is determined to be an Indian custodian, a proceeding that involves the involuntary removal of the Indian child from the Indian custodian requires the same proof as the removal of the child from a natural parent, except when the removal is for the purpose of returning the child to a natural parent.[130] This is proof again of Congress's cognizance of the important role extended family members play in the rearing of Indian children.

Active Efforts: Remedial Services and Rehabilitative Programs

There is nothing unique about requiring a state foster care placement agency to provide services to families whose children have been removed because of neglect or abuse in the home.[131] Title IV-E of the Social Security Act requires reasonable efforts to reunite a family by the provision of services to the family. The ICWA, however, requires that "active" services be provided "before" the removal of the Indian child in an attempt to avoid the necessity of removal.[132] The legislative history of the ICWA evinces a clear congressional bent for energetic efforts to be made by state agencies in Indian communities for the development of culturally relevant programs designed to address the problems that lead to the removal of Indian children.[133] Some examples included home counseling, homemaker care, residential treatment facilities, and day care.[134] Of course, there is a universal need for these types of services, not only in Indian communities but in all communities. Congress mandated a showing that such services were offered to an Indian family before a foster care placement, as opposed to a showing that such services were offered as part of a case service plan entered into by the parent after placement.[135] These services should commence promptly after a family is referred to an agency,[136] and it has been held that active efforts must be provided in a case where a child has been placed in his own home as part of a juvenile court case.[137] In the case of an emergency removal, however, most courts have held that the state would not need to demonstrate compliance with § 1912(d) before removal of the Indian child, only as part of the foster care and termination proceedings,[138] although one court has ruled that an active efforts finding is required under a state ICWA law.[139] The courts have also held that § 1912(d) does not apply in voluntary foster care placement or termination proceedings,[140] although there may be an exception to this rule if the agency should have known that the voluntary placement would turn into an involuntary placement unless active efforts were provided during the voluntary placement.[141]

25 U.S.C. § 1912(d) does not explicitly provide for a standard of proof, as do subsections (e) and (f), which has led to a split of authority in terms of the standard to apply. Some have ruled that the same standard applicable to the particular proceeding, that is, clear and convincing evidence for foster care placements and beyond a reasonable doubt for TPR proceedings, applies to the showing that subsection (d) has been satisfied.[142] The BIA guidelines indicate that

the Department of Interior views these cases favorably.[143] Other courts have ruled that a lesser standard of the proof applies; in the context of a TPR proceeding, this has generally been a clear and convincing evidence standard.[144] In general, there must be a finding that not only have active efforts been provided but also that they have been unsuccessful.[145] The regulations require that active efforts be documented on the record[146] and courts have not been hesitant to remand cases to the trial court when there has been inadequate documentation.[147] At least one court has held that a trial court must make an active efforts finding at every hearing if the child is in an out-of-home placement.[148] Failure to meet active efforts has also been raised on appeal, even when not raised before the trial court.[149]

The BIA regulations provide significant detail in terms of the types of remedial and rehabilitative services a state should attempt to provide to avoid the need for the breakup of an Indian family. The following are examples of the services needed to meet the active efforts requirement:

(1) Conducting a comprehensive assessment of the circumstances of the Indian child's family, with a focus on safe reunification as the most desirable goal
(2) Identifying appropriate services and helping the parents to overcome barriers, including actively assisting the parents in obtaining such services[150]
(3) Identifying, notifying, and inviting representatives of the Indian child's tribe to participate in providing support and services to the Indian child's family and in family team meetings, permanency planning, and resolution of placement issues
(4) Conducting or causing to be conducted a diligent search for the Indian child's extended family members, and contacting and consulting with extended family members to provide family structure and support for the Indian child and the Indian child's parents

(5) Offering and employing all available and culturally appropriate family preservation strategies and facilitating the use of remedial and rehabilitative services provided by the child's tribe
(6) Taking steps necessary to keep siblings together whenever possible
(7) Supporting regular visits and trial home visits of the Indian child in the most natural setting possible as well as trial home visits of the Indian child during any period of removal, consistent with the need to ensure the safety, health, and welfare of the child
(8) Identifying community resources, including housing, financial, transportation, mental health, substance abuse, and peer support services and actively assisting the Indian child's parents or, when appropriate, the child's family in utilizing and accessing those resources
(9) Monitoring progress and participation in services
(10) Considering alternative ways of addressing the needs of the Indian child's parents and, where appropriate, the family, if services do not exist or if existing services are not available
(11) Providing post-reunification services and monitoring[151]

The regulations stress that active efforts should be conducted in partnership with the resources of the extended family and tribe.[152] Of course, if the custody proceeding arises in a venue distant from where such resources can be tapped, access to these resources may be challenging, although since the Covid-19 pandemic there are more resources available remotely. In addition, in many cities, urban Indian cultural centers exist that may have the human resources available to assist and advise state social services agencies in the implementation of the ICWA.

A few issues have arisen in this area that may be relevant in an ICWA case. The first issue is whether active efforts is more than the reasonable efforts required by Title IV-E. Although the regulations do not explicitly address this issue, they emphasize that active efforts must be "affirmative, active and timely" and list a number of examples that arguably go beyond the reasonable efforts requirement.[153] To the extent that case law has defined the reasonable efforts requirement in a more passive manner, this would be a clear distinction between the two standards. Most of the case law has agreed with the conclusion that active efforts requires more than reasonable efforts.[154] Cases have described the active efforts requirement in various ways. For example, courts have said that active efforts requires "timely affirmative steps";[155] a vigorous and concerted level of casework;[156] active, not passive efforts;[157] mandates the social worker to "take the client through the plan rather than requiring that the plan be performed on its own";[158] and creates a "heightened responsibility."[159] The regulations also emphasize that "active efforts should be provided in a manner consistent with the prevailing social and cultural conditions and way of life of the Indian child's tribe" to the maximum extent possible,[160] and courts have noted that the ICWA, as embodied in the active efforts requirement, emphasizes familial and tribal connections, not permanency per se.[161] The guidelines add that they should be provided at the earliest point possible.[162]

The second issue is whether the aggravated circumstance exception to the provision of reasonable efforts, enacted as part of the ASFA,[163] also applies to active efforts. The aggravated circumstance exception provides that reasonable efforts do not need to be provided when a parent has abandoned, tortured, or chronically or sexually abused the child; if the parent has been previously convicted of certain crimes, including murder, voluntary manslaughter of another child, or felony assault on a child; or has had rights terminated to a sibling of the child.[164] It should be noted that some states and the District of Columbia merely adopted the federal mandatory aggravated circumstances when they passed ASFA enabling legislation, whereas a majority of states adopted a variety of other optional aggravated circumstances that permit state court judges to relieve state child welfare agencies of the obligation to provide reasonable efforts.[165]

Most cases have held that the exceptions to reunification efforts in the ASFA do not apply to ICWA proceedings. These cases have found that the ASFA does not supersede ICWA requirements.[166] These conclusions would seem to be supported by standard principles of statutory construction.[167]

Nonetheless, although the specific exceptions to the reasonable efforts requirement have not been applied to the active efforts requirement, there are circumstances where courts have found that the active efforts requirement has been met even where services actually provided have been limited. Specifically, courts have held that the active efforts requirement is satisfied if the parent–child relationship is "beyond repair";[168] efforts to provide services would be "futile"[169] (although at least one court has rejected application of the "futility doctrine" in ICWA cases);[170] the parent is not amenable to services,[171] although in that situation it is relevant how the agency responded to the parent's failure to cooperate;[172] or the parent will not be able to care for the child in the foreseeable future.[173] However, incarceration of a parent does not eliminate the requirement that active efforts be provided to that parent,[174] although the nature of the efforts required may be different.[175] In addition, while emphasizing that the ICWA statute does not contain any exceptions to the active efforts requirement, the commentary to the regulations suggests that the ASFA factors may be considered as part of determining whether the active efforts requirement has been met in a given case.[176]

The final issue involves the meaning of the U.S. Supreme Court decision in *Adoptive Couple v. Baby Girl*.[177] In the context of a contested private adoption, the Court in *Baby Girl* held that § 1912(d) of the ICWA does not apply when an Indian parent "abandons" a child prior to birth and the parent has never had prior physical or legal custody.[178] Stated differently, the Court found that the breakup of an Indian family only referred to the "discontinuance of a relationship," and when a father "abandons" a child and has had no legal or physical custody, there is no relationship to discontinue.[179] The Court found that the focus of § 1912(d) is on the "removal" of Indian children from their families and does not include "transfer of the child to an Indian parent."[180]

Based upon this interpretation, the Court found that § 1912(d) did not apply to the circumstances in that case.[181] The Court suggested that applying the active efforts requirement in private adoptions, such as the one in the *Baby Girl* case, would "place vulnerable Indian children at a unique disadvantage in finding a permanent and loving home" because of the obligation that it would place upon prospective adoptive parents.[182] In reaching this holding, the Court clearly characterized the actions of the father in that case as "abandonment" of the child, although the court never defined the term.[183] As the dissent pointed out, the term "abandonment" is a term of art in child and family law and one that varies greatly from state to state.[184]

Much of the Court's analysis of § 1912(d) was based on the specific facts of this case, in particular the voluntary adoption context from which it arose.[185] In fact, the Court stated "[s]ection 1912(d) is a sensible requirement when applied to state social workers who might otherwise be too quick to remove Indian children from their Indian families."[186] This statement may indicate that the Court's interpretation in this case should not be applied in traditional involuntary state child welfare proceedings. Of note, one of the five justices in the 5–4 majority (Justice Breyer) wrote a concurrence where he emphasized the narrowness of the court's holding, opining that "we should decide here no more than is necessary."[187]

Although the regulations do not explicitly address the opinion, their approach seems consistent with a narrow reading of this case.[188]

Nonetheless, a few courts, particularly in Montana, have applied this decision outside the context of a contested voluntary adoption and did not apply the active efforts requirement in guardianship and involuntary termination cases to fathers who had never had custody and had not been involved with their children for extended periods of time, although other courts have disagreed.[189] Thus, although it appears to be raised infrequently, this may be an ongoing issue in future cases and fathers of Indian children who want to protect their rights under the ICWA should remain actively engaged throughout pregnancy and after the birth of their child. Furthermore, they should seek to formally establish legal or physical custody before or immediately after the birth of a child by utilizing any legal mechanisms that are available or required. Of note, the regulations define custody as "physical or legal custody under any applicable tribal law or tribal custom or state law."[190] Thus, tribes may be able to address the potential ramifications of this decision at least partially through amendments to tribal codes that address the rights of unwed fathers of tribal children.

It should be noted that courts have applied the active efforts requirement to Indian custodians even where previous active efforts were provided to a parent,[191] extensions of the agency's legal custody where physical custody remains with the parents,[192] and § 1916(a) proceedings,[193] although it has also been held not to apply to a hearing on a petition to change a foster care placement to a guardianship where an active efforts showing was made at the time of the permanency hearing when the court approved guardianship as the permanency plan.[194] Active efforts must be provided to both parents, and courts have declined to terminate a parent's rights when active efforts were not provided to that parent, even though they were provided for the other parent.[195]

In cases where an agency is not involved, active efforts by the party seeking placement are still required.[196] Examples of cases where active efforts have been required include stepparent adoptions,[197] a private termination proceeding,[198] and efforts by relatives to obtain custody of the child.[199] Active efforts in a non-agency case might consist of "informal private initiatives aimed at promoting contact by a parent with the child and encouraging that parent to embrace his or her responsibility to support and supervise the child."[200]

Thus, those involved in ICWA cases, attorneys, and others should be prepared to demonstrate active efforts to provide remedial and rehabilitative services to an Indian family, even if in similar circumstances no showing of reasonable efforts under the ASFA would be required, though there may potentially be arguments made in a very limited number of cases that active efforts need not be provided.

Qualified Expert Testimony

Before a court can order the foster care placement of an Indian child, the court must be persuaded by clear and convincing evidence that continued custody by the parent or Indian custodian will result in serious emotional or physical damage to the child, and that finding must be supported by the testimony of "qualified expert witnesses" (QEWs).[201] QEW testimony is also required prior to the termination of parental rights.[202] Although this term is not defined in the statute, the legislative history proclaims that the term is designed to require more from a witness than the "normal social worker qualifications."[203] The regulations specifically preclude the social worker regularly assigned to the child from serving as the QEW.[204]

The purpose of the qualified expert testimony requirement is "to provide the Court with knowledge of the social and cultural aspects of Indian life to diminish the risk of any cultural bias."[205] It is also intended "to prevent courts from basing their decision solely upon the testimony of social workers who possessed neither specialized professional education nor the familiarity with Native culture necessary to distinguish between cultural variations in child-rearing practices and actual abuse and neglect."[206]

The BIA regulations further flesh out the Department of the Interior's understanding of the qualifications of an expert witness for ICWA cases. A QEW must be qualified to testify regarding whether the child's continued custody by parent or Indian custodian is likely to result in serious emotional or physical damage to the child and should be qualified to testify as to the prevailing social and cultural standards of the Indian child's tribe.[207] Thus, there are essentially two key questions to answer in regard to whether a person can serve as a Qualified Expert Witness:

(1) Is the individual qualified to testify regarding the statutory standard?
(2) Does the individual have the required cultural knowledge or, if not, it is appropriate given the facts of the case to invoke the narrow exception to the general rule requiring knowledge of the cultural and social standards of the Indian child's tribe?

In regard to the first question, most courts that have addressed the requirement of qualified expert testimony have concluded that social workers with some experience working with Indian children qualify as experts under the ICWA, notwithstanding their lack of formal training or education in the field.[208] In addition, many courts (often citing the last category of QEW listed in the definition in the 1979 BIA guidelines, now superseded) have ruled that persons with specialized knowledge over and above that of a normal social worker qualify as a QEW.[209] In practice, the requirement of qualified expert testimony has expanded the potential pool of witnesses in ICWA cases to include those Indian persons who otherwise would not qualify as experts under state law,[210] and it has been generally understood that "there is no specific educational or career requirement to be a qualified expert witness."[211] Among those that have served as QEWs "include tribal elders, college professors, tribal appointed individuals, teachers, tribal professionals, certain child protective services workers, tribal council members, retired human services workers, traditional healers, healthcare professionals, tribal chiefs, and members of tribal organizations.[212] Indeed, the regulations specifically encourage the court or any party to request assistance of the Indian child's tribe,[213] a potential source for many of the different types of QEWs just described.

Nonetheless, since the adoption of the 2016 regulations, at least some courts have scrutinized more closely whether a witness is qualified to testify about the statutory standard and declined to recognize certain individuals as being capable of testifying in regard to the standard who might have been found to be qualified prior to the 2016 regulations,[214] and it may be important to lay a careful foundation for a QEW's ability to testify to the standard if the QEW's qualifications are likely to be challenged. At least one court has addressed this issue by allowing for the aggregation of the testimony of multiple QEWs, one that testified based upon subject matter expertise and another that testified about relevant social and cultural standards.[215]

A literal reading of the ICWA would permit only those QEWs who testify in favor of a foster care placement or termination of parental rights to introduce testimony at trial. Many Indian parents and tribes, however, have used the broad definition of qualified expert testimony to offer evidence to counter a contention that an Indian child should be removed from his or her home.[216] In those cases it appears that the state court is not entitled to give greater weight to a witness merely because of academic achievement, but must give equal or more weight to lay witnesses with a particularized knowledge of Indian customs and traditions.[217]

As noted, in terms of the second question, the new regulations indicate that QEWs "should" have knowledge of the prevailing social and cultural standards of the Indian child's tribe, further explaining in the guidelines that while this should normally be the case there may be limited circumstances where the knowledge is "plainly irrelevant" to the proceeding—for example, if the issue at hand is sexual abuse.[218] Some states have enacted laws that require a showing of expertise in Indian child-rearing practices before a person is qualified as an expert witness, which the commentary recognizes as a legitimate exercise of state power.[219] A few courts have imposed a similar requirement, with one court noting that "[s]pecific behavior patterns will often need to be placed in the context of the total culture to determine whether they are likely to cause emotional harm."[220] The 2016 guidelines also state that knowledge of closely related tribes may be sufficient in some circumstances, presumably implying that knowledge of a totally different tribal culture would not meet the standard.[221]

The failure to offer QEW testimony is grounds for reversing a dispositional order by a state court[222] and it has been held that failure to call a QEW in an ICWA proceeding cannot be classified as harmless error.[223] Testimony must be provided in terms of both parents if TPR is being sought for both parents.[224] Similarly, where the QEW does not offer testimony regarding the statutory standard, this can also be the basis for the reversal of a termination order.[225] In this regard, some courts have required that the QEW be specifically asked whether there is the likelihood of emotional and physical damage to the child if the parent were to have custody, which seems to be the approach of the regulations as well, although not all courts have agreed that specific questions related to the standard of proof must be met, provided the QEW testimony supports the court's conclusion.[226] In addition, where a QEW does not have cultural expertise and it is relevant to the case before the court, this is yet another circumstance where it is appropriate for the court to find that the standard for termination of parental rights has not been met.[227]

Most courts have held that the testimony by the QEW must support the decision to place a child in foster care or to terminate parental rights, although they have not required that the QEW's testimony be the sole basis for that court's conclusion.[228] In that regard, courts have held that the QEW must address future harm, not just past harm.[229]

Some courts have been critical of the use of experts who only conduct a paper review of the record of the child custody proceedings and are not actively involved in working with the family involved, and the guidelines agree with this perspective, but others have accepted such testimony as valid.[230] Where challenged, testimony from the QEW by affidavit alone, as opposed to in-person testimony, has also been found not to meet the statutory standard.[231] A few courts have held that the failure of a parent to object at trial to the state's failure to call qualified expert witnesses bars appeal of that issue.[232] However, other courts have found that 25 U.S.C. § 1914 allows these issues to be raised on appeal even where they were not raised in the lower court.[233]

In some cases, QEW testimony based upon an understanding of the social and cultural values of the Indian child's tribe may be relevant to other issues such as whether active efforts have been met, which is one of the criteria that must be satisfied before a non-emergency removal of a child or a termination of parental rights.[234]

Thus, in considering the nature of QEW testimony that is required, it is important for a practitioner to review the new regulations, any applicable state law, and the case law and statutes in the state where the child custody proceeding is taking place, particularly to the extent it addresses issues not explicitly addressed by the regulations.

Serious Emotional or Physical Damage

To accomplish a foster care placement of an Indian child, the petitioning party must demonstrate by clear and convincing evidence that the continued custody by the parent or Indian custodian would likely result in serious emotional or physical damage to the child.[235] In many states this standard is a modification of the state standards for the removal of children, some of which focus on the best interest of the child and the abilities of the parents to conform their behavior to what is expected of an adequate parent.[236] The focus in ICWA cases, on the other hand, is on whether the actions of the parents or Indian custodian have or will likely result in serious emotional or physical harm to the child.

The legislative history makes it pervasively clear that Congress attributed many unwarranted removals to cultural ignorance on the part of the courts and social workers making the decisions. In many cases children were removed because the family did not conform to the decision-maker's stereotype of what a proper family should be.[237]

If the state criteria for removal includes additional, more onerous standards on the petitioning party than proving serious emotional or physical damage to the child, the ICWA demands that the higher standard be the basis for a foster care placement.[238] However, if the state standard requires less than such proof, the ICWA precludes its use under *Holyfield* because of the Supreme Court's admonition there against the use of state standards that conflict with the policy behind the enactment of the ICWA.[239] Some states have applied a preponderance of the evidence standard for the state-required elements of proof required for a finding that a child is subject to the court's child welfare jurisdiction, while using the clear and convincing evidence required by the ICWA to determine if the child should be removed from the home.[240] It has also been held that a finding that removal is necessary under the ICWA standards must be based upon evidence presented to the court, and not unsworn statements made at review hearings.[241] The evidence must also show a causal connection between conditions in the home and serious physical or emotional harm to the child in order for an out of home placement to occur or parental rights to be terminated.[242]

Practitioners should examine their state laws defining abused or neglected children with an eye toward determining whether the state criteria for defining an abused or neglected child would satisfy the ICWA standard. For example, most states define an abused or neglected child as one who has been abandoned by his or her parent.[243] This is one of the criteria that was perhaps cited most often by non-Indian social workers in support of the removal of Indian children who had been placed with extended family members, such as grandparents, to be raised.[244] Clearly, the mere fact that a parent has placed a child with another person, be it a relative or not, and the other person has the primary responsibility to raise that child does not satisfy the ICWA criteria for a foster care placement. Otherwise, the ICWA's granting of a protected status to the Indian custodian would be rendered superfluous.

Other states require foster care placement when a child has been sexually abused in the home of the parent or other relative.[245] Proof of sexual abuse would almost certainly satisfy the ICWA criteria, although QEW testimony would still be required.

It is in areas where non-Indian social workers and judges tend to be culturally naive that state courts should tread carefully. These areas include the exercise of parental responsibilities by individuals other than the parents even where the parent is still a custodial parent.[246] A judge or social worker, unsophisticated in the traditions and cultures of Indian people, may conclude that the abdication of certain supervisory functions by a parent means that the child is being subjected to the threat of physical or emotional harm. The requirement of qualified expert testimony in those types of cases becomes a sine qua non if a judge wishes to comply with the ICWA.[247]

It is currently unsettled whether the ICWA standard for a foster care placement applies in those cases where the parent has not had custody of the child. There are a number of cases that have held that it does apply.[248] Many ICWA cases have arisen in situations where children have been removed from non-Indian mothers of children whose fathers are Indian but have had little or no contact with the children.[249]

In *Adoptive Couple v. Baby Girl*,[250] however, the U.S. Supreme Court ruled that the standard for proving termination of parental rights did not apply in a voluntary adoption to a nonconsenting father who never had prior legal or physical custody based upon language in that section (§ 1912(f)) that references "continued custody of the child by the parent." This has led at least one court to rule based upon *Baby Girl* that § 1912(e), which governs foster care placements, should be interpreted in the same way because the language in the two sections is similar.[251] In so doing, it did not consider the admonition in Justice Breyer's concurrence (Justice Breyer was the fifth vote in a 5–4 decision) that the Court had decided no more than was necessary to decide the case before it,[252] nor the Court's focus on the specific facts of the case that involved a voluntary adoption, which could suggest that the Court's holding should not be expanded beyond the context of a TPR that is taking place in a voluntary adoption case.[253]

Finally, it is important to observe that any parent, Indian or non-Indian, of an Indian child can claim the protections of the ICWA, including the higher standard of proof for placement of an Indian child in foster care.[254] The exception to that rule, of course, is the mostly rejected Existing Indian Family Exception to the ICWA, discussed in Chapter 2, where certain courts have held that the ICWA should not apply unless the Indian child is being removed from an Indian family or Indian cultural setting.

The higher standard also does not apply when the child is being moved in order to return the child to the biological parent or to the Indian custodian that had custody prior to removal.[255]

Termination of Parental Rights

The most drastic remedy a court can order for the neglect and abuse of a child is the termination of the parents' rights. As the Supreme Court noted in *Santosky v. Kramer*,[256] "parents retain a vital interest in preventing the irretrievable destruction of their family life." That interest requires, at a minimum, that the state require clear and convincing evidence to support a finding that the parental rights should be terminated.[257] The Supreme Court, however, rejected the parents' arguments in *Santosky* that the termination of parental rights was such a drastic remedy that a "beyond a reasonable doubt" standard should be mandated in all cases by the 14th Amendment's Due Process Clause.[258]

Nonetheless, the ICWA requires that to support a termination of parental rights a petitioning party must establish, by evidence beyond a reasonable doubt, that the continued custody of the parents or Indian custodian would result in serious emotional or physical harm to the child.[259] As with a foster care placement, the burden rests with the petitioning party to demonstrate that remedial services and rehabilitative programs have been provided to prevent the breakup of the Indian family.[260] Some courts have held that this must be established based upon a clear and convincing evidentiary standard, some have required and the guidelines recommend a showing beyond a reasonable doubt, and a handful of courts have required only a mere preponderance of the evidence.[261] The finding that the continued custody of the child by the parent or custodian would result in serious emotional or physical harm must be supported by the testimony of a QEW.[262] Most courts have ruled that the QEW testimony must support, at least inferentially, a legal conclusion that the ICWA standard for termination has been met, although courts are split as to whether the QEW must be asked a specific question related to whether the statutory standard has been met.[263]

Many courts have held that both the state and federal standards for termination have to be met in the case of an Indian child.[264] Thus, practitioners should refer to state law to determine what other showings a petitioning party must demonstrate to support a termination of parental rights (e.g., least restrictive alternative, all rehabilitative services after placement have been exhausted, and best interest of the child), because these factors would also have to be demonstrated to support termination if required by state law.[265] These required findings would be in addition to the ultimate finding under the ICWA that serious emotional or physical damage would befall the Indian child.[266] With respect to the required showings under state law to support a termination of parental rights, most courts appear to apply the state burden of proof rather than the standard under the ICWA.[267] The refusal to apply the federal standards under the ICWA is a ground for reversal of a termination order, however, notwithstanding adherence to state law.[268] Of note, it has been held that § 1912(f) applies to circumstances where an adoption has been vacated or set aside and a biological parent or prior Indian custodian is petitioning for return of custody pursuant to 25 U.S.C. § 1916(a).[269] It has also been held that a court is required to obtain a conclusive determination from an Indian tribe of tribal eligibility before proceeding with termination proceedings when there is a reason to believe the child may be an Indian child.[270]

The BIA regulations are virtually silent as to family circumstances that would constitute serious emotional or physical harm to a child. They emphasize, however, that the agency must show a causal connection between conditions in the home and serious physical or emotional harm to the child in order for parental rights to be terminated.[271] They also cite several conditions that would not justify such a finding, specifically noting that evidence of poverty, single parenting, inadequate housing, substance abuse, or nonconforming social behavior cannot meet the standard of proof unless the causal connection can be shown.[272]

A number of courts have ruled that the ICWA TPR standard includes a requirement for a showing that there is a likelihood of future harm and that it is unlikely that the conduct of the parents will change.[273] Courts have also held that termination cannot be based solely on past conduct uninformed by current circumstances.[274]

Among the factors that courts have considered as relevant to a finding that the termination of parental rights is appropriate are alcoholism,[275] a nomadic lifestyle,[276] mental illness,[277] sexual abuse,[278] abandonment,[279] failure to comply with a case plan,[280] failure to visit,[281] need for stability of the child,[282] trauma associated with removing the child from foster/prospective adoptive parents,[283] and abhorrent living conditions.[284] A review of these cases does not reveal any pattern for the type of evidence presented, although one could argue that one of the considerations seems to be the need for stability in the child's lifestyle.

In *Adoptive Couple v. Baby Girl*, the U.S. Supreme Court, relying upon the phrase "continued custody" in § 1912(f), held that the ICWA TPR standard did not apply to a nonconsenting father in a voluntary adoption case when that father never had prior legal or physical custody.[285] A few courts have applied that holding to a termination of parental rights decision in a purely involuntary context based upon the statutory analysis in *Baby Girl*,[286] but at least one court has declined to apply it in an involuntary proceeding based largely upon the cautionary language in Justice Breyer's concurrence, opining that the analysis in *Baby Girl* might apply in some involuntary cases but not in others.[287] See discussion of *Adoptive Couple v. Baby Girl* in Chapter 1.

Many courts have expressly held that a trial court must make explicit rulings with regard to the required showings under the ICWA in order to satisfy the federal law, and that it is inappropriate for an appellate court to review the record to make an independent determination, although not all courts have so ruled.[288] In general, courts have ruled that 25 U.S.C. § 1914 allows appellate challenges to TPR based upon violations of the ICWA even if not raised before the trial court.[289] In terms of standards of review on appeal, there have been a number of articulations, including whether a "reasonable factfinder" or "reasonable person" could have concluded that the evidence met the statutory standard,[290] whether there was "substantial evidence" to support the finding,[291] and whether the factual findings below were "clearly erroneous."[292]

Title IV-E, in provisions adopted as part of the ASFA, compels a state agency to file a termination of parental rights petition in order to continue receiving federal matching dollars to fund the child's placement in certain circumstances. The filing of a petition is mandatory when the child has been in foster care for 15 out of the 22 preceding months, and when the parent has committed serious abuse upon the child or a sibling or has abandoned the child. The only three exceptions to the rule that the state agency must file when these circumstances are met are when (1) the child is being cared for by a relative; (2) the state has documented a compelling reason that filing a termination petition would not be in the child's best interest; or (3) the situation calls for services to be provided to a non-offending parent and those services have not yet been provided.[293] Other provisions in the ASFA that could impact placements of Indian children include the reasonable efforts/active efforts dichotomy already discussed earlier in this chapter, the fiscal incentive scheme for states that encourages adoptive placements of children,[294] and the permanency hearing requirements. The ASFA requires a permanency hearing within 12 months.[295]

These provisions of the ASFA must be reconciled with the specific provisions of the ICWA governing foster care placement proceedings and termination issues. Implementing the policies and procedures underlying the ASFA is not generally anathema to the goals of Congress when it enacted the ICWA in most situations.[296] The potential problems that arise occur mostly when ASFA is rigidly applied, for example, when the permanency hearing is viewed as a deadline for reunification rather than a hearing to review a permanency plan that involves multiple options. Merely because a child has been in extended foster care is not sufficient proof that the continued custody of the parent would result in serious emotional or physical harm to the child, which is the ICWA standard. Therefore, a petition to terminate parental rights in regard to an Indian child founded exclusively upon the ASFA 15-month rule would most likely be denied by a state court unless concomitant proof is submitted to comply with ICWA requirements.[297] One court has noted that even though a petition for termination cited the language in the ASFA that a child had been in substitute care for 15 out of the preceding 22 months as the sole basis for termination, termination was appropriate in that case only because other evidence existed that met the ICWA standard for termination.[298] State courts cannot apply a strict mathematical test to termination proceedings if Indian children are involved because nothing in the ASFA expresses the intent to override ICWA requirements. Arguably, if ICWA requirements cannot be met, that would be a compelling reason for not filing a petition because it would not advance the best interests of the child (one of the exceptions to the ASFA filing requirement).

In terms of the permanency hearing provision, there is no inherent conflict between those provisions and ICWA objectives, especially if Indian tribes receive notice of these permanency hearings and are allowed input into permanency decisions and the permanency hearing is not viewed as a de facto deadline for reunification efforts. Moreover, the requirements of the ASFA emphasize the need for state and private agencies to recruit more Indian foster and adoptive homes for Native children and, in fact, federal law requires that state agencies make efforts to recruit foster homes that reflect their service population.[299] It should be noted that permanency under the ASFA is not always synonymous with termination of parental rights and adoption, as the ASFA also permits permanent guardianships and placements with relatives as accepted types of permanency placements.[300] The U.S. Department of Health and Human Services has also recognized that adoption (clearly a permanent placement) is possible without termination of parental rights.[301] A permanent placement that does not involve TPR may often be in better accord with ICWA objectives of keeping Indian children within extended Native families and communities than termination proceedings and adoptive placements, which many times lead to non-Indian adoptive placements because of the lack of recruitment efforts for Native families.

Voluntary Proceedings

The ICWA was enacted not only to censure the unwarranted involuntary removal of Indian children from their families but also to make the common practice of voluntary displacement more difficult.[302] Congress pointed to instances of Indian parents voluntarily signing away custody of their children under threats by state and federal social services agencies to terminate their cash welfare payments.[303] Thus, although concerns about involuntary removals by state agencies were a major impetus for the ICWA, it is clear that "voluntary" adoptions of Indian children were likewise of great concern to Congress based upon the evidence it considered.[304]

Congressional hearings were replete with testimony about public and private agencies and private attorneys and their sometimes overzealous pursuit of Indian children for adoption by non-Indians.[305] Indeed, Congress found that many "voluntary" consents were not truly voluntary.[306] Consents in voluntary adoption cases were sometimes "coerced" or induced by "trickery."[307] In addition, particular concerns were expressed about the failure of adoption agencies to utilize Indian families for placement.[308]

To prevent these types of abuses, in the ICWA, Congress made it more difficult for a parent or custodian to execute a voluntary termination of parental rights by requiring some semblance of formality in the act and by permitting the Indian parent or custodian to regain custody of the child under certain circumstances.[309]

In this way the pernicious removal of Indian children from their families under the guise of a "voluntary" act would, one hopes, be curtailed. In fact, the regulations specifically define a proceeding as "voluntary" only if the parent or Indian custodian is acting "of his or her own free will, without a threat of removal by a State agency."[310] A number of cases have likewise held that consent that occurs in the context of an involuntary proceeding does not transform an involuntary case into a voluntary one.[311]

Moreover, Congress applied the ICWA to voluntary placements with both public and private agencies, including the placement preferences.[312] This is not surprising given the concerns expressed about coercive practices and the failure of adoption agencies to utilize Indian homes for placements. It is clear that the intent of ICWA to provide a home for Indian children that adequately reflects their cultural values and traditions would not be realized if private agencies were to arrange adoptions based on the ability of the adoptive parents to pay the fee to the agency.[313]

Finally, as discussed previously, it should be noted that although notice to the tribe is not required in voluntary proceedings, the party seeking placement must take all reasonable steps to confirm the child's status. This may include contacting the tribe.[314] Obviously, if a tribe is contacted about a voluntary placement, the chances are increased that the tribe may become involved in the proceeding.

Voluntary Foster Care Placements

Section 1913 of the ICWA governs the procedures for a voluntary foster care placement.[315] It is important to remember that not all voluntary placements are governed by the provisions of the ICWA. The definition of "foster care placement" contained in the ICWA explicitly excludes placements in which the parent can regain custody of the child upon demand.[316] The regulations define "upon demand" to mean that "the parent or Indian custodian can regain custody simply upon verbal request, without any formalities or contingencies," such as formal court proceedings, signing of agreements, or repayment of the child's expenses.[317] The definition of "upon demand" makes clear that any time that a court is invoked or any other formal action is required by the parent or Indian custodian to regain custody, the provisions in § 1913 apply.

Certain placements that may not initially be governed by the ICWA may be converted into such by the actions of the party with whom custody was vested. For example, if an Indian mother temporarily places her child with a social services agency because of some family emergency and after the emergency desists the agency refuses to return the child, the provisions of the ICWA govern, even though the original intent of the parties may have been to permit return upon demand. Custody would then have to be returned to the mother under the provisions of § 1913(b), although the placement may not have been a foster care placement under the act when initially done.[318] On the other hand, if an involuntary proceeding is commenced and the parent or Indian custodian admits to the petition alleging that the child is abused or neglected, the parent or custodian would not be entitled to revoke his or her admission or consent and demand the return of custody of the child under § 1913(b).[319] Such a proceeding would clearly be governed by the involuntary procedures set out in § 1912.[320] If, however, as part of an involuntary proceeding the parent consents to the termination of parental rights as a disposition, at least one court has held that the parent retains the right to withdraw that consent, provided that it is done before an order terminating parental rights is entered, even if the consent has become irrevocable under state law.[321] Of course, the state cannot rely upon a consent that is meant to be temporary to alleviate the need for a showing of active efforts under § 1912(d), nor the need to produce evidence justifying the foster care placement under § 1912(e) or termination of parental rights under § 1912(f).[322]

Necessity of Consent

For purposes of the execution of a voluntary consent to foster care placement, the Indian custodian is treated in much the same way as the parent, with the ICWA requiring the valid consent of either for a legal placement.[323] The legislative history is unclear on whether each would have to consent to a foster care placement in a case where the Indian custodian has the custody of the child, but the use of the disjunctive "or" in the language of § 1913(a) indicates that consent need be given only by the party with the custody of the child for a lawful foster care placement.[324] This is not true, however, for a consent to termination of parental rights, which can only be given by a parent (although in some cases, an Indian custodian may obtain parental rights through tribal law or custom even where the biological parents' rights have not been terminated and, in that case, presumably the Indian custodian's consent would be needed).

For a valid consent to be given, the consent must be (1) given in writing; (2) recorded before a judge of a court of competent jurisdiction; (3) certified to by the presiding judge that the consequences of the consent were fully explained; (4) certified to by the court that the parent or custodian understood the explanation in English or had the explanation translated into a language understood by the person; and (5) executed after the child is ten days old.[325] The consent should be executed in open court unless the parent requests confidentiality.[326]

Court of Competent Jurisdiction

In *Holyfield* the Supreme Court held that a state court was not a court of competent jurisdiction to accept a voluntary termination of parental rights executed by a reservation-domiciled Indian.[327] Therefore, for a state court to be a court of competent jurisdiction under the provisions of § 1913(a) the state court must have jurisdiction under the provisions of § 1911.[328]

If the parent and child are domiciled off the reservation, the state court and possibly the tribal court would have the authority to accept a consent to foster care placement or termination of parental rights.[329] A tribe's governing ordinances, including its constitution and code, may authorize the tribal court to continue to exercise jurisdiction over its members when they venture off the reservation.[330] An inquiry with the tribal court would be a possible manner of finding out this information.

Type of Consent

The consent form in Appendix F is a typical form that can be used both for the consent to foster care placement and to termination of parental rights. It not only explains the consequences of the act to the parent or custodian but also clarifies the rights of the parent or custodian after execution of the consent form. It also gives the parent or custodian the option of recommending a placement. This recommendation, as discussed in Chapter 5, is entitled to a certain amount of deference by the court.[331]

It should be noted that in some tribal courts this type of consent form is not necessary because tribal law, and not the ICWA, governs child custody proceedings in tribal court.[332] Any time a voluntary consent is executed in the tribal court, it is safe practice to assume that the child has become a ward of the tribal court and any future proceedings involving the child should be commenced in the tribal court.[333]

If the natural parent or custodian does not understand the English language, the ICWA mandates that the state court provide translation into a language that the parent or custodian can understand.[334] There are various persons, both on and off reservations, who still speak and write Native languages. The best way to find a fluent speaker would be to contact the Indian child's tribe or another tribe that speaks the same language. Certain federal agencies, including the Department of the Interior, may also be helpful in locating translators of Native languages.

Withdrawal of Consent

Section 1913(b) of the ICWA permits an Indian parent or custodian to withdraw consent to a foster care placement by filing a written document with the court and directs that upon said withdrawal the child shall be returned to the parent or custodian.[335] There is no provision in § 1913(b) allowing a court to refuse to return custody on the basis that it would not be in the best interest of the child to be returned.[336] Section 1913(b) should be compared to §§ 1916 and 1920, both of which allow a state court to refuse to restore the custody of the child to the parent or custodian if certain conditions are met.[337]

The rights secured to an Indian parent or custodian under § 1913(b) cannot, of course, be exercised if the state court has already entered an order terminating that parent or custodian's rights.[338] Before that time, however, § 1913(b) permits a parent who has executed a consent to foster care placement to withdraw that consent and regain custody of the child.[339] This includes the right of the parent to withdraw a conditional consent to adoption if the state or private agency then attempts to place the child with a family other than the one specified by the parent.[340] It has been held, however, that the agency and the tribe do not have the right to withdraw consent independent from the parent's right.[341]

Whereas § 1913(b) governs the situation when a parent has lawfully placed a child in foster care pursuant to the provisions of the ICWA, § 1920 controls when a party has obtained custody in violation of § 1913(a) or has wrongfully kept custody after the termination of a voluntary placement.[342] In that situation, the ICWA directs the state court to decline to exercise jurisdiction over any petition filed by the party wrongfully obtaining custody and also directs the court to restore custody to the parent or guardian "unless returning the child . . . would subject the child to a substantial and immediate danger or threat of danger."[343] It is somewhat strange that the ICWA mandates the unconditional return of custody to a parent who executed a lawful consent to a foster care placement but permits a party who unlawfully obtained custody to argue against a return of custody. This scheme seems to reward those entities that illegally gain custody of Indian children by providing them with a mechanism to avoid a return of custody, whereas parties that lawfully obtained custody must return the child upon demand without inquiry into whether return would be dangerous to the child.[344]

Of course, if a public or private agency that was voluntarily vested with a foster care placement is desirous of avoiding a return of the child, an involuntary proceeding may be started by that agency, provided that the agency can satisfy the standards of proof for an involuntary foster care placement. That option does not seem available to an agency that illegally obtained or retained custody, because § 1920 commands that the state court decline to exercise jurisdiction over any proceeding commenced by such a party.[345]

A revocation of consent may occur at any time for any reason.[346] Congress chose this route because of its grave concern over the abuses associated with "voluntary" placements that were in no sense voluntary.[347] If state rules prohibit the return of custody of the child after the revocation of a voluntary placement, they are superseded by ICWA and are inapposite.[348]

Voluntary Termination of Parental Rights Proceedings

The same provisions that govern voluntary foster care placements control the voluntary termination of a parent's or Indian custodian's parental rights. In order to terminate the parental rights of the parent of an Indian child, the requirements of § 1913(a) must be followed, as well as state law requirements if they provide for additional procedural requirements or a higher standard of proof.[349] For example, in certain states the parental rights of a parent may not be voluntarily terminated except upon a showing that it would be in the best interest of the child.[350] Such a standard prohibits a parent from terminating parental rights merely to avoid the obligations of parenthood. Arguably, this is a higher state standard, which would apply to the voluntary termination of an Indian parent's rights.[351]

As with voluntary foster care placements, there are provisions under the ICWA permitting parents to withdraw consent to a voluntary termination of parental rights or to an adoptive placement by filing a written document with the court for any reason "prior to a final decree of termination or adoption, as the case may be, and the child shall be returned to the parent."[352] If the parent does withdraw consent before an order of termination or adoption, that parent has an unqualified right to regain custody of the child,[353] although at least one court has stated that the right to regain custody would be contingent upon the parent having custody before executing the consent.[354] Even when the consent to termination of parental rights is executed as part of an involuntary proceeding, the right to withdraw consent exists, although the right to reclaim custody of the child may not.[355]

The ICWA has elevated the rights of an Indian custodian to those of a parent in many respects, but less so in the area of termination of parental rights, which is consistent with holdings of the Supreme Court, which has declined to recognize that the rights of extended family are synonymous with those of the parents.[356] Because § 1913(a) merges together both voluntary foster care placements and termination of parental rights and references both consents by parents and Indian custodians, some have read this to provide Indian custodians with parental rights similar to a parent. This is an unlikely reading of the statute, however, and it is more likely that the reference to consent by the Indian custodian applies to a voluntary foster care placement and not termination of parental rights, although there might be an exception in a case where tribal law or custom recognizes parental rights in an Indian custodian. Certainly, there is no indication that Congress intended to supplant the rights of natural parents to custody of their children by elevating the rights of Indian custodians to that of a parent and in fact it would probably be unconstitutional to do so. Thus, even though the language of § 1913(a) could be read to require consent to termination only by the party with custody of the child, a more reasonable interpretation is that the parents' rights remain intact until a valid termination order is entered, and that an Indian custodian has no right to consent to the termination of the rights of a parent. Interestingly, the regulations do recognize the right of an Indian custodian to withdraw consent to adoption, but not to termination, which may be meant to address a situation where all parental rights have been terminated, or no parents are living, and the Indian custodian has the authority to consent to an adoption.[357] But generally, except in the case of a traditional customary adoption (or comparable state process), which may take place without a termination of parental rights, an adoption cannot be granted unless the rights of all recognized parents have been terminated, either voluntarily by the parent or involuntarily.[358]

After the entry of a final decree of adoption an Indian parent cannot withdraw consent unless he or she can demonstrate that the consent was obtained through "fraud or duress."[359] Upon a showing of such, the court can set aside an adoption unless it has been effective for more than two years, or longer if state law permits it to be invalidated even after two years.[360] In light of the requirement that a parent appear before a judge of competent jurisdiction to execute a consent to termination or adoptive placement, it appears difficult to make the required showing of fraud or duress to set aside an adoption.[361] This may explain the dearth of case law on this particular provision. One court has held that a putative father cannot use this provision to challenge an adoption that took place without his knowledge as such does not involve fraud or duress in the execution of a consent.[362]

Several courts have addressed the effect on voluntary proceedings of the discovery, after the act of consent takes place, that the child involved is Indian. Most have held that the consent to termination or adoption should be judged by the standards of state law and not the ICWA, even in one case when the mother suggested that she was of Indian heritage.[363] A decision from Oregon, however, has held that a natural mother of an Indian child can revoke her consent to adoption, which had become irrevocable under state law, if the child becomes an Indian child before the finalization of an adoption.[364]

Full Faith and Credit

Tribal courts have a somewhat anomalous existence in the federalist scheme concocted by the framers of the Constitution, notwithstanding the framers' liberal use of the Iroquois Confederacy as a model for the United States' system of government. Tribal courts are not state courts for purposes of the constitutional full faith and credit clause.[365] Some state and federal courts have concluded that they are territorial courts for purposes of the federal full faith and credit statute,[366] but this point of view is clearly not a universal one.[367]

To eliminate any confusion over the deference a state court must grant a tribal court's judgment in a child custody proceeding, the ICWA unequivocally provides at § 1911(d) that the United States, every state and federal territory, and every Indian tribe must give full faith and credit to the "public acts, records, and judicial proceedings of any Indian tribe applicable to Indian child custody proceedings to the same extent that those entities give full faith and credit to the public acts, records, and judicial proceedings of any other entity."[368]

Before a public act, record, or order from a judicial proceeding is entitled to full faith and credit under § 1911(d), there must be a finding that the document is related to a child custody proceeding.[369] In addition, several courts have held that § 1911 does not mandate blind allegiance to a tribal court order but instead permits a state court to look beyond an order to determine whether the issuing court had jurisdiction over the subject matter and parties when it entered the order, much the same way state courts are permitted to examine the jurisdictional basis for a state court's entry of an order.[370] Full faith and credit has also been denied where the court found that an essential party was not notified and thus deprived of due process, which would be another ground for denying full faith and credit of a state judgment as well.[371] A tribal court judgment should clearly be honored if it pertains to a child custody proceeding, however, provided that the tribal court had jurisdiction to enter the order when it did and accorded the parties basic due process.[372]

If an Indian tribe makes a determination that a child is a member of that tribe, that finding is entitled to absolute allegiance even if the child in question has no Indian blood.[373] Granting full faith and credit to a document or court order should be distinguished from the question of whether a proper evidentiary foundation has been laid to admit a document or court order into evidence, the answer to which may lie in the state's rules of evidence and not in the ICWA.[374] Most records of Indian tribes are admissible under the public records or business records exception to the hearsay rule, and most tribal court orders should be authenticated in a way that conforms to the state's recognition of foreign judgments act.[375] One court, however, has ruled inadmissible an affidavit from a tribal official asserting that a child is eligible for membership.[376]

Although this exact holding is not addressed in the regulations, it would be appear that this decision is probably contrary to the procedures required and contemplated by the regulations.[377]

Some tribes have attempted to preempt a state court's exercise of its jurisdiction by making an Indian child who is not resident or domiciled on the reservation a ward of the tribal court and arguing that such an order precludes state court jurisdiction under § 1911(a).[378] This practice has been spurned by some state courts, which have looked beyond the order to conclude that the tribal court lacked jurisdiction to act and have therefore declined to honor the particular order, but other courts have recognized such orders.[379] It should be noted, however, that the Uniform Child Custody Jurisdiction Enforcement Act (UCCJEA)[380] may require a tribal court order to be given full faith and credit in circumstances beyond those covered by ICWA.[381] Finally, while certain states may have statutes or case law governing the recognition of tribal court judgments that honor the judgments under the doctrine of comity, not full faith and credit,[382] such statutes would appear to be preempted in ICWA child custody proceedings.[383]

Interestingly, § 1911(d) requires tribal courts to grant full faith and credit to other tribal court orders but not to state court orders.[384] Indeed, a tribal court need not defer to a state court's findings with respect to a child custody proceeding made before the case is transferred to a tribal court, as the ICWA does not require such. Of course, the tribal court may want to recognize the state court's proceedings that took place before transfer, because they may inform future decisions pertaining to the child and family and because conceivably the failure to do so could negatively influence tribal court transfer requests in future proceedings.

Some advocates have attempted to use the axioms set out in the ICWA to argue for transfers of jurisdiction among tribal courts as well as from state to tribal courts. The ICWA does not seem to create a mechanism for such transfers, although tribal law may allow such transfers.

This chapter has examined the various procedural requirements of the ICWA. The next chapter will explore another critical objective of Congress in enacting the ICWA: the placement of Indian children with their relatives and in homes that reflect their unique cultural and traditional heritages.

Endnotes

1. *Compare In re* H.D., 729 P.2d 1234 (Kan. Ct. App. 1986) (failure to give tribe notice of termination proceeding renders the proceeding null and void) *and* Nicole K. v. Super. Ct., 53 Cal. Rptr. 251 (Ct. App. 2007) (same) *with In re* Veronica G., 157 Cal. App. 4th 179, 68 Cal. Rptr. 3d 465 (Ct. App. 2007) (failure to give notice not jurisdictional) *and In re* C.I. Morris, 807 N.W.2d 857 (Mich. 2012) (same).
2. 42 U.S.C. §§ 620 *et seq.* and 42 U.S.C. §§ 670 *et seq.* These provisions of the Social Security Act have been amended several times since the first edition of this book. Among the most well-known sets of amendments are the Adoption and Safe Families Act of 1997, the Fostering Connections to Success and Increasing Adoptions Act of 2008, and the Family First Prevention Services Act of 2018. These are discussed in the text of the book as appropriate.
3. An example would be the requirement that the party petitioning for a foster care placement or termination of parental rights utilize a "qualified expert witness" to support a removal or termination. *See* 25 U.S.C. § 1912(e) (foster care placements) and 25 U.S.C. § 1912(f) (termination of parental rights).
4. 25 U.S.C. § 1921. *See, e.g., In re* Spears, 872 N.W.2d 85 (Mich. Ct. App. 2015) (Michigan state statute that provides for only limited reasons to deny a motion to transfer to tribal court must be applied by trial court

even though the standard is narrower than what is contained in Bureau of Indian Affairs (BIA) guidelines implementing the ICWA); *In re* Interest of D.S.P., 166 Wis. 2d 464, 480 N.W.2d 234 (Wis. 1992) (court holds that state must not only prove serious emotional or physical harm may befall child if termination is not ordered, but also abandonment under state law, although abandonment may be demonstrated by clear and convincing evidence only).

5. For example, Wisconsin and Michigan have adopted a state law definition for who can qualify as a qualified expert witness (QEW) that is more stringent than many of the state cases that have interpreted who can be a qualified expert witness for ICWA purposes. *Compare* Wis. Stat. § 48.028(g) and Mich. Comp. Laws § 712B.17 (both requiring that a QEW have specific knowledge of the Indian child's tribe's culture and child-rearing practices) *with In re* M.C.M., 180 P.3d 688 (Okla. Ct. App. 2007) (no requirement that the QEW have special knowledge of Indian life when the person is a professional person with substantial education and expertise and testifies on matters not implicating cultural bias). See generally Chapter 1, the section on state ICWAs.
6. *See* S.D. Codified Laws § 26-8A-21 (requiring the provision of remedial and rehabilitative services to a family before removal of a child from the home).
7. *See, e.g., In re* Brandon M., 54 Cal. App. 4th 1387 (1997) (The ICWA does not occupy the field of child custody and adoption, even as to Indian children, and other child welfare laws should be applied unless there is a conflict between those laws and the ICWA.); *In re* J.S.B. Jr., 2005 SD 3, 691 N.W.2d 611 (S.D. 2005) (exceptions to reasonable efforts requirement enacted in the Adoption and Safe Families Act do not override the ICWA active efforts requirement).
8. 42 U.S.C. § 671(a)(16) and *id.* § 675(5).
9. *See* Mississippi Band of Choctaw Indians v. Holyfield, 490 U.S. 30, 49 (1989); 25 U.S.C. § 1901(3); S. Rep. No. 95-597, at 51 (1977). It is well-settled that parens patriae authority extends beyond territorial boundaries. *See* Alfred L. Snapp & Son, Inc. v. Puerto Rico, 458 U.S. 592 (1982) (Puerto Rico, as parens patriae, has right to intervene in Virginia state court to

protect the health and safety of Puerto Rican workers in Virginia.); *see also* State of Alaska v. Native Vill. of Curyung, 151 P.3d 388, 402 (Alaska 2006) (tribe has right as parens patriae to bring suit to prevent future violations of the ICWA).

10. 25 U.S.C. § 1911(c).
11. *Id.* § 1911(b).
12. *See, e.g., In re* H.D., 729 P.2d 1234 (Kan. Ct. App. 1986).
13. 25 U.S.C. § 1912(a); 25 C.F.R. § 23.11(a).
14. *Compare In re* K.A.B.E., 325 N.W.2d 840 (S.D. 1982); In Interest of H.D., 729 P.2d 1234 (Kan. App. 1986); *In re* A.G., 2005 MT 81, 109 P.3d 756 (Mont. 2005); *In re* M.C.P., 571 A.2d 627 (Vt. 1989) *and In re* Kahlen W., 233 Cal. App. 3d 1414, 285 Cal. Rptr. 507 (Cal. App. 5th Dist. 1991) *with In re* Veronica G., 157 Cal. App. 4th 179, 68 Cal. Rptr. 3d 465 (Cal. App. 1st Dist. 2007); *In re* K.B., 173 Cal. App. 4th 1275, 93 Cal. Rptr. 751 (Cal. App. 2d Dist. 2009); *and In re* Morris, 491 Mich. 81, 815 N.W.2d 62 (2012). If, however, it is determined that the tribe that claims entitlement to notice is not the "Indian child's tribe," a failure to give notice does not deprive the trial court of jurisdiction. *See In re* M.C.P., 571 A.2d 627 (Vt. 1989); People *ex rel.* Dep't of Social Servs. in Interest of C.H., 510 N.W.2d 119 (S.D. 1993). A California court has also held that a tribe that appeared to assert its interests waived the lack of proper notice by appearing. *In re* Krystle D., 37 Cal. Rptr. 2d 132, 30 Cal. App. 4th 1778 (Cal. App. 6th Dist. 1994).
15. 25 C.F.R. § 23.124(b).
16. Dep't of the Interior, Bureau of Indian Affairs, Final Rule Indian Child Welfare Act Proceedings, 81 Fed. Reg. 38778, 38834 (June 14, 2016); BIA GUIDELINES FOR IMPLEMENTING THE INDIAN CHILD WELFARE ACT § D.1 (Dec. 2016).
17. *In re* Dependency of Colnar, 757 P.2d 534 (Wash. App. 1988); *In re* Baby Boy Doe, 849 P.2d 925 (Idaho 1993); In the Interest of C.H., 510 N.W.2d 119 (S.D. 1993).
18. *In re* A.U., 141 Cal. App. 4th 326 (2006) (failure of state agency to give notice to several tribes after mother and relatives self-identified as Indian violates notice provisions of ICWA); *see also In re* Dependency of T.L.G., 108 P.3d 156 (Wash. App. 2005).

19. 25 C.F.R. § 23.108; *In re* Adoption of Riffle, 922 P.2d 510, 512 (Mont. 1996) (Tribal determination on membership is conclusive.).
20. 25 C.F.R. §§ 23.11, 23.107.
21. *Id.* § 23.107(c).
22. *See In re* J.L., 10 Cal. App. 5th 913, 217 Cal. Rptr. 3d 201 (Cal. App. 4th 2017) (vague assertion does not trigger notice requirement); *In re* Joseph P., 140 Cal. App. 4th 1524 (Cal. App. 5th 2006) (determining that the ICWA did not apply during foster care proceedings based upon information provided by father and father's new assertion that he was Mohican from New York during termination proceedings did not trigger new notice requirement); *In re* T.D., 890 So. 2d 473 (Fla. App. 2004) (finding mother's assertion of Indian ancestry at time of termination hearing not sufficient to invoke the ICWA, but court cautions state to do a better job of determining ICWA applicability early in proceedings); *In re* Guardianship of J.O., 327 N.J. Super. 304, 743 A.2d 341 (N.J. App. 2000); *In re* Ariana R.G., 657 N.W.2d 363 (Wis. 2003) (holding father's vague self-identification not sufficient to trigger notice requirements).
23. *See In re* T.A., 883 N.E.2d 639 (Ill. App. 2008) (which lists and discusses cases from various jurisdictions that have reached different conclusions on whether mere suspicion is enough to trigger the notice requirement).
24. *In re* Morris, 491 Mich. 81, 815 N.W.2d 62 (2012).
25. *In re* Gabriel G., 206 Cal. App. 4th 1160, 142 Cal. Rptr. 3d 344 (Cal. App. 2d 2012); *but see In re* Austin J., 47 Cal. App. 5th 870, 261 Cal. Rptr. 3d 297 (2020) (vague assertion not enough to find reason to know).
26. J.J. & A.J. v. State, 2011 UT App. 398, 266 P.3d 850 (Utah Ct. App. 2011).
27. Jimmy E. v. State of Alaska, Dep't of Health & Soc. Servs., 529 P.3d 504 (2023); *In re* Z.J.G., 196 Wn.2d 152, 471 P.3d 853 (2020); *see also* M.Y. v. Texas Dep't of Fam. & Protective Servs., 667 S.W.3d 502 (Tex. App. 2023) (Notice should have been provided when mother stated that she had Indian heritage from two tribal nations and a grandmother who is registered with the Cherokee tribe.).
28. People in Interest of E.A.M. v. D.R.M., 516 P.3d 924 (Colo. 2022); *In re* P.H., Jr., 98 Cal. App. 5th 992, 317 Cal. Rptr. 3d 197 (2024). The specific

holding in Colorado that there may not be reason to know even when specific tribes have been identified has been changed by statute, although the reason to know standard in Colorado is still stricter than in some other states, like Washington. COLO. REV. STAT. § 19-1.2-107(3)(b)(VIII).

29. 25 C.F.R. § 23.107 summarizes the need to use due diligence to make a status inquiry to all tribes that may be the Indian child's tribe and this requirement is explained further in the BIA GUIDELINES, *supra* note 16, § B.1. 25 C.F.R. § 23.111 is the section of the regulations that specifically addresses the formal notice requirement.
30. BIA GUIDELINES, *supra* note 16, § B.1.
31. 25 U.S.C. § 1912(a).
32. 25 C.F.R. § 23.111(e).
33. *See In re* H. Wardia Minor, 2022 WL 2288586 (Mich. Ct. App. 2022) (finding that assertion of heritage required notice to the BIA, but was not reason to know and did not require application of the statute to the mother).
34. *In re* Morris, 491 Mich. 81, 815 N.W.2d 62 (2012).
35. *See In re* Custody of C.C.R.S., 872 P.2d 1337 (Colo. App. 1993), *aff'd*, 892 P.2d 246 (1995), *cert. den. sub. nom.* C.R.S. v. T.A.M., 512 U.S. 837 (1995) (naked allegation by mother that she is one-half Indian not sufficient to invoke notice); *In re* Adoption of Baby Boy W., 831 P.2d 643 (Okla. 1992) (mere fact that father was listed in school records as Indian did not warrant finding that ICWA applied); *In re* Interest of A.M., 235 Neb. 506, 455 N.W.2d 572 (Neb. 1990) (burden rests with parents to prove they are Indian). Whether all of these cases are still good law in view of the requirements in the regulations is questionable.
36. *See In re* Kahlen W., 285 Cal. Rptr. 507 (Cal. App. 5th Dist. 1991).
37. *People ex rel.* J.O., 170 P.3d 840 (Colo. Ct. App. Div. V, 2007).
38. *In re* K.S., 448 S.W.2d 521 (Tex. Ct. App. 2014) (where tribe received actual notice and timely intervened, failure to strictly comply with § 1912(a) notice requirement does not invalidate trial court proceeding); *but see In re* Custody of C.C.M., 149 Wash. App. 184, 202 P.3d 971 (Wash. Ct. App. 2009) (where tribe only allowed limited intervention, this does not cure the lack of notice).

39. *In re* L.A.G., 393 Mont. 146, 429 P.3d 629 (2018), *reh'g. denied.*
40. *See* People in Interest of Z.C., 487 P.3d 1044 (Colo. App. 2019); *In re* I.G., 133 Cal. App. 4th 1246, 35 Cal. Rptr. 3d 427 (Cal. App. 1st Dist. 2006); *In re* Jonathan S., 129 Cal. App. 4th 334, 28 Cal. Rptr. 3d 495 (4th Dist. Cal. 2005); *In re* Brooke C., 127 Cal. App. 4th 377, 25 Cal. Rptr. 3d 590 (2d Dist. 2005); Family Independence Agency v. Hosler, 245 Mich. App. 126, 133, 626 N.W.2d 921, 924 (2001); *In re* R.E.K.F., 698 N.W.2d 147 (Iowa 2005).
41. *See, e.g., In re* B.R., 97 Cal. Rptr. 3d 890 (Cal. App. 2009); *In re* Interest of J.J.C., 302 S.W.3d 896 (Tex. Ct. App. 2009); People *ex rel.* J.O., 170 P.3d 840 (Colo. Ct. App. Div. V, 2007); State of New Mexico v. Marlene, 215 P.3d 43 (N.M. 2009).
42. 25 C.F.R. § 23.111(a)(2).
43. *See, e.g., In re* K.G., 270 N.C. App. 423, 840 S.E.2d 914 (2020).
44. *See, e.g., In re* M.T., 401 Mont. 518, 474 P.3d 820 (2020) (When mother identified herself as Cherokee, notice must be sent to all three federally recognized Cherokee tribes.); *Accord In re* N.G., 27 Cal. App. 5th 474, 238 Cal. Rptr. 3d 304 (2018).
45. 25 C.F.R. § 23.111(b)(1).
46. *Id.* § 23.111(e). The statute actually refers to notice to the Secretary of the Interior. 25 U.S.C. § 1912(a).
47. *See, e.g., In re* J.T., 65 Cal. Rptr. 320 (Ct. App. 1st Dist. 2007) .
48. *In re* J.J., 454 N.W.2d 317 (S.D. 1990).
49. *See In re* R.E.K.F., 698 N.W.2d 147, 150 (Iowa 2005) (noting that the state ICWA law, Iowa Code § 232B.5, required notice to the Seneca Nation of a pending child custody proceeding).
50. 25 U.S.C. § 1912(a).
51. 25 C.F.R. § 23.2.
52. *See* Catholic Social Services, Inc. v. C.A.A., 783 P.2d 1159 (Alaska 1989), *cert. denied*, 495 U.S. 948 (1990); People in Interest of J.J., 454 N.W.2d 317 (S.D. 1990); Navajo Nation v. Supe. Ct., 47 F. Supp. 2d 1233 (E.D. Wash. 1999); Duncan v. Wiley, 657 P.2d 1212 (Okla. App. 1982).
53. 25 C.F.R. § 23.124(b).

54. BIA GUIDELINES, *supra* note 16, § I.3.
55. 25 U.S.C. § 1911(c). A tribe is also entitled to intervene in a custody dispute between a grandparent and parent. *In re* Custody of A.K.H., 502 N.W.2d 790 (Minn. Ct. App. 1993).
56. 25 U.S.C. § 1912(a). For example, although the California Court of Appeals held that an Indian tribe was entitled to intervene in a declaratory judgment action filed by an Indian mother who had been raised in a non-Indian adoptive home who was seeking a judgment that the ICWA did not apply to her attempts to place her child in a non-Indian home for adoption, the court also suggested that the tribe there was not entitled to notice and that the mother could determine the child's fate notwithstanding the wishes of the tribe. *In re* Baby Girl A., 230 Cal. App. 3d 1611, 282 Cal. Rptr. 105 (Cal. App. 4th Dist. 1991).
57. BIA GUIDELINES, *supra* note 16, § D.1.
58. 25 U.S.C. § 1915(e); 25 C.F.R. § 23.141.
59. 25 U.S.C. § 1912(a); 25 C.F.R. § 23.11(a). Regulations now require that notice be sent to the Department of the Interior in all cases, not just when tribal identity cannot be ascertained. *See* 25 C.F.R. § 23.11(a).
60. *See* S.D. CODIFIED LAWS § 15-6-4d (requiring personal service to commence an action).
61. 25 U.S.C. § 1912(a).
62. 25 C.F.R. § 23.111(d).
63. *See In re* Nikki R., 106 Cal. App 4th 844, 131 Cal. Rptr. 256 (4th Dist. 2003); *In re* Asia L., 107 Cal. App. 4th 498, 132 Cal. Rptr. 2d 733 (1st Dist. 2003); *In re* Suzanna L., 104 Cal. App. 4th 223, 127 Cal. Rptr. 2d. 860 (4th Dist. 2002); *In re* H.A., 103 Cal. App, 4th 1206, 128 Cal. Rptr. 2d 12 (5th Dist. 2002); *In re* Jeffrey A., 103 Cal. App. 4th 1103, 127 Cal. Rptr. 2d 314 (3d Dist. 2002); *In re* Jennifer A., 103 Cal. App. 4th 692, 127 Cal. Rptr. 2d 54 (4th Dist. 2002); *In re* Jonathan D., 92 Cal. App. 4th 105, 111 Cal. Rptr. 2d 628 (3d Dist. 2001); B.H. v. People *ex rel.* X.H., 138 P.3d 299 (Col. 2006); *In re* N.A.H., 418 N.W.2d 310 (S.D. 1988); *In re* B.J.E., 422 N.W.2d 597 (S.D. 1988); *In re* S.Z., 325 N.W.2d 53 (S.D. 1982). In apparent response to the burgeoning number of child custody decisions being rendered by California

trial courts that were reversed because of defective or no notice at all, several of the Courts of Appeal in California adopted an appellate rule permitting remand for appropriate notice without overturning the results of the child custody proceeding. If notice is served and there is no finding by the trial court that the children involved are covered by the ICWA, the lower court decision is affirmed. If the children are determined to be covered by the ICWA, the lower court orders are vacated and the matter remanded for new hearings. *In re* Francisco W., 139 Cal. App. 4th 695, 705, 43 Cal. Rptr. 3d 171, 177 (Cal. App. 4th Dist. 2006); *see also In re* Merrick V., 122 Cal. App. 4th 1449 (Cal. App. 3d Dist. 2003). Other states have adopted this approach as well. *See, e.g.,* In Interest of R.E.K.F., 698 N.W.2d 147 (Iowa 2005).

64. *In re* D.T, 113 Cal. App. 4th 1449, 5 Cal. Rptr. 3d 893 (3d Dist. 2003).
65. In the Interest of N.D.C., 210 P.3d 494 (Colo. Ct. App. 2009).
66. *Id.* (grandmother); *In re* A.G., 139 Cal. Rptr. 3d 727 (Cal. Ct. App. 1st Dist. 2012).
67. *In re* Christian P., 207 Cal. App. 4th 1266 (Cal. Ct. App. 2d Dist. 2012).
68. *See, e.g, In re* C.B., 117 Cal. Rptr. 3d 896 (Cal. App. 2010); *In re* S.E., 217 Cal. App. 4th 610 (Cal. App. 2013).
69. *In re* E.J.B., 375 N.C. 95, 846 S.E.2d 472 (2020).
70. *In re* I.W., 180 Cal. App. 4th 1517, 103 Cal. Rptr. 3d 538 (Cal. App. 6th Dist. 2009).
71. *In re* Morris, 491 Mich. 81, 815 N.W.2d 62 (2012); *In re* K.T., 990 N.E.2d 1260 (Ill. App. 2013).
72. 25 C.F.R. § 23.111(a)(2).
73. *See, e.g., In re* E.J.B., 375 N.C. 95, 846 S.E.2d 472 (2020); People in Interest of Z.C., 487 P.3d 1044 (Colo. App. 2019).
74. *In re* A.E., 749 P.2d 450 (Colo. App. 1987); *In re* Adoption of Crews, 825 P.2d 305 (Wash. 1992). Of course, if the state court or the parties involved should have known that the child involved was an Indian but still failed to provide notice, the proceedings would be invalid.
75. *In re* B.J.E., 422 N.W.2d 597 (S.D. 1988); *but cf.* People in the Interest of T.M.W., 208 P.3d 272 (Colo. Ct. App. 2009) (fact that another sibling was

previously found to be ineligible does not alleviate notice obligation for second sibling); 25 C.F.R. § 23.11.

76. *See* 25 U.S.C. § 1916(b), which, construed broadly, requires a new notice to the tribe each time a placement is changed. *See also* People in Interest of S.R.M., 153 P.2d 438, 442 (Colo. App. 1995) (court erred by terminating parental rights after failing to give notice to an Indian tribe that had failed to intervene after receiving notice of a foster care placement).
77. *See* 25 U.S.C. § 1911(c); *In re* Adoption Petition of Begay, 765 P.2d 1178 (N.M. App. 1988); *In re* J.J., 454 N.W.2d 317, 331 (S.D. 1990).
78. *Compare* 25 U.S.C. § 1911(c) granting intervention rights in all foster care and termination proceedings *with* 25 U.S.C. § 1912(a) mandating notice only in "any involuntary proceeding."
79. *See* 25 U.S.C. § 1911(c).
80. *In re* J.R.S., 690 P.2d 10 (Alaska 1984) (permitting an Indian tribe and extended family members to intervene in an adoptive placement proceeding); A.B.M. v. M.H. & A.H., 651 P.2d 1170 (Alaska 1982); *In re* Baby Girl A., 230 Cal. App. 3d 1611, 282 Cal. Rptr. 105 (Cal. App. 4th Dist. 1991); *In re* Custody of A.K.H., 502 N.W.2d 790 (Minn. Ct. App. 1993).
81. *See, e.g.*, Rosalind M. v. Alaska DFCS, 555 P.3d 505 (Alaska 2024) (affirming trial court's ruling denying foster family motion to intervene because their motion was based upon an argument precluded by the ICWA regulations); *In re* B.P., 328 Or. App. 267, 538 P.3d 577 (2013) (upholding discretion of tribal court to deny petition to intervene by foster family); *In re* H.N.B. & A.J.B., 619 N.W.2d 340 (Iowa 2000) (denying permissive intervention to a former foster care provider and noting that the provider's husband did not meet the definition of an Indian person under the ICWA); *but see In re* C.G.L., 28 S.W.2d 502 (Mo. App. 2000) (granting intervention status to extended family members entitled to preference under adoption placement preferences in an adoption proceeding).
82. 42 U.S.C. § 675G.
83. *See id.*, which would apply to ICWA proceedings because it does not appear to be inconsistent with the goals of the ICWA.

84. *See* 25 U.S.C. § 1911(c), stating that only the Indian child's tribe has the right to intervene as a matter of right.
85. *In re* J.J., 454 N.W.2d 317 (S.D. 1990). Cases may also arise where the siblings in a particular case are members of different tribes so that several tribes may have a mandatory right of intervention.
86. *See In re* Kirk v. Klamath Tribe, 170 Or. App. 106, 11 P.3d 701 (Ct. App. 2000) (holding that under state regulations an Indian tribe where children are not enrolled or eligible not entitled to participate in permanency planning for the children).
87. *See* 25 U.S.C. § 1912(c).
88. *Id. See also* J.P.H. v. Florida Dept. of Children and Families, 30 So. 3d 560 (Fla. Ct. App. 2010) (tribe has right to intervene and is not required to be represented by a member of the state bar; the ICWA preempts state prohibitions on the unauthorized practice of law); *In re* N.N.E., 752 N.W.2d 1 (Iowa 2008) (tribe can intervene without an attorney); *In re* Interest of Elias L., 277 Neb. 1023 (Neb. Sup. Ct. 2009) (The ICWA preempts state law that requires that tribe be represented by an attorney).
89. The South Dakota Supreme Court, in recognition that tribes may not have legal counsel in all child custody proceedings, enacted a court rule authorizing the tribe to designate a non-attorney to represent it in ICWA proceedings. S.D. Codified Laws § 26-8A-33 (2007).
90. BIA Guidelines, *supra* note 16, § A.3. If local rules of court prohibit appearances by a person other than an attorney for a tribe, those local rules are superseded by the policy of the ICWA allowing tribes the right to participate in ICWA cases. State *ex rel.* Juvenile Dep't of Lane Cnty. v. Shuey, 119 Or. App. 185, 850 P.2d 378 (Or. App. 1993) (ICWA preempts state rule that group of persons may only appear in court through counsel). In many states, out-of-state attorneys who are representing tribes in Indian Child Welfare cases are permitted to appear *pro hac vice* as of right, often without the need to associate with local attorneys. *See, e.g.*, Neb. Rev. Stat. 43-1504(3); Arizona Court r. 39a; Colorado Court r. 205.3(8); Kansas Court r. 116; Michigan Court r. 8.126; Minnesota Court r. 3.06; Oregon UTCR 3.170; Washington, APR 8; and Wisconsin Court r. SCR 10.03(4).

91. *In re* Custody of C.C.M., 149 Wash. App. 184, 202 P.3d 971 (Wash. Ct. App. 2009).
92. In Interest of J.J.T., 544 S.W.3d 874 (Tex. Ct. App. 2017).
93. *See* 25 U.S.C. § 1911(c). Most courts do not list the tribe as a party in the caption of the proceedings, however.
94. 25 U.S.C. § 1912(c).
95. *See* Ressler v. C.B., 205 N.D. 216, 707 N.W.2d 705 (2005) for the proposition that permitting intervention is not an appealable final order. *See In re Baby Girl A.*, 230 Cal. App. 3d 1611 (Cal. App. 1991) for an example where a denial of the tribe's motion for intervention was appealed.
96. 25 U.S.C. § 1912(b). Failure to appoint counsel is the basis for a reversal of any action taken by a trial court. *See In re* J.W., 742 P.2d 1171 (Okla. App. 1987).
97. 25 U.S.C. § 1912(b).
98. *Id.* The statute provides that appointment of counsel for the child depends on the best interest of the child. One court has held that the ICWA, however, does not mandate the appointment of a guardian ad litem for an incompetent Indian parent. *In re* D.S.P., 458 N.W.2d 823 (1990), *aff'd*, 480 N.W.2d 234 (Wis. 1992).
99. 25 C.F.R. § 23.13 speaks of the appointment of counsel in any child custody proceeding, not just those initiated by the state.
100. *See* 25 U.S.C. § 1912(b) requiring the state court to appoint counsel "in any case the Court determines indigency."
101. *In re* I.T.S., 490 P.3d 127 (Okla. 2021) (Mother's court-appointed counsel was discharged at the conclusion of the disposition hearing, which left her without legal representation until counsel was reappointed following the filing of State's petition to terminate her parental rights over two years later; lower court judgment reversed because ICWA requires court-appointed counsel for the parent at all stages of the child custody proceeding.).
102. 455 U.S. 745 (1982). The Supreme Court has, however, refused to find that the right to counsel is a due process right in a termination proceeding. Lassiter v. Dep't of Soc. Servs., 452 U.S. 18 (1981).
103. *See Lassiter,* 452 U.S. at 34.

104. The procedure for seeking reimbursement from the Department of the Interior is set out in 25 C.F.R. § 23.13.
105. *In re* the Welfare of the Child of S.L.J., 782 N.W.2d 549 (Minn. Ct. App. 2010).
106. It should be noted that this was updated in the 2016 regulations and practitioners should be sure to refer to the most recent version of this regulation.
107. *See* 25 C.F.R. § 23.13(b)(6).
108. *In re* R.D.C. *ex rel.* C.E.D., 8 Indian Law Rptr. 5071 (1981).
109. 25 U.S.C. § 1912 (b) (state court may appoint attorney for the child if it finds that it is in the child's best interest).
110. *See, e.g.*, ARIZ. REV. STAT. § 8-221(I).
111. *See* 25 C.F.R. § 23.13(b)(3).
112. In the Interest of D.H. Jr., 401 P.3d 163 (Kan. Ct. App. 2017).
113. *See* 25 U.S.C. § 1912(e),(f).
114. For instance, ICWA requires that active efforts be made to prevent the breakup of an Indian family, 25 U.S.C. § 1912(d), and Title IV-E requires the state to make reasonable efforts to avoid a removal of a child from his or her home. 42 U.S.C. § 671(a)(13). These standards are not identical but are conceptually similar. *See* discussion associated with footnotes 153 and 154.
115. *In re* E.M., 466 N.W.2d 168 (S.D. 1991) (holding state court must not only demonstrate that ICWA standards are met but also that termination is the least restrictive alternative); *In re* D.S.P., 166 Wis. 2d 464, 480 N.W.2d 234 (Wis. 1992) (holding trial court must not only apply ICWA standard in termination proceeding but must also apply relevant state law, which is not superseded by the ICWA).
116. 25 U.S.C. § 1922.
117. 25 C.F.R. § 23.113; BIA GUIDELINES, *supra* note 16, § C.1.
118. *In re* Dependency of A.W, 24 Wn. App. 2d 76, 519 P.3d 262 (Wash. Ct. App. 2022).
119. 25 C.F.R. § 23.113(a).
120. *Id.* § 23.113(c); BIA GUIDELINES, *supra* note 16, § C.3.

121. 25 C.F.R. § 23.113(b). A federal district court ruled that the procedures followed in a county of South Dakota, which effectively prevented parents from presenting evidence at the emergency hearing stage, violated the ICWA and Due Process Clause. Oglala Sioux Tribe v. Van Hunnik, 100 F. Supp. 3d 749 (D.S.D. 2015). On appeal, the case was overturned on procedural grounds. Oglala Sioux Tribe v. Fleming, 904 F.3d 603 (2018).
122. 25 C.F.R. § 23.113(d).
123. *Id.* § 23.113(e); BIA GUIDELINES, *supra* note 16, § C.5.
124. *See, e.g.*, State *ex rel.* Children, Youth & Families Dep't v. Marlene C., 149 N.M. 315, 248 P.3d 863 (2011); Interest of A.M., 570 S.W.3d 860 (Tex. Ct. App. 2018).
125. *In re* Dependency of J.M.W., 199 Wn.2d 837, 841, 514 P.3d 186 (2022) (interpreting the Washington ICWA).
126. BIA GUIDELINES, *supra* note 16, § C.9; 25 C.F.R. § 23.113(d)(3); *see also* Interest of A.M., 570 S.W.3d 860 (Tex. Ct. App. 2018).
127. 25 U.S.C. § 1912(d).
128. *Id.* § 1912(e).
129. *See id.* § 1911(b).
130. 25 U.S.C. § 1916(b) stipulates that any further placement of an Indian child, after the initial removal and placement, shall also be subject to the requirements of the ICWA, except when the child is returned to the parent or Indian custodian from whom the child was originally removed.
131. *See* 42 U.S.C. § 671(a)(15)(B).
132. *See* 25 U.S.C. § 1912(d).
133. Indian Child Welfare Act of 1977: Hearing on S. 1214 before the Senate Select Committee on Indian Affairs, 95th Cong., at 117–18.
134. *Id.*
135. *See* 25 U.S.C. § 1912(d).
136. *See, e.g.*, State *ex rel.* CYFD v. Eric E., 544 P.3d 307 (N.M. Ct. App. 2023) (agency must start active efforts promptly after referral to the agency; where voluntary placement agreement was entered into and it was clear that if no active efforts were provided an involuntary proceeding would likely be

required, the active efforts requirement was triggered at the time that the voluntary placement was made).

137. *In re* Interest of Shayla H., 289 Neb. 473, 855 N.W.2d 774 (2014).
138. *See, e.g.*, State *ex rel.* Children, Youth & Families Dep't v. Marlene C., 149 N.M. 315, 248 P.3d 863 (2011). State *ex rel.* Juv. Dep't v. Charles, 688 P.2d 1354 (Or. App. 1984).
139. *In re* Dependency of J.M.W., 199 Wn.2d 837, 841, 514 P.3d 186 (2022) (interpreting the Washington ICWA).
140. *See* B.R.T. v. Exec. Dir., 391 N.W.2d 594 (N.D. 1986); *but see* NEB. CODE § 43-1506(4) requiring active efforts under state law when there is a voluntary placement.
141. State *ex rel.* CYFD v. Eric E., 544 P.3d 307 (N.M. Ct. App. 2023).
142. State *ex. rel.* CYFD v. Maisie Y., 489 P.3d 964 (N.M. Ct. App. 2021) (State must prove that active efforts were provided beyond a reasonable doubt in a termination case.); *In re* B.Y., 393 Mont. 530, 432 P.3d 129 (2018) (remanded case and ordered the trial court to "document in detail" if the Department met its burden of providing active efforts by clear and convincing evidence prior to removal and beyond a reasonable doubt prior to termination); *In re* Welfare of M.S.S., 465 N.W.2d 412 (Minn. Ct. App. 1991) (finding state failed to demonstrate beyond a reasonable doubt that remedial services had been provided when the state failed to place Indian child with a relative who could care for the child). *Accord In re* L.N.W., 457 N.W.2d 17 (Iowa App. 1990); *cf.* People *ex rel.* L.O.L., 197 P.3d 291, 294 (Colo. Ct. App. 2008) (In an ICWA case, all relevant criteria for termination determination must be established by proof beyond a reasonable doubt.).
143. BIA GUIDELINES, *supra* note 16, § E.6.
144. *In re* Annette P., 589 A.2d 924 (Me. 1991) (clear and convincing evidence of active efforts in a termination proceeding); *In re* Roe, 281 Mich. App. 88, 764 N.W.2d 789 (Mich. Ct. App. 2008) (same); *In re* Vaughn R., 770 N.W.2d 795 (Wis. Ct. App. 2009) (same); *In re* Walter W., 744 N.W.2d 55 (Neb. 2008) (clear and convincing evidence, but at least some of the efforts must be culturally relevant); *In re* Dependency of A.M., 106 Wn.

App. 123, 22 P.3d 828 (Wash. Ct. App. 2001) (clear, cogent, and convincing evidence required); *In re* Interest of Nery V. v. Mario V., 22 Neb. App. 959, 864 N.W.2d 728 (Neb. Ct. App. 2015) (clear and convincing standard in a termination proceeding, preponderance of the evidence standard in a foster care placement proceeding); *but see* K.N. v. State, 856 P.2d 468 (Alaska 1993) (preponderance of the evidence in all proceedings); *In re* Doe, 342 P.3d 632 (Idaho 2015) (same).

145. *See In re* T.S., 315 P.3d 1030 (Okla. Ct. Civ. App. 2014); In the Interest of J.I.H., 768 N.W.2d 168 (S.D. 2009).
146. 25 C.F.R. § 23.120(b). The Department of Interior recommends that the State agency include in its documentation, the issues the family is facing that the State agency is targeting with the active efforts (which should be the issues threatening the breakup of the family or preventing reunification), a list of active efforts the State agency determines would best address the issues and the reasoning for choosing those specific active efforts, dates, persons contacted, and other details evidencing how the State agency provided active efforts, and the results of the active efforts provided and, where the results were less than satisfactory, whether the State agency adjusted the active efforts to better address the issues. BIA GUIDELINES, *supra* note 16, § E.6.
147. Bill S. v. DHSS, 436 P.3d 976 (Alaska 2019); *In re* B.Y., 393 Mont. 530, 432 P.3d 129 (2018).
148. *In re* Dependency of G.J.A., 197 Wn.2d 868, 888, 489 P.3d. 631 (2021). This is a recommended practice in the BIA guidelines, but not explicitly required by the regulations. BIA GUIDELINES, *supra* note 16, § E.5.
149. Dep't of Health & Hum. Servs. v. J.G., 260 Or. App. 500, 317 P.3d 936 (2014).
150. The requirement to search for extended family and enlist them in providing support for the child and family is in addition to and separate from the requirement to place the child with extended family as a preferred placement when removal is required. *Cf.* Interest of M.D., 920 N.W.2d 496 (S.D. 2018) (compliance with placement preferences is generally not a factor in determining whether active efforts were made).

151. 25 C.F.R. § 23.2.
152. *Id.*
153. *Id.*
154. Winston J. v. State, 134 P.3d 343, 347 n.18 (Alaska 2006); K.M. v. V.K.L., 512 P.2d 132 (Colo. 2022); *In re* J.L., 770 N.W.2d 853, 865 (Mich. 2009); *In re* Welfare of Children of S.W., 727 N.W.2d 144, 150 (Minn. Ct. App. 2007); *In re* A.N., 106 P.3d 556, 560 (Mont. 2005); *In re* Interest of Walter W., 744 N.W.2d 55, 61 (Neb. 2008); State of New Mexico v. Yodell B., 367 P.3d 881 (N.M. Ct. App. 2015) (citing 2015 BIA guidelines); *In re* J.S., 177 P.3d 590, 593 (Okla. Civ. App. 2008); Dep't of Human Services v. K.C.J., 207 P.3d 423, 425 (Or. Ct. App. 2009); People in Interest of P.S.E., 816 N.W.2d 110, 115 (S.D. 2012); *In re* C.D., 200 P.3d 194, 205 (Utah Ct. App. 2008). *Contra* Adoption of Hannah S., 142 Cal. App. 4th 988, 998, 48 Cal. Rptr. 3d 605, 612 (2006).
155. *See, e.g., In re* G.S., 312 Mont. 108, 59 P.3d 1063 (Mont. 2012); Letitia v. Super. Ct., 81 Cal. App. 4th 1009, 1016, 97 Cal. Rptr. 2d 303 (Cal. App. 2000).
156. *In re* D.S., 806 N.W.2d 458 (Iowa Ct. App. 2011); *see also In re* Welfare of Child of E.A.C., 812 N.W.2d 165, 174 (Minn. Ct. App. 2012) ("a rigorous and concerted level of case work that uses the prevailing social and cultural values, conditions and way of life of the Indian child's tribe . . .").
157. *See, e.g.*, Christina v. State of Alaska, 254 P.3d 1095 (Alaska 2011); *In re* Roe, 281 Mich. App. 88, 764 N.W.2d 789 (Mich. Ct. App. 2008); *In re* S.H.E., 2012 SD 88 (S.D. 2012); *In re* C.D., 200 P.3d 194, 205 (Utah Ct. App. 2008); *see also In re* J.S., 177 P.3d 590, 593 (Okla. Civ. App. 2008) ("requires leading the horse to water").
158. *In re* K.B. & T.B., 370 Mont. 254, 301 P.3d 836 (Mont. 2013); *but see* Jude M. v. DHSS, 394 P.3d 543 (Alaska 2017) (services provided by third parties can be included as part of the active efforts provided by the agency).
159. *See, e.g.*, Carson P. *ex rel.* Foreman v. Heineman, 240 F.R.D. 456, 474, 500 (D. Neb. 2007); *In re* Roe, 281 Mich. App. 88, 764 N.W.2d 789 (Mich. Ct. App. 2008); *In re* Welfare of Children of S.W., 727 N.W.2d 144, 150 (Minn. App. 2007); *In re* Walter W., 274 Neb. 859, 744 N.W.2d 55 (2008).

160. 25 C.F.R. § 23.2; *see also, e.g., In re* Dependency of G.J.A., 197 Wn.2d 868, 888, 489 P.3d. 631 (2021).

161. *In re* Dependency of G.J.A., 197 Wn.2d 868, 888, 489 P.3d. 631 (2021); State ex rel. CYFD v. Eric E., 544 P.3d 307 (N.M. Ct. App. 2023).

162. BIA GUIDELINES, *supra* note 16, § E.5.

163. Pub. Law No. 105-89. The ASFA was enacted in 1997 in response to a growing dissatisfaction with the child welfare system and the length of time some children were spending in substitute care. One of the goals of Congress was to narrow the "reasonable efforts" requirement of federal law and to remove the obligation of states to provide "reasonable efforts" in certain circumstances when the requirement conflicted with the safety of a child and the need of the child for a permanent placement outside the parental home. As one court has stated the "ASFA establishes a child protection system that subordinates parental rights to the paramount concern for the health and safety of the child[.]" State *ex rel.* D.B., 670 N.W.2d 67 (S.D. 2003); *see also* New Jersey v. A.R.G., 361 N.J. Super. 46, 824 A.2d 213, 233 (2003). The ASFA is the congressional response to concerns that the preexisting law acted as a barrier to the adoption of abused and neglected children. H.R. REP. NO. 105-77, at 8 (1997).

164. Specifically, 42 U.S.C. § 671(a)(15)(D) mandates that a state need not provide reasonable efforts in the following circumstances:

> (D) reasonable efforts of the type described in subparagraph (B) shall not be required to be made with respect to a parent of a child if a court of competent jurisdiction has determined that—(i) the parent has subjected the child to aggravated circumstances (as defined in State law, which definition may include but need not be limited to abandonment, torture, chronic abuse, and sexual abuse); (ii) the parent has—(I) committed murder (which would have been an offense under section 1111(a) Title 18, if the offense had occurred in the special maritime or territorial jurisdiction of the United States) of another child of the parent; (II) committed voluntary manslaughter (which would have been an offense under section 1112(a) of Title 18, if the offense

had occurred in the special maritime or territorial jurisdiction of the United States) of another child of the parent; (III) aided or abetted, attempted, conspired, or solicited to commit such a murder or such a voluntary manslaughter; or (IV) committed a felony assault that results in serious bodily injury to the child or another child of the parent; or (iii) the parental rights of the parent to a sibling have been terminated involuntarily.

165. It should be noted that this statute mandates that services need not be provided in certain circumstances (mandatory aggravated circumstances) and leaves the definition of other aggravated circumstances to the states (optional aggravated circumstances). *See* 42 U.S.C. § 671(a)(15)(D)(1). The National Conference of State Legislatures maintains a web page that reveals the wide diversity of "optional aggravated circumstances" enacted by state legislatures in response to the ASFA, http://www.ncsl.org. One state, Montana, explicitly exempted Indian children from coverage under the ASFA. MONT. CODE ANN. § 41-3-423(2) (2005).

166. *In re* J.L., 770 N.W.2d 853, 865 (Mich. 2009); *In re* Interest of Jamyia M., 18 Neb. App. 679, 791 N.W.2d 343 (Neb. Ct. App. 2010); *In re* J.S.B. Jr., 2005 SD 3, 691 N.W.2d 611 (S.D. 2005); *but see* J.S. v. State, 50 P.3d 388 (Alaska 2002).

167. In general, specific legislative enactments take precedence over general statutory enactments, *see, e.g.*, Morton v. Mancari, 417 U.S. 535, 550–51 (1974), and Indian-specific statutes are to be liberally interpreted for the benefit of the people on whose behalf they were enacted, *see, e.g.*, Ramah Navajo Sch. Bd. v. Bureau of Revenue, 458 U.S. 832, 838 (1982). *See generally* DAVID SIMMONS & JACK TROPE, P.L. 105-89 ADOPTION AND SAFE FAMILIES ACT OF 1997: ISSUES FOR TRIBES AND STATES SERVING INDIAN CHILDREN 6–7 (The National Resource Center for Organizational Improvement 1999).

168. *See, e.g.*, Adoption of Arnold, 50 Mass. App. Ct 743, 741 N.E.2d 456 (Mass. App. 2001) (court did not err in terminating father's parental rights for sexual abuse notwithstanding lack of services to him); *In re* T.H., 105 P.3d 354 (Okla. App. 2005) (severe abuse inflicted upon children warranted waiving remedial services).

169. *See, e.g., In re* K.B., 173 Cal. App. 4th 1275, 93 Cal. Rptr. 751 (Cal. App. 2d Dist. 2009) (finding that further efforts would be futile because father was a multiple sex offender and incarcerated); *see also* In the Interest of A.V. and J.V., 297 P.3d 1019 (Colo. Ct. App. 2012).
170. *In re* Dependency of G.J.A., 197 Wn.2d 868, 888, 489 P.3d. 631 (2021) (in rejecting futility doctrine, the Court noted that generational trauma may be a reason why parents may not cooperate with the state agency).
171. *See, e.g., In re* William G., 89 Cal. App. 4th 423, 107 Cal. Rptr. 2d 436 (Cal. App. 2001) (rejecting father's argument that termination inappropriate because he was denied rehabilitative efforts when he refused to avail himself of such efforts); Roy S. v. State of Alaska, 278 P.3d 886 (Alaska 2012) (holding that active efforts requirement had been met because parents had intentionally "evaded" the department).
172. Mona J. v. State, Dep't of Health & Soc. Servs., 511 P.3d 553 (Alaska 2022).
173. *In re* Welfare of Children of S.W., 727 N.W.2d 144 (Minn. Ct. App. 2007). At least one court has suggested that what constitutes a "reasonable period of time" may be different in an ICWA case if warranted by tribal culture or childrearing practices. *In re* E.G.M., 230 N.C. App. 196, 750 S.E.2d 857 (2013). It should also be noted that this principle does not eliminate the requirement that active efforts be made in the case of incarcerated parents. *See, e.g.,* Daschiell v. State, 222 P.3d 841 (Alaska 2009); *In re* Cari B., 327 Ill. App. 3d 743, 763 N.E.2d 917 (Ill. App. 2002); *In re* D.S.B., 2013 MT 112, 300 P.3d 702 (Mont. 2013); *In re* A.W., 284 P.3d 1233 (Or. Ct. App. 2012). The nature of the services to be provided, however, may be impacted by the incarceration. *See, e.g., In re* S.H.E., 2012 SD 88, 824 N.W.2d 420 (S.D. 2012) (holding that because father is incarcerated, services provided to non-incarcerated mother can be included as active efforts toward father because they were designed to prevent the breakup of the Indian family and, if successful, would have precluded the termination of the father's parental rights).
174. *See, e.g., In re* N.D.M., 288 N.C. App. 554, 886 S.E.2d. 640 (2023); A.A. v. Dep't of Family & Youth Servs., 982 P.2d 256, 261 (Alaska 1999).
175. Anton K. v. Alaska DCFS, 554 P.3d 456 (Alaska 2024).

176. In the commentary to the regulations, the Department states that the factors in the ASFA may be considered by a court in determining whether sufficient active efforts have taken place in a given case. Dep't of the Interior, Bureau of Indian Affairs, Final Rule Indian Child Welfare Act Proceedings, 81 Fed. Reg. 38778, 38814 (June 14, 2016).
177. 133 S. Ct. 2552 (2013).
178. *Id.* at 2559.
179. *Id.*
180. *Id.*
181. *Id.* at 2564.
182. *Id.* at 2563–64. The Court did not attempt to explain whether and how the "reasonable efforts" requirement in Title IV-E might be applicable to the birth father in this case or in similar cases.
183. *Id.* at 2562–63. Of course, attorneys for the father were not in agreement that he had "abandoned" the child. *See* Jack Trope & Adrian Smith, *The Continued Protection of Indian Children and Families After* Adoptive Couple v. Baby Girl: *What the Case Means and How to Respond*, 2 Am. Indian L.J. 434 (2014) at 442–46 for a summary of the underlying facts of the case.
184. *Id.* at 2576 n.3 (Sotomayor, J., dissenting). *See also* Child Welfare Information Gateway, *State Statutes: Definitions of Child Abuse and Neglect* (2022), https://www.childwelfare.gov/resources/definitions-child-abuse-and-neglect/ (last visited Aug. 10, 2025). Approximately 19 states and the District of Columbia include abandonment in their definitions of abuse or neglect, generally as a type of neglect. Approximately 24 states, Guam, Puerto Rico, and the Virgin Islands provide definitions for abandonment that are separate from the definition of neglect. *Id.* at 5. Child Welfare Information Gateway, *State Statutes: Grounds for Involuntary Termination of Parental Rights* (2021), https://www.childwelfare.gov/resources/grounds-involuntary-termination-parental-rights/ (last visited Aug. 10, 2025). The grounds for involuntary termination of parental rights are specific circumstances under which the child cannot safely be returned home because of risk of harm by the parent or the inability of

the parent to provide for the child's basic needs. Each state is responsible for establishing its own statutory grounds, and these vary by state. The most common statutory grounds for determining parental unfitness include Abandonment of the child. *Id.* at 2.

185. 133 S. Ct. at 2563.
186. *Id.*
187. *Id.* at 2571. It should be noted that there is nothing in the opinion that would preclude active efforts in any case. The Court's holding was only that it is not required in certain circumstances.
188. 25 C.F.R. § 23.120 (prior to ordering an involuntary placement or termination of parental rights, the court must conclude that active efforts have been made).
189. *In re* P.T.D., 392 Mont. 376, 424 P.3d 619 (2018); *In re* J.S., 374 Mont. 329, 321 P.3d 103 (Mont. 2014); *In re* S.B.C., 377 Mont. 400, 340 P.3d 534 (2014); *In re* G.V., 2016 OK CIV APP 6 (Okla. Ct. Civ. App. 2015); *but see In re* Beers, 325 Mich. App. 653, 926 N.W.2d. 832 (2018) (quoting Justice Breyer's opinion as a reason to limit *Baby Girl* to the type of fact pattern that was present in the *Baby Girl* case).
190. 25 C.F.R. § 23.2.
191. *In re* C.D., 200 P.3d 194 (Utah Ct. App. 2008).
192. *In re* Interest of Shayla H., 289 Neb. 473, 855 N.W.2d 774 (2014).
193. *In re* Welfare of Child of E.A.C., 812 N.W.2d 165 (Minn. Ct. App. 2012), *rev. denied*. 25 U.S.C. § 1916(a) provides that a parent or Indian custodian may petition for return of a child if a final decree of adoption has been set aside and that the court shall grant the petition unless it is not in the best interests of the child.
194. Dep't of Health & Hum. Servs. v. J.G., 260 Or. App. 500, 317 P.3d 1936 (Or. Ct. App. 2014).
195. Ronan F. v. DFCS, 539 P.3d 507 (Alaska 2023).
196. Haaland v. Brackeen, 599 U.S. 255, 143 S. Ct. 1609, 1633 (2023).
197. *In re* the Petition of N.B., 199 P.3d 16 (Colo. Ct. App. 2007), *cert. denied*, 2008 WL 757927; *In re* Adoption of T.A.W., 186 Wash. 2d 828, 383 P.3d 492 (2016).

198. S.S. v. Stephanie H., 241 Ariz. 419, 388 P.3d 569 (Ariz. Ct. App. 2017), *cert. denied*, 538 U.S. 959 (2017).
199. O'Brien v. Delaplain, 556 P.3d 1170 (Alaska 2024).
200. S.S. v. Stephanie H., 241 Ariz. 419, 388 P.3d 569 (Ariz. Ct. App. 2017) *cert. denied*, 538 U.S. 959 (2017). *See also* O'Brien v. Delaplain, 556 P.3d 1170 (Alaska 2024) (Aunt and uncle met the active efforts requirement by attempting to set up counseling for the children and family, scheduling weekly video chats, paying the child's mother to visit her child and allowing her to stay with them while visiting, and by seeking to assist the mother in finding housing and employment near their home.).
201. 25 U.S.C. § 1912(e).
202. *Id.* § 1912(f).
203. H. Rep. No. 95-1386, at 22, *reprinted in* 1978 U.S.C.C.A.N. 7530.
204. 25 C.F.R. § 23.122(c). The issue of whether a supervisor can be a QEW is an open question that has been raised in some cases, *see, e.g.*, Garris v. Arkansas Dep't of Hum. Servs., 619 S.W.3d 67 (Ark. App. 2021) (ruling that the issue had not been preserved for appeal), and is one of the issues that may be addressed in a state ICWA. *See, e.g.*, Wash. Rev. Code § 13.38.130 (Washington state law prohibits supervisor from being a QEW.).
205. *In re* Custody of S.E.G., 507 N.W.2d 872, 844 (Minn. Ct. App. 1993); *In re* T.H., 105 P.3d 354 (Okla. App. 2005) (member of Indian children's tribe not required to have educational qualifications for expert testimony).
206. Thomas H. v. State of Alaska, 184 P.3d 9 (Alaska 2008).
207. 25 C.F.R. § 23.122(a).
208. *See, e.g.*, L.G. v. Dep't of Health & Soc. Servs., 14 P.3d 946 (Alaska 2001) (social worker familiar with Native culture suffices).
209. *See, e.g.*, Brenda O. v. Arizona Dep't of Econ. Security, 244 P.3d 574 (Ariz. Ct. App. 2010); People *ex rel.* K.D., 155 P.3d 634 (Colo. Ct. App. 2007); *In re* Guardianship of L.N.P., 294 P.3d 904 (Wyo. 2013).
210. *See In re* T.W., 2003 MT 197N, 77 P.3d 553 (2003) (tribal elder could testify in ICWA case even though she was not degreed in substance abuse or social work field).

211. Elizabeth Low, *Keeping Cultural Bias Out of the Courtroom: How ICWA "Qualified Expert Witnesses" Make a Difference*, 44 AM. INDIAN L. REV. 43, 61 (2019).
212. *Id.*
213. 25 C.F.R. § 23.122(b); BIA GUIDELINES, *supra* note 16, § G.2.
214. *See, e.g.*, CYFD v. Douglas B., 511 P.3d 357 (N.M. Ct. App. 2021) (Although QEW had been the tribe's ICWA caseworker for five years and been qualified as a QEW more than 50 times, had knowledge of the tribe's cultural and social practices, and held a bachelor's degree in criminal justice, she had not explained how this background qualified her to express an opinion regarding the likelihood of future emotional or physical damage to the child.); Oliver N. v. State of Alaska, 444 P.3d 171 (Alaska 2019) (Tribal elder, although qualified to testify to tribal cultural standards and childrearing norms, could not be qualified as a QEW because his extensive life experience as a community leader and grandfather was insufficient to qualify him to testify about the likelihood of harm should the child be returned to the father.); Adoption of Leonard, 103 Mass. App. Ct. 419, 218 N.E.3d 673 (2023) (Native lawyer experienced in ICWA and trained in Indian studies who did not have any training in social work, psychology or counseling was not qualified to opine on the likelihood of harm if the child was returned to the mother's custody.).
215. *See, e.g.*, O'Brien v. Delaplain, 556 P.3d 1170 (Alaska 2024).
216. *See, e.g.*, *In re* Interest of Birdhead, 331 N.W.2d 785 (Neb. 1983).
217. *State ex rel.* Juv. Dep't v. Charles, 688 P.2d 1354 (Or. App. 1984).
218. 25 C.F.R. § 23.122(a); BIA GUIDELINES, *supra* note 16, § G.2; *see also, e.g.*, State of Alaska v. Cissy, 513 P.3d 999 (Alaska 2022) (Based upon the regulations and guidelines, the court narrowed the scope of prior cases allowing QEW testimony by individuals who did not have the requisite cultural knowledge and opined that the circumstances where a QEW need not have cultural knowledge are "very limited."); *but cf.* In Interest of Cameron L. and David L., 32 Neb. App. 578, 3 N.W.3d 376 (2024); In the Interest of M.S., 624 N.W.2d 678 (N.D. 2001); Geiss v. State, 69 P.3d 1226

(Okla. Civ. App. 2003); and *In re* Lucas, 33 P.3d 1001 (Or. Ct. App. 2001) as examples of cases where the QEW was not required to have specialized knowledge of Indian cultural practices because cultural bias was not an issue. *See also* O'Brien v. Delaplain, 556 P.3d 1170 (Alaska 2024), where the court allowed for the aggregation of the testimony of QEWs, one with specialized knowledge in her field of expertise and other with knowledge about cultural and social standards.

219. *See, e.g.*, MICH. COMP. LAWS § 712B.17(1) and WIS. STAT. § 48.028(g); BIA GUIDELINES, *supra* note 16, § G.2.

220. *In re* Brandon T., 164 Cal. App. 4th 1400, 1414 (Cal. App. 2008); *see also In re* the Welfare of M.S.S., 465 N.W.2d 412, 417 (Minn. App. 1991); *In re* K.H. & K.L.E., 294 Mont. 466, 981 P.2d 1190 (Mont. 1999); State *ex rel.* Juv. Dep't v. Charles, 688 P.2d 1354 (Or. App. 1984); Michigan Indian Family Preservation Act, M.C.L.A. § 712B.17; WIS. STAT. § 48.028(g).

221. BIA GUIDELINES, *supra* note 16, § G.2; *see also In re* M.H., 691 N.W.2d 622 (S.D. 2005) (reversing a termination of parental rights order based upon the testimony of a former tribal prosecutor and director of ICWA program for two Dakota tribes in case involving Lakota children); *In re* Welfare of Children of S.W., 727 N.W.2d 144 (Minn. Ct. App. 2007) (expert member of larger consortium that includes parent's tribe qualifies as QEW even though not a member of the Indian child's tribe).

222. *See, e.g.*, *In re* K.S.D., 2017 ND 289, 904 N.W.2d 479 (2017); *In re* K.H. & K.L.E., 294 Mont. 466, 981 P.2d 1190 (Mont. 1999); Doty-Jabbar v. Dallas Cnty., 19 S.W.3d 870, 877 (Tex. App. 5th Dist. 2000); *see also In re* Welfare of S.R.K. & O.A.K, 911 N.W.2d 821 (Minn. 2018), *rev. denied* (where QEW testified that continued custody by the mother would cause serious emotional or physical harm to the child, but did not provide similar testimony regarding the father, the court reversed the termination of parental rights in regard to the father and remanded the case); In the Interest of D.L.N.G., 2019 WL 3214151 (Tex. Ct. App. 2019) (applied the QEW to appointment of foster parents as managing conservators and reversed and remanded the case since there has been no QEW testimony before the trial court); Navajo Nation v. Dep't of Child Safety, 246 Ariz. 463, 441 P.3d 982

(2019) (as QEW requirement applies to petition for permanent guardianship, case must be vacated and remanded because no QEW testimony had been offered).

223. *In re* Tamika R., 973 A.2d 547 (R.I. 2009).
224. *In re* Welfare of S.R.K. & O.A.K, 911 N.W.2d 821 (Minn. 2018).
225. In the Interest of T.W., B.S., H.S., & H.W., 2022 WL 2293919 (Tex. Ct. App. 2022).
226. *In re* McCarrick/Lamoreaux, 307 Mich. App. 436, 861 N.W.2d 303 (Mich. App. 2014), *vacated on other grounds*, 495 Mich. 986, 844 N.W.2d 126 (2014); *In re* E.G.M., 230 N.C. App. 196, 750 S.E.2d 857 (2013); 25 C.F.R. § 23.122(a); *but see* Steven H. v. Arizona Dep't of Econ. Security, 190 P.3d 180 (Ariz. 2008) (QEW must address future harm, but expert testimony need not recite the specific language of the statute).
227. State of Alaska v. Cissy, 513 P.3d 999 (Alaska 2022).
228. *In re* I.W., 2018 OK Civ. App. 6, 419 P.3d 362 (2017) (where QEW was unsure about whether continued custody by the father would result in serious physical or emotional harm to the child, the agency has not met its burden of proof); *In re* Payne/Pumphrey/Fortson, 311 Mich. App. 49, 874 N.W.2d 205 (2015), *app. denied*, 498 Mich. 869, 866 N.W.2d 458 (2015) (where QEW testified that continued custody of child would not cause serious emotional or physical harm to the child, § 1912(f) standard not met); In the Interest of M.F., 225 P.3d 1177 (Kan. 2010) (QEW opinion must support the ultimate finding of the court); Thomas H. v. State of Alaska, 184 P.3d 9 (Alaska 2008) (QEW testimony must support a TPR decision, but need not be the sole basis for the decision); Steven H. v. Arizona Dep't of Econ. Security, 190 P.3d 180 (Ariz. 2008) (same).
229. *Steven H.*, 190 P.3d 180.
230. *See* C.J. v. Dep't of Health & Soc. Servs., 18 P.3d 1214 (Alaska 2001) (reversing a termination of parental rights because the doctor who testified to the serious emotional harm that would befall the child only conducted a paper review of the case); BIA Guidelines, *supra* note 16, § G.2, *but see* In the Interest of Cameron L. & David L., 32 Neb. App. 578, 3 N.W.3d 376 (2024) (QEW need not have personal contact with the parents); J.A.

v. Alaska, 50 P.3d 395 (Alaska 2002) (finding hypothetical questions to experts who reviewed file only and did not work with mother sufficient to support evidence by qualified expert witness); *In re* A.N., 106 P.3d 556 (Mont. 2005) (allowing expert to testify based solely on paper review of file without visiting with any of the parties to the case); S.S. v. State, 2002 UT App. 340, 57 P.3d 1130 (Utah Ct. App. 2002) (finding paper review by expert combined with participation in staffings on case satisfied the ICWA).

231. Interest of A.P., 2022 ND 131, 976 N.W.2d 244 (2022).
232. *In re* Riva M., 235 Cal. App. 3d 403, 286 Cal. Rptr. 592 (Cal. App. 4th Dist. 1991); *In re* R.L.F., 437 N.W.2d 599 (Iowa Ct. App. 1989); *In re* Inquiry into K.M.G. and J.G., 309 Mont. 529, 43 P.3d 983 (2002) (holding parents' failure to object to questions to alleged expert witness bars appellate review).
233. *See In re* S.M.H., 103 P.3d 976, 982 (Kan. Ct. App. 2005).
234. In the Interest of K.B., 2024 UT App. 114, 557 P.3d 210 (2024).
235. 25 U.S.C. § 1912(e).
236. *See, e.g.*, Mont. Code. Ann. § 41-3-6002 (2005).
237. H.R. Rep. No. 95-1386, at 10 (1978), *reprinted in* 1978 U.S.C.C.A.N. 7530.
238. *See* 25 U.S.C. § 1921.
239. Mississippi Band of Choctaw Indians v. Holyfield, 490 U.S. 30, 44 (1989).
240. *See, e.g., In re* Interest of Emma J., 789 N.W.2d 528 (Neb. Ct. App. 2010).
241. Diego K. v. Alaska Dep't of Health & Soc. Servs., 411 P.3d 622, 628 (Alaska 2018).
242. 25 C.F.R. § 23.121(c); see discussion in Termination of Parental Rights later in this chapter for further information about this requirement.
243. *See, e.g.*, N.M. Stat. Ann. § 32A-4-2, defining abandonment as any child left with another person for a period of three months or more.
244. H.R. Rep. No. 95-1386, at 10 (1978), *reprinted in* 1978 U.S.C.C.A.N. 7530.
245. *See* Colo. Rev. Stat. § 19-3-604(b)(VI).
246. H.R. Rep. No. 95-1386, at 10 (1978), *reprinted in* 1978 U.S.C.C.A.N. 7530.
247. Dep't of the Interior, Bureau of Indian Affairs, Final Rule Indian Child Welfare Act Proceedings, 81 Fed. Reg. 38778, 38829 (June 14, 2016).

248. *See In re* Appeal in Coconino Cnty. Juvenile Action J-10175, 736 P.2d 829 (Ariz. App. 1987); *In re* Adoption of Baade, 462 N.W. 2d 485 (S.D. 1990).
249. *See In re* Adoption of a Child of Indian Heritage, 543 A.2d 925 (N.J. 1988).
250. 570 U.S. 637, 133 S. Ct. 2552 (2013).
251. *In re* J.S., 374 Mont. 329, 321 P.3d 103 (2014).
252. 133 S. Ct. at 2571.
253. *See* Trope & Smith, *supra* note 183; see further discussion about *Adoptive Couple v. Baby Girl* at pages 24–26.
254. *See, e.g., In re* J.J.G., 32 Kan. App. 448, 83 P.3d 1264 (Kan. App. 2004) (non-Indian father can appeal notice deficiency issue under the ICWA); *In re* Adoption of Micah H., 295 Neb. 213, 887 N.W.2d 859 (2018) (ICWA and NICWA applied to non-Indian father).
255. *See* 25 U.S.C. § 1916(b); *cf. In re* E.R. v. J.R. et al., 18 Cal. App. 5th 891, 227 Cal. Rptr. 3d 264 (Ct. App. 1st Dist., Div. 4, Cal. 2017) (holding that after a minor's mother revoked the maternal uncle's Indian custodian status for purposes of ICWA, the uncle no longer was party to the case and lacked standing to make objections in the proceedings).
256. 455 U.S. at 753 (1982).
257. *Id.* at 769.
258. *Id.*
259. 25 U.S.C. § 1912(f).
260. *See id.* § 1912(d).
261. *See* footnotes 142–144.
262. 25 U.S.C. § 1912(f).
263. *See* footnotes 226 and 228.
264. In the Interest of R.H., 693 S.W.3d 846 (Tex. Ct. App. 2024), *rev. denied*; Valerie M. v. Arizona Dep't of Econ. Security, 198 P.3d 1203 (Ariz. 2009); In the Interest of H.A.M., 25 Kan. App. 2d 289, 961 P.2d 716 (1998); *In re* Bluebird, 411 S.E.2d 820 (N.C. App. 1992); *In re* Dependency of Roberts, 732 P.2d 528 (Wash. App. 1987); *In re* Interest of D.S.P., 166 Wis. 2d 464, 480 N.W.2d 234 (Wis. 1992). In these cases, the courts seem to use a hybrid burden of proof scheme, with state grounds having to be proven by clear and convincing evidence but evidence beyond a reasonable doubt being

required for the showing of serious emotional or physical harm required by § 1912(f) of the ICWA. *See also* New York City Dep't of Soc. Servs. on Behalf of Oscar C., Jr. v. Oscar C., 192 A.D.2d 280, 600 N.Y.S.2d 957 (N.Y.A.D. 2 Dep't 1993) (court holds that at adjudication preponderance of the evidence standard for court findings of fact did not conflict with ICWA); *but see In re* W.D.H., 43 S.W.3d 30 (Tex. App. 2001) (holding that ICWA preempted the state standard).

265. *Id.*
266. *See* 25 U.S.C. § 1912(f).
267. *See* footnote 264.
268. *In re* H.T., 378 Mont. 206, 343 P.3d 159 (2015) (where court below stated that requirements were met by clear and convincing evidence, as opposed to beyond a reasonable doubt, this violates the ICWA and the case must be remanded); *In re* W.D.H., 43 S.W.3d 30 (Tex. App. 2001); Doty-Jabbar v. Dallas Cnty., 19 S.W.3d 870 (Tex App. 2000) (holding failure to adhere to federal standards on qualified expert witnesses and burden of persuasion commanded reversal of a termination of parental rights over Indian child).
269. *In re* Welfare of Child E.A.C., 812 N.W.2d 165 (Minn. Ct. App. 2012).
270. *In re* L.D., 391 Mont. 33, 414 P.3d 768 (2018).
271. 25 C.F.R. § 23.121(c).
272. *Id.* § 23.121(d).
273. Larry W. v. State Dep't of Health & Soc. Servs., 208 P.3d 156 (Alaska 2009); Steven H. v. Arizona Dep't of Econ. Security, 190 P.3d 180 (Ariz. 2008).
274. *In re* Roe, 764 N.W.2d 789 (Mich. Ct. App. 2008).
275. People *ex rel.* T.I., 2005 SD 125, 707 N.W.2d 826 (S.D. 2005); *In re* S.D., 402 N.W.2d 346 (S.D. 1987).
276. D.W.H. v. Cabinet for Human Resources, 706 S.W.2d 840 (Ky. App. 1986); *In re* Bluebird, 411 S.E.2d 820 (N.C. App. 1992).
277. K.N. v. State, 856 P.2d 468 (Alaska 1993).
278. Adoption of Arnold, 50 Mass. Ct. App. 743, 741 N.E.2d 456 (2001); *In re* J.J., 454 N.W.2d 317 (S.D. 1990).
279. *In re* Adoption of Baade, 462 N.W.2d 485 (S.D. 1990).

280. *In re* Annette P., 589 A.2d 924 (Me. 1991); *In re* A.R.P., 519 N.W.2d 56 (S.D. 1994); *In re* P.B., 371 N.W.2d 366 (S.D. 1989).
281. K.N. v. State, 856 P.2d 468 (Alaska 1993).
282. *In re* the Welfare of T.J.J. & G.L.J., 366 N.W.2d 651 (Minn. Ct. App. 1985).
283. *In re* Bluebird, 411 S.E.2d 820 (N.C. App. 1992); *In re* T.C., 984 A.2d 549 (Pa. Super. Ct. 2009). This particular reason for termination should be closely scrutinized in view of the new BIA regulations. In the section of the regulations dealing with placement preferences, the regulations indicate that deviation from the placement preferences should not occur solely because of bonding or attachment in a non-preferred placement made in violation of the ICWA. 25 C.F.R. § 23.132(e). In so doing, the BIA noted in its commentary that "the concepts of bonding and attachment can have serious limitations in court determinations." Dep't of the Interior, Bureau of Indian Affairs, Final Rule Indian Child Welfare Act Proceedings, 81 Fed. Reg. 38778, 38846 (June 14, 2016). *See also* In the Interest of A.R., 310 P.3d 1007 (Colo. Ct. App. 2012) (attachment to foster parents is not an adequate reason to deviate from the placement preferences). If bonding and attachment is viewed as a questionable ground for deviating from the placement preferences, it would seem to be even a stronger case that it would be a questionable rationale for imposing the severe sanction of termination of parental rights.
284. *See* State v. D.N., 2003 Okla. Ct. App. 92, 71 P.3d 43.
285. 133 S. Ct. at 2560–62.
286. *In re* Adoption of Micah H., 295 Neb. 213, 887 N.W.2d 859 (2018); *In re* P.T.D., 392 Mont. 376, 424 P.3d 619 (2018); *In re* S.B.C., 377 Mont. 400, 340 P.3d. 534 (2014).
287. *In re* Beers, 325 Mich. App. 653, 926 N.W.2d 832 (2018).
288. *See In re* S.M.H., 33 Kan. App. 424, 103 P.3d 976 (Kan. App. 2005); *In re* Sabriena B., 9 Neb. App. 888 (Neb. App. 2001) (holding failure to properly plead all required showings under the ICWA in a termination proceeding is subject to dismissal in state court even if state shows all necessary elements); *but see In re* M.R.G., 322 Mont. 60, 97 P.3d 1085 (2004) (holding failure of trial court to articulate standard for termination of parental rights

of Indian mother not reversible error when the record supported a finding beyond a reasonable doubt).

289. *See, e.g.*, G.L. v. Dep't of Child. & Families, 80 So. 3d 1065 (Fla. Ct. App. 2012); *In re* H.T., 378 Mont. 206, 343 P.3d 159 (2015); *In re* Interest of J.J.C., 302 S.W.3d 896 (Tex. Ct. App. 2009).
290. *In re* K.B. & T.B., 370 Mont. 254, 301 P.3d 836 (2013); *In re* T.W.F., 351 Mont. 233, 210 P.2d 174 (2009).
291. Idaho Dep't of Health & Welfare v. Doe (2011–20), 152 Idaho 797, 275 P.3d 23 (Ct. App. 2012).
292. *In re* C.B., 316 P.3d 177 (Mont. Sup. Ct. 2014); *see also In re* A.R.F., 2021 UT. App. 31, 484 P.3d 1185 (2021) (because TPR is factually intense, appellate court should provide a "high degree of deference" to the trial court).
293. 42 U.S.C. § 675(5)(E)(i)–(iii).
294. *Id.* § 673b.
295. *Id.* § 675(C).
296. *See* State *ex rel.* D.B., 2003 SD 113, 670 N.W.2d 67 (reconciling the ASFA and the ICWA in a termination proceeding and thus avoiding any resolution of potential conflicts between the two); *see also* Simmons & Trope, *supra* note 167.
297. *See* 25 U.S.C. § 1912(f).
298. *See* State v. Regina S., 11 Neb. App. 919, 664 N.W.2d 470 (2003).
299. 42 U.S.C. § 622(b)(7).
300. *Id.* § 675(5)(C).
301. *See* ACYF-CB-PA-01-01 (2001).
302. H.R. Rep. No. 95-1386, at 10 (1978), *reprinted in* 1978 U.S.C.C.A.N. 7530.
303. *Id.*
304. As Senator Abourezk, sponsor of the ICWA, observed, "[p]artly because of the decreasing numbers of Anglo children available for adoption and changing attitudes about interracial adoptions, the demand for Indian children has increased dramatically." 123 Cong. Rec. 21043 (1977). *See also Problems that American Indian Families Face in Raising Their Children and How These Problems Are Affected by Federal Action or Inaction: Hearings*

Before the Subcomm. on Indian Affairs, S. Comm. on Interior and Insular Affairs, 93rd Cong. (1974) [hereinafter 1974 Senate Hearing] at 146 ("[Indian] Infants under 1 year old are adopted at [a] rate . . . 139 percent greater than the rate of non-Indians in the state of Minnesota.").

305. *See, e.g.*, 1974 Senate Hearing, *supra* note 304, at 70 (referring to the adoption system as a "grey market" because "there's tremendous pressure to adopt Indian children, or have Indian children adopted out") (testimony of Bertram Hirsch for the Association on American Indian Affairs); *id.* at 161 (calling for "an investigation of agencies who deal with the Indian adoptions and make them accountable for the methods they use for transporting Indian children across the state lines and the Canadian borders") (testimony of Esther Mays, Native American Child Protection Council); *Indian Child Welfare Act of 1977: Hearing on S. 1214 Before the S. Select Committee on Indian Affairs*, 95th Cong. at 359, *viz.* [hereinafter 1977 Senate Hearing] ("Private adoption . . . process involves doctors and private attorneys who arrange for adoptions of their Indian client's children to a non-Indian through their attorney directly through a court. . . . All of us are aware of the adoption black market that has blossomed due to the effects of modern family planning efforts. Some people will pay thousands of dollars for a child. It is also well-known that Indian children have always been a prize catch in the field of adoption.") (statement of Don Milligan, State of Washington, Dep't of Soc. & Health Servs.).

306. H.R. Rep. No. 95 1386, at 11 (1978), *reprinted in* 1978 U.S.C.C.A.N. 7530.

307. *See, e.g.*, 1974 Senate Hearing, at 23 and 222–23 (testimony about woman who was tricked into signing a form that she was told would allow two non Indian women to take her child for a short visit, but which in reality was a consent to adoption, and a discussion of parents who have been "induced to waive their parental rights voluntarily without understanding the implications") As Senator Abourezk summarized, it was asserted that "in many cases they [parents] were lied to, they were given documents to sign, and they were deceived about the contents of the documents." 1974 Senate Hearing, at 463.

308. *See, e.g.*, 1974 Senate Hearing, at 61 ("[W]elfare agencies tend to think of adoption too quickly without having other options available. . . . Once you're at the point of thinking about adoption . . . welfare agencies are not making adequate use of the Indian communities themselves. They tend to look elsewhere for adoption type of homes.") (testimony of Dr. Carl Mindell, a child psychiatrist at Albany Medical College); *id.* at 116 ("The standards that have been established by adoption agencies have created an additional burden . . . as they are white status quo oriented. . . . As you well know, this automatically leaves the Indian out.") (statement of Mel Sampson, Northwest Affiliated Tribes); 1977 Senate Hearing, at 271 ("Through various ways, the State of Washington public assistance and private placing agencies can completely go around the issue and place without contact to that child's tribe, until the action is completed and irreversible," noting that of 136 Colville adoptions in the last ten years, only 20 went to Indian families and 31 were out of state.) (testimony of Virgil Gunn, Colville Business Council); 1974 Senate Hearing, at 147 (testimony of Leon Cook).
309. 25 U.S.C. § 1913(b) mandates that if an Indian parent revokes a voluntary consent, even one done in compliance with § 1913(a), the parent is entitled to regain the child upon demand.
310. 25 C.F.R. § 23.2.
311. *In re* J.M., 218 P.3d 1213 (Mont. 2009); *In re* Welfare of M.G., 201 P.3d 354 (Wash. App. 2009).
312. *See* Doe v. Hughes, 838 P.2d 804 (Alaska 1992) (court holds that it is malpractice for an attorney representing adoptive parents not to obtain consent under the ICWA from natural mother even in case where child born by artificial insemination).
313. *See* Catholic Social Services v. C.A.A., 789 P.2d 1159 (Alaska 1989).
314. 25 C.F.R. § 23.124(b). See discussion about notice in voluntary proceedings at pages 139–140.
315. 25 U.S.C. § 1913.
316. *See id.* § 1903(1)(i).
317. 25 C.F.R. § 23.2; BIA GUIDELINES, *supra* note 16, § L.20.

318. *See, e.g., In re* Adoption of K.L.R.F., 515 A.2d 33 (Pa. Super. 1986). Of course, if the foster care placement is preceded by the filing of a petition alleging abuse and neglect by the custodian, the fact that the parent or custodian admits to the petition does not render that a "voluntary" placement. C.E.H. v. L.M.W., 837 S.W.2d 947 (Mo. App. W.D. 1992) (finding mother is not entitled to regain custody by withdrawing consent made in an involuntary removal proceeding).
319. *See* C.E.H. v. L.M.W., 837 S.W.2d 947 (Mo. App. W.D. 1992); *but see In re* J.R.S., 690 P.2d 10 (Alaska 1984) (parent could revoke consent to foster care placement entered in an involuntary proceeding).
320. *See* 25 U.S.C. § 1912(e).
321. *See In re* J.R.S., 690 P.2d 10 (Alaska 1984) (parent could revoke relinquishment of parental rights entered in an involuntary proceeding). The fact that a parent withdraws a consent to termination does not, however, entitle the parent to the automatic return of the custody of the child. Harvick v. Harvick, 828 P.2d 769 (Alaska 1992) (mother who withdraws consent to termination not entitled to return of custody from natural father who had been vested with custody).
322. *Cf.* State of New Mexico v. Marlene, 215 P.3d 43 (N.M. 2009).
323. 25 U.S.C. § 1913(a).
324. *Id.*
325. *Id.* § 1913(a).
326. *Id.* § 23.125(d).
327. *Mississippi Band of Choctaw Indians v. Holyfield*, 490 U.S. 30, 48 (1989).
328. 25 U.S.C. §§ 1911, 1913(a).
329. A tribal court's authority to do so would be governed by the tribal constitution and law establishing the legal jurisdictional principles for the court to act. *See generally* the Full Faith and Credit section later in this chapter discussing state recognition of tribal court judgments involving Indian children not domiciled or residing in Indian country.
330. *See In re* M.R.D.B., 241 Mont. 455, 787 P.2d 1219 (Mont. 1990) (tribal court has exclusive jurisdiction over adoption proceeding after natural

mother withdraws consent to adoption in state court and tribal court makes child ward of court); *In re* D.L.L. & C.L.L., 291 N.W.2d 278 (S.D. 1980) (tribal court retains exclusive jurisdiction over minor Indian children who are wards of the tribal court even though they live off the reservation).

331. *See, e.g., In re* Adoption of F.H., 851 P.2d 1361 (Alaska 1993) (court states that a parent's preference for placement is good cause for deviating from placement preference provisions of the ICWA).
332. A majority of Tribal Codes include provisions regarding abused and neglected children, and it is clear that the ICWA applies in state courts, not tribal courts.
333. *See* 25 U.S.C. § 1911(a).
334. 25 U.S.C. § 1913(a), requiring the presiding judge to certify that the consent was explained in a language understood by the parent if English is not understood.
335. *See id.* § 1913(b); 25 C.F.R. § 23.127.
336. *Id.* Return of custody is mandated and not left up to the discretion of a court or the person to whom temporary placement was made.
337. 25 U.S.C. § 1916(a) permits a court to return custody to the parent of a child who was adopted if the adoption is subsequently set aside unless a showing is made that such a return would be "contrary to the best interests of the child." 25 U.S.C. § 1920 requires a state court to restore custody of an Indian child to a parent or Indian custodian when it finds that the child was wrongfully removed from the parent or custodian, or a person wrongfully retained custody of the child after a visit or temporary placement, unless it can be demonstrated that a return of custody would "subject a child to a substantial and immediate danger or threat of danger."
338. *See In re* J.R.S., 690 P.2d 10 (Alaska 1984); *In re* Kiogma, 472 N.W.2d 13 (Mich. App. 1991), *cert. denied*, 112 S. Ct. 952 (1992); B.R.T. v. Exec. Dir., 391 N.W.2d 594 (N.D. 1986).
339. 25 U.S.C. § 1913(b).
340. *See* Cheree L. v. Ariz. Dep't of Econ. Sec., 66 P.3d 1248 (Ariz. App. 2003).
341. *In re* J.J.W. & E.L.W., 320 Mich. App. 88, 902 N.W.2d. 901 (2017), *rev'd on other grounds sub. nom., In re* Williams, 501 Mich. 289, 915 N.W.2d 328 (2018).

342. *See* 25 U.S.C. § 1920.
343. *Id.*
344. *Id.*
345. An argument perhaps could be mounted by a person or placement agency that it should be permitted to file a petition based upon grounds other than the voluntary placement of the child with that person or agency (drug use by the parent seeking to regain custody, for example), but § 1920 seems to foreclose that filing if the person or agency has wrongfully refused to return a child when requested by a parent or custodian.
346. 25 C.F.R. § 23.125(b).
347. *See* notes 304–308.
348. *But see In re* Adoption of Infant Boy Crews, 825 P.2d 305 (Wash. 1992) (if termination becomes final under state law prior to mother becoming member of tribe, she cannot revoke consent).
349. *See* 25 U.S.C. § 1913(a).
350. For example, courts sometimes refuse to permit a noncustodial parent to voluntarily terminate his/her parental rights to avoid the obligation of paying child support, and nothing in the ICWA indicates that such a practice should be permitted for Indian children, even though § 1913 seems to permit the voluntary termination without a justification for so doing.
351. *See* 25 U.S.C. § 1921.
352. 25 U.S.C. § 1913(c). The regulations clarify that revocation of a consent to termination of parental rights must take place before there is a final decree of termination, whereas revocation of a consent to a voluntary adoption may take place until there is a final decree of adoption. 25 C.F.R. § 23.128(a), (b).
353. *See* Quinn v. Walters, 845 P.2d 206 (Or. App. 1993), *rev'd on other grounds*, 881 P.2d 795 (Or. 1994) (appellate court's order setting aside adoption because natural mother withdrew consent prior to adoption reversed on ground that natural mother's use of an affidavit from tribe alleging that she was enrolled member was inadmissible hearsay and therefore mother failed to show that child was eligible for membership with tribe).
354. *In re* Custody of S.B.R., 719 P.2d 154 (Wash. App. 1986); *see also* Harvick v. Harvick, 828 P.2d 769 (Alaska 1992) (mother not entitled to return of custody from father merely because she revoked a consent to adoption).

355. Although 25 U.S.C. § 1913(c) permits a parent to revoke a consent to termination of parental rights or adoption prior to either action being approved by the state court and custody restored to that parent, if the child has already been adjudicated a neglected or abused child in a foster care placement proceeding, the state court is not required to restore custody to a parent who revokes a consent to termination or adoption because the parent did not have legal custody prior to the execution of the voluntary consent.
356. *See* Moore v. City of East Cleveland, 431 U.S. 494 (1977).
357. *Compare* 25 C.F.R. § 23.128(a) and 25 C.F.R. § 23.128(b). Of note, unlike the section dealing with foster care placements (25 U.S.C. § 1913(b)), 25 U.S.C. § 1913(c) recognizes only the right of a parent to withdraw a consent to termination or adoption and regain custody of a child.
358. The failure to provide a parent with the right to challenge a TPR proceeding would appear to violate the due process rights of parents recognized in *Santosky v. Kramer*, 455 U.S. 745 (1982). For an example of a statute recognizing tribal customary adoption, *see* CAL. WELF. & INST. CODE § 366.24.
359. 25 U.S.C. § 1913(d).
360. *See id.*
361. 25 U.S.C. § 1913(a) requires the parent or Indian custodian to appear before a court of competent jurisdiction to lawfully consent to a foster care placement or termination of parental rights.
362. *In re* Adoption of Child of Indian Heritage, 543 A.2d 925, 938 (N.J. 1988).
363. *In re* Nery V., 20 Neb. App. 798, 832 N.W.2d 909 (2013); *In re* Adoption of Infant Boy Crews, 825 P.2d 305 (Wash. 1992).
364. Quinn v. Walters, 845 P.2d 206 (Or. App. 1993), *rev'd on other grounds*, 881 P.2d 795 (Or. 1994). The Oregon Supreme Court reversed the appellate court's finding that the ICWA applied to the adoption, but did not address the propriety of the court's ruling on the right to withdraw consent.
365. Dement v. Oglala Sioux Tribal Court, 874 F.2d 510 (8th Cir. 1989).
366. *See* 28 U.S.C. § 1738.
367. *See* Sheppard v. Sheppard, 655 P.2d 895 (Idaho 1982); *In re* Adoption of Buehl, 555 P.2d 1334 (Wash. 1976).
368. 25 U.S.C. § 1911(d).

369. *Id.*
370. *See In re* Defender, 435 N.W.2d 717 (S.D. 1989) (state court can determine whether tribal court had personal jurisdiction over mother before granting comity to tribal court custody order); *see also In re* Welfare of R.I., 402 N.W.2d 173 (Minn. App. 1987) (state court need not defer to tribal court order finding that child is ward of tribal court in situation where tribal court had no jurisdiction).
371. *In re* Adoption of K.L.J. and K.P.J., 266 N.C. App. 289, 831 S.E.2d 114 (N.C. Ct. App. 2019) (full faith and credit not appropriate because guardians were not notified of and did not participate in the tribal court proceeding); Starr v. George, 175 P.3d 50 (Alaska 2008) (when paternal grandparents had been granted visitation rights by state court and had filed a petition for custody, failure of tribal court to give notice to paternal grandparents of maternal grandparents adoption petition in tribal court violated due process and precluded recognition of the tribal court order on the basis of full faith and credit); *see also, e.g.,* State Dep't of Pub. Safety v. Fann, 864 P.2d 533, 536 n.5 (Alaska 1993) explaining the general principle that full faith and credit need not be accorded to any foreign judgment when due process not provided.
372. *See, e.g.*, Peidlow v. Williams, 459 P.3d 1136 (Alaska 2020).
373. *In re* Dependency & Neglect of A.L., 442 N.W.2d 233 (S.D. 1989).
374. *See* Quinn v. Walters, 881 P.2d 795 (Or. 1994), *reversing* 845 P.2d 206 (Or. App. 1993).
375. For example, the North Dakota Supreme Court has enacted a rule, Rule 7.2, governing full faith and credit for tribal court orders, including how the tribal court order should be registered with the state court, *see* N.D.S. Ct. Rule 7.2(c), although the court notes that the rule should not apply to orders it must honor under federal law.
376. Quinn v. Walters, 881 P.2d 795, 801 (Or. 1994), *reversing* 845 P.2d 206 (Or. App. 1993).
377. 25 C.F.R. § 23.108; BIA GUIDELINES, *supra* note 16, § B.7.
378. *See* Brown *ex rel.* Brown v. Rice, 760 F. Supp. 1459 (D. Kan. 1991) (federal court has jurisdiction to resolve parents' claim that tribal court lacks

jurisdiction where tribal law did not permit such jurisdiction even under the ICWA).

379. *Compare In re* Adoption of T.R.M., 525 N.E.2d 298 (Ind. 1988) (tribal court has exclusive jurisdiction on the basis of an order of wardship by the tribal court only if the domicile or residence of the Indian child is on the reservation), *In re* W.L., 260 Mont. 325, 859 P.2d 1019 (Mont. 1993) (state court does not lose jurisdiction under the ICWA because of mother's move to reservation), *and In re* J.D.M.C., 739 N.W.2d 796 (S.D. 2007) (no full faith and credit where tribe made a child domiciled off reservation a ward of the tribal court) *with* Kaltag Tribal Council v. Jackson, 344 Fed. Appx. 324 (9th Cir. 2009) (holding adoption judgment issued by tribal court entitled to full faith and credit because reservation status is not a requirement of jurisdiction when tribal members are involved), Alaska v. Native Vill. of Tanana, 249 P.3d 734 (Alaska 2011) (Tribes have concurrent jurisdiction outside of Indian country and child custody proceedings that they initiate for children so residing may be entitled to full faith and credit.), and *In re* M.R.D.B., 241 Mont. 455, 787 P.2d 1219 (Mont. 1990) (tribal court has exclusive jurisdiction over adoption proceeding when natural mother withdraws consent to adoption in state court and tribal court has made child ward of tribal court). *See also* Johnson v. Jones, Case No. 6:05-CV-1256-Orl-22KRS (order dated Nov. 3, 2005) (in an unpublished order, a federal court upheld a Minnesota tribal court's authority to remove an Indian child domiciled in Florida under the Tribal Code).
380. https://www.uniformlaws.org/viewdocument/final-act-34?CommunityKey=4cc1b0be-d6c5-4bc2-b157-16b0baf2c56d (later amended to address international custody orders in 2013).
381. *See* Holly C. v. Tohono O'odham Nation, 247 Ariz. 495, 452 P.3d 725 (Ariz. Ct. App. 2019) (The UCCJEA requires deference to another state or tribe's jurisdiction, but only when the other state or tribe has exercised jurisdiction substantially in compliance with the UCCJEA.); *cf.* C.L. v. Z.M.F. H., 18 A.3d 1175 (Pa. Sup. Ct. 2011) (In custody case between parents where child had no "home state" within the meaning of the UCCJEA, the state

court was required to defer to the jurisdiction of the Pine Ridge Tribal Court since it was the first court to exercise jurisdiction.). For more information, see also Chapter 3, note 7. The exact circumstances in which the UCCJEA requires full faith and credit of a tribal court order are beyond the scope of this book.

382. *See, e.g.*, S.D. CODIFIED LAWS 1-1-25; *see also, e.g.*, Mashantucket Pequot Gaming Enter. v. Malhotra, 326 N.J. Super. 134, 740 A.2d 703 (1999).
383. *See* 25 U.S.C. § 1911(d).
384. *Id.* Nothing in 25 U.S.C. § 1911(d) or the federal full faith and credit law, 28 U.S.C. § 1738, mandates that tribal courts grant the same preclusive effect to state court judgments as federal courts are required to do under federal law.

Placement Provisions of the ICWA

5

This chapter will focus on the Indian Child Welfare Act's (ICWA's) placement preferences set out in 25 U.S.C. § 1915 and will include a discussion of the regulations' interplay with the ICWA's statutory language and case law regarding the placement preferences. This chapter focuses on foster care placement and preadoptive placement preferences, adoptive placement preferences, tribal placement preferences, and good cause to deviate from the placement preferences.

As part of the special relationship between Congress and Indian tribes and tribal members, it is the United States' responsibility, as trustee, to ensure the protection of Indian children who are members of, or are eligible for membership in, an Indian tribe.[1] At the time of the ICWA's enactment in 1978, an estimated 25 to 35 percent of all Indian children had been separated from their families and placed in foster care, adoptive homes, or in institutions, and 90 percent of adoptive placements were with nonrelative, non-Indian families.[2] Recall that the ICWA serves to protect the best interests of Indian children by promoting the stability and security of Indian tribes and families and to establish minimum federal standards when removal is necessary to place those Indian children with families in homes that reflect the unique values and cultures of the Indian tribes.[3] Congress also found that the wholesale removal of Indian children by nontribal governmental agencies and placement in nonrelative, non-Native homes constituted a serious threat to the tribe's existence as an ongoing self-governing sovereign.[4] The placement preferences in the ICWA address these concerns and also codify best practices in child welfare by favoring extended family placements, a practice now required for all children ever since 2008, and placement within a child's broader community and culture, whenever possible.[5]

However, for decades, various state courts and agencies have interpreted the ICWA in conflicting ways, resulting in the ICWA being applied contrary to congressional intent, and although progress has been made, the data indicates that Indian children continue to be placed in non-Indian homes in large numbers.[6] The regulations sought to address this ongoing problem by clarifying issues relating to the placement preferences, particularly what constitutes good cause to deviate from those placement preferences.[7]

The U.S. Supreme Court addressed the essential nature of the statutory placement preferences and stated in *Holyfield* that "the most important substantive requirements imposed upon state courts" are the placement preferences expressed in § 1915 of the act.[8] Those provisions reflect the congressional realization that even if the Indian child's bond to the parents or Indian custodian is severed, state courts must make every effort not to dissolve that tie between the child and his or her tribe because that association will protect the integrity and future viability of the tribe itself and provide protective factors for that child.[9] Although applying such a directive may sometimes seem awkward in situations in which the Indian child has not resided in an Indian family, the majority of courts have stated that the placement preference provisions must be followed, including, if relatives are not available, the preferences with tribal members and Indian families that connect the child with his or her Indian culture, provided that good cause to the contrary does not exist.[10]

The placement preferences in the ICWA and the regulations underscore that best practices in child welfare cases where a child is removed from a parent favor placing the child with the extended family or within a child's broader kinship community, something that is true for all children, not just Indian children.[11]

The ICWA placement preferences are listed in two precise paradigms—one paradigm sets forth foster care placements/preadoptive placements (which by definition includes guardianships) and one paradigm sets forth adoptive placements. Both paradigms are enumerated in an exact order of preference. A state court must make a finding that no placement exists at the top of the list before moving down the placement preferences list, unless the court makes a detailed finding there is evidence to establish good cause to deviate from the placement preference paradigm.[12]

While a tribe may not always support a particular placement preference, most often tribes are strong advocates for the placement of an Indian child in accordance with the provisions of § 1915, sometimes even despite a parental effort to avoid such a placement.[13] Of course, the placement provisions of the ICWA should never become subservient to the provisions seeking to limit removals of Indian children from their homes, as both areas were of equal importance to Congress.

The ICWA's placement preferences do not explicitly apply in emergency proceedings. The guidelines recommend, however, that states make emergency placements in accordance with the ICWA's placement paradigms whenever possible and as soon as possible following removal of the Indian child, as this may prevent subsequent disruptions.[14]

The ICWA's Statutory Mandate Regarding Placement Preferences

As noted, the ICWA's placement preferences are listed in descending order starting with the most preferred and moving to the least preferred.[15] Each placement preference should be considered in the order the ICWA requires and state agencies and other placement agencies should make efforts to identify and assist extended family and tribal members with preferred placements.[16] Giving a preference means more than prioritization and connotes the active bestowal of advantages of some over others.[17] Thus, the state should provide individuals with preferred placement status with at least enough information about the ICWA proceeding to allow the person(s) to avail themselves of the placement preferences.[18]

It should be noted that § 1915(b) also directs a state court, state agency, or private agency to place an Indian child in the least restrictive setting that closely approximates his or her family, including taking into account sibling attachment, and that is within a reasonable proximity to his or her home.[19] Presumably, the proximity requirement is designed to promote reunification with the child's parent(s), which is the first priority when a child is removed (see discussion of active efforts requirement in Chapter 4).

The ICWA requires the states to maintain records evidencing the efforts made to comply with the placement preferences and that those records be made available at any time upon request of the secretary or the Indian child's tribe,[20] and this requirement is underscored in situations where a party seeks good cause to deviate from the ICWA placement preferences based upon unavailability.[21] The agency must document the efforts made to comply with the placement preferences whenever the placement departs from the placement preferences.[22] The fact that no federally recognized tribe is located within a state does not equate to no family members or members of tribes residing within a state.[23] Further, the standards for determining whether a placement preference is unavailable must conform to the prevailing social and cultural standards of the Indian community.[24]

Tribes may supplant tribal placement preferences in the place of the ICWA's placement preferences.[25] If an Indian child's tribe establishes a different order of placement preferences by tribal resolution, the agency or court effecting the placement shall follow the tribal placement preferences so long as the placement is the least restrictive setting appropriate to the needs of the child, as provided in subsection (b) of 25 U.S.C. § 1915. Thus, the order of placement preferences established by a tribal resolution or by a tribal-state agreement could change the placement preference structure set out in the ICWA.[26] Although some have asserted that a tribe may eliminate the good cause exception to the ICWA placement preferences when it passes a resolution because the language in the ICWA statute regarding a tribal resolution setting forth a tribal placement preference does not include the good cause language, dicta in the recent Supreme Court case of *Adoptive Couple v. Baby Girl* suggests that if the tribe adopts a different order of preference, the good cause exception would still apply.[27] A few courts have also refused to abide by a tribal resolution in a couple of instances, notwithstanding the broad language in the ICWA statute and regulations, specifically cases where the tribal resolution has prohibited the adoption of tribal members by non Indians.[28]

The ICWA's Foster Care and Preadoptive Placement Preferences

The placement preference provisions for foster care and preadoptive placements are set out at § 1915(b) of the ICWA.[29] These provisions apply to both voluntary and involuntary foster care placements,

placements that may sometimes lead to a termination of parental rights, guardianships, and preadoptive placements.[30]

In the absence of good cause to the contrary discussed as follows, and considering the requirement that a child be placed in a family setting within reasonable proximity to his or her home, in any foster care or preadoptive placement an Indian child shall be placed with

(1) a member of the Indian child's extended family;
(2) a foster home licensed, approved, or specified by the Indian child's tribe;
(3) an Indian foster home licensed or approved by an authorized non-Indian licensing authority; or
(4) an institution for children approved by an Indian tribe or operated by an Indian organization, which has a program suitable to meet the Indian child's needs.[31]

The preference of a parent may be considered where appropriate (see good cause discussion as follows) and a court shall "give weight" to a parent's request for anonymity in applying the preferences.[32]

An Indian tribe plays a vital role in the implementation of the foster care placement preferences not only because many of the preferences refer to homes or institutions licensed by the tribe but also because an Indian tribe may be in possession of information about the child's extended family members or other placements that is otherwise unavailable to the state court.[33] The ICWA does not prefer an Indian relative over a non-Indian relative under § 1915(b)(i).[34] A review of the definition of "extended family member," contained at § 1903(2), reveals that the definition encompasses various relatives of the child without regard to race, unless the tribe defines the term in another manner.[35] Therefore, a state court would be in compliance with the ICWA by placing the child in a non-Indian relative's home, provided that placement is consistent with the prevailing social and cultural standards of the Indian community.[36] Although mandated by the ICWA, at least one court has held that failure to follow the placement provisions will not vitiate an otherwise valid termination of parental rights.[37]

One of the major problems confronting social workers who attempt to comply with the placement preference provisions for foster care, however, is the eligibility of the family for foster care payments under Title IV-E of the Social Security Act. To be eligible for payments, the family must be licensed as a foster home by the state.[38] The very conditions that are illegitimate considerations to deny placement under the ICWA may very well disqualify the family from licensing. However, § 1931(b) seems to partially address this problem by stating that "for purposes of qualifying for assistance under a federally-assisted program," licensing by a tribal entity should be deemed the equivalent of licensing by the state, thereby giving families the possible option to pursue tribal licensure.[39] Some tribes and states are attempting a reciprocal recognition of licensing standards so more Indian families can be recruited as foster homes.[40] In addition, tribal-state Title IV-E agreements that provide for payment of tribal foster homes through the Title IV-E program are becoming more frequent and almost half of the tribes are covered by such agreements.[41] The Fostering Connections to Success and Increasing Adoptions Act of 2008 requires states to negotiate Title IV-E agreements in good faith with tribes.[42] That law also provides tribes with the option to apply directly to the Secretary of Health and Human Services to receive federal funding to support the administration of their own foster care, adoption assistance, and guardianship assistance programs under Title IV-E of the act, although as of the date of the publishing of this book, only a small number of tribes have been approved for direct funding.[43]

Adoptive Placements

The ICWA has placement preference criteria specifically for adoptive placements. The same provisions discussed with respect to foster care and preadoptive placements—including the right of the tribe to alter the preference provisions by resolution, the right of the parent to request anonymity and to suggest a placement, and the good cause to the contrary grounds for deviating from the placement preferences—apply equally to adoptive placements.[44] The Indian child and the Indian child's tribe become the primary benefactor of the adoption placement provisions of the ICWA as the parents and Indian custodians have usually left the scene by way of a parental rights termination.[45]

In the absence of good cause to the contrary, a preference shall be given for the adoption of an Indian child to

(1) a member of the Indian child's extended family;
(2) other members of the Indian child's tribe; or
(3) other Indian families.[46]

This is the order of preference a state court must follow in adoption cases, unless the tribe has altered it by resolution or if a state court makes detailed findings that good cause exists to deviate from the placement preferences.[47] The ICWA does not bar the adoption of an Indian child by a non-Indian couple if good cause is present unless the tribe adopts a resolution banning such adoptions, which at least two courts have ruled even then is not binding.[48] The first preference for adoption may in fact be a non-Indian family when a non-Indian is a member of the child's extended family. Of note, the U.S. Supreme Court has raised an issue as to when adoption placement preferences are activated and it would be prudent for a person who is a preferred placement who wants to adopt to take action as soon as possible to make that known to the court.[49]

Good Cause to Deviate from Placement Preferences

Although Congress enacted the ICWA to protect the best interests of Indian children, the ICWA provides state courts and state agencies with the discretion to deviate from the foster care, preadoptive, and adoptive placement preferences upon a detailed finding of "good cause to the contrary." If circumstances exist wherein an Indian child's needs cannot be met through an ICWA preferred placement, the state court may find good cause to deviate from the ICWA placement preferences.[50] However, what constitutes good cause to deviate from the placement preferences is a limited exception, rather than a broad category that would swallow the rule to adhere to the placement preferences.[51] Thus, the regulations lay out five specific possible grounds for good cause that should normally be the basis for a good cause to deviate decision by a state court.[52] The good cause exception to the placement preferences is the most frequently litigated area of the ICWA.[53]

Burden of Proof

If any party asserts that good cause not to follow the placement preferences exists, the reasons for that belief or assertion must be stated orally on the record or be provided in writing to the parties to the child custody proceeding and the court.[54] The regulations recommend and most case law requires that the party seeking departure from the placement preferences bear the burden of proving by clear and convincing evidence that there is "good cause" to depart from the placement preferences.[55]

Factors to Consider Regarding Good Cause to Deviate

Five factors upon which a state court can base a determination of good cause to deviate from the ICWA placement preferences are set out in the regulations.[56] A court's determination of good cause to depart from the placement preferences must be made on the record or in writing and should be based on one or more of the following considerations:

(1) The request of one or both Indian child's parents, if they attest that they have reviewed the placement options, if any, that comply with the order of preference
(2) The request of the child, if the child is of sufficient age and capacity to understand the decision that is being made
(3) The presence of a sibling attachment that can be maintained only through a particular placement
(4) The extraordinary physical, mental, or emotional needs of the Indian child, such as specialized treatment services that may be unavailable in the community where families who meet the placement preferences live
(5) The unavailability of a suitable placement after a determination by the court that a diligent search was conducted to find suitable placements meeting the preference criteria, but none has been located[57]

The court's analysis must conform to the prevailing social and cultural standards of the Indian community in which the Indian child's parent or extended family resides or with which the Indian child's parent or extended family members maintain social and cultural ties.[58] Good cause to depart from the placement preferences cannot be based on the socioeconomic status of any placement relative to another placement.[59] Further, a deviation from the placement preferences may not be based solely on the ordinary bonding or attachment that flowed from time spent in a nonpreferred placement that was made in violation of the ICWA.[60]

The first good cause exception is an apparent attempt to implement that section of the ICWA, § 1915(c), directing a state court to consider the wishes of the parent, when appropriate, in making placement decisions.[61] The regulations emphasize that the choice must be a knowing one in that a birth parent must attest that he or she has reviewed the placement options that comply with the ICWA's placement preferences and has selected an alternative placement.[62] The guidelines emphasize that this means reviewing the actual preferred placements that are available and not just the general categories.[63] The text of the statute, the guidelines, and some case law make clear that a court is not required to follow a parent's request, but instead provide that it may consider the parent's request to be good cause when appropriate.[64] If both parents make different placement requests then both requests must be considered.[65] While the request of the parent is a consideration for the court, the request might carry more weight in a foster care placement than in an adoptive placement because in case of an adoption the parent usually has had or will have his or her parental rights terminated.[66] Thus, especially in the latter case, the parent's desire to control the placement of the child should not normally supersede the right of the tribe or extended family members to assert a placement that would serve the overall purpose of the ICWA.[67] Nonetheless, many courts have cited to the preference of the parent as a ground for deviating from the adoptive placement preferences of the ICWA.[68]

The second possible basis for good cause is the request of the child, if the child is of sufficient age and capacity to understand the decision that is being made.[69] Since no guidance is offered on "sufficient age and capacity," state courts would look to state statutory or case law on this issue.

The third exception is when the presence of a sibling attachment can be maintained through a placement together.[70] However, if it is not possible to place the siblings together, then the Indian child should be placed, if possible, in a setting that is within a reasonable proximity to the sibling.[71] In addition, if the sibling is age 18 or older, that sibling might qualify as a preferred placement, as extended family.

Extraordinary physical, mental, or emotional needs may also be grounds for good cause to deviate from the ICWA placement preferences. The meaning of this phrase is not defined in the regulations, but recent case law indicates that bonding alone does not constitute an extraordinary physical, mental, or emotional need of the child.[72] Although the regulations do not absolutely prohibit the consideration of bonding and attachment, the commentary notes that bonding and attachment may have serious limitations in court determinations.[73] The guidelines also emphasize that the benefits of any such relationship must be weighed against the long-term benefits to the child of maintaining connections with extended family and the tribal community.[74] As noted previously, bonding cannot be the sole basis for departing from the preferences if it follows from time spent in a nonpreferred placement made in violation of the ICWA, which makes explicit the admonition by the U.S. Supreme Court that courts should not "reward those who obtain custody, whether lawfully or otherwise, and maintain it during any ensuing (and protracted) litigation," by treating relationships established by temporary, non-ICWA-compliant placements as a reason to depart from the ICWA's mandates.[75]

The guidelines note that beneficial connections between an Indian child and potential preferred placements can be facilitated to ease the transition. Facilitating transitions between a temporary nonpreferred placement and the ICWA preferred placement allows the child the opportunity to develop additional bonds with these preferred placements that will ease any transitions.[76]

Finally, a good cause determination may be made based upon the unavailability of a suitable placement after a determination by the court that a diligent search was conducted to find suitable placements meeting the preference criteria but none had been located.[77]

A diligent search would require some contact with those preferred placements (that also meet the requirements for a least-restrictive setting within a reasonable proximity in a foster care placement), taking into account the child's special needs.[78] It also includes working with the Indian child's tribe to identify family members and tribal community placements.[79]

If a state court properly makes a finding that good cause exists not to adhere to the ICWA placement preferences, the placement would comply with the ICWA.[80]

Perhaps the most common reasons for deviating from the placement preferences in the case law has been parental preference[81] (directly addressed in the 2016 regulations) or a finding that it is in the best interest of the Indian child to deviate.[82] The commentary specifically addresses the latter issue cautioning that good cause should not "devolve into a free-ranging 'best interests' determination," noting that the legislative history of the ICWA indicates that Congress was skeptical of using vague standards like best interests and intended the exception to be a narrow one.[83]

Post-Placement Issues

The ICWA continues to play a role in child custody proceedings involving Indian children even after a foster care or adoptive placement has been affected.[84]

Removal from Foster Home

If an Indian child is removed from a foster home or other institution, the placement preference criteria apply to any future placements, unless the removal from the foster home is for the purpose of returning the child to his or her parent or Indian custodian.[85] This provision of the ICWA prevents state courts from initially effecting a placement in compliance with the ICWA and then removing the child from that home for placement in one that may not comply with the placement provisions. Every placement of an Indian child must be made in accordance with the placement preference provisions unless the child is being returned to the parents or Indian custodian.[86]

Vacation of Adoption Decree

If an adoption decree is set aside under state law or the adoptive parents voluntarily terminate their parental rights, the biological parent or prior Indian custodian may petition the court for a return of custody and custody shall be restored unless there is a showing that return would not be in the best interest of the child.[87] If the return of custody is opposed, the hearing to determine whether custody shall be returned must comply with § 1912.[88]

This is a very interesting provision of the ICWA that has been discussed infrequently.[89] It grants rights only to the biological parent of the child and to the prior Indian custodian and not to an Indian who previously adopted the child, who would be a parent under the ICWA.[90]

Record of Placements

Each state that places an Indian child in either foster care or in an adoptive placement shall keep records of each placement along with efforts exerted by the state agency to comply with the placement preference provisions of the ICWA.[91] Such records will be made available to either the Indian child's tribe or the Department of the Interior upon request, notwithstanding any state law requiring the confidentiality of such proceedings.[92] This requirement would appear to extend to private agency placements, provided that the state court plays some role in the placement of the Indian child. The provision does not require the records to be maintained at a central location, but other federal law may mandate such. The existence of this requirement imposed on the state may prove useful to any

Indian tribe who wants information about a specific adoption or the ICWA advocate wishing to demonstrate a systematic violation of the placement provisions of the law.[93]

Right of Indian Child to Discover Tribal Affiliation

A miscellaneous provision of the ICWA, but one that would be of great importance to an Indian child adopted by a non-Indian family, is the provision allowing an adult adopted child to apply to the state court where he or she was adopted for information relating to the tribal affiliation of his or her parents and any other information assisting the child in establishing the child's relationship with an Indian tribe.[94] If the child is not aware of which court granted the adoption, the child should inquire with the Bureau of Indian Affairs, because that agency is charged with the responsibility of keeping a central registry of adoptions involving Indian children.[95]

Endnotes

1. 25 U.S.C. § 2501 (1978); *see also* Dep't of the Interior, Bureau of Indian Affairs, Indian Child Welfare Act Proceedings, 81 Fed. Reg. 38778, 38779 (June 14, 2016).
2. H.R. Rep. No. 95-1386, at 9 (1978), *reprinted in* 1978 U.S.C.C.A.N. 7530, 7531; *see also* Jack Trope & Adrian T. Smith, *The Continued Protection of Indian Children and Families After Adoptive Couple v. Baby Girl: What the Case Means and How to Respond*, 2 Am. Indian L.J. 434 (2014), https://indian-affairs.org/uploads/5/4/7/6/54761515/trope-and-smith.pdf (noting the data from the 1970s indicated that Indian foster care placement rates ranged by state from 2.4 to 22.4 times the non-Native rate, with the percentage of Indian children placed in non-Native foster homes ranging from 53 percent to 97 percent, and that the adoption rate for Native children was eight times that of non-Native children and, of those, 90 percent of the Native children were placed in non-Native homes).
3. 25 U.S.C. § 1902 (1978).

4. 124 Cong. Rec. H38103.
5. 42 U.S.C. § 671(a)(19); *see also* Elaine Farmer & Sue Moyers, Kinship Care: Fostering Effective Family and Friends Placements (2008).
6. Casey Family Programs, *Native American and Alaska Native Children 2020 Data Overview* (Aug. 3, 2022), https://www.casey.org/native-american-alaska-native-data-overview-2022/; *see also* Nat'l Indian Child Welfare Ass'n, *ICWA Compliance Summary and Review of Existing Literature* (Feb. 15, 2024), https://www.nicwa.org/news/icwa-compliance-summary-and-review-of-existing-literature/.
7. *See* 25 U.S.C. § 23.132 (How is a determination of "good cause" to depart from the placement preferences made?).
8. Mississippi Band of Choctaw Indians v. Holyfield, 490 U.S. 30, 36 (1989).
9. *Id.*; *see also* Center for Native Child & Family Resilience, Enhancing Child and Family Resilience in Indian Country, https://cncfr.jbsinternational.com/sites/default/files/uploads/CNCFR_LitReview_Brief.pdf (last visited July 28, 2025); *see also* T.D. LaFromboise et al., *Family, Community, and School Influences on Resilience Among American Indian Adolescents in the Upper Midwest*, 34 J. Cmty. Psych. 193 (2006).
10. *See, e.g.*, *In re* Alexandria P., 204 Cal. Rptr. 3d 617 (Ct. App. 2d Dist., Div. 5 Cal. 2016) (upholding finding that there was not good cause to depart from ICWA's placement preferences and place the Indian child with foster parents, rather than with child's extended family, based upon evidence regarding the child's ability to navigate and develop new attachments, the adverse effects of foster parents' unwillingness or inability to support child's relationship with extended family, and that the extended family offered child a better opportunity to maintain a relationship with her siblings and access to her cultural identity); *In re* Appeal in Coconino Juvenile Action No. J-10175, 736 P.2d 829 (Ariz. Ct. App. 1987) (rejecting as a ground for deviating from the placement preferences a trial court's determination that introducing an Indian child into an Indian family would cause cultural shock to the child because of the child's upbringing in non-Indian families); *cf. In re* M.K.T., 368 P.3d 771 (S. Ct. Okla. 2016) (In order to find good cause to deviate from the placement preferences, the State needed to show (1) a serious emotional

or physical need of the Native American child, (2) a course of action for remedying that need via the non-ICWA-compliant placement, and (3) some fact or facts showing that the ICWA-compliant placement was inconsistent with the child's needed plan or treatment.).

11. *See* ANNIE E. CASEY FOUND., VARIATIONS IN THE USE OF KINSHIP DIVERSION AMONG CHILD WELFARE AGENCIES 8 (2019), https://www.aecf.org/resources/variations-in-the-use-of-kinship-diversion-among-child-welfare-agencies ("[K]inship care placements . . . appear more stable than placements in non-kin care."); Marc A. Winokur et al., *Kinship Care for the Safety, Permanency, and Well-Being of Children Removed from the Home for Maltreatment*, COCHRANE DATABASE SYS. REV. (2014) (kinship care results in fewer behavioral problems, fewer mental health disorders, and better well-being, while minimizing trauma); *see also* NAT'L COUNCIL ON JUVENILE & FAM. CT. JUDGES, *ADOPTION AND PERMANENCY GUIDELINES: IMPROVING COURT PRACTICE IN CHILD ABUSE AND NEGLECT CASES 10–11* (2000); CHILD WELFARE LEAGUE OF AMERICA, STANDARD OF EXCELLENCE FOR ADOPTION SERVICES 1.10 (2000). In the case of Indian children, the importance of extended family was explicitly recognized by the U.S. Supreme Court in *Mississippi Band of Choctaw Indians v. Holyfield*, 490 U.S. 30, 35 n.4 (U.S. 1989) ("One of the particular points of concern was the failure of non-Indian child welfare workers to understand the role of the extended family in Indian society. The House Report on the ICWA noted: 'An Indian child may have scores of, perhaps more than a hundred, relatives who are counted as close, responsible members of the family. Many social workers, untutored in the ways of Indian family life or assuming them to be socially irresponsible, consider leaving the child with persons outside the nuclear family as neglect and thus as grounds for terminating parental rights.' At the conclusion of the 1974 Senate hearings, Senator Abourezk noted the role that such extended families played in the care of children: 'We've had testimony here that in Indian communities throughout the Nation there is no such thing as an abandoned child because when a child does have a need for parents for one reason or another, a relative or a friend will take that child in. It's the extended family concept.'" (citations

omitted)); *see also* Wisconsin Potowatomies of Hannahville Indian Cmty. v. Houston, 393 F. Supp. 719 (W.D. Mich. 1973) (discussing custom of extended family and tribe assuming responsibility for care of orphaned children).

12. 25 U.S.C. § 1915(a), (b); *see In re* Welfare of Children of L.K. and A.S., 9 N.W.3d 174 (Minn. Ct. App. 2024) (holding that the placement preferences are hierarchical and state courts may only place the child with someone in a lower-ranked group when there is no available placement in a higher ranked group).
13. *In re* T.S.W., 276 P.3d 133 (S. Ct. Kan. 2012) (mother's wish that child not be placed with any member of father's family, together with her wish that child be placed with non-Native American family, by itself, was not good cause to deviate from ICWA's placement preference statute); *In re* Baby Girl Jane Doe, 865 P.2d 1090 (Mont. 1993) (holding mother's desire to see that child is placed with non-Indian family does not override tribe's efforts to gain placement of child with Indian family).
14. BIA Guidelines for Implementing the Indian Child Welfare Act § C.6 (Dec. 2016).
15. 25 U.S.C. § 1915(a), (b); *see also* 25 C.F.R. §§ 23.130(a)(1), 23.131(b)(1); *see also* Haaland v. Brackeen, 599 U.S. 255, 143 S. Ct. 1609, 1624 (2023) ("ICWA's placement preferences . . . are hierarchical: State courts may only place the child with someone in a lower-ranked group when there is no available placement in the higher-ranked groups.").
16. 25 U.S.C. 1915(a), (e); *In re* N.J., 104 Cal. App. 5th 96 (Ct. App. 2d Dist., Div. 4, Cal. 2024) (reversing the trial court's finding of good cause based upon the child's bond with the caregiver given the extensive failures by DCFS to place the child with a preferred placement in spite of the aunt's early and repeated requests for placement and court orders requiring an assessment of the aunt which were ignored); Native Village of Tununak v. State, Dep't of Health & Soc. Servs. (*Tununak II*), 334 P.3d 165, 177–78 (Alaska 2014) (before a court may entertain an argument of good cause to deviate from the ICWA's placement preferences, the court must inquire about the existence of and the state's efforts to comply with achieving

suitable and preferred placements); *In re* T.S.W., 276 P.3d 133, 142–44 (Kan. 2012) (reversing a lower court's decision finding good cause to deviate from the ICWA's placement preferences based, in part, on the adoption agency's failure to make adequate efforts to identify potential preferred placements); *In re* D.W., 795 N.W.2d 39, 44–45 (S.D. 2011) (scrutinizing the state's efforts to obtain a suitable ICWA preferred placement); *In re* Jullian B., 82 Cal. App. 4th 1337, 1347 (Cal. Ct. App. 2000) (The ICWA requires a state to search diligently for a placement that falls within the ICWA's statutory preferences.); 25 C.F.R. § 23.132(c)(5) (unavailability of preferred placement after a diligent search is one of the grounds for deviating from a preferred placement); *but see* Haaland v. Brackeen, 599 U.S. 255 (burden is on the tribe or other objecting party to produce a higher-ranked placement, and not the agency). The *Brackeen* court did not seek to harmonize this observation with the regulation cited earlier; nor did it invalidate the regulation.

17. 81 Fed. Reg. 38839 (citing Black's Law Dictionary 1369, 10th ed. 2014).
18. 81 Fed. Reg. 38841.
19. *See* 25 U.S.C. § 1915(b); 25 C.F.R. § 23.131(a). *In re* D.A., 314 Or. App. 385, 499 P.3d 876 (Ct. App. OR 2021), the Oregon Court of Appeals analyzed how these requirements fit together. The court found that Congress built some give and take into the three requirements of § 1915(b) as they relate to one another. The first requirement—that an Indian child be placed in the least restrictive setting that most approximates a family and in which any special needs of the child may be met—is the most unequivocal. The second requirement—that an Indian child be placed within reasonable proximity to the child's home, taking into account any special needs of the child—contains some wiggle room by virtue of the word "reasonable." And the third requirement—that an Indian child be placed in one of four legislatively preferred types of placements—also contains wiggle room in that there is an express exception for situations in which the juvenile court determines that "good cause" exists not to use a preferred placement. The court found that Texas was reasonably proximate for the children given the circumstances, that is, it was the most family-like setting, it allowed the children to stay together,

the Tribe supported the placement, and since the children are no longer on a plan of reunification, but durable guardianship, the distance between Oregon and Texas was not unreasonable. *See also In re* Anthony T., 146 Cal. Rptr. 3d 124 (Ct. App. 4th Dist. 2012) (Foster home placement of five-month-old Indian child in dependency proceeding was not "within reasonable proximity to his or her home" given that travel from child's home to the placement took two and a half hours by car, mother could not legally drive and there was no evidence that the tribe could help mother travel to child, and that therefore the twice a week visits recommended could not reasonably be achieved in view of mother's other responsibilities and commitments if the child were placed in the preferred placement.).

20. 25 U.S.C. § 1915(e), 25 C.F.R. § 23.132(c)(5). *See also* 81 Fed. Reg. at 38839.
21. 25 C.F.R. § 23.132(c)(5).
22. *Id.* § 23.141.
23. 81 Fed. Reg. 38841.
24. 25 U.S.C. § 1915(d); *see also* 81 Fed. Reg. 38846 (nothing in the rule eliminates other requirements under state or federal law for determining the safety of a placement).
25. 25 U.S.C. § 1915(c); 25 C.F.R. § 23.129(a); 25 C.F.R. § 23.130(b); 25 C.F.R. § 23.133(c). Questions have been raised about whether this authority may be exercise by a resolution pertaining to all child welfare cases involving a tribe's children or whether this can be done on a case-by-case basis. *See In re* Jullian B., 99 Cal. Rptr. 2d 241 (Cal. App. 2000) (while tribe can alter preferences generally, it cannot designate a specific placement in a specific case). Thus, to ensure that tribal preferences are honored, a tribe should consider adopting a resolution applicable to all cases.
26. 25 C.F.R. § 23.131; *see also* comment at 81 Fed. Reg. 38840.
27. 133 S. Ct. 2552, 2564 n.11.
28. *In re* Laura F., 99 Cal. Rptr. 2d 859 (Ct. App. 2000) (holding tribal resolution barring non-Indians from adopting tribal members did not supersede state's right to place Indian child with non-Indian because such would violate state public policy.) *Cf.* Adoptive Couple v. Baby Girl, 570 U.S., 637,

133 S. Ct. 2552 (2013) (placement preferences do not bar a non-Indian family from adopting an Indian child when no other eligible candidates have sought to adopt the Indian child).

29. *See* 25 U.S.C. § 1915(b).
30. *Id.*
31. 25 U.S.C. § 1915(b).
32. *Id.* § 1915(c).
33. *Cf. In re* Custody of A.K.H., 502 N.W.2d 790 (Minn. Ct. App. 1993) (significant reason for finding that the tribe is entitled to intervene in custody dispute between grandparent and parent is because the tribe can prepare a home study of the proposed custodian which takes into account the cultural and social standards in the Indian community).
34. 25 U.S.C. § 1915(b)(i).
35. *Id.* § 1903(2).
36. *Id.* § 1915(d).
37. *See* Interest of J.W., 528 N.W.2d 657 (Ct. App. Iowa 1995) (Noncompliance with placement preferences does not require reversal of a termination order, as the remedial provisions of § 1914 do not apply to violations of § 1915.).
38. 42 U.S.C. § 672.
39. 25 U.S.C. § 1931(b).
40. Minnesota, for example, entered into a memorandum of understanding with all the Indian tribes in that state governing foster care recruiting and licensing as well as Title IV-E payments made by the counties for tribal placements. *See* https://tribalinformationexchange.org/wp-content/uploads/2019/03/Minnesota-Tribal State-Agreement.pdf; *see also* COLO. REV. STAT. § 26-6-102(4), (14), and (21), as amended in 2021, which includes tribal licensed homes in the Colorado state definitions of "foster care home" and "kinship foster care home" to make it easier for state and county social workers to place children in tribal homes and provide payments to those homes.
41. *See* JACK F. TROPE & SHANNON KELLER O'LOUGHLIN, A SURVEY AND ANALYSIS OF SELECT TITLE IV-E TRIBAL-STATE AGREEMENTS (Ass'n on Am. Indian Affairs, Mar. 2014), http://www.narf.org/nill/resources

/title-iv-e/20140320_title_iv-e_report.pdf. These agreements also may provide for administrative and training costs for tribes and touch upon a variety of other topics, including the ICWA.

42. 42 U.S.C. § 671(a)(32). The ICWA also allows for agreements between states regarding ICWA implementation, including issues of jurisdiction. 25 U.S.C. § 1919(a). These agreements describe how the ICWA will be implemented and may address services provided to American Indian/Alaska Native children in non-kinship out-of-home care. They may also specify procedures, roles, and responsibilities for tribal notification when the state receives a referral for an Indian child, when and how state or tribal law enforcement is involved, the roles of the BIA and state and tribal courts, and guidance dealing with transfers of jurisdiction to tribes that have their own child protection programs and courts, among other things. *See* SHANNON KELLER O'LOUGHLIN, A SURVEY AND ANALYSIS OF TRIBAL-STATE INDIAN CHILD WELFARE ACT AGREEMENTS (Ass'n on Am. Indian Affairs, June 2017), https://www.indian-affairs.org/uploads/8/7/3/8/87380358/icwa_tribal-state_agreements_report.pdf. For additional information see https://api.childwelfare.gov/topics/tribal-child-welfare/tribal-state-partnerships/?top=1528.
43. 42 U.S.C. § 679c; as of October 29, 2024, 20 tribes had been approved for direct funding. *See* https://www.acf.hhs.gov/cb/resource/tribes-with-approved-title-iv-e-plans.
44. 25 U.S.C. § 1915(b).
45. *Id.* § 1915(a). This may not be totally true in the case of a voluntary open adoption or a customary adoption.
46. *Id.*
47. *Id.* § 1913(a).
48. *See supra* note 28.
49. Adoptive Couple v. Baby Girl, 570 U.S. 637 (2013).
50. 25 U.S.C. § 1915(a), (b); 25 C.F.R. § 21.132(c)(4).
51. BIA GUIDELINES, *supra* note 14, § H.4.
52. 25 C.F.R. § 132(c). The Guidelines recognize that there may be "extraordinary circumstances where there is good cause to deviate from the placement preferences based on some reason outside of the five specially-listed factors,"

BIA Guidelines, *supra* note 14, § H.4., and that limited exception was utilized in one case to find good cause to deviate from the placement preferences where two and a half years had passed after removal of an 11-month-old child before the child was identified as an Indian child, even more time passed before the alternative placement [a non-Indian who had adopted the child's sibling] was identified as a preferred placement, and the child would suffer significant trauma if the bonds with her current family were broken. Alexandra K. v. Dep't of Child Safety, 2019 WL 258095 (Ariz. Ct. App. 2019).

53. 81 Fed. Reg. 38839.
54. 25 C.F.R. § 23.132.
55. *Id.*; *see* Gila River Indian Cmty. v. Dep't of Child Safety, 363 P.3d 148 (Ariz. 2015); *In re* Adoption of Baby Girl B, 67 P.3d 359 (Okla. 2003) (For purposes of applying the preferential scheme described in the ICWA regarding the preadoption placement of a child, the party proposing to deviate from the placement guidelines must establish good cause to do so by clear and convincing evidence.); Native Village of Tununak v. State, 303 P.3d 431 (Alaska 2013), *vacated in part on other grounds*, 334 P.3d 165 (Alaska 2014) (clear and convincing evidence applies to deviation from the ICWA placement preferences); *cf.* Taryn M. v. State of Alaska, 529 P.3d 523 (S. Ct. Alaska 2023) (suggesting that a clear and convincing standard applied to a determination whether a preferred placement is suitable); *but see* Fresno Cnty. v. Dep't of Child. & Fam. Servs. v. Super. Ct., 19 Cal. Rptr. 3d 155 (Cal. App. 2004) (applying substantial evidence test).
56. 25 C.F.R. § 23.132.
57. *Id.* § 23.132(c).
58. *Id.* § 23.132(c)(5).
59. *Id.* § 23.132(d).
60. *Id.* § 23.132(e).
61. This good cause exception is also referenced in the statutory language of the ICWA itself at 25 U.S.C. § 1915(c), which is the section of the ICWA authorizing tribes to alter the placement preferences by resolution.
62. 25 C.F.R. § 23.132(c)(1).

63. BIA Guidelines, *supra* note 14, § H.4.
64. 25 U.S.C. § 1915(c); BIA Guidelines, *supra* note 14, § H.4; *In re* T.S.W., 276 P.3d 133 (Kan. 2012).
65. BIA Guidelines, *supra* note 14, § H.4; note that a guardian ad litem's requests is not covered under the language of the ICWA. 25 U.S.C. § 1915(c).
66. *In re* C.B.D. & P.MP., 387 Mont. 347 (S. Ct. Mont. 2017) (holding that a mother who had previously terminated her parental rights had no standing to challenge the ICWA placement preferences); *cf.* Molly O. v. State Dep't of Health & Soc. Servs., Off. of Children's Servs., 320 P.3d 303 (Alaska 2014) (foster parents have no standing to challenge the ICWA's placement provisions); *but see* Navajo Nation v. Dep't of Child Safety, 2022 WL 402700 (Ariz. Ct. App. 2022) (in finding good cause to deviate from the placement preferences, the court considered the views of mother whose rights had been terminated since mother was going to have continued contact with the child and the nonpreferred placement also kept the child connected with his extended family and culture).
67. *See In re* Baby Girl Jane Doe, 865 P.2d 1090, 1095 (Mont. 1993) (held that tribe's right to enforce statutory preferences for adoptive placement of Indian children prevailed over mother's statutorily recognized interest in anonymity).
68. *See, e.g., In re* Baby Girl A., 282 Cal. Rptr. 105 (Ct. App. 1991) (in employing placement preferences of ICWA, Indian tribe's interest in voluntary adoption of minor who was only part Indian and living off the reservation was not as great as interest of parents); *In re* Adoption of Baby Boy J. 944 N.Y.S.2d 871 (N.Y. Sur. Ct. 2012) (finding good cause to deviate from the ICWA placement preferences when mother requested that a child be adopted by non-Indian couple where mother did not reside on reservation and foster parents would inform *Baby J.* of American Indian heritage); *cf. In re* N.N.E., 752 N.W.2d (Iowa 2008) (finding that parents have a fundamental right to raise children and that the Iowa ICWA, which did not allow court to utilize good cause to deviate from state's placement preferences, was unconstitutional and contrary to the provision in the ICWA allowing a parent's wishes to be a consideration under the ICWA).

69. 25 C.F.R. § 23.132.
70. *Id.* § 23.132(c)(3).
71. *Id.* § 23.131(a)(3).
72. *In re* Alexandria P., 1 Cal. App. 5th 331 (Ct. App. 2d Dist. Div. 5 Cal. 2016) (upholding trial court decision that foster parents had not shown good cause to depart from ICWA's placement preferences and which had ordered child removed from foster parents' custody and placed with extended family); *but see In re* K.R.C., I.A.C., Children, DHS v. 3 Affiliated Tribes, 236 Or. App. 535 (2011) (children will suffer serious harm if removed from foster parents due to bonding).
73. 81 Fed. Reg. 38846, referencing Comments of Casey Family Programs, et al., at 6 n.9 (citing literature including David E. Arrendondo & Leonard P. Edwards, *Attachment, Bonding, and Reciprocal Connectedness*, 2 J. CTR. FOR FAM. CHILD. & CTS. 109, 110–11 (2000) discussing the ways that bonding and attachment theory "may mislead courts"); *see also* People *ex rel.* A.R., 310 P.3d 1007 (Colo. App. 2012) (attachment not valid reason for deviation).
74. BIA GUIDELINES, *supra* note 14, § H.5.
75. *Holyfield*, 490 U.S. at 54 (citation omitted).
76. 81 Fed. Reg. 38846; BIA GUIDELINES, *supra* note 14, § H.5.
77. 25 C.F.R. § 23.132(c)(5); *In re* D.W., 795 N.W.2d 39 (SD 2011) (finding that the Department of Social Services had made a diligent search to locate an ICWA compliant placement and had worked with the tribe to locate an ICWA placement and that failure to find a placement for three and a half years amounted to good cause to deviate from the ICWA placement preferences).
78. 81 Fed. Reg. 38841.
79. BIA GUIDELINES, *supra* note 14, § H.4.
80. 81 Fed. Reg. 38798.
81. *See, e.g., In re* Adoption of B.G.J., 111 P.3d 651 (Kan. App. 2005), *aff'd*, 133 P.3d 1 (2006) (Good cause existed for deviation from adoptive placement preferences when mother preferred that child be adopted by prospective adoptive parents, four prospective adoptive placements with mother's

relatives were not suitable and child and prospective adoptive parents shared strong bond.)

82. *See, e.g., In re* Adoption of Baby Girl B., 67 P.3d 359 (Okla. Civ. App. 2003) (For purposes of determining whether good cause exists to depart from pre-adoptive placement scheme described in the ICWA, a child's best interest is a factor to consider, albeit not the sole criterion, because other factors, including those set forth in the statutes and the Bureau of Indian Affairs Guidelines, must also be considered.); *but see In re* Adoption of Riffle, 922 P.2d 510 (Mont. 1996) ("Good cause" exception to the ICWA's adoptive placement preferences, which presume that Indian child's best interests are best served by adoptive placement with extended family member, did not permit district court to conduct independent "best interest" analysis under state law to determine whether there was "good cause" not to follow ICWA placement preference.); *In re* Custody of S.E.G., 521 N.W.2d 357 (Minn. 1994) (utilizing best interests test is inappropriate).
83. 81 Fed. Reg. 38847.
84. 25 C.F.R. § 1213(d); 25 U.S.C. §§ 1914, 1916.
85. 25 U.S.C. § 1916(b).
86. *In re* Alexandria P., 176 Cal. Rptr. 3d 468 (Cal. App. 2014) (A tribe's consent to a foster care placement does not waive the requirement of adhering to the ICWA adoption placement preferences.).
87. 25 U.S.C. § 1916(a).
88. *Id.* § 1912.
89. *See In re* Adoption of a Child of Indian Heritage, 543 A.2d 925 (N.J. 1988) (Trial court did not abuse its discretion by refusing to vacate judgment of adoption for child, who may have been eligible for membership in Indian tribe, where court found that the putative father had done nothing to assert parental rights during the first 21 months of child's life.).
90. 25 U.S.C. § 1903(9).
91. *Id.* § 1915(e).
92. *Id.*
93. 42 U.S.C. § 671.

94. 25 U.S.C. §§ 1917, 1951; *see also* 25 C.F.R. § 23.71(b) for BIA's requirements to assist adult Indian adoptees; *In re* Adoption of Mellinger, 672 A.2d 197, 288 N.J. Super. Ct. 191 (N.J. App. 1996) (The ICWA provision allowing adopted Indian child access to state court records preempts state confidentiality law.); *In re* Adoption of Linda J.W., 682 N.Y.S.2d 565 (N.Y. Fam. Ct. 1998) (court holds that Canadian Indian entitled to have her adoption records released to Canadian band under the ICWA); *cf. In re* Adoption of Rebecca, 601 N.Y.S.2d 682 (N.Y. Sur. Ct. 1993) (the court held that the child there had a right to discover her tribal affiliation but that the information regarding the adoption would only be released to the Oneida Nation, the tribe with which she was attempting to enroll); *In re* Hanson, 470 N.W.2d 669 (Mich. App. 1991), 188 Mich. App. 392 (1991) (held that absent consent from the biological parents, a court should release information regarding the adult adoptee to the tribe responsible for enrollment issues and request that the tribe keep the information relative to the biological parents confidential to protect privacy).
95. 25 U.S.C. § 1951.

6 Collateral Challenges to ICWA Determinations

25 U.S.C. § 1914 permits any Indian child, tribe, and parent or Indian custodian from whose custody the child has been removed to petition a court of competent jurisdiction to invalidate a child custody proceeding if it violates §§ 1911, 1912, or 1913 of the act.[1] This provision seems to grant those parties, either alone or in concert, a federal court cause of action to collaterally attack an order that violates the Indian Child Welfare Act (ICWA). The availability of that remedy has proven less widely available than anticipated, however, for the reasons discussed herein. Of note, § 1914 is not available to a party who wishes to challenge a placement preference issue collaterally.[2]

Unfortunately, § 1914 does not explicitly confer on the federal courts subject matter jurisdiction to review state court ICWA decisions, unlike other provisions of federal law that do.[3] It is apparent from the legislative history that Congress did intend to allow some type of collateral review of ICWA decisions,[4] but the language of § 1914 does not unambiguously express that federal courts would have that authority.[5] The courts that have addressed this issue have found that jurisdiction may still lie under 28 U.S.C. § 1331, although that can be a contested issue.[6] Decisions by the Ninth and Tenth Circuits illustrate the divergent approaches of different federal circuit courts in regard to § 1914.

The Ninth Circuit in *Doe v. Mann*[7] held that § 1914 of the ICWA was an exception to the Rooker-Feldman doctrine, a rule derived from *Rooker v. Fidelity Trust*[8] and *District of Columbia Court of Appeals v. Feldman*[9] that bars federal courts, with the exception of the U.S. Supreme Court, from essentially serving as an appellate court to review state court decisions based on federal law. The court found that § 1914, in combination with the federal jurisdiction vested by the federal question statute, 28 U.S.C. § 1331, conferred jurisdiction on a federal district court to review alleged state court violations of §§ 1911–1913 of the ICWA.[10] The court reached that conclusion by the process of elimination, finding that Congress could not have intended the language of § 1914 referring to a "court of competent jurisdiction" as meaning a state or tribal court because tribal courts have no authority to overturn state court decisions and state courts would be barred by the doctrine of res judicata from questioning a final decision of another state court; thus, Congress must have intended some limited federal court authority.[11] After finding that it had the authority under § 1914, the court went on to conclude that the California state court properly exercised jurisdiction under § 1911 to terminate the parental rights of an Indian mother residing on an Indian reservation in California.[12] In a later case, a federal district court in the Ninth Circuit allowed a § 1914 challenge to a foster care placement based upon a claim of ineffective counsel in the state court proceeding, citing *Doe v. Mann.*[13]

By contrast, although in a subsequent case the Tenth Circuit appeared to allow for the use of § 1914 to challenge the validity of a parental consent (although it ultimately ruled against the parent),[14] and a federal district court in that circuit has utilized § 1914 to invalidate a mother's consent to a termination of parental rights,[15] in most cases the Tenth Circuit has found that the merits of a § 1914 claim could not be reached because of the requirement in 28 U.S.C. § 1738 that a federal court grant full faith and credit to the judgment of state courts.[16] That section requires that a federal court grant preclusive effect to a state court decision, provided that there is identity of parties and the issues sought to be litigated in federal court were litigated in the state forum.[17] Thus, it appears that a case brought in the Tenth Circuit to review a state court's application and disposition of a child custody proceeding under the ICWA may be barred by res judicata, provided that the issues were litigated in state court.[18]

There are several potential ways to avoid this outcome, but they are risky. One would be for a party to seek federal court intervention before the state court acts, possibly under 28 U.S.C. § 1331 (federal question jurisdiction) or even under 42 U.S.C. § 1983, seeking to enjoin the state court from taking action in violation of the ICWA. Such an action would obviously be met with an argument that the Anti-Injunction Act prohibits a federal court from enjoining a state court from taking action on a matter clearly within its jurisdiction,[19] and at least one court has ruled that the abstention doctrine precluded the use of § 1983 to challenge the handling by one South Dakota county of emergency child welfare proceedings involving Indian children.[20]

A second potential strategy would be for an interested party with standing, such as a tribe, to intentionally not participate in the state court proceeding to avoid the identity of parties requirement for the application of the full faith and credit clause. Choosing this route is dangerous, however, especially because the failure of the tribe to participate in the state court proceedings may translate into the loss of input into important decisions, including placement decisions.

Of course, a federal court may not be the only court of competent jurisdiction where an action can be brought under § 1914. If the child in question was domiciled on a reservation at the time of the commencement of some child custody proceeding in state court and the state court nonetheless exercised jurisdiction, the tribal court may be an available forum to bring an action to invalidate the state court order.[21] Obtaining the tribal court order and having it enforced are two different matters, however, and some type of federal court intervention, possibly under 28 U.S.C. § 1331 to declare that the tribal court order is entitled to deference, may be necessary.[22] A federal court decision from the Western District of Oklahoma recognized that a federal court may exercise jurisdiction under § 1331 to declare that a tribal court has exclusive jurisdiction over an Indian child.[23]

In addition, practitioners should not foreclose the possibility of state courts being utilized under § 1914. In some cases, Indian tribes have been found to have standing under § 1914 to petition a state court to invalidate an adoption that took place in state court.[24] Indeed, if new evidence becomes available that was not reasonably obtainable at the time of the state court proceeding, a state court might be an appropriate forum for an invalidation action. For example, if a state agent knows that the child in question is possibly Indian but withholds that information from the court, the parent, child, or tribe may be able to use § 1914 to invalidate all proceedings held in state court in violation of the ICWA, although one court has held that such jurisdiction does not lie.[25] Section 1914 has also been used to allow litigants to raise ICWA violations at the state appellate stage even though the issues were not raised before the trial court,[26] and has been utilized as a basis for a tribe to appeal the trial court judgment even where the parent has not appealed.[27]

There does not appear to be any statute of limitations associated with the use of § 1914, as compared to § 1913(d), which permits a collateral challenge against an adoption obtained through fraud or duress but only if the challenge is brought within two years.[28] Of course, in a case where the § 1914 challenge is brought based upon a violation of § 1913(d), presumably those provisions would be read in pari materia.[29] At least one state court has utilized state limitations periods to limit § 1914 challenges.[30] A federal court decision denied a motion to dismiss, however, based upon a state statute of limitations.[31] It did not make a specific holding on whether there is a statute of limitations pertaining to the use of § 1914, but opined that at a minimum (referencing § 1913(d)), any statute of limitations that might be imposed would have to be at least two years.[32]

Federal court jurisdiction does seem to lie to challenge tribal court determinations in child custody proceedings if the litigants challenge the tribal court's jurisdictional authority.[33] One court has even held that a federal court can intervene to remove from a tribal court's jurisdiction a child who had been wrongfully transferred to the tribal court's jurisdiction without notice to the natural parents.[34]

In short, although there are potential avenues for collateral challenges to ICWA decisions, the path to success for such challenges can be daunting and vary according to jurisdiction. Thus, in general, such strategies should generally be considered as a last resort when other efforts have failed or would be futile.

Endnotes

1. 25 U.S.C. § 1914. The prior custody requirement has generally been understood to apply to removal of the child from either the physical or legal custody of a parent. *See In re* the Adoption of B.B., 2017 UT 59, 417 P.3d 1 (2017). It has been held that a stepparent lacks standing to file a § 1914 petition. *See In re* Kerby, 13 P.3d 523 (Or. Ct. App. 2000).
2. Placement provisions governed by § 1915 cannot be challenged under § 1914.

3. For example, federal courts are explicitly vested with habeas corpus jurisdiction to review violations of the Indian Civil Rights Act. *See* 25 U.S.C. § 1303.
4. H.R. Rep. No. 95-1386, at 23 (1978), *reprinted in* 1978 U.S.C.C.A.N. 7530.
5. The ICWA does not define the term "court of competent jurisdiction" that is utilized in 25 U.S.C. § 1914, leaving that issue up to judicial resolution. Although it could mean a state or tribal court, it is hard to envision why one state trial court would have the authority to overrule a decision of another trial judge under § 1914 in lieu of an appeal of the challenged decision, except in some limited circumstances. It is also difficult to conceive of tribal court authority to overturn a state court decision unless the state court may have unlawfully assumed jurisdiction over a reservation-domiciled child or a ward of the tribal court in express violation of 25 U.S.C. § 1911(a).
6. *See* Roman Nose v. New Mexico Dep't of Human Resources, 967 F.2d 435 (10th Cir. 1992).
7. 415 F.3d 1038 (9th Cir. 2005), *cert. denied*, 126 S. Ct. 1911 (2006).
8. 263 U.S. 413 (1923).
9. 460 U.S. 462 (1983).
10. Doe v. Mann, 415 F.3d 1038, 1045 (9th Cir. 2005).
11. *Id.* at 1045.
12. *Id.* at 1058.
13. Kirk v. Baldovinus, 2010 WL 2763283 (N.D. Cal. 2010).
14. Nielson v. Ketchum, 640 F.3d 1117 (10th Cir. 2011).
15. Adoption of C.D.K., 629 F. Supp. 1258 (D. Utah 2009).
16. *See* 28 U.S.C. § 1738; *see, e.g.*, Kickapoo Tribe of Oklahoma v. Rader, 822 F.2d 1493 (10th Cir. 1987); Kiowa Tribe of Oklahoma v. Lewis, 777 F.2d 587 (10th Cir. 1985); Navajo Nation v. Dist. Ct., 624 F. Supp. 130 (D. Utah 1985), *dismissed as moot*, 831 F.2d 929 (10th Cir. 1987); Yancey v. Thomas, 441 Fed. Appx. 552 (10th Cir. 2011). *See also* Morrow v. Winslow, 94 F.3d 1386 (10th Cir. 1996) (natural father of Indian child barred by doctrine of abstention from invoking federal court jurisdiction to enjoin Oklahoma state

court proceeding, which had declared that his consent to adoption was not necessary under Oklahoma law because he had abandoned child).

17. *See* 28 U.S.C. § 1738.
18. *See Kickapoo Tribe of Oklahoma*, 822 F.2d at 1501.
19. *See* 28 U.S.C. § 2283.
20. Oglala Sioux v. Fleming, 904 F.3d 603 (8th Cir. 2018), *reversing* Oglala Sioux Tribe v. Van Hunnik, 100 F. Supp. 3d 749 (D.S.D. 2015), which had held that the South Dakota process was a civil rights violation under § 1983.
21. The Supreme Court in *Holyfield v. Mississippi Band of Choctaw Indians*, 490 U.S. 30, 51 n.26 stated that when a reservation-domiciled child is involved the tribal court is the only court with jurisdiction.
22. The Supreme Court has recognized that the extent of a tribal court's jurisdiction is a matter of federal law and raises a federal question under 28 U.S.C. § 1331. *See* Nat'l Farmers Union Ins. Co. v. Crow Tribe of Indians, 105 S. Ct. 2447 (1985). The U.S. Court of Appeals for the Eighth Circuit has also held that a federal court may properly exercise jurisdiction over a dispute between parties with conflicting tribal and state court custody orders, provided that tribal court remedies are exhausted. *See* Dement v. Oglala Sioux Tribal Ct., 874 F.2d 510 (8th Cir. 1989).
23. *See* Comanche Indian Tribe of Oklahoma v. Hovis, 847 F. Supp. 871 (W.D. Okla. 1994); *but see* Fletcher v. Florida, 858 F. Supp. (M.D. Fla. 1994) (dismissing claims of Indian mother against various state and private officials brought under various federal civil rights statutes for alleged violations of the ICWA).
24. *See, e.g., In re* Petition of Phillip A.C. v. Tlingit & Haida Tribes of Alaska, 122 Nev. 1284, 149 P.3d 51 (Nev. S.Ct. 2006); *but cf.* Interest of A.M., 570 S.W.3d. 860 (Tex. Ct. App. 2018) (defects in temporary orders do not allow a § 1914 challenge to a final judgment).
25. In Slone v. Inyo Cnty. Juv. Ct., 282 Cal. Rptr. 126 (Ct. App. 1991), the court rejected an attempt to invoke the superior court's jurisdiction to reverse a juvenile court's application of the ICWA.

26. *See, e.g., In re* Enrique P., 709 N.W.2d 676 (Neb. App. 2006).
27. In the Interest of S.E. & B.E., 527 S.W.3d 894 (Mo. Ct. App. 2017).
28. *See* 25 U.S.C. § 1913(d).
29. *Id.*
30. *See In re* Adoption of Erin G., 140 P.3d 886 (Alaska 2006), *cert. denied sub nom.* Daniel L. v. Grant, 127 S. Ct. 591 (2006).
31. Kirk v. Baldovinus, 2010 WL 2763283 (N.D. Cal. 2010).
32. *Id.*
33. *See* LaBeau v. Dakota, 815 F. Supp. 1074 (W.D. Mich. 1993) (habeas corpus jurisdiction lies in federal court to challenge tribal court's assumption of jurisdiction); Sandman v. Dakota, 816 F. Supp. 448 (W.D. Mich. 1992).
34. Brown *ex rel.* Brown v. Rice, 760 F. Supp. 1459 (D. Kan. 1991).

7 Funding ICWA Programs

Funding for tribes and tribal organizations to operate Indian Child Welfare Act (ICWA) programs has been of utmost concern since the enactment of the ICWA. Indian tribes and organizations need funding to provide the variety of services required to establish and maintain an effective child welfare assistance program. Title II of the ICWA recognizes a broad scope of activities that may be conducted by Indian tribes and organizations.[1] Some of these services include the licensing of foster homes, the delivery of services to families to avoid displacement of children, the provision of legal services and advice for both the tribe and entities involved in ICWA proceedings, and the education and training of tribal court personnel to implement the ICWA.[2] This is a very ambitious agenda for any tribe delving into the ICWA arena.

Funding for tribal ICWA programs has historically been a patchwork where programs pull together resources from a variety of different sources. There are a few main sources of federal funding that a tribe or tribal organization may access to operate ICWA programs, exclusive of any money the tribe may provide from its own revenue sources. First, under Title II of the ICWA the Secretary of Interior is authorized to make grants to Indian tribes and organizations, including off-reservation programs, for the establishment and operation of child welfare programs and implementation of child welfare codes.[3] The grants for on-reservation programs are directed at the delivery of services to reservation families or near-reservation families, while the off-reservation grants are geared toward allowing the payment of foster care subsidies in a manner comparable to the states, as well as ancillary services to those families.[4]

Since 1994, ICWA funds have been awarded to tribes on a formula grant basis.[5] Of note, the definition of "Indian" in § 1934 is broader than that in the substantive portion of the ICWA, which allows tribes at their discretion to service some individuals who may not be covered by the ICWA definition of Indian.[6] There has also been a small amount of funding available to tribes to implement the Indian Child Protection and Family Violence Prevention Act,[7] a law that was enacted in 1990 but that was not funded for many years.[8]

A second source of funding for tribes is Title IV-B of the Social Security Act.[9] Title IV-B, Part I funds general child welfare services, including activities to promote the safety and well-being of children and prevent child abuse and neglect.[10] An "Indian tribal organization" may receive Title IV-B, Part 1 funds directly from the federal government if it "has a plan for child welfare services approved under this subpart" and 3 percent has been set aside for tribes under this part.[11] This section has been implemented by a tribal-specific regulation, which specifies how tribes need to comply with the requirements of Title IV-B, Part 1.[12]

Title IV-B, Part 2, provides funding for child welfare services designed to prevent the breakup of or to reunify the family, as well as funding to support adoptive families.[13] There is a 3 percent allocation for tribes that is awarded on a formula basis.[14] Part II also includes a court improvement program that tribes access on a competitive grant basis, with funds set aside specifically for tribal courts.[15]

Title IV-B is a matching funds program, meaning that the entity that receives funding must provide a fiscal match to the amount provided by the federal government.[16] Title II of ICWA specifically authorizes ICWA grants to be used as the match for a grant under Title IV-B, as can relevant funds from Pub. Law 95-638 contracts.[17] See discussion about Pub. Law 95-638 contracts later in this chapter. Title II also prohibits the Secretary of Health and Human Services (HHS) from denying funding under Title IV-B because a tribe has received funding under Title II of the ICWA.[18]

Since 2008, tribes, tribal organizations, and tribal consortia at their option can apply directly to HHS to administer the Title IV-E foster care and adoption assistance program and receive direct funding from HHS.[19] Title IV-E provides for foster care, guardianship, and adoption assistance payments and related administrative and training expenses,[20] and in 2018 new sections were added to the law by the Family First Prevention Services Act that allow for the use of Title IV-E funds for prevention services under some circumstances.[21] Unlike the other funding sources, Title IV-E is an entitlement program, which means that it is not subject to appropriations.[22] Rather, tribes and states are entitled to receive a partial reimbursement of all money that they spend for eligible purposes.[23] Thus, it is a more stable source of funding than other available federal resources. Tribes already possess the authority to license foster homes, which in turn renders those homes eligible for any federally assisted program, including Title IV-E.[24] Except in limited circumstances, tribal plans for administration of the program must fulfill similar requirements as the statute sets out for state plans.[25] One significant difference is that tribes can also receive funding for culturally adapted prevention programs, whereas states can only receive funding for evidence-based prevention programs listed on a federal Clearinghouse.[26]

Tribal–state agreements are an alternative to direct funding from the federal government. When tribes request to enter into a Title IV-E agreement with a state, the state is required to negotiate with the tribe in good faith.[27] The requirement to negotiate was added in 2008. Prior to that, there was no affirmative obligation for the state to enter into cooperative agreements with tribes for the pass-through of Title IV-E monies, although some tribal-state agreements were voluntarily negotiated prior to the 2008 amendments.[28]

Under Pub. Law 95-638, tribes may also contract to provide services that would otherwise be provided by the federal government.[29] This may include the Bureau of Indian Affairs Social Service program. That program covers a number of areas beyond child welfare, but the funding from that program is sometimes used to supplement other sources of funding for tribal child welfare programs.[30] There are also a variety of other small federal sources that provide funding to a limited number of tribes—for example, some states pass through Title XX Social Services block grant money to tribes.[31]

Many tribes receive direct federal funding for the Temporary Assistance to Needy Families (TANF) program.[32] Among other things, those funds can be used to promote assistance to needy families so that children can be cared for in their own homes.[33] One type of TANF grant is a child-only grant that can be paid to relative caregivers.[34] Another program that has funded some tribal child welfare related activities is the Tiwahe Social Services initiative, which is designed to promote systems change in services provided to children and families by incorporating tribal customs and values into a tribe's social services programming.[35]

There are also some instances where states have provided tribes with state funds to operate their tribal child welfare programs. One mechanism has been to provide the nonfederal match for foster care maintenance payments for those tribes who are operating Title IV-E through an agreement with the state.[36] In other cases, states have simply included tribes as recipients of funds in state child welfare programs that assist all children in the state.[37]

Of course, tribes can also use funds from their own revenue sources to support child welfare programs, although most do not have the financial capacity to fully and adequately fund a comprehensive child welfare program.

Thus, it is apparent that Indian tribes and tribal organizations, as well as urban Indian programs that work in the ICWA field, need to be creative in accessing multiple sources of funding to support their ICWA programs fully and carry out the huge responsibilities recognized by Congress when it enacted the ICWA. Only with adequate funding for tribes will the problems that frequently lead to the removal of Indian children from their homes be redressed.

Endnotes

1. 25 U.S.C. §§ 1931–1932.
2. *Id.*
3. *Id.*
4. *Id.*
5. 25 C.F.R. § 23.25, as amended by 59 Fed. Reg. at 2248, converted the competitive grant award process for Indian tribes into a noncompetitive funding process. In FY 2024, $17.848 million was appropriated for ICWA grants for tribes. *See* U.S. Dep't of the Interior, Budget Justifications and Performance Information, FY 2025, at IA-ST-1.
6. *See* 25 U.S.C. § 1603(c), incorporated into Title II of ICWA by 25 U.S.C. § 1934; *compare* 25 U.S.C. § 1603(c) *with* 25 U.S.C. § 1903(8). At some point, these inconsistent definitions raised a question whether terminated tribes might be eligible for funding under ICWA, but this does not seem to have materialized.
7. 25 U.S.C. §§ 3201 *et seq.*

8. *See* testimony by National Indian Child Welfare Association for FY 2024 and 2025 to the United States House of Representatives, Committee on Appropriations, Subcommittee on Interior, Environment, & Related Agencies at https://www.congress.gov/118/meeting/house/115411/witnesses/HHRG-118-AP06-Wstate-MartinA-20230308.pdf and https://indianz.com/News/wp-content/uploads/2024/05/16/HHRG-118-AP06-Wstate-MartinA-20240508.pdf.
9. 42 U.S.C. §§ 620 *et seq.* This law now requires states to include in their Title IV-B plans a description of the specific measures the state has taken to comply with ICWA after consultation with tribal entities. 42 U.S.C. § 622(b)(9). Recent 2024 amendments have added much more specificity to this provision, requiring states to include information about "how the State will ensure timely notice to Indian tribes of State custody proceedings involving Indian children, foster care or adoptive placement of Indian children, and case recordkeeping as such matters relate to jurisdiction, termination of parental rights, and active efforts." The law also requires states to make a more concerted effort to recruit minority foster families, which may assist in recruitment of Indian foster families. 42 U.S.C. § 622(b)(7).
10. 42 U.S.C. § 620-628b.
11. *Id.* § 628.
12. 45 C.F.R. § 1357.40. In 2023, 172 tribes and tribal consortia (including Alaska Native nonprofit corporations) received more than $7.36 million under Title IV-B, Part I. *See* https://acf.gov/sites/default/files/documents/cb/FY%202023%20Allotment%20Tables%20for%20Tribes.pdf.
13. 42 U.S.C. §§ 629 *et seq.*
14. *Id.* § 629f(b)(3). In 2023, 126 tribes and tribal consortia (including Alaska Native nonprofit corporations) received more than $10.43 million under Title IV-B, Part II. https://acf.gov/sites/default/files/documents/cb/FY%202023%20Allotment%20Tables%20for%20Tribes.pdf.

15. 42 U.S.C. § 629h(c)(3)(A)(iv).
16. *See id.* § 622.
17. 25 U.S.C. § 1931 (b) (Title Ill of ICUA); 25 U.S.C. § 5325(j) (P.L. 93-638 Contracting).
18. *Id.*
19. 42 U.S.C. § 679c; as of August 8, 2024, 20 tribes have been approved for direct federal funding, although not all tribes have implemented the program. https://www.acf.hhs.gov/cb/grant-funding/tribes-approved-title-iv-e-plans.
20. 42 U.S.C. §§ 670 *et seq.*
21. Pub. Law No. 115-123, §§ 50701–50782. This new program has not yet been fully implemented. As of February 3, 2025, 43 states and four tribes of the tribes receiving direct federal funding have been approved to operate a Family First program. https://www.acf.hhs.gov/cb/data/status-submitted-title-iv-e-prevention-program-five-year-plans.
22. *See* 42 U.S.C. § 674(a)(1-3); *id.* § 673(d).
23. *Id.*
24. *See* 25 U.S.C. § 1931(b).
25. *See* 42 U.S.C. § 679c.
26. *See* and *compare* 42 U.S.C. § 671(e)(4) *with* 42 U.S.C. § 679c(c)(1)(E)(i). *See also* Administration for Children & Families, Child Welfare Policy Section 8.6 (recognizing that tribes accessing Title IV-E through tribal–state agreements also have the ability to receive funding for culturally based prevention programs).
27. 42 U.S.C. § 671(a)(32); ICWA also authorizes states and tribes to enter into cooperative agreements respecting the care and custody of Indian children. 25 U.S.C. § 1919(a).
28. *See* Trope & O'Loughlin, *A Survey and Analysis of Select Title IV-E Tribal State Agreements* (Rockville, MD: Association on American Indian Affairs, Mar. 2014) at 1, https://narf.org/nill/resources/title-iv-e/.

29. 25 U.S.C. §§ 450 *et seq.*
30. *See, e.g.*, U.S. Dep't of the Interior, Budget Justifications and Performance Information for Fiscal Year 2016, at IA-HS-1-4.
31. *See, e.g.*, Oregon Dep't of Human Services Legislative Commission on Indian Affairs 2015 Government-to-Government Report (Dec. 2015). Title XX can be found at 42 U.S.C. §§ 1397–1397f.
32. 42 U.S.C. § 612. As of 2020, there were 75 approved tribal TANF programs serving nearly half of the 574 federally recognized tribes. https://www.cbpp.org/research/income-security/tribal-tanf.
33. https://www.acf.hhs.gov/ofa/programs/tribal/tribal-tanf.
34. Craig W. Abbey, Welfare Reform: TANF Cash Benefits (Washington D.C.: Congressional Research Service, Mar. 2001).
35. In FY 2024, Congress appropriated $44.5 million for the Tiwahe program. *See* Testimony of Deb Haaland, Secretary, U.S. Department of the Interior before the Subcommittee on Interior, Environment and Related Agencies, Committee on Appropriations, United States Senate, May 8, 2024, https://www.doi.gov/ocl/interior-budget-18#:~:text=The%202025%20BIA%20budget%20contains,above%20the%202024%20CR%20level. Ten tribes were full participants in the program and another ten tribes received seed grants. *See* https://www.bia.gov/tiwahe; *see also* U.S. Dep't of the Interior, Budget Justifications and Performance Information, FY 2025, at IA-HS-2.
36. Trope & O'Loughlin, *supra* note 28, at 36 (lists states that pay entire maintenance payment, both the federal and nonfederal share).
37. *Id.* at 9 (agreements between the State of Minnesota and Leech Lake and White Earth Bands of Ojibwe).

8 ICWA: After Almost Half a Century

More than 45 years have passed since the Indian Child Welfare Act (ICWA) became binding on all state courts and agencies in this country. Without a doubt, the ICWA has had an impact, but at the same time it is certainly true that the expectations of its authors have not yet been fully realized.

When the ICWA was passed in 1978, it was novel in many respects. It required active efforts to keep families together or reunify them and provided for preferred placements with relatives at a time when much of the prevailing attitude was that it was best to remove children from environments that (in the eyes of the larger society) were detrimental to the children. Uprooting such children to entirely new environments and separating them from their larger family was often considered best for the child.

Those perspectives have now been largely rejected. Since 2008, to receive federal funding, all agencies must first seek to identify relative placements, and kinship guardianship is now funded by the federal government.[1] In 2018, Congress changed federal law to provide preventive services as part of the Title IV-E entitlement program to keep children with their parents whenever possible.[2] Indeed, many national child welfare organizations now have endorsed the principles of the ICWA—keeping children with parents whenever possible, placing them with relatives if they must be removed, and maintaining the connection of children with their communities and cultures—as the gold standard in child welfare that should be provided to all children.[3]

In addition, the ICWA has also served as an educational device for many state court judges and social services agencies in this country that ignored or perhaps never paused to reflect on the specific needs of Indian children and their unique circumstances. Many lawyers representing the interests of Indian tribes and parents in ICWA cases will acknowledge that often the key to obtaining a fair application of the ICWA is to educate the judge about why the law exists. Implementing the ICWA supports a broader objective of educating predominantly non-Indian judges about Indian tribes and children in a manner that promotes multicultural understanding and sensitivity.

The ICWA has also played a primary role in strengthening tribal courts and other tribal institutions, thereby increasing the esteem by which those entities are held in the eyes of the tribal and non-Indian community alike. Tribal courts play a critical role in the implementation of the ICWA, and most tribes have accepted this role by enhancing their court systems and social services agencies in a manner that redounds to the benefit of all who interact with those entities. In fact, some tribes, particularly tribes in states subject to Pub. Law 83-280 (P.L. 280), resurrected their court systems in response to the enactment of the ICWA, which has led to an extension of those tribes' sovereign authorities. Tribes have also used this opportunity to examine the value of more traditional forms of dispute resolution. It is perhaps not coincidental that after the enactment of the ICWA, the federal courts began issuing decisions recognizing the role tribal courts play in the American system of jurisprudence by deferring to the authority of tribal courts.[4]

A byproduct of these developments has been increasing dialogue between state and tribal judges and officials that has extended beyond the ICWA into other areas of mutual concern, such as recognition of one another's judgments and cooperative agreements to enhance the welfare of Indian children. In many states, discussion regarding the ICWA has been the lure for state and tribal court judges to convene to discuss the state of the law and working arrangements for its implementation. Those discussions have inevitably extended into other areas of concern and have led to state and tribal court fora in some states, where meetings are held regularly to resolve matters of mutual concern.

The ICWA has also led to the enactment of many state laws pertaining to Indian children and families (sometimes referred as state ICWAs) that often provide protections that are stronger than the federal law. This is a result of successful education and advocacy efforts by tribes targeted at state legislators. The ICWA has certainly been a catalyst for these efforts.

For all its successes, however, the law has fallen short of its remedial goals. Although the out-of-home placement rate is lower than it was prior to 1978, Indian children are still removed from their parents, guardians, and custodians at almost three times the rate of non-Indians, even though the rate of substantiated abuse and neglect of Indian child is comparable to (only slightly higher than) the rate for non-Indian children.[5] In addition, a slight majority of Indian children are still placed in non-Native, nonrelative homes, which is significantly less than the estimated 90 percent before enactment, but still far greater than expected.[6] Part of this is the challenge in recruiting Native American foster homes and sometimes the reluctance of families to get involved. One need only peruse a small number of ICWA cases, however, to know that sometimes there are family members willing and able to take a child who are unsuccessful in that quest. The U.S. Supreme Court's *Adoptive Couple v. Baby Girl* decision is perhaps the most well-known and most publicized example of this occurring.[7]

Thus, although the data shows that we have seen some improvement from the situation as it was in 1978, it also suggests that racism or at least cultural insensitivity and biases continue to play a role in some child welfare decisions. It is a paradox that while policies supported by federal and state policymakers and child welfare experts have in general moved toward the principles incorporated in the ICWA, many child welfare organizations have recognized ICWA as the gold standard in child welfare, and there was overwhelming support for ICWA from states and parent's and children's attorneys, among others, when ICWA's constitutionality was recently challenged unsuccessfully in the *Haaland v. Brackeen* case,[8] at the same time implementation at the case level continues to fall short of ICWA's goals. One recent development seeking to address these issues is the development of ICWA courts in a number of jurisdictions. Those courts include judges and advocates specially assigned to ICWA cases who are knowledgeable about and committed to the principles of the law, including making special efforts to involve tribes as an integral part of the court proceedings.[9]

In part, the reason for the gap between ICWA's goals and its outcomes may also be because there are limitations inherent in ICWA that limit its ability to achieve its lofty remedial goals. ICWA is a procedural statute for a substantive problem. The underlying problems that may lead to the separation of Indian children from their families are not only the byproducts of faulty state institutions but also the result of multigenerational social ills and trauma that may impact the family. These ills and trauma, many of which can be directly tied to the introduction of alcohol and drugs into the lives of Native Americans and the destruction of the lifestyle of Native Americans by non-Indians, must be redressed if Indian children and families are going to remain fully intact.

When confronted with the removal of Indian children, many state court judges have no benchmark to judge "traditional Native American culture" against except that particular judge's perceptions of that culture, which in many cases is stereotypical and may not be positive because of the stark reality that family law judges most often see families in crisis. The concepts embodied in the ICWA, of traditional Native American child-rearing practices preserving the unique values of Indian culture, can seem overly idealistic when considered in light of the panoply of social problems that sometimes confront Indian families.

Those social problems receive little, if any, attention in the ICWA, except in Title II where limited funding is made available for Indian tribes. Although some important recent progress has been made in making additional resources available to tribes through Title IV-B, Title IV-E, Pub. Law 93-638 contracts with the Bureau of Indian Affairs, and other federal programs, funding continues to be insufficient for most tribes to be able to comprehensively deal with the day-to-day problems associated with transferring state court cases and intervening in those cases, much less to confront all of the underlying issues that may impact families.

The ICWA must not be viewed as a panacea then, but simply as a piece in a larger puzzle that includes addressing the challenges faced by Native American families—particularly challenges related to historical trauma, substance abuse, and poverty. The ICWA was a law designed to eliminate state institutional practices that led to the breakup of Indian families and was not designed to redress the social ills that lead to family disintegration nor to comprehensively attack all of the root causes for the displacement of Indian children. This is an ongoing challenge for federal, state, and tribal governments, a challenge that is being acknowledged more frequently by all levels of government.

In the end, one has to marvel at the grand design and ambitious objective sought by the enactment of the ICWA. It sought to convince courts and agencies that keeping children with their families, communities, and cultures was in their best interest. It also sought to achieve a larger goal of preserving distinct tribal cultures across this country by protecting the children of those cultures. It was a recognition that cultural attachment is a right of Indian children worthy of congressional protection.

Indeed, it is the children who receive the protections of ICWA who will eventually decide the fate of Native American cultures and traditions. If ICWA works as intended, whether they embrace their traditions will be their decision and not the result of a system that alienates them from their families and cultures.

Endnotes

1. 42 U.S.C. § 673(d).
2. Pub. Law No. 115-123, Title VII.
3. *See* brief of Casey Family Programs et al., https://turtletalk.blog/wp-content/uploads/2022/08/cfpamicus.pdf.
4. *See, e.g.,* Nat'l Farmers Union Ins. Cos. v. Crow Tribe of Indians, 471 U.S. 845, 105 S. Ct. 2447 (1985); Iowa Mutual Ins. Co. v. LaPlante, 480 U.S. 9, 107 S. Ct. 971 (1987).
5. Analysis based upon publicly available data from the 2011–2021 Adoption and Foster Care Analysis Reporting System (AFCARS). This is not a perfect measure of the placement of Native children, as it is based upon self-identification, which may be different than the definition of Indian child in ICWA, which is based upon tribal membership. The AFCARS have been

amended to include the specific identification of Native children covered by the ICWA, so future data should more accurately reflect the impact of the ICWA requirements. See Chapter 1, text associated with footnotes 115–118.

6. *Id.*
7. 570 U.S. 637, 133 S. Ct. 2552 (2013).
8. *See* State A.G.'s, Family Defenders and National Association of Counsel for Children's briefs, https://turtletalk.blog/2022/08/21/amicus-briefs-in-haaland-v-brackeen/. Twenty-three states and the District of Columbia (including states as diverse as Utah, California, South Dakota, and Oregon) filed a brief in support of ICWA's constitutionality, whereas only two states joined Texas (one of the parties) in arguing that it was unconstitutional.
9. https://www.ncjfcj.org/child-welfare-and-juvenile-law/icwa-courts/.

Appendix A

Indian Child Welfare Act of 1978 (25 U.S.C. §§ 1901–63, P.L. 95-608)

§ 1901. Congressional findings

Recognizing the special relationship between the United States and the Indian tribes and their members and the Federal responsibility to Indian people, the Congress finds—

(1) that clause 3, section 8, article I of the United States Constitution provides that "The Congress shall have Power * * * To regulate Commerce * * * with Indian tribes and, through this and other constitutional authority, Congress has plenary power over Indian affairs;
(2) that Congress, through statutes, treaties, and the general course of dealing with Indian tribes, has assumed the responsibility for the protection and preservation of Indian tribes and their resources;
(3) that there is no resource that is more vital to the continued existence and integrity of Indian tribes than their

children and that the United States has a direct interest, as trustee, in protecting Indian children who are members of or are eligible for membership in an Indian tribe;

(4) that an alarmingly high percentage of Indian families are broken up by the removal, often unwarranted, of their children from them by nontribal public and private agencies and that an alarmingly high percentage of such children are placed in non-Indian foster and adoptive homes and institutions; and

(5) that the States, exercising their recognized jurisdiction over Indian child custody proceedings through administrative and judicial bodies, have often failed to recognize the essential tribal relations of Indian people and the cultural and social standards prevailing in Indian communities and families.

§ 1902. Congressional declaration of policy

The Congress hereby declares that it is the policy of this Nation to protect the best interests of Indian children and to promote the stability and security of Indian tribes and families by the establishment of minimum Federal standards for the removal of Indian children from their families and the placement of such children in foster or adoptive homes which will reflect the unique values of Indian culture, and by providing for assistance to Indian tribes in the operation of child and family service programs.

§ 1903. Definitions

For the purposes of this chapter, except as may be specifically provided otherwise, the term—

(1) "child custody proceeding" shall mean and include—

  i. "foster care placement" which shall mean any action removing an Indian child from its parent or Indian custodian for temporary placement in a foster home or institution or the home of a guardian or conservator where the parent or Indian custodian cannot have the child returned upon demand, but where parental rights have not been terminated;

ii. "termination of parental rights" which shall mean any action resulting in the termination of the parent-child relationship;

iii. "preadoptive placement" which shall mean the temporary placement of an Indian child in a foster home or institution after the termination of parental rights, but prior to or in lieu of adoptive placement; and

iv. "adoptive placement" which shall mean the permanent placement of an Indian child for adoption, including any action resulting in a final decree of adoption. Such term or terms shall not include a placement based upon an act which, if committed by an adult, would be deemed a crime or upon an award, in a divorce proceeding, of custody to one of the parents.

(2) "extended family member" shall be as defined by the law or custom of the Indian child's tribe or, in the absence of such law or custom, shall be a person who has reached the age of eighteen and who is the Indian child's grandparent, aunt or uncle, brother or sister, brother-in-law or sister-in-law, niece or nephew, first or second cousin, or stepparent;

(3) "Indian" means any person who is a member of an Indian tribe, or who is an Alaska Native and a member of a Regional Corporation as defined in 1606 of title 43;

(4) "Indian child" means any unmarried person who is under age eighteen and is either (a) a member of an Indian tribe or (b) is eligible for membership in an Indian tribe and is the biological child of a member of an Indian tribe;

(5) "Indian child's tribe" means (a) the Indian tribe in which an Indian child is a member or eligible for membership or (b), in the case of an Indian child who is a member of or eligible for membership in more than one tribe, the Indian tribe with which the Indian child has the more significant contacts;

(6) "Indian custodian" means any Indian person who has legal custody of an Indian child under tribal law or custom or under State law or to whom temporary physical care, custody, and control has been transferred by the parent of such child;

(7) "Indian organization" means any group, association, partnership, corporation, or other legal entity owned or controlled by Indians, or a majority of whose members are Indians;

(8) "Indian tribe" means any Indian tribe, band, nation, or other organized group or community of Indians recognized as eligible for the services provided to Indians by the Secretary because of their status as Indians, including any Alaska Native village as defined in section 1602(c) of title 43;

(9) "parent" means any biological parent or parents of an Indian child or any Indian person who has lawfully adopted an Indian child, including adoptions under tribal law or custom. It does not include the unwed father where paternity has not been acknowledged or established;

(10) "reservation" means Indian country as defined in section 1151 of title 18 and any lands, not covered under such section, title to which is either held by the United States in trust for the benefit of any Indian tribe or individual or held by any Indian tribe or individual subject to a restriction by the United States against alienation;

(11) "Secretary" means the Secretary of the Interior; and

(12) "tribal court" means a court with jurisdiction over child custody proceedings and which is either a Court of Indian Offenses, a court established and operated under the code or

custom of an Indian tribe, or any other administrative body of a tribe which is vested with authority over child custody proceedings.

§ 1911. Indian tribe jurisdiction over Indian child custody proceedings

(a) Exclusive jurisdiction

An Indian tribe shall have jurisdiction exclusive as to any State over any child custody proceeding involving an Indian child who resides or is domiciled within the reservation of such tribe, except where such jurisdiction is otherwise vested in the State by existing Federal law. Where an Indian child is a ward of a tribal court, the Indian tribe shall retain exclusive jurisdiction, notwithstanding the residence or domicile of the child.

(b) Transfer of proceedings; declination by tribal court

In any State court proceeding for the foster care placement of, or termination of parental rights to, an Indian child not domiciled or residing within the reservation of the Indian child's tribe, the court, in the absence of good cause to the contrary, shall transfer such proceeding to the jurisdiction of the tribe, absent objection by either parent, upon the petition of either parent or the Indian custodian or the Indian child's tribe: Provided, That such transfer shall be subject to declination by the tribal court of such tribe.

(c) State court proceedings; intervention

In any State court proceeding for the foster care placement of, or termination of parental rights to, an Indian child, the Indian custodian of the child and the Indian child's tribe shall have a right to intervene at any point in the proceeding.

(d) Full faith and credit to public acts, records, and judicial proceedings of Indian tribes

The United States, every State, every territory or possession of the United States, and every Indian tribe shall give full faith and credit to the public acts, records, and judicial proceedings of any Indian tribe applicable to Indian child custody proceedings to the same extent that such entities give full faith and credit to the public acts, records, and judicial proceedings of any other entity.

§ 1912. Pending court proceedings

(a) Notice; time for commencement of proceedings; additional time for preparation

In any involuntary proceeding in a State court, where the court knows or has reason to know that an Indian child is involved, the party seeking the foster care placement of, or termination of parental rights to, an Indian child shall notify the parent or Indian custodian and the Indian child's tribe, by registered mail with return receipt requested, of the pending proceedings and of their right of intervention. If the identity or location of the parent or Indian custodian and the tribe cannot be determined, such notice shall be given to the Secretary in like manner, who shall have fifteen days after receipt to provide the requisite notice to the parent or Indian custodian and the tribe. No foster care placement or termination of parental rights proceeding shall be held until at least ten days after receipt of notice by the parent or Indian custodian and the tribe or the Secretary: Provided, That the parent or Indian custodian or the tribe shall, upon request, be granted up to twenty additional days to prepare for such proceeding.

(b) Appointment of counsel

In any case in which the court determines indigency, the parent or Indian custodian shall have the right to court-appointed counsel in any removal, placement, or termination proceeding. The court may, in its discretion, appoint counsel for the child upon a finding that such appointment is in the best interest of the child. Where State law makes no provision for appointment of counsel in such proceedings, the court shall promptly notify the Secretary upon appointment of counsel, and the Secretary, upon certification of the presiding judge, shall pay reasonable fees and expenses out of funds which may be appropriated pursuant to section 13 of this title.

(c) Examination of reports or other documents

Each party to a foster care placement or termination of parental rights proceeding under State law involving an Indian child shall have the right to examine all reports or other documents filed with the court upon which any decision with respect to such action may be based.

(d) Remedial services and rehabilitative programs; preventive measures

Any party seeking to effect a foster care placement of, or termination of parental rights to, an Indian child under State law shall satisfy the court that active efforts have been made to provide remedial services and rehabilitative programs designed to prevent the breakup of the Indian family and that these efforts have proved unsuccessful.

(e) Foster care placement orders; evidence; determination of damage to child

No foster care placement may be ordered in such proceeding in the absence of a determination, supported by clear and convincing evidence, including testimony of qualified expert witnesses, that the continued custody of the child by the parent or Indian custodian is likely to result in serious emotional or physical damage to the child.

(f) Parental rights termination orders; evidence; determination of damage to child

No termination of parental rights may be ordered in such proceeding in the absence of a determination, supported by evidence beyond a reasonable doubt, including testimony of qualified expert witnesses, that the continued custody of the child by the parent or Indian custodian is likely to result in serious emotional or physical damage to the child.

§ 1913. Parental rights; voluntary termination

(a) Consent; record; certification matters; invalid consents

Where any parent or Indian custodian voluntarily consents to a foster care placement or to termination of parental rights, such consent shall not be valid unless executed in writing and recorded before a judge of a court of competent jurisdiction and accompanied by the presiding judge's certificate that the terms and consequences of the consent were fully explained in detail and were fully understood by the parent or Indian custodian. The court shall also certify that either the parent or Indian custodian fully understood the explanation in English or that it was interpreted into a language that the parent or Indian custodian understood. Any consent given prior to, or within ten days after, birth of the Indian child shall not be valid.

(b) Foster care placement; withdrawal of consent

Any parent or Indian custodian may withdraw consent to a foster care placement under State law at any time and, upon such withdrawal, the child shall be returned to the parent or Indian custodian.

(c) Voluntary termination of parental rights or adoptive placement; withdrawal of consent; return of custody

In any voluntary proceeding for termination of parental rights to, or adoptive placement of, an Indian child, the consent of the parent may be withdrawn for any reason at any time prior to the entry of a final decree of termination or adoption, as the case may be, and the child shall be returned to the parent.

(d) Collateral attack; vacation of decree and return of custody; limitations

After the entry of a final decree of adoption of an Indian child in any State court, the parent may withdraw consent thereto upon the grounds that consent was obtained through fraud or duress and may petition the court to vacate such decree. Upon a finding that such consent was obtained through fraud or duress, the court shall vacate such decree and return the child to the parent. No adoption which has been effective for at least two years may be invalidated under the provisions of this subsection unless otherwise permitted under State law.

§ 1914. Petition to court of competent jurisdiction to invalidate action upon showing of certain violations

Any Indian child who is the subject of any action for foster care placement or termination of parental rights under State law, any parent or Indian custodian from whose custody such child was removed, and the Indian child's tribe may petition any court of competent jurisdiction to invalidate such action upon a showing that such action violated any provision of sections 1911, 1912, and 1913 of this title.

§ 1915. Placement of Indian children

(a) Adoptive placements; preferences

In any adoptive placement of an Indian child under State law, a preference shall be given, in the absence of good cause to the contrary, to a placement with (1) a member of the child's extended family; (2) other members of the Indian child's tribe; or (3) other Indian families.

(b) Foster care or preadoptive placements; criteria; preferences

Any child accepted for foster care or preadoptive placement shall be placed in the least restrictive setting which most approximates a family and in which his special needs, if any, may be met. The child shall also be placed within reasonable proximity to his or her home, taking into account any special needs of the child. In any foster care or preadoptive placement, a preference shall be given, in the absence of good cause to the contrary, to a placement with—

i. a member of the Indian child's extended family;
ii. a foster home licensed, approved, or specified by the Indian child's tribe;
iii. an Indian foster home licensed or approved by an authorized non-Indian licensing authority; or
iv. a institution for children approved by an Indian tribe or operated by an Indian organization which has a program suitable to meet the Indian child's needs.

(c) Tribal resolution for different order of preference; personal preference considered; anonymity in application of preferences

In the case of a placement under subsection (a) or (b) of this section, if the Indian child's tribe shall establish a different order of preference by resolution, the agency or court effecting the placement shall follow such order so long as the placement is the least restrictive setting appropriate to the particular needs of the child, as provided in subsection (b) of this section. Where appropriate, the preference of the Indian child or parent shall be considered: Provided, That where a consenting parent evidences a desire for anonymity, the court or agency shall give weight to such desire in applying the preferences.

(d) Social and cultural standards applicable

The standards to be applied in meeting the preference requirements of this section shall be the prevailing social and cultural standards of the Indian community in which the parent or extended family resides or with which the parent or extended family members maintain social and cultural ties.

(e) Record of placement; availability

A record of each such placement, under State law, of an Indian child shall be maintained by the State in which the placement was made, evidencing the efforts to comply with the order of preference specified in this section. Such record shall be made available at any time upon the request of the Secretary or the Indian child's tribe.

§ 1916. Return of custody

(a) Petition; best interests of child

Notwithstanding State law to the contrary, whenever a final decree of adoption of an Indian child has been vacated or set aside or the adoptive parents voluntarily consent to the termination of their parental rights to the child, a biological parent or prior Indian custodian may petition for return of custody and the court shall grant such petition unless there is a showing, in a proceeding subject to the provisions of section 1912 of this title, that such return of custody is not in the best interests of the child.

(b) Removal from foster care home; placement procedure

Whenever an Indian child is removed from a foster care home or institution for the purpose of further foster care, preadoptive, or adoptive placement, such placement shall be in accordance with the provisions of this chapter, except in the case where an Indian child is being returned to the parent or Indian custodian from whose custody the child was originally removed.

§ 1917. Tribal affiliation information and other information for protection of rights from tribal relationship; application of subject of adoptive placement; disclosure by court

Upon application by an Indian individual who has reached the age of eighteen and who was the subject of an adoptive placement, the court which entered the final decree shall inform such individual of the tribal affiliation, if any, of the individual's biological parents and provide such other information as may be necessary to protect any rights flowing from the individual's tribal relationship.

§ 1918. Reassumption of jurisdiction over child custody proceedings

(a) Petition; suitable plan; approval by Secretary

Any Indian tribe which became subject to State jurisdiction pursuant to the provisions of the Act of August 15, 1953 (67 Stat. 588), as amended by title IV of the Act of April 11, 1968 (82 Stat. 73, 78), or pursuant to any other Federal law, may reassume jurisdiction over child custody proceedings. Before any Indian tribe may reassume jurisdiction over Indian child custody proceedings, such tribe shall present to the Secretary for approval a petition to reassume such jurisdiction which includes a suitable plan to exercise such jurisdiction.

(b) Criteria applicable to consideration by Secretary; partial retrocession

(1) In considering the petition and feasibility of the plan of a tribe under subsection (a) of this section, the Secretary may consider, among other things:

i. whether or not the tribe maintains a membership roll or alternative provision for clearly identifying the persons who will be affected by the reassumption of jurisdiction by the tribe;

ii. the size of the reservation or former reservation area which will be affected by retrocession and reassumption of jurisdiction by the tribe;

iii. the population base of the tribe, or distribution of the population in homogeneous communities or geographic areas; and

iv. the feasibility of the plan in cases of multitribal occupation of a single reservation or geographic area.

(2) In those cases where the Secretary determines that the jurisdictional provisions of section 1911(a) of this title are not feasible, he is authorized to accept partial retrocession which will enable tribes to exercise referral jurisdiction as provided in section 1911(b) of this title, or, where appropriate, will allow them to exercise exclusive jurisdiction as provided in section 1911(a) of this title over limited community or geographic areas without regard for the reservation status of the area affected.

(c) Approval of petition; publication in Federal Register; notice; reassumption period; correction of causes for disapproval

If the Secretary approves any petition under subsection (a) of this section, the Secretary shall publish notice of such approval in the Federal Register and shall notify the affected State or States of such approval. The Indian tribe concerned shall reassume jurisdiction sixty days after publication in the Federal

Register of notice of approval. If the Secretary disapproves any petition under subsection (a) of this section, the Secretary shall provide such technical assistance as may be necessary to enable the tribe to correct any deficiency which the Secretary identified as a cause for disapproval.

(d) Pending actions or proceedings unaffected

Assumption of jurisdiction under this section shall not affect any action or proceeding over which a court has already assumed jurisdiction, except as may be provided pursuant to any agreement under section 1919 of this title.

§ 1919. Agreements between States and Indian tribes

(a) Subject coverage

States and Indian tribes are authorized to enter into agreements with each other respecting care and custody of Indian children and jurisdiction over child custody proceedings, including agreements which may provide for orderly transfer of jurisdiction on a case-by-case basis and agreements which provide for concurrent jurisdiction between States and Indian tribes.

(b) Revocation; notice; actions or proceedings unaffected

Such agreements may be revoked by either party upon one hundred and eighty days' written notice to the other party. Such revocation shall not affect any action or proceeding over which a court has already assumed jurisdiction, unless the agreement provides otherwise.

§ 1920. Improper removal of child from custody; declination of jurisdiction; forthwith return of child: danger exception

Where any petitioner in an Indian child custody proceeding before a State court has improperly removed the child from custody of the parent or Indian custodian or has improperly retained custody after a visit or other temporary relinquishment of custody, the court shall decline jurisdiction over such petition and shall forthwith return the child to his parent or Indian custodian unless returning the child to his parent or custodian would subject the child to a substantial and immediate danger or threat of such danger.

§ 1921. Higher State or Federal standard applicable to protect rights of parent or Indian custodian of Indian child

In any case where State or Federal law applicable to a child custody proceeding under State or Federal law provides a higher standard of protection to the rights of the parent or Indian custodian of an Indian child than the rights provided under this subchapter, the State or Federal court shall apply the State or Federal standard.

§ 1922. Emergency removal or placement of child; termination; appropriate action

Nothing in this subchapter shall be construed to prevent the emergency removal of an Indian child who is a resident of or is domiciled on a reservation, but temporarily located off the reservation, from his parent or Indian custodian or the emergency placement of such child in a foster home or institution, under applicable State law, in order to prevent imminent physical damage or harm to the child. The State authority, official, or agency involved shall insure that the emergency removal or placement terminates immediately when such removal or placement is no longer necessary to prevent imminent physical damage or harm to the child and shall expeditiously initiate a child custody proceeding subject to the provisions of this subchapter, transfer the child to the jurisdiction of the appropriate Indian tribe, or restore the child to the parent or Indian custodian, as may be appropriate.

§ 1923. Effective date

None of the provisions of this subchapter, except sections 1911(a), 1918, and 1919 of this title, shall affect a proceeding under State law for foster care placement, termination of parental rights, preadoptive placement, or adoptive placement which was initiated or completed prior to one hundred and eighty days after November 8, 1978, but shall apply to any subsequent proceeding in the same matter or subsequent proceedings affecting the custody or placement of the same child.

§ 1931. Grants for on or near reservation programs and child welfare codes

(a) Statement of purpose; scope of programs

The Secretary is authorized to make grants to Indian tribes and organizations in the establishment and operation of Indian child and family service programs on or near reservations and in the preparation and implementation of child welfare codes. The objective of every Indian child and family service program shall be to prevent the breakup of Indian families and, in particular, to insure that the permanent removal of an Indian child from the custody of his parent or Indian custodian shall be a last resort. Such child and family service programs may include, but are not limited to—

(1) a system for licensing or otherwise regulating Indian foster and adoptive homes;

(2) the operation and maintenance of facilities for the counseling and treatment of Indian families and for the temporary custody of Indian children;

(3) family assistance, including homemaker and home counselors, day care, afterschool care, and employment, recreational activities, and respite care;

(4) home improvement programs;

(5) the employment of professional and other trained personnel to assist the tribal court in the disposition of domestic relations and child welfare matters;
(6) education and training of Indians, including tribal court judges and staff, in skills relating to child and family assistance and service programs;
(7) a subsidy program under which Indian adoptive children may be provided support comparable to that for which they would be eligible as foster children, taking into account the appropriate State standards of support for maintenance and medical needs; and
(8) guidance, legal representation, and advice to Indian families involved in tribal, State, or Federal child custody proceedings.

(b) Non-Federal matching funds for related Social Security or other Federal financial assistance programs; assistance for such programs unaffected; State licensing or approval for qualification for assistance under federally assisted program

Funds appropriated for use by the Secretary in accordance with this section may be utilized as non-Federal matching share in connection with funds provided under titles IV-B and XX of the Social Security Act [42 U.S.C. 620 et seq., 1397 et seq.] or under any other Federal financial assistance programs which contribute to the purpose for which such funds are authorized to be appropriated for use under this chapter. The provision or possibility of assistance under this chapter shall not be a basis for the denial or reduction of any assistance otherwise authorized under titles IV-B and XX of the Social Security Act or any other federally assisted program. For purposes of qualifying for assistance under a federally assisted program, licensing or approval of foster or adoptive homes or institutions by an Indian tribe shall be deemed equivalent to licensing or approval by a State.

§ 1932. Grants for off-reservation programs for additional services

The Secretary is also authorized to make grants to Indian organizations to establish and operate off-reservation Indian child and family service programs which may include, but are not limited to—

(1) a system for regulating, maintaining, and supporting Indian foster and adoptive homes, including a subsidy program under which Indian adoptive children may be provided support comparable to that for which they would be eligible as Indian foster children, taking into account the appropriate State standards of support for maintenance and medical needs;
(2) the operation and maintenance of facilities and services for counseling and treatment of Indian families and Indian foster and adoptive children;
(3) family assistance, including homemaker and home counselors, day care, afterschool care, and employment, recreational activities, and respite care; and
(4) guidance, legal representation, and advice to Indian families involved in child custody proceedings.

§ 1933. Funds for on and off reservation programs

(a) Appropriated funds for similar programs of Department of Health and Human Services; appropriation in advance for payments

In the establishment, operation, and funding of Indian child and family service programs, both on and off reservation, the Secretary may enter into agreements with the Secretary of Health and Human Services, and the latter Secretary is hereby authorized for such purposes to use funds appropriated for similar programs of the Department of Health and Human Services: Provided, That authority to make payments pursuant to such agreements shall be effective only to the extent and in such amounts as may be provided in advance by appropriation Acts.

(b) Appropriation authorization under section 13 of this title

Funds for the purposes of this chapter may be appropriated pursuant to the provisions of section 13 of this title.

§ 1934. "Indian" defined for certain purposes

For the purposes of sections 1932 and 1933 of this title, the term "Indian" shall include persons defined in section 1603(c) of this title.

§ 1951. Information availability to and disclosure by Secretary

(a) Copy of final decree or order; other information; anonymity affidavit; exemption from Freedom of Information Act

Any State court entering a final decree or order in any Indian child adoptive placement after November 8, 1978, shall provide the Secretary with a copy of such decree or order together with such other information as may be necessary to show—

(1) the name and tribal affiliation of the child;
(2) the names and addresses of the biological parents;
(3) the names and addresses of the adoptive parents; and
(4) the identity of any agency having files or information relating to such adoptive placement. Where the court records contain an affidavit of the biological parent or parents that their identity remain confidential, the court shall include such affidavit with the other information. The Secretary shall insure that the confidentiality of such information is maintained and such information shall not be subject to the Freedom of Information Act (5 U.S.C. 552), as amended.

(b) Disclosure of information for enrollment of Indian child in tribe or for determination of member rights or benefits; certification of entitlement to enrollment

Upon the request of the adopted Indian child over the age of eighteen, the adoptive or foster parents of an Indian child, or an Indian tribe, the Secretary shall disclose such information as may be necessary for the enrollment of an Indian child in the tribe in which the child may be eligible for enrollment or for determining any rights or benefits associated with that membership. Where the documents relating to such child contain an affidavit from the biological parent or parents requesting anonymity, the Secretary shall certify to the Indian child's tribe, where the information warrants, that the child's parentage and other circumstances of birth entitle the child to enrollment under the criteria established by such tribe.

§ 1952. Rules and regulations

Within one hundred and eighty days after November 8, 1978, the Secretary shall promulgate such rules and regulations as may be necessary to carry out the provisions of this chapter.

§ 1961. Locally convenient day schools

(a) Sense of Congress

It is the sense of Congress that the absence of locally convenient day schools may contribute to the breakup of Indian families.

(b) Report to Congress; contents, etc.

The Secretary is authorized and directed to prepare, in consultation with appropriate agencies in the Department of Health and Human Services, a report on the feasibility of providing Indian children with schools located near their homes, and to submit such report to the Select Committee on Indian Affairs of the United States Senate and the Committee on Interior and Insular Affairs of the United States House of Representatives within two years from November 8, 1978. In developing this report the Secretary shall give particular consideration to the provision of educational facilities for children in the elementary grades.

§ 1962. Copies to the States

Within sixty days after November 8, 1978, the Secretary shall send to the Governor, chief justice of the highest court of appeal, and the attorney general of each State a copy of this chapter, together with committee reports and an explanation of the provisions of this chapter.

§ 1963. Severability

If any provision of this chapter or the applicability thereof is held invalid, the remaining provisions of this chapter shall not be affected thereby.

Appendix B

Code of Federal Regulations

Title 25 – Indians

Part 23: Indian Child Welfare Act

Subpart A - Purpose, Definitions, and Policy

§ 23.2 Definitions.

Act means the Indian Child Welfare Act (ICWA), Pub. L. 95–608, 92 Stat. 3069, 25 U.S.C. 1901 *et seq.*

Active efforts means affirmative, active, thorough, and timely efforts intended primarily to maintain or reunite an Indian child with his or her family. Where an agency is involved in the child-custody proceeding, active efforts must involve assisting the parent or parents or Indian custodian through the steps of a case plan and with accessing or developing the resources necessary to satisfy the case plan. To the maximum extent possible, active efforts should be provided in a manner consistent with the prevailing social and cultural conditions and way of life of the Indian child's Tribe and should be conducted in partnership with the Indian child and the Indian child's parents, extended family members, Indian custodians, and Tribe. Active efforts are to be tailored to the facts and circumstances of the case and may include, for example:

(1) Conducting a comprehensive assessment of the circumstances of the Indian child's family, with a focus on safe reunification as the most desirable goal;
(2) Identifying appropriate services and helping the parents to overcome barriers, including actively assisting the parents in obtaining such services;
(3) Identifying, notifying, and inviting representatives of the Indian child's Tribe to participate in providing support and services to the Indian child's family and in family team meetings, permanency planning, and resolution of placement issues;
(4) Conducting or causing to be conducted a diligent search for the Indian child's extended family members, and contacting and consulting with extended family members to provide family structure and support for the Indian child and the Indian child's parents;
(5) Offering and employing all available and culturally appropriate family preservation strategies and facilitating the use of remedial and rehabilitative services provided by the child's Tribe;
(6) Taking steps to keep siblings together whenever possible;
(7) Supporting regular visits with parents or Indian custodians in the most natural setting possible as well as trial home visits of the Indian child during any period of removal, consistent with the need to ensure the health, safety, and welfare of the child;
(8) Identifying community resources including housing, financial, transportation, mental health, substance abuse, and peer

support services and actively assisting the Indian child's parents or, when appropriate, the child's family, in utilizing and accessing those resources;

(9) Monitoring progress and participation in services;

(10) Considering alternative ways to address the needs of the Indian child's parents and, where appropriate, the family, if the optimum services do not exist or are not available;

(11) Providing post-reunification services and monitoring.

Assistant Secretary means the Assistant Secretary—Indian Affairs, the Department of the Interior.

Bureau of Indian Affairs (BIA) means the Bureau of Indian Affairs, the Department of the Interior.

(1) *Child-custody proceeding.* "Child-custody proceeding" means and includes any action, other than an emergency proceeding, that may culminate in one of the following outcomes:

(i) *Foster-care placement,* which is any action removing an Indian child from his or her parent or Indian custodian for temporary placement in a foster home or institution or the home of a guardian or conservator where the parent or Indian custodian cannot have the child returned upon demand, but where parental rights have not been terminated;

(ii) *Termination of parental rights,* which is any action resulting in the termination of the parent-child relationship;

(iii) *Preadoptive placement,* which is the temporary placement of an Indian child in a foster home or institution after the termination of parental rights, but prior to or in lieu of adoptive placement; or

(iv) *Adoptive placement,* which is the permanent placement of an Indian child for adoption, including any action resulting in a final decree of adoption.

(2) An action that may culminate in one of these four outcomes is considered a separate child-custody proceeding from an action that may culminate in a different one of these four outcomes. There may be several child-custody proceedings involving any given Indian child. Within each child-custody proceeding, there may be several hearings. If a child is placed in foster care or another out-of-home placement as a result of a status offense, that status offense proceeding is a child-custody proceeding.

Consortium means an association or partnership of two or more eligible applicants who enter into an agreement to administer a grant program and to provide services under the grant to Indian residents in a specific geographical area when it is administratively feasible to provide an adequate level of services within the area.

Continued custody means physical custody or legal custody or both, under any applicable Tribal law or Tribal custom or State law, that a parent or Indian custodian already has or had at any point in the past. The biological mother of a child has had custody of a child.

Custody means physical custody or legal custody or both, under any applicable Tribal law or Tribal custom or State law. A party may demonstrate the existence of custody by looking to Tribal law or Tribal custom or State law.

Domicile means: (1) For a parent or Indian custodian, the place at which a person has been physically present and that the person regards as home; a person's true, fixed, principal, and permanent home, to which that person intends to return and remain indefinitely even though the person may be currently residing elsewhere. (2) For an Indian child, the domicile of the Indian child's parents or Indian custodian or guardian. In the case of an Indian child whose parents are not married to each other, the domicile of the Indian child's custodial parent.

Emergency proceeding means and includes any court action that involves an emergency removal or emergency placement of an Indian child.

Extended family member is defined by the law or custom of the Indian child's Tribe or, in the absence of such law or custom, is a person who has reached age 18 and who is the Indian child's grandparent, aunt or uncle, brother or sister, brother-in-law or sister-in-law, niece or nephew, first or second cousin, or stepparent.

Grant means a written agreement between the BIA and the governing body of an Indian tribe or Indian organization wherein the BIA provides funds to the grantee to plan, conduct or administer specific programs, services, or activities and where the administrative and programmatic provisions are specifically delineated.

Grantee means the tribal governing body of an Indian tribe or Board of Directors of an Indian organization responsible for grant administration.

Grants officer means an officially designated officer who administers ICWA grants awarded by the Bureau of Indian Affairs, the Department of the Interior.

Hearing means a judicial session held for the purpose of deciding issues of fact, of law, or both.

Indian means any person who is a member of an Indian tribe, or who is an Alaska Native and a member of a Regional Corporation as defined in section 7 of the Alaska Native Claims Settlement Act, 43 U.S.C. 1606.

Indian child means any unmarried person who is under age 18 and either: (1) Is a member or citizen of an Indian Tribe; or (2) Is eligible for membership or citizenship in an Indian Tribe and is the biological child of a member/citizen of an Indian Tribe.

Indian child's Tribe means: (1) The Indian Tribe in which an Indian child is a member or eligible for membership; or (2) In the case of an Indian child who is a member of or eligible for membership in more than one Tribe, the Indian Tribe described in § 23.109.

Indian custodian means any Indian who has legal custody of an Indian child under applicable Tribal law or custom or under applicable State law, or to whom temporary physical care, custody, and control has been transferred by the parent of such child. An Indian may demonstrate that he or she is an Indian custodian by looking to Tribal law or Tribal custom or State law.

Indian foster home means a foster home where one or more of the licensed or approved foster parents is an "Indian" as defined in 25 U.S.C. 1903(3).

Indian organization, solely for purposes of eligibility for grants under subpart D of this part, means any legally established group, association, partnership, corporation, or other legal entity which is owned or controlled by Indians, or a majority (51 percent or more) of whose members are Indians.

Indian preference means preference and opportunities for employment and training provided to Indians in the administration of grants in accordance with section 7 (b) of the Indian Self-Determination and Education Assistance Act (25 U.S.C. 450).

Indian tribe means any Indian tribe, band, nation, or other organized group or community of Indians federally recognized as eligible for the services provided to Indians by the Secretary because of their status as Indians, including any Alaska Native village as defined in section 3 (c) of the Alaska Native Claims Settlement Act, 43 U.S.C. 1602 (c).

Involuntary proceeding means a child-custody proceeding in which the parent does not consent of his or her free will to the foster-care, preadoptive, or adoptive placement or termination of parental rights or in which the parent consents to the foster-care, preadoptive, or adoptive placement under threat of removal of the child by a State court or agency.

Off-reservation ICWA program means an ICWA program administered in accordance with 25 U.S.C. 1932 by an off-reservation Indian organization.

Parent or *parents* means any biological parent or parents of an Indian child, or any Indian who has lawfully adopted an Indian child, including adoptions under Tribal law or custom. It does not include an unwed biological father where paternity has not been acknowledged or established.

Reservation means Indian country as defined in 18 U.S.C 1151 and any lands, not covered under that section, title to which is held by the United States in trust for the benefit of any Indian Tribe or individual or held by any Indian Tribe or individual subject to a restriction by the United States against alienation.

Secretary means the Secretary of the Interior or the Secretary's authorized representative acting under delegated authority.

Service areas solely for newly recognized or restored Indian tribes without established reservations means those service areas congressionally established by Federal law to be the equivalent of a reservation for the purpose of determining the eligibility of a newly recognized or restored Indian tribe and its members for all Federal services and benefits.

State court means any agent or agency of a state, including the District of Columbia or any territory or possession of the United States, or any political subdivision empowered by law to terminate parental rights or to make foster care placements, preadoptive placements, or adoptive placements.

Status offenses mean offenses that would not be considered criminal if committed by an adult; they are acts prohibited only because of a person's status as a minor (*e.g.*, truancy, incorrigibility).

Subgrant means a secondary grant that undertakes part of the obligations of the primary grant, and assumes the legal and financial responsibility for the funds awarded and for the performance of the grant-supported activity.

Technical assistance means the provision of oral, written, or other relevant information and assistance to prospective grant applicants in the development of their grant proposals. Technical assistance may include a preliminary review of an application to assist the applicant in identifying the strengths and weaknesses of the proposal, ongoing program planning, design and evaluation, and such other program-specific assistance as is necessary for ongoing grant administration and management.

Title II means title II of Public Law 95–608, the Indian Child Welfare Act of 1978, which authorizes the Secretary to make grants to Indian tribes and off-reservation Indian organizations for the establishment and operation of Indian child and family service programs.

Tribal court means a court with jurisdiction over child-custody proceedings and which is either a Court of Indian Offenses, a court established and operated under the code or custom of an Indian Tribe, or any other administrative body of a Tribe vested with authority over child-custody proceedings.

Tribal government means the federally recognized governing body of an Indian tribe.

Upon demand means that the parent or Indian custodian can regain custody simply upon verbal request, without any formalities or contingencies.

Value means face, par, or market value, or cost price, either wholesale or retail, whichever is greater.

Voluntary proceeding means a child-custody proceeding that is not an involuntary proceeding, such as a proceeding for foster-care, preadoptive, or adoptive placement that either parent, both parents, or the Indian custodian has, of his or her or their free will, without a threat of removal by a State agency, consented to for the Indian child, or a proceeding for voluntary termination of parental rights. [59 FR 2256, Jan. 13, 1994, as amended at 81 FR 38864, June 14, 2016]

Subpart I—Indian Child Welfare Act Proceedings
Source: 81 FR 38867, June 14, 2016, unless otherwise noted.

General Provisions

§ 23.101 What is the purpose of this subpart?
These regulations clarify the minimum Federal standards governing implementation of the Indian Child Welfare Act (ICWA) to ensure that ICWA is applied in all States consistent with the Act's express language, Congress's intent in enacting the statute, and to promote the stability and security of Indian tribes and families.

§ 23.102 What terms do I need to know?
The following terms and their definitions apply to this subpart. All other terms have the meanings assigned in § 23.2.

Agency means a nonprofit, for-profit, or governmental organization and its employees, agents, or officials that performs, or provides services to biological parents, foster parents, or adoptive parents to assist in the administrative and social work necessary for foster, preadoptive, or adoptive placements.

Indian organization means any group, association, partnership, corporation, or other legal entity owned or controlled by Indians or a Tribe, or a majority of whose members are Indians.

§ 23.103 When does ICWA apply?
(a) ICWA includes requirements that apply whenever an Indian child is the subject of:

(1) A child-custody proceeding, including:

(i) An involuntary proceeding;

(ii) A voluntary proceeding that could prohibit the parent or Indian custodian from regaining custody of the child upon demand; and

(iii) A proceeding involving status offenses if any part of the proceeding results in the need for out-of-home placement of the child, including a foster-care, preadoptive, or adoptive placement, or termination of parental rights.

(2) An emergency proceeding.

(b) ICWA does not apply to:

(1) A Tribal court proceeding;

(2) A proceeding regarding a criminal act that is not a status offense;

(3) An award of custody of the Indian child to one of the parents including, but not limited to, an award in a divorce proceeding; or

(4) A voluntary placement that either parent, both parents, or the Indian custodian has, of his or her or their free will, without a threat of removal by a State agency, chosen for the Indian child and that does not operate to prohibit the child's parent or Indian custodian from regaining custody of the child upon demand.

(c) If a proceeding listed in paragraph (a) of this section concerns a child who meets the statutory definition of "Indian child," then ICWA will apply to that proceeding. In determining whether ICWA applies to a proceeding, the State court may not consider factors such as the participation of the parents or the Indian child in Tribal cultural, social, religious, or political activities, the relationship between the Indian child and his or her parents, whether the parent ever had custody of the child, or the Indian child's blood quantum.

(d) If ICWA applies at the commencement of a proceeding, it will not cease to apply simply because the child reaches age 18 during the pendency of the proceeding.

§ 23.104 What provisions of this subpart apply to each type of child-custody proceeding?

[Author's Note: A table detailing what sections of this subpart apply to each type of child-custody proceeding identified in §23.103(a) can be found at: https://www.gpo.gov/fdsys/pkg/CFR-2017-title25-vol1/xml/CFR-2017-title25-vol1-part23.xml#seqnum23.101]

§ 23.105 How do I contact a Tribe under the regulations in this subpart?

To contact a Tribe to provide notice or obtain information or verification under the regulations in this subpart, you should direct the notice or inquiry as follows:

(a) Many Tribes designate an agent for receipt of ICWA notices. The BIA publishes a list of Tribes' designated Tribal agents for service of ICWA notice in the **Federal Register** each year and makes the list available on its website at *www.bia.gov*.

(b) For a Tribe without a designated Tribal agent for service of ICWA notice, contact the Tribe to be directed to the appropriate office or individual.

(c) If you do not have accurate contact information for a Tribe, or the Tribe contacted fails to respond to written inquiries, you should seek assistance in contacting the Indian Tribe from the BIA local or regional office or the BIA's Central Office in Washington, DC (see *www.bia.gov*).

§ 23.106 How does this subpart interact with State and Federal laws?

(a) The regulations in this subpart provide minimum Federal standards to ensure compliance with ICWA.

(b) Under section 1921 of ICWA, where applicable State or other Federal law provides a higher standard of protection to the rights of the parent or Indian custodian than the protection accorded under the Act, ICWA requires the State or Federal court to apply the higher State or Federal standard.

Pretrial Requirements

§ 23.107 How should a State court determine if there is reason to know the child is an Indian child?

(a) State courts must ask each participant in an emergency or voluntary or involuntary child-custody proceeding whether the participant knows or has reason to know that the child is an Indian child. The inquiry is made at the commencement of the proceeding and all responses should be on the record. State courts must instruct the parties to inform the court if they subsequently receive information that provides reason to know the child is an Indian child.

(b) If there is reason to know the child is an Indian child, but the court does not have sufficient evidence to determine that the child is or is not an "Indian child," the court must:

(1) Confirm, by way of a report, declaration, or testimony included in the record that the agency or other party used due diligence to identify and work with all of the Tribes of which there is reason to know the child may be a member (or eligible for membership), to verify whether the child is in fact a member (or a biological parent is a member and the child is eligible for membership); and

(2) Treat the child as an Indian child, unless and until it is determined on the record that the child does not meet the definition of an "Indian child" in this part.

(c) A court, upon conducting the inquiry required in paragraph (a) of this section, has reason to know that a child involved in an emergency or child-custody proceeding is an Indian child if:

(1) Any participant in the proceeding, officer of the court involved in the proceeding, Indian Tribe, Indian organization, or agency informs the court that the child is an Indian child;

(2) Any participant in the proceeding, officer of the court involved in the proceeding, Indian Tribe, Indian

organization, or agency informs the court that it has discovered information indicating that the child is an Indian child;

(3) The child who is the subject of the proceeding gives the court reason to know he or she is an Indian child;

(4) The court is informed that the domicile or residence of the child, the child's parent, or the child's Indian custodian is on a reservation or in an Alaska Native village;

(5) The court is informed that the child is or has been a ward of a Tribal court; or

(6) The court is informed that either parent or the child possesses an identification card indicating membership in an Indian Tribe.

(d) In seeking verification of the child's status in a voluntary proceeding where a consenting parent evidences, by written request or statement in the record, a desire for anonymity, the court must keep relevant documents pertaining to the inquiry required under this section confidential and under seal. A request for anonymity does not relieve the court, agency, or other party from any duty of compliance with ICWA, including the obligation to verify whether the child is an "Indian child." A Tribe receiving information related to this inquiry must keep documents and information confidential.

§ 23.108 Who makes the determination as to whether a child is a member, whether a child is eligible for membership, or whether a biological parent is a member of a Tribe?

(a) The Indian Tribe of which it is believed the child is a member (or eligible for membership and of which the biological parent is a member) determines whether the child is a member of the Tribe, or whether the child is eligible for membership in the Tribe and a biological parent of the child is a member of the Tribe, except as otherwise provided by Federal or Tribal law.

(b) The determination by a Tribe of whether a child is a member, whether a child is eligible for membership, or whether a biological parent is a member, is solely within the jurisdiction and authority of the Tribe, except as otherwise provided by Federal or Tribal law. The State court may not substitute its own determination regarding a child's membership in a Tribe, a child's eligibility for membership in a Tribe, or a parent's membership in a Tribe.

(c) The State court may rely on facts or documentation indicating a Tribal determination of membership or eligibility for membership in making a judicial determination as to whether the child is an "Indian child." An example of documentation indicating membership is a document issued by the Tribe, such as Tribal enrollment documentation.

§ 23.109 How should a State court determine an Indian child's Tribe when the child may be a member or eligible for membership in more than one Tribe?

(a) If the Indian child is a member or eligible for membership in only one Tribe, that Tribe must be designated as the Indian child's Tribe.

(b) If the Indian child meets the definition of "Indian child" through more than one Tribe, deference should be given to the Tribe in which the Indian child is already a member, unless otherwise agreed to by the Tribes.

(c) If an Indian child meets the definition of "Indian child" through more than one Tribe because the child is a member in more than one Tribe or the child is not a member of but is eligible for membership in more than one Tribe, the court must provide the opportunity in any involuntary child-custody proceeding for the Tribes to determine which should be designated as the Indian child's Tribe.

(1) If the Tribes are able to reach an agreement, the agreed-upon Tribe should be designated as the Indian child's Tribe.

(2) If the Tribes are unable to reach an agreement, the State court designates, for the purposes of ICWA, the Indian

Tribe with which the Indian child has the more significant contacts as the Indian child's Tribe, taking into consideration:

i. Preference of the parents for membership of the child;
ii. Length of past domicile or residence on or near the reservation of each Tribe;
iii. Tribal membership of the child's custodial parent or Indian custodian; and
iv. Interest asserted by each Tribe in the child-custody proceeding;
v. Whether there has been a previous adjudication with respect to the child by a court of one of the Tribes; and
vi. Self-identification by the child, if the child is of sufficient age and capacity to meaningfully self-identify.

(3) A determination of the Indian child's Tribe for purposes of ICWA and the regulations in this subpart do not constitute a determination for any other purpose.

§ 23.110 When must a State court dismiss an action?

Subject to 25 U.S.C. 1919 (Agreements between States and Indian Tribes) and § 23.113 (emergency proceedings), the following limitations on a State court's jurisdiction apply:

(a) The court in any voluntary or involuntary child-custody proceeding involving an Indian child must determine the residence and domicile of the Indian child. If either the residence or domicile is on a reservation where the Tribe exercises exclusive jurisdiction over child-custody proceedings, the State court must expeditiously notify the Tribal court of the pending dismissal based on the Tribe's exclusive jurisdiction, dismiss the State-court child-custody proceeding, and ensure that the Tribal court is sent all information regarding the Indian child-custody proceeding, including, but not limited to, the pleadings and any court record.

(b) If the child is a ward of a Tribal court, the State court must expeditiously notify the Tribal court of the pending dismissal, dismiss the State-court child-custody proceeding, and ensure that the Tribal court is sent all information regarding the Indian child-custody proceeding, including, but not limited to, the pleadings and any court record.

§ 23.111 What are the notice requirements for a child-custody proceeding involving an Indian child?

(a) When a court knows or has reason to know that the subject of an involuntary foster-care-placement or termination-of-parental-rights proceeding is an Indian child, the court must ensure that:

(1) The party seeking placement promptly sends notice of each such child-custody proceeding (including, but not limited to, any foster-care placement or any termination of parental or custodial rights) in accordance with this section; and

(2) An original or a copy of each notice sent under this section is filed with the court together with any return receipts or other proof of service.

(b) Notice must be sent to:

(1) Each Tribe where the child may be a member (or eligible for membership if a biological parent is a member) (*see* § 23.105 for information on how to contact a Tribe);

(2) The child's parents; and

(3) If applicable, the child's Indian custodian.

(c) Notice must be sent by registered or certified mail with return receipt requested. Notice may also be sent via personal service or electronically, but such alternative methods do not replace the requirement for notice to be sent by registered or certified mail with return receipt requested.

(d) Notice must be in clear and understandable language and include the following:

(1) The child's name, birthdate, and birthplace;
(2) All names known (including maiden, married, and former names or aliases) of the parents, the parents' birthdates and birthplaces, and Tribal enrollment numbers if known;
(3) If known, the names, birthdates, birthplaces, and Tribal enrollment information of other direct lineal ancestors of the child, such as grandparents;
(4) The name of each Indian Tribe in which the child is a member (or may be eligible for membership if a biological parent is a member);
(5) A copy of the petition, complaint, or other document by which the child-custody proceeding was initiated and, if a hearing has been scheduled, information on the date, time, and location of the hearing;
(6) Statements setting out:
    i. The name of the petitioner and the name and address of petitioner's attorney;
    ii. The right of any parent or Indian custodian of the child, if not already a party to the child-custody proceeding, to intervene in the proceedings.
    iii. The Indian Tribe's right to intervene at any time in a State-court proceeding for the foster-care placement of or termination of parental rights to an Indian child.
    iv. That, if the child's parent or Indian custodian is unable to afford counsel based on a determination of indigency by the court, the parent or Indian custodian has the right to court-appointed counsel.
    v. The right to be granted, upon request, up to 20 additional days to prepare for the child-custody proceedings.

vi. The right of the parent or Indian custodian and the Indian child's Tribe to petition the court for transfer of the foster-care-placement or termination-of-parental-rights proceeding to Tribal court as provided by 25 U.S.C. 1911 and § 23.115.
vii. The mailing addresses and telephone numbers of the court and information related to all parties to the child-custody proceeding and individuals notified under this section.
viii. The potential legal consequences of the child-custody proceedings on the future parental and custodial rights of the parent or Indian custodian.
ix. That all parties notified must keep confidential the information contained in the notice and the notice should not be handled by anyone not needing the information to exercise rights under ICWA.

(e) If the identity or location of the child's parents, the child's Indian custodian, or the Tribes in which the Indian child is a member or eligible for membership cannot be ascertained, but there is reason to know the child is an Indian child, notice of the child-custody proceeding must be sent to the appropriate Bureau of Indian Affairs Regional Director (see *www.bia.gov*). To establish Tribal identity, as much information as is known regarding the child's direct lineal ancestors should be provided. The Bureau of Indian Affairs will not make a determination of Tribal membership but may, in some instances, be able to identify Tribes to contact.

(f) If there is a reason to know that a parent or Indian custodian possesses limited English proficiency and is therefore not likely to understand the contents of the notice, the court must provide language access services as required by Title VI of the Civil Rights Act and other Federal laws. To secure such translation or interpretation support, a court may contact or direct a party to contact the

Indian child's Tribe or the local BIA office for assistance in locating and obtaining the name of a qualified translator or interpreter.
(g) If a parent or Indian custodian of an Indian child appears in court without an attorney, the court must inform him or her of his or her rights, including any applicable right to appointed counsel, right to request that the child-custody proceeding be transferred to Tribal court, right to object to such transfer, right to request additional time to prepare for the child-custody proceeding as provided in § 23.112, and right (if the parent or Indian custodian is not already a party) to intervene in the child-custody proceedings.

§ 23.112 What time limits and extensions apply?

(a) No foster-care-placement or termination-of-parental-rights proceeding may be held until at least 10 days after receipt of the notice by the parent (or Indian custodian) and by the Tribe (or the Secretary). The parent, Indian custodian, and Tribe each have a right, upon request, to be granted up to 20 additional days from the date upon which notice was received to prepare for participation in the proceeding.
(b) Except as provided in 25 U.S.C. 1922 and § 23.113, no child-custody proceeding for foster-care placement or termination of parental rights may be held until the waiting periods to which the parents or Indian custodians and to which the Indian child's Tribe are entitled have expired, as follows:

(1) 10 days after each parent or Indian custodian (or Secretary where the parent or Indian custodian is unknown to the petitioner) has received notice of that particular child-custody proceeding in accordance with 25 U.S.C. 1912(a) and § 23.111;
(2) 10 days after the Indian child's Tribe (or the Secretary if the Indian child's Tribe is unknown to the party seeking placement) has received notice of that particular

child-custody proceeding in accordance with 25 U.S.C. 1912(a) and § 23.111;

(3) Up to 30 days after the parent or Indian custodian has received notice of that particular child-custody proceeding in accordance with 25 U.S.C. 1912(a) and § 23.111, if the parent or Indian custodian has requested up to 20 additional days to prepare for the child-custody proceeding as provided in 25 U.S.C. 1912(a) and § 23.111; and

(4) Up to 30 days after the Indian child's Tribe has received notice of that particular child-custody proceeding in accordance with 25 U.S.C. 1912(a) and § 23.111, if the Indian child's Tribe has requested up to 20 additional days to prepare for the child-custody proceeding.

(c) Additional time beyond the minimum required by 25 U.S.C. 1912 and § 23.111 may also be available under State law or pursuant to extensions granted by the court.

§ 23.113 What are the standards for emergency proceedings involving an Indian child?

(a) Any emergency removal or placement of an Indian child under State law must terminate immediately when the removal or placement is no longer necessary to prevent imminent physical damage or harm to the child.

(b) The State court must:

(1) Make a finding on the record that the emergency removal or placement is necessary to prevent imminent physical damage or harm to the child;

(2) Promptly hold a hearing on whether the emergency removal or placement continues to be necessary whenever new information indicates that the emergency situation has ended; and

(3) At any court hearing during the emergency proceeding, determine whether the emergency removal or placement is no longer necessary to prevent imminent physical damage or harm to the child.

(4) Immediately terminate (or ensure that the agency immediately terminates) the emergency proceeding once the court or agency possesses sufficient evidence to determine that the emergency removal or placement is no longer necessary to prevent imminent physical damage or harm to the child.

(c) An emergency proceeding can be terminated by one or more of the following actions:

(1) Initiation of a child-custody proceeding subject to the provisions of ICWA;

(2) Transfer of the child to the jurisdiction of the appropriate Indian Tribe; or

(3) Restoring the child to the parent or Indian custodian.

(d) A petition for a court order authorizing the emergency removal or continued emergency placement, or its accompanying documents, should contain a statement of the risk of imminent physical damage or harm to the Indian child and any evidence that the emergency removal or placement continues to be necessary to prevent such imminent physical damage or harm to the child. The petition or its accompanying documents should also contain the following information:

(1) The name, age, and last known address of the Indian child;

(2) The name and address of the child's parents and Indian custodians, if any;

(3) The steps taken to provide notice to the child's parents, custodians, and Tribe about the emergency proceeding;

(4) If the child's parents and Indian custodians are unknown, a detailed explanation of what efforts have been made to locate and contact them, including contact with the appropriate BIA Regional Director (see *www.bia.gov*);

(5) The residence and the domicile of the Indian child;

(6) If either the residence or the domicile of the Indian child is believed to be on a reservation or in an Alaska Native village, the name of the Tribe affiliated with that reservation or village;

(7) The Tribal affiliation of the child and of the parents or Indian custodians;

(8) A specific and detailed account of the circumstances that led the agency responsible for the emergency removal of the child to take that action;

(9) If the child is believed to reside or be domiciled on a reservation where the Tribe exercises exclusive jurisdiction over child-custody matters, a statement of efforts that have been made and are being made to contact the Tribe and transfer the child to the Tribe's jurisdiction; and

(10) A statement of the efforts that have been taken to assist the parents or Indian custodians so the Indian child may safely be returned to their custody.

(e) An emergency proceeding regarding an Indian child should not be continued for more than 30 days unless the court makes the following determinations:

(1) Restoring the child to the parent or Indian custodian would subject the child to imminent physical damage or harm;

(2) The court has been unable to transfer the proceeding to the jurisdiction of the appropriate Indian Tribe; and

(3) It has not been possible to initiate a "child-custody proceeding" as defined in § 23.2.

§ 23.114 What are the requirements for determining improper removal?

(a) If, in the course of any child-custody proceeding, any party asserts or the court has reason to believe that the Indian child may have been improperly removed from the custody of his or her parent or Indian custodian, or that the Indian child has been improperly retained (such as after a visit or other temporary relinquishment of custody), the court must expeditiously determine whether there was improper removal or retention.

(b) If the court finds that the Indian child was improperly removed or retained, the court must terminate the proceeding and the child must be returned immediately to his or her parent or Indian custodian, unless returning the child to his parent or Indian custodian would subject the child to substantial and immediate danger or threat of such danger.

Petitions To Transfer to Tribal Court

§ 23.115 How are petitions for transfer of a proceeding made?

(a) Either parent, the Indian custodian, or the Indian child's Tribe may request, at any time, orally on the record or in writing, that the State court transfer a foster-care or termination-of-parental-rights proceeding to the jurisdiction of the child's Tribe.

(b) The right to request a transfer is available at any stage in each foster-care or termination-of-parental-rights proceeding.

§ 23.116 What happens after a petition for transfer is made?

Upon receipt of a transfer petition, the State court must ensure that the Tribal court is promptly notified in writing of the transfer petition. This notification may request a timely response regarding whether the Tribal court wishes to decline the transfer.

§ 23.117 What are the criteria for ruling on transfer petitions?

Upon receipt of a transfer petition from an Indian child's parent, Indian custodian, or Tribe, the State court must transfer the child-custody proceeding unless the court determines that transfer is not appropriate because one or more of the following criteria are met:

(a) Either parent objects to such transfer;
(b) The Tribal court declines the transfer; or
(c) Good cause exists for denying the transfer.

§ 23.118 How is a determination of "good cause" to deny transfer made?

(a) If the State court believes, or any party asserts, that good cause to deny transfer exists, the reasons for that belief or assertion must be stated orally on the record or provided in writing on the record and to the parties to the child-custody proceeding.

(b) Any party to the child-custody proceeding must have the opportunity to provide the court with views regarding whether good cause to deny transfer exists.

(c) In determining whether good cause exists, the court must not consider:

(1) Whether the foster-care or termination-of-parental-rights proceeding is at an advanced stage if the Indian child's parent, Indian custodian, or Tribe did not receive notice of the child-custody proceeding until an advanced stage;
(2) Whether there have been prior proceedings involving the child for which no petition to transfer was filed;
(3) Whether transfer could affect the placement of the child;
(4) The Indian child's cultural connections with the Tribe or its reservation; or
(5) Socioeconomic conditions or any negative perception of Tribal or BIA social services or judicial systems.

(d) The basis for any State-court decision to deny transfer should be stated orally on the record or in a written order.

§ 23.119 What happens after a petition for transfer is granted?

(a) If the Tribal court accepts the transfer, the State court should expeditiously provide the Tribal court with all records related to the proceeding, including, but not limited to, the pleadings and any court record.

(b) The State court should work with the Tribal court to ensure that the transfer of the custody of the Indian child and of the proceeding is accomplished smoothly and in a way that minimizes the disruption of services to the family.

Adjudication of Involuntary Proceedings

§ 23.120 How does the State court ensure that active efforts have been made?

(a) Prior to ordering an involuntary foster-care placement or termination of parental rights, the court must conclude that active efforts have been made to prevent the breakup of the Indian family and that those efforts have been unsuccessful.

(b) Active efforts must be documented in detail in the record.

§ 23.121 What are the applicable standards of evidence?

(a) The court must not order a foster-care placement of an Indian child unless clear and convincing evidence is presented, including the testimony of one or more qualified expert witnesses, demonstrating that the child's continued custody by the child's parent or Indian custodian is likely to result in serious emotional or physical damage to the child.

(b) The court must not order a termination of parental rights for an Indian child unless evidence beyond a reasonable doubt is presented, including the testimony of one or more qualified expert witnesses, demonstrating that the child's continued custody by the child's parent or Indian custodian is likely to result in serious emotional or physical damage to the child.

(c) For a foster-care placement or termination of parental rights, the evidence must show a causal relationship between the particular conditions in the home and the likelihood that continued custody of the child will result in serious emotional or physical damage to the particular child who is the subject of the child-custody proceeding.

(d) Without a causal relationship identified in paragraph (c) of this section, evidence that shows only the existence of community or family poverty, isolation, single parenthood, custodian age, crowded or inadequate housing, substance abuse, or nonconforming social behavior does not by itself constitute clear and convincing evidence or evidence beyond a reasonable doubt that continued custody is likely to result in serious emotional or physical damage to the child.

§ 23.122 Who may serve as a qualified expert witness?

(a) A qualified expert witness must be qualified to testify regarding whether the child's continued custody by the parent or Indian custodian is likely to result in serious emotional or physical damage to the child and should be qualified to testify as to the prevailing social and cultural standards of the Indian child's Tribe. A person may be designated by the Indian child's Tribe as being qualified to testify to the prevailing social and cultural standards of the Indian child's Tribe.

(b) The court or any party may request the assistance of the Indian child's Tribe or the BIA office serving the Indian child's Tribe in locating persons qualified to serve as expert witnesses.

(c) The social worker regularly assigned to the Indian child may not serve as a qualified expert witness in child-custody proceedings concerning the child.

§ 23.123 [Reserved]

Voluntary Proceedings

§ 23.124 What actions must a State court undertake in voluntary proceedings?

(a) The State court must require the participants in a voluntary proceeding to state on the record whether the child is an Indian child, or whether there is reason to believe the child is an Indian child, as provided in § 23.107.

(b) If there is reason to believe the child is an Indian child, the State court must ensure that the party seeking placement has taken all reasonable steps to verify the child's status. This may include contacting the Tribe of which it is believed the child is a member (or eligible for membership and of which the biological parent is a member) to verify the child's status. As described in § 23.107, where a consenting parent requests anonymity, a Tribe receiving such information must keep relevant documents and information confidential.

(c) State courts must ensure that the placement for the Indian child complies with §§ 23.129-23.132.

§ 23.125 How is consent obtained?

(a) A parent's or Indian custodian's consent to a voluntary termination of parental rights or to a foster-care, preadoptive, or adoptive placement must be executed in writing and recorded before a court of competent jurisdiction.

(b) Prior to accepting the consent, the court must explain to the parent or Indian custodian:

(1) The terms and consequences of the consent in detail; and

(2) The following limitations, applicable to the type of child-custody proceeding for which consent is given, on withdrawal of consent:

i. For consent to foster-care placement, the parent or Indian custodian may withdraw consent for any reason, at any time, and have the child returned; or

ii. For consent to termination of parental rights, the parent or Indian custodian may withdraw consent for any reason, at any time prior to the entry of the final decree of termination and have the child returned; or

iii. For consent to an adoptive placement, the parent or Indian custodian may withdraw consent for any reason, at any time prior to the entry of the final decree of adoption, and have the child returned.

(c) The court must certify that the terms and consequences of the consent were explained on the record in detail in English (or the language of the parent or Indian custodian, if English is not the primary language) and were fully understood by the parent or Indian custodian.

(d) Where confidentiality is requested or indicated, execution of consent need not be made in a session of court open to the public but still must be made before a court of competent jurisdiction in compliance with this section.

(e) A consent given prior to, or within 10 days after, the birth of an Indian child is not valid.

§ 23.126 What information must a consent document contain?

(a) If there are any conditions to the consent, the written consent must clearly set out the conditions.

(b) A written consent to foster-care placement should contain, in addition to the information specified in paragraph (a) of this section, the name and birthdate of the Indian child; the name of the Indian child's Tribe; the Tribal enrollment number for the parent and for the Indian child, where known, or some other indication of the child's membership in the Tribe; the name, address, and other identifying information of the consenting parent or Indian custodian; the name and address of the person or entity, if any, who arranged the placement; and the name and address of the prospective foster parents, if known at the time.

§ 23.127 How is withdrawal of consent to a foster-care placement achieved?

(a) The parent or Indian custodian may withdraw consent to voluntary foster-care placement at any time.

(b) To withdraw consent, the parent or Indian custodian must file a written document with the court or otherwise testify before the court. Additional methods of withdrawing consent may be available under State law.

(c) When a parent or Indian custodian withdraws consent to a voluntary foster-care placement, the court must ensure that the Indian child is returned to that parent or Indian custodian as soon as practicable.

§ 23.128 How is withdrawal of consent to a termination of parental rights or adoption achieved?

(a) A parent may withdraw consent to voluntary termination of parental rights at any time prior to the entry of a final decree of termination.

(b) A parent or Indian custodian may withdraw consent to voluntary adoption at any time prior to the entry of a final decree of adoption.

(c) To withdraw consent prior to the entry of a final decree of adoption, the parent or Indian custodian must file a written document with the court or otherwise testify before the court.

Additional methods of withdrawing consent may be available under State law.

(d) The court in which the withdrawal of consent is filed must promptly notify the person or entity who arranged any voluntary preadoptive or adoptive placement of such filing, and the Indian child must be returned to the parent or Indian custodian as soon as practicable.

Dispositions

§ 23.129 When do the placement preferences apply?

(a) In any preadoptive, adoptive, or foster-care placement of an Indian child, the placement preferences specified in § 23.130 and § 23.131 apply.

(b) Where a consenting parent requests anonymity in a voluntary proceeding, the court must give weight to the request in applying the preferences.

(c) The placement preferences must be applied in any foster-care, preadoptive, or adoptive placement unless there is a determination on the record that good cause under § 23.132 exists to not apply those placement preferences.

§ 23.130 What placement preferences apply in adoptive placements?

(a) In any adoptive placement of an Indian child under State law, where the Indian child's Tribe has not established a different order of preference under paragraph (b) of this section, preference must be given in descending order, as listed below, to placement of the child with:

(1) A member of the Indian child's extended family;

(2) Other members of the Indian child's Tribe; or

(3) Other Indian families.

(b) If the Indian child's Tribe has established by resolution a different order of preference than that specified in ICWA, the Tribe's placement preferences apply.

(c) The court must, where appropriate, also consider the placement preference of the Indian child or Indian child's parent.

§ 23.131 What placement preferences apply in foster-care or preadoptive placements?

(a) In any foster-care or preadoptive placement of an Indian child under State law, including changes in foster-care or preadoptive placements, the child must be placed in the least-restrictive setting that:

(1) Most approximates a family, taking into consideration sibling attachment;
(2) Allows the Indian child's special needs (if any) to be met; and
(3) Is in reasonable proximity to the Indian child's home, extended family, or siblings.

(b) In any foster-care or preadoptive placement of an Indian child under State law, where the Indian child's Tribe has not established a different order of preference under paragraph (c) of this section, preference must be given, in descending order as listed below, to placement of the child with:

(1) A member of the Indian child's extended family;
(2) A foster home that is licensed, approved, or specified by the Indian child's Tribe;
(3) An Indian foster home licensed or approved by an authorized non-Indian licensing authority; or
(4) An institution for children approved by an Indian Tribe or operated by an Indian organization which has a program suitable to meet the child's needs.

(c) If the Indian child's Tribe has established by resolution a different order of preference than that specified in ICWA, the Tribe's placement preferences apply, so long as the placement is the least-restrictive setting appropriate to the particular needs of the Indian child, as provided in paragraph (a) of this section.

(d) The court must, where appropriate, also consider the preference of the Indian child or the Indian child's parent.

§ 23.132 How is a determination of "good cause" to depart from the placement preferences made?

(a) If any party asserts that good cause not to follow the placement preferences exists, the reasons for that belief or assertion must be stated orally on the record or provided in writing to the parties to the child-custody proceeding and the court.

(b) The party seeking departure from the placement preferences should bear the burden of proving by clear and convincing evidence that there is "good cause" to depart from the placement preferences.

(c) A court's determination of good cause to depart from the placement preferences must be made on the record or in writing and should be based on one or more of the following considerations:

(1) The request of one or both of the Indian child's parents, if they attest that they have reviewed the placement options, if any, that comply with the order of preference;

(2) The request of the child, if the child is of sufficient age and capacity to understand the decision that is being made;

(3) The presence of a sibling attachment that can be maintained only through a particular placement;

(4) The extraordinary physical, mental, or emotional needs of the Indian child, such as specialized treatment services that may be unavailable in the community where families who meet the placement preferences live;

(5) The unavailability of a suitable placement after a determination by the court that a diligent search was conducted to find suitable placements meeting the preference criteria, but none has been located. For purposes of this analysis, the standards for determining whether a placement is unavailable must conform to the prevailing social and cultural standards of the Indian community in which

the Indian child's parent or extended family resides or with which the Indian child's parent or extended family members maintain social and cultural ties.

(d) A placement may not depart from the preferences based on the socioeconomic status of any placement relative to another placement.

(e) A placement may not depart from the preferences based solely on ordinary bonding or attachment that flowed from time spent in a non-preferred placement that was made in violation of ICWA.

Access

§ 23.133 Should courts allow participation by alternative methods?

If it possesses the capability, the court should allow alternative methods of participation in State-court child-custody proceedings involving an Indian child, such as participation by telephone, videoconferencing, or other methods.

§ 23.134 Who has access to reports and records during a proceeding?

Each party to an emergency proceeding or a foster-care-placement or termination-of-parental-rights proceeding under State law involving an Indian child has a right to timely examine all reports and other documents filed or lodged with the court upon which any decision with respect to such action may be based.

§ 23.135 [Reserved]

Post-Trial Rights & Responsibilities

§ 23.136 What are the requirements for vacating an adoption based on consent having been obtained through fraud or duress?

(a) Within two years after a final decree of adoption of any Indian child by a State court, or within any longer period of time permitted by the law of the State, the State court may invalidate the voluntary adoption upon finding that the parent's consent was obtained by fraud or duress.

(b) Upon the parent's filing of a petition to vacate the final decree of adoption of the parent's Indian child, the court must give notice to all parties to the adoption proceedings and the Indian child's Tribe and must hold a hearing on the petition.

(c) Where the court finds that the parent's consent was obtained through fraud or duress, the court must vacate the final decree of adoption, order the consent revoked, and order that the child be returned to the parent.

§ 23.137 Who can petition to invalidate an action for certain ICWA violations?

(a) Any of the following may petition any court of competent jurisdiction to invalidate an action for foster-care placement or termination of parental rights under state law where it is alleged that 25 U.S.C. 1911, 1912, or 1913 has been violated:

(1) An Indian child who is or was the subject of any action for foster-care placement or termination of parental rights;

(2) A parent or Indian custodian from whose custody such child was removed; and

(3) The Indian child's Tribe.

(b) Upon a showing that an action for foster-care placement or termination of parental rights violated any provision of 25 U.S.C. 1911, 1912, or 1913, the court must determine whether it is appropriate to invalidate the action.

(c) To petition for invalidation, there is no requirement that the petitioner's rights under ICWA were violated; rather, a petitioner may challenge the action based on any violations of 25 U.S.C. 1911, 1912, or 1913 during the course of the child-custody proceeding.

§ 23.138 What are the rights to information about adoptees' Tribal affiliations?

Upon application by an Indian who has reached age 18 who was the subject of an adoptive placement, the court that entered the final decree of adoption must inform such individual of the Tribal affiliations, if any, of the individual's biological parents and provide such other information necessary to protect any rights, which may include Tribal membership, resulting from the individual's Tribal relationship.

§ 23.139 Must notice be given of a change in an adopted Indian child's status?

(a) If an Indian child has been adopted, the court must notify, by registered or certified mail with return receipt requested, the child's biological parent or prior Indian custodian and the Indian child's Tribe whenever:

(1) A final decree of adoption of the Indian child has been vacated or set aside; or
(2) The adoptive parent has voluntarily consented to the termination of his or her parental rights to the child.

(b) The notice must state the current name, and any former name, of the Indian child, inform the recipient of the right to petition for return of custody of the child, and provide sufficient information to allow the recipient to participate in any scheduled hearings.

(c) A parent or Indian custodian may waive his or her right to such notice by executing a written waiver of notice and filing the waiver with the court.

(1) Prior to accepting the waiver, the court must explain the consequences of the waiver and explain how the waiver may be revoked.
(2) The court must certify that the terms and consequences of the waiver and how the waiver may be revoked were explained in detail in English (or the language of the parent or Indian custodian, if English is not the primary language), and were fully understood by the parent or Indian custodian.

(3) Where confidentiality is requested or indicated, execution of the waiver need not be made in a session of court open to the public but still must be made before a court of competent jurisdiction in compliance with this section.
(4) The biological parent or Indian custodian may revoke the waiver at any time by filing with the court a written notice of revocation.
(5) A revocation of the right to receive notice does not affect any child-custody proceeding that was completed before the filing of the notice of revocation.

Recordkeeping

§ 23.140 What information must States furnish to the Bureau of Indian Affairs?

(a) Any State court entering a final adoption decree or order in any voluntary or involuntary Indian-child adoptive placement must furnish a copy of the decree or order within 30 days to the Bureau of Indian Affairs, Chief, Division of Human Services, 1849 C Street NW., Mail Stop 4513 MIB, Washington, DC 20240, along with the following information, in an envelope marked "Confidential":

(1) Birth name and birthdate of the Indian child, and Tribal affiliation and name of the Indian child after adoption;
(2) Names and addresses of the biological parents;
(3) Names and addresses of the adoptive parents;
(4) Name and contact information for any agency having files or information relating to the adoption;
(5) Any affidavit signed by the biological parent or parents asking that their identity remain confidential; and
(6) Any information relating to Tribal membership or eligibility for Tribal membership of the adopted child.

(b) If a State agency has been designated as the repository for all State-court adoption information and is fulfilling the duties described in paragraph (a) of this section, the State courts in that State need not fulfill those same duties.

§ 23.141 What records must the State maintain?

(a) The State must maintain a record of every voluntary or involuntary foster-care, preadoptive, and adoptive placement of an Indian child and make the record available within 14 days of a request by an Indian child's Tribe or the Secretary.

(b) The record must contain, at a minimum, the petition or complaint, all substantive orders entered in the child-custody proceeding, the complete record of the placement determination (including, but not limited to, the findings in the court record and the social worker's statement), and, if the placement departs from the placement preferences, detailed documentation of the efforts to comply with the placement preferences.

(c) A State agency or agencies may be designated to be the repository for this information. The State court or agency should notify the BIA whether these records are maintained within the court system or by a State agency.

§ 23.142 How does the Paperwork Reduction Act affect this subpart?

The collections of information contained in this part have been approved by the Office of Management and Budget under 44 U.S.C. 3501 *et seq*. and assigned OMB Control Number 1076-0186. Response is required to obtain a benefit. A Federal agency may not conduct or sponsor, and you are not required to respond to, a collection of information unless the form or regulation requesting the information displays a currently valid OMB Control Number. Send comments regarding this collection of information, including suggestions for reducing the burden, to the Information Collection Clearance Officer—Bureau of Indian Affairs, 1849 C Street N.W., Washington, DC 20240.

Effective Date

§ 23.143 How does this subpart apply to pending proceedings?

None of the provisions of this subpart affects a proceeding under State law for foster-care placement, termination of parental rights, preadoptive placement, or adoptive placement that was initiated prior to December 12, 2016, but the provisions of this subpart apply to any subsequent proceeding in the same matter or subsequent proceedings affecting the custody or placement of the same child.

Severability

§ 23.144 What happens if some portion of this part is held to be invalid by a court of competent jurisdiction?

If any portion of this part is determined to be invalid by a court of competent jurisdiction, the other portions of the part remain in effect. For example, the Department has considered separately whether the provisions of this part apply to involuntary and voluntary proceedings; thus, if a particular provision is held to be invalid as to one type of proceeding, it is the Department's intent that it remains valid as to the other type of proceeding.

Appendix C

Guidelines for Implementing the Indian Child Welfare Act, December 2016

The reader is referred to the entire version of the *Guidelines for Implementing the Indian Child Welfare Act, December 2016*, which can be found at https://www.bia.gov/bia/ois/dhs/icwa or https://www.westlaw.com/Browse/Home/AdministrativeDecisionsGuidance/FederalAdministrative-DecisionsGuidance/DepartmentoftheInterior/GuidelinesforImplementingtheIndianChildWelfareAct?contextData=(sc.Default)&transitionType=Default&VR=3.0&RS=cblt1.0. The guidelines further clarify the meaning of both the Indian Child Welfare Act and the regulations. For your convenience and reference, we provide as follows the table of contents to inform you of the contents of the guidelines.

Appendix D

State Codes Addressing Indian Child Welfare

The authors would like to thank and acknowledge Hannah Ditzenberger of the National Conference of State Legislatures for allowing us to reprint materials that she has developed. (Of note: Since N.C.S.L. developed its compilation of state statutes, Colorado passed a comprehensive ICWA bill and C.R.S. 19-1-126 has been replaced with C.R.S. 19-1.2-101 through 19-1.2-132. There may have been or may be in the future other changes to state laws. Thus, the practitioner should not assume that this list is complete, comprehensive, and up-to-date, and should always do an independent review of state statutes, as well as court rules where they exist.)

Below is a chart of state statutes related to Indian children in child welfare systems that NCSL identified.

State	State Statutes
Alabama	**Code of Ala. § 12-15-314** Dispositions for dependent children
Alaska	**Alaska Stat. § 25.23.060** Adoption: Execution of consent; consent as power of attorney **Alaska Stat. § 25.23.173** Indian child adoption reports **Alaska Stat. § 47.14.100** Powers and duties of department over care of child **Alaska Stat. § 47.14.300** Multidisciplinary child protection teams **Alaska Stat. § 47.70.010** Interstate Compact on the Placement of Children
Arizona	**A.R.S. § 8-105.01** Adoption; racial preferences; prohibition; exception **A.R.S. § 8-106** Adoption **A.R.S. § 8-815** Indian child welfare act inquiry **A.R.S. § 8-515.05** Removal of child from foster parent's home; requirements; notification; review **A.R.S. § 8-817** Initial screening and safety assessment and investigation protocols

	A.R.S. § 8-535 Notice of initial hearing; waiver; guardian ad litem **A.R.S. § 8-841** Dependency petition; service; preliminary orders; hearing **A.R.S. § 8-453** Powers and duties of the director **A.R.S. § 8-872** Permanent guardianship; procedure **A.R.S. § 8-874** Appointment of successor permanent guardian
Arkansas	**A.C.A. § 9-27-325** Juvenile Code – Hearings – Generally
California	**Cal Fam Code § 170, 175, 177, 180, 185** Indian Children Determination as to Indian tribe; Legislative findings and declarations; Indian child custody proceeding; Applicable law, Indian child custody proceeding; Indian child custody proceeding; Tribal participation **Cal Fam Code § 3041, 3404** Additional requirements for custody granted to nonparent; Custody proceedings involving Indian children **Cal Fam Code § 7660.5** Voluntary waiver of father's right to notice of adoption proceedings; Rights of Indian tribes **Cal Fam Code § 7822** Abandoned child **Cal Fam Code § 7892.5** Declaration of freedom for Indian child from custody or control of parent **Cal Fam Code § 7907.3, 7911.1** Interstate Compact on Placement of Children, Application to Indian child **Cal Fam Code § 7950** Order of placement preference; Consideration of race, color, or national origin; Application of Indian Child Welfare Act **Cal Fam Code § 8606.5, 8616.5, 8619, 8619.5, 8620** Consent to adoption by Indian child's parents; Postadoption contact agreements; Children of Indian ancestry (adoption); Petition for return of custody where adoption decree vacated or set aside; Inquiry into tribal status of child when relinquishing for adoption or executing adoption placement agreement **Cal Gov Code § 12019.40** Tribal Nation Grant Fund Program purpose **Cal Health & Saf Code § 1250.10, 1562.01**

	Psychiatric residential treatment facilities; Facility requirements; Regulations **Cal Health & Saf Code § 1505** California Community Child Care Facilities Act; Facilities exempt from licensing requirements **Cal Pen Code § 11166** Duty to report; Mandated reporters; Punishment for violation **Cal Prob Code § 1449, 1459, 1459.5, 1460.2, 1474, 1500.1** Guardianship, Conservatorship, and Other Protective Proceedings: Definitions; Legislative findings and declarations; Notice; Inability to afford counsel; Consent to nomination of guardian; Investigation and report by court-designated officer; Referrals to child welfare services agency **Cal Wel & Inst Code § 224 to 224.7; 305.5; 306.6; 309; 315; 317; 352; 358.1; 361; 361.2; 361.5; 361.7; 361.31; 366.24; 366.26** Delinquents and Wards of Juvenile Court: Indian child custody proceedings; Determination as to Indian tribe; Notice of hearings; Intervention; Full faith and credit; Testimony of qualified expert witness; State Department of Social Services programs to facilitate tribal participation in Indian child custody proceedings; Domicile of Indian child; Participation in dependency proceeding; Investigation by social worker when minor taken into temporary custody; Detention hearing; Appointment of counsel for parent or guardian unable to afford counsel; Appointment of counsel for child or nonminor dependent; Initial hearing; Continuance; Contents of social study; Limitations on control of parent, guardian, or Indian custodian; Foster care and placement with relative; Family reunification services; Involuntary foster care placement of or termination of parental rights over Indian child; Placement of Indian child; Tribal customary adoption to be considered as option when assessing children; Procedures for conducting hearings to terminate parental rights or determine adoption, guardianship, or placement of children adjudged dependent children of juvenile court **Cal Wel & Inst Code § 4096** Interagency placement committees and placement into short-term residential therapeutic programs, community treatment facility or out-of-state residential facility **Cal Wel & Inst Code § 10553.1; 10553.12; 10553.13-14** Agreement with Indian tribe to provide child welfare services or assistance under AFDC-FC program; Authority of federally recognized tribe; Tribally Approved Homes Compensation Program **Cal Wel & Inst Code § 16001.9** Rights of minors and nonminors in foster care **Cal Wel & Inst Code § 16500.9** Assistance for counties in complying with federal Indian Child Welfare Act.
Colorado	**C.R.S. 19-1-126** Compliance with the federal "Indian Child Welfare Act of 1978". **C.R.S. 19-2.5-502** Petitition initiation – petition form and content **C.R.S. 19-3-212**

	Notice of rights and remedies for families. **C.R.S. 19-3-602; 19-3-612** Motion for termination - separate hearing - right to counsel - no jury trial; Reinstatement of the parent-child legal relationship **C.R.S. 19-5.5-103** Uniform Unregulated Child Custody Transfer Act: Limits on applicability.
Connecticut	**C.G.S.A. § 17a-6g** Indian Child Welfare Act. Application to actions and proceedings involving an Indian child. **C.G.S.A. § 46b-116 to § 46b-116aa** Connecticut Indian Child Welfare Act **C.G.S.A. § 45a-706a** Application to actions and proceedings involving an Indian child
Delaware	**DE ST TI 31 § 381** Interstate Compact for the Placement of Children
Florida	**West's F.S.A. § 409.408** Interstate Compact for the Placement of Children **West's F.S.A. § 39.0137** Federal law; rulemaking authority
Georgia	**GA ST § 39-4A-7** Interstate Compact for the Placement of Children **GA ST § 15-11-100.1, 15-11-260.1** Dependency proceedings: Construction with federal law; Termination of parental rights: Construction with federal law
Idaho	**I.C. § 32-1704** De Facto Custodian Act: Commencement of Proceedings **I.C. § 16-1501** Adoption of children **I.C. § 16-1645** Child Protective Act: Exemption
Indiana	**IC 31-28-6-1** Interstate Compact for the Placement of Children **IC 31-9-2-58.4** Family law and juvenile law: Definitions
Iowa	**I.C.A. §§ 232B.1 to 232B.14** Iowa Indian Child Welfare Act
Kansas	**K.S.A. 38-2202 to 2203** Definitions; Jurisdiction; application of the Indiana child welfare act; age of child, presumptions; precedence of certain orders
Kentucky	**KRS § 615.030** Interstate compact for the placement of children
Louisiana	**LSA-Ch.C. Art. 103.1** Applicability of Indian Child Welfare Act **LSA-Ch.C. Art. 767.1, 767.2,**

	Federal Indian Child Welfare Act inquiry; Reason to know a child is an Indian child; federal Indian Child Welfare Act **LSA-Ch.C. Art. 749** Families in need of services: Contents of petition
Maine	**18-C M.R.S.A. § 5-213** Guardianship of Minor: Indian Child Welfare Act of 1978 and Maine Indian Child Welfare Act **18-C M.R.S.A. § 9-107** Adoption: Indian Child Welfare Act of 1978 and Maine Indian Child Welfare Act **22 M.R.S.A. § 3941 to 3955** Maine Indian Child Welfare Act
Michigan	**M.C.L.A. 712B.1 to 712B.41** Michigan Indian Family Preservation Act
Minnesota	**M.S.A. §§ 260.751 to 836** Minnesota Indian Family Preservation Act **M.S.A. § 260D.011** Child in voluntary foster care for treatment: Compliance with federal Indian Child Welfare Act and Minnesota Indian Family Preservation Act **M.S.A. § 260E.015** Reporting of maltreatment of minors: Compliance with federal Indian Child Welfare Act and Minnesota Indian Family Preservation Act **M.S.A. § 259.201** Adoption: Compliance with federal Indian Child Welfare Act and Minnesota Indian Family Preservation Act
Mississippi	**Miss. Code Ann. § 93-15-125** Termination of Parental Rights Law: Compliance with Indian Child Welfare Act **Miss. Code Ann. § 93-17-3** Adoption: Compliance with Indian Child Welfare Act
Montana	**MCA 41-3-1301 to 1329** Montana Indian Child Welfare Act **MCA 41-3-109** Child Abuse and Neglect: Proceedings subject to Indian Child Welfare Acts **MCA 42-2-102** Adoption of Child: Proceedings subject to Indian Child Welfare Acts
Nebraska	**Neb. Rev. Stat. §§ 43-1501 to 1516** Nebraska Indian Child Welfare Act **Neb.Rev.St. § 71-1906 to 1906.01** Native American foster homes; legislative intent; rules and regulations **Neb.Rev.St. § 43-263, 246** Juvenile Code: Issuance of process

	Neb.Rev.St. § 43-1103 Interstate Compact for the Placement of Children
Nevada	**N.R.S. 125E.010 to 125E.370** Custody of Indian Children **N.R.S. 127.1861, 1865** Adoption of Children: Petition to vacate order or decree of adoption of Indian child; Adoption records of Indian child to be provided to Indian child's tribe or United States Secretary of the Interior upon request **N.R.S. 62D.210** Proceedings Involving Indian Children
New Hampshire	**N.H. Rev. Stat. § 170-A:1** Interstate Compact for the Placement of Children.
New Mexico	**N. M. S. A. 1978 § 32A–28–1 to § 32A–28–42** Indian Family Protection Act **N. M. S. A. 1978, § 32A-4-28** Termination of parental rights; adoption decree **N. M. S. A. 1978, § 32A-5-4** Adoptions: Application of the federal Indian Child Welfare Act of 1978
New York	**NY SOC SERV § 39** Department and State Board of Social Welfare: Indian affairs
North Carolina	**N.C.G.S.A. § 143B-139.5A** Collaboration between Division of Social Services and Commission of Indian Affairs on Indian Child Welfare Issues **N.C.G.S.A. § 48-1-108** Adoptees subject to Indian Child Welfare Act **N.C.G.S.A. § 48-3-605** Consent to adoption: Execution of consent: procedures **N.C.G.S.A. § 7B-506** Hearing to determine need for continued nonsecure custody
North Dakota	**NDCC, 27–19.1–01 to 27–19.1–06** Indian Child Welfare **NDCC, 27-20.2-15** Indian child welfare--Active efforts and procedures
Oklahoma	**10 Okl.St.Ann. §§ 40.1 to 40.9** Indian Child Welfare Act **10 Okl.St.Ann. § 577** Interstate Compact for the Placement of Children--Enactment of compact—Text
Oregon	**O.R.S. §§ 419B.600 to 419B.665** Indian Child Welfare **O.R.S. § 419B.305, 517, 529** Hearing on petition alleging jurisdiction; inquiry concerning Indian child; protective custody; continuance; Mediation; Prospective adoptive parents

	O.R.S. § 419B.171, 452 Report of person taking child into custody; report to be sent to parents or tribe **O.R.S. § 419B.365, 366** Petition for guardianship; Rights of limited participation in guardianship proceeding; Indian child considerations **O.R.S. § 109.302; 350; 382** Parental consent; requirements concerning Indian child; Judgment of adoption or readoption; Petition to vacate judgment of adoption of Indian child
South Carolina	**SC ST § 27-16-80** Catawba Indian Claims Settlement Act
South Dakota	**SDCL § 25-6-24** Adoption: Due regard to be afforded Indian Child Welfare Act **SDCL § 25-5A-36** Voluntary Termination of Parental Rights: Due regard to be afforded Indian Child Welfare Act **SDCL § 26-7A-15, 15.1** Notice to parents, guardian, or custodian of child taken into temporary custody; Proceedings under certain chapters to which the Indian Child Welfare Act applies **SDCL § 26-8A-32** Protection of Children from Abuse or Neglect: Due regard to be afforded Indian Child Welfare Act **SDCL § 1-36-38** Indian Child Welfare Advisory Council
Tennessee	**T. C. A. § 37-1-101** Construction and application; compliance with Indian Child Welfare Act **T. C. A. § 36-1-111** Pre-surrender request for home study or preliminary home study; surrender of child; consent for adoption by parent; effect of surrender; form of surrender; waiver of interest
Utah	**U.C.A. 1953 § 26B-1-233** Indian Child Welfare Act Liaison--Appointment--Qualifications—Duties **U.C.A. 1953 § 26B-2-129** Licensure of tribal foster homes **U.C.A. 1953 § 80-2-1006** Sharing of records with Indian tribe under agreement **U.C.A. 1953 § 78B-6-107** Compliance with the Interstate Compact on Placement of Children--Compliance with the Indian Child Welfare Act **U.C.A. 1953 § 80-2a-101 (5)** Definitions of relative
Vermont	**15A V.S.A. §§ 1-107, 3-304, 2-406**

	Adoption Act: Proceedings subject to Indian Child Welfare Act, Content of Petition, Content of consent or relinquishment **33 V.S.A. § 5120** Juvenile Proceedings: Indian Child Welfare Act **33 V.S.A. § 5255, 5307** Temporary care hearings **33 V.S.A. § 5907** Interstate Compact on the Placement of Children
Washington	**Wash. Rev. Code §§ 13.38.01 to 13.38.190** Indian Child Welfare Act **Wash. Rev. Code § 13.34.040** Petition to court to deal with dependent child--Application of federal Indian child welfare act **Wash. Rev. Code §§ 13.34.132** Petition seeking termination of parent-child relationship **Wash. Rev. Code § 13.36.030** Guardianship petition--Requirements--Contents--Application of Indian child welfare act, federal servicemembers civil relief act, Washington service members' civil relief act **Wash. Rev. Code §§ 26.33.040, 45, 150** Petitions--Application of federal Indian child welfare act--Requirements--Federal servicemembers civil relief act statement and findings; Delay or denial of adoption on basis of race, color, or national origin prohibited; Petition for adoption **Wash. Rev. Code §§ 26.33.090, 160** Petition for relinquishment--Hearing--Temporary custody order--Notice--Order of relinquishment; Consent to adoption--When revocable—Procedure **Wash. Rev. Code § 74.13.621** Kinship care oversight committee
West Virginia	**W. Va. Code, § 48-22-303** Content of consent or relinquishment
Wisconsin	**Wis. Stat. §§ 48.01, 028, 31, 42, 48, 63, 88, 255, 977, 981** Children's Code: Intent, custody of Indian children, petition, termination of parental rights, authority of department, appointment of guardian, abused and neglected children, notice of hearing, Procedure, Restrictions on placements **W.S.A. 48.485** Transfer of Indian children to department for adoption **W.S.A. 48.831** Appointment of guardian for child without a living parent for adoptability finding **W.S.A. 48.837** Placement of children with nonrelatives for adoption

	W.S.A. 938.028 Indian juvenile welfare
Wyoming	**W.S.1977 § 14-3-401** Child Protection Act **W.S.1977 §§ 14-6-701 to 14-6-715** Wyoming Indian Child Welfare Act

For additional information please contact Hannah Ditzenberger, Policy Associate, Children and Families Program, hannah.ditzenberger@ncsl.org

Appendix E

Indian Entities Recognized and Eligible to Receive Services from the United States Bureau of Indian Affairs

The reader is referred to the *Federal Register Notice of Indian Entities Recognized and Eligible to Receive Services from the United States Bureau of Indian Affairs* (89 Fed. Reg. 99899), which is the current official listing of all federally recognized tribes in the United States, pursuant to the Federally Recognized Indian Tribe List Act of 1994 (Pub. Law 103-454, 108 Stat. 4791-4792). The reader is advised to contact the Bureau of Indian Affairs' contact person listed in the federal register notice for any additions and updates to the list, because occasionally the list changes before a new list is published. For additional contact information for federally recognized tribes, visit https://www.bia.gov.

Indian Child Welfare Act: Designated Tribal Agents for Service of Notice

The reader is referred to *Indian Child Welfare Act: Designated Tribal Agents for Service of Notice*, which designates an agent other than a tribal chairman for service of notice of proceedings under the act. See current list at https://www.bia.gov/bia/ois/dhs/icwa.

Directory of Contact Information for Tribal Justice Systems

The reader is referred to https://naicja.wildapricot.org/our-programs/directory for a directory of contact information for tribal justice systems.

Appendix F

Forms

MOTION TO INTERVENE

IN THE ______________ COURT FOR
______________ COUNTY, STATE OF ________

In the Matter of: ________,	)	Case No.
	)	
DOB: ____________,	)	MOTION TO INTERVENE
	)	
	)	
A Person Under Eighteen Years of Age.	)	
________________________	)	

COMES NOW the Petitioner, ________, the undersigned, and moves the Court to permit the Petitioner to intervene in this matter, a child custody proceeding involving an Indian child as defined by the Indian Child Welfare Act of 1978, 25 U.S.C. § 1903(1). As grounds for this motion, the Tribe states:

1. The child is an "Indian child" as defined by the Indian Child Welfare Act, 25 U.S.C. § 1903(4), in that the child is under age eighteen, date of birth ________________, and is a member of the Tribe, or is eligible for membership in the Tribe and the biological child of a member.
2. The ________________ is an "Indian tribe" as defined by the Indian Child Welfare Act, 25 U.S.C. § 1903(8), and this fact is entitled to judicial notice by virtue of publication in the Federal Register [list most recent publication of tribes entitled to federal services and benefits].
3. The Tribe is "the Indian child's tribe" as defined by the Indian Child Welfare Act, 25 U.S.C. § 1903(5), in that the child is a member of, or eligible for membership in, the Tribe.
4. This is a child custody proceeding as defined by the Indian Child Welfare Act, 25 U.S.C. § 1903(1).
5. The Indian Child Welfare Act, 25 U.S.C. § 1911(c) and 25 C.F.R. §23.111(c)(6)(ii-iii), gives the Indian child's tribe the right to intervene in this proceeding.

WHEREFORE, Petitioner requests the Court to grant the Motion to Intervene in the above-captioned proceeding.

______________, Signature

I hereby certify that a true and correct copy of this Motion was mailed to the opposing party, this __________ day of __________, 20 ___.

By:

MOTION TO TRANSFER JURISDICTION AND DISMISS CASE

IN THE ______________ COURT FOR ____________ COUNTY, STATE OF _________

In the Matter of: ________,	)	Case No.
	)	
DOB: ___________,	)	MOTION TO
	)	TRANSFER
	)	JURISDICTION AND
	)	DISMISS THE CASE
An Indian Person Under Eighteen	)	
Years of Age.	)	
____________________________	)	

COMES NOW the Petitioner, (parent, the Indian custodian, or the Indian child's Tribe), the undersigned, and petitions the Court to transfer this action (foster care proceeding or termination of parental rights proceeding unless state's version or interpretation of the ICWA allows transfer in other proceedings) to the ______ Tribal Court, (city)___________, (state)_________ , and to dismiss this state court proceeding pursuant to the Indian Child Welfare Act, 25 U.S.C. § 1911(b). As grounds therefore, the Petitioner states:

1. The child is an "Indian child" as defined by the Indian Child Welfare Act, 25 U.S.C. § 1903(4), in that the child is under eighteen years of age, unmarried date of birth ________, and the child is a member of the Tribe or is eligible for membership in the Tribe and the biological child of a member.
2. The ____________ is an "Indian tribe" as defined by the Indian Child Welfare Act, 25 U.S.C. § 1903(8), and this fact is

entitled to judicial notice by virtue of publication in the Federal Register, [list most recent publication of tribes entitled to federal services and benefits].

3. The Tribe is "the Indian child's tribe" as defined by the Indian Child Welfare Act, 25 U.S.C. § 1903(5), in that the child is a member of, or eligible for membership in, the Tribe.
4. This is a child custody proceeding as defined by the Indian Child Welfare Act, 25 U.S.C. § 1903(1).
5. The Indian Child Welfare Act, 25 U.S.C. § 1911(b), requires that the state court transfer this matter involving an Indian child to the jurisdiction of the Tribe, absent good cause to the contrary.
6. Good cause does not exist to deny transfer of this proceeding.

WHEREFORE Petitioner requests;

1. The Court to transfer the above-captioned proceeding to the ________Tribal Court, _______________ (address), ______ (city)_______, _______(state)_________; and
2. The Court promptly notify the Tribal Court in writing of the filing of the transfer petition and request the Tribal Court to timely notify this Court as to whether the Tribal Court wishes to decline the transfer; and
3. If the Tribal Court accepts the transfer, this Court shall expeditiously provide the Tribal court with all records related to the proceeding; and the Court shall dismiss this case relinquishing jurisdiction over this matter.

_______________, Signature

I hereby certify that a true and correct copy of this Motion was mailed to the opposing party this __________ day of _________, 20_____.

By:

CONFIDENTIAL

NOTICE OF CHILD CUSTODY PROCEEDING FOR INDIAN CHILD

Attorney or Party without Attorney	Court Use Only
Name: ______________________	
Address: ______________________	
Telephone Number: ______________	
E-mail Address (Optional): __________	
Attorney For (If applicable): _________	
State Bar No. (If applicable): _________	

XXXX COURT OF [STATE],
COUNTY OF: ______________________
Address: ______________________
Branch Name: ______________________
Telephone No.: ______________________

CASE NAME:	CASE NO.:

THIS IS A NOTICE OF CHILD CUSTODY PROCEEDING FOR INDIAN CHILD

TO *(Check all that apply)*

___ Parents or legal guardians ____ Indian custodians
___ Tribes* ____ BIA Regional Director

THAT based on the petition, a copy of which is attached to this notice, a child-custody proceeding under the Indian Child Welfare Act (25 U.S.C. §§ 1901 *et seq*) has been initiated for the following child: (*a separate notice must be filed for each child)*

Name: ______________________________________

Date of Birth: ___/___/___ Place of Birth: ____________

FOR the following proceeding: *(Check all that apply)*
___ Juvenile ___ Dependency ___ Delinquency
___ Declaration of Freedom from Control of Parent
___ Adoption ___ Custody ___ Guardianship
___ Termination of Parental Rights
___ Voluntary relinquishment of child by parent

WITH potential consequences of this proceeding are:
(*Describe here*) ________________________________

____

A HEARING WILL BE HELD on:
Date: ______ Time: ______ Location: ______ Room: ______

Type of Hearing: ________________________________

Address and telephone number of court: ________________

TRIBES
The child is or may be a member (or the child of a member) of the following Indian Tribes: (*List each*)

____

____

*Notice to the Tribe must be sent to the designated agent for service of ICWA notices.

Under the Indian Child Welfare Act:

- The parent or Indian custodian has the right to intervene in the proceedings.
- The child's Indian tribe has the right to intervene at any time in a State court proceeding for a foster care placement or termination of a parental right.

- If the Indian parent(s) or, if applicable, Indian custodian(s) is unable to afford counsel based on a determination of indigency by the court, counsel will be appointed to represent the parent or Indian custodian where authorized by State law.
- Where state law makes no provision for appointment of counsel in such proceedings, the court shall promptly notify the Secretary upon appointment of counsel, and the Secretary, upon certification of the presiding judge, shall pay reasonable fees and expenses out of the funds which may be appropriated.
- The parent, Indian custodian, and Tribe have the right to be granted, upon request, a specific amount of additional time (up to 20 additional days) to prepare for the proceedings due to circumstances of the particular case.
- The parent, Indian custodian, and Tribe have the right to petition the court for transfer of the proceeding to tribal court under 25 U.S.C. § 1911(b), absent objection by either parent and subject to declination by the tribal court.
- The parent(s) and Indian custodian(s) have the right to receive information regarding the potential legal consequences of the child-custody proceeding on their parental and custodial rights, including information directly from the court when not represented by an attorney, and the right to request language access services if not proficient in English.
- The parent, Indian custodian, and tribe have the right to expect that information will be kept confidential.

INFORMATION ON THE CHILD

a. The child's birth certificate is: ____ attached ____ unavailable

b. A copy of the Tribal registration card of _______ the child ____ the parent is attached ____ unavailable

c. Biological relative information is listed below.

(Indicate if any information is unknown or does not apply. Do not use the abbreviation "N/A")

Biological Mother	**Biological Father**
Name (include unmarried, married, and former names or aliases):	Name (include unmarried, married, and former names or aliases):
Current address:	Current address:
Former address:	Former address:
Birth date and place:	Birth date and place:
Tribe and location:	Tribe and location:
Tribal membership or enrollment number, if known:	Tribal membership or enrollment number, if known:
If deceased, date and place of death:	If deceased, date and place of death:
Additional information:	Additional information:

INFORMATION ON THE CHILD (CONTINUED)

Mother's Biological Mother (Child's Maternal Grandmother)	**Father's Biological Mother (Child's Paternal Grandmother)**
Name (include unmarried, married, and former names or aliases):	Name (include unmarried, married, and former names or aliases):
Current address:	Current address:

Former address:	Former address:
Birth date and place:	Birth date and place:
Tribe and location:	Tribe and location:
Tribal membership or enrollment number, if known:	Tribal membership or enrollment number, if known:
If deceased, date and place of death:	If deceased, date and place of death:
Mother's Biological Father (Child's Maternal Grandfather)	**Father's Biological Father (Child's Paternal Grandfather)**
Name (include unmarried, married, and former names or aliases):	Name (include unmarried, married, and former names or aliases):
Current address:	Current address:
Former address:	Former address:
Birth date and place:	Birth date and place:
Tribe and location:	Tribe and location:
Tribal membership or enrollment number, if known:	Tribal membership or enrollment number, if known:
If deceased, date and place of death:	If deceased, date and place of death:

INFORMATION ON THE CHILD (CONTINUED)

Mother's Biological Grandmother (Child's Maternal Great-grandmother)	**Mother's Biological Grandmother (Child's Maternal Great-grandmother)**
Name (include unmarried, married, and former names or aliases):	Name (include unmarried, married, and former names or aliases):
Current address:	Current address:
Former address:	Former address:
Birth date and place:	Birth date and place:
Tribe and location:	Tribe and location:
Tribal membership or enrollment number, if known:	Tribal membership or enrollment number, if known:
If deceased, date and place of death:	If deceased, date and place of death:

Mother's Biological Grandfather (Child's Maternal Great-grandfather)	**Mother's Biological Grandfather (Child's Maternal Great-grandfather)**
Name (include unmarried, married, and former names or aliases):	Name (include unmarried, married, and former names or aliases):
Current address:	Current address:

Former address:	Former address:
Birth date and place:	Birth date and place:
Tribe and location:	Tribe and location:
Tribal membership or enrollment number, if known:	Tribal membership or enrollment number, if known:
If deceased, date and place of death:	If deceased, date and place of death:

INFORMATION ON THE CHILD (CONTINUED)

Father's Biological Grandmother (Child's Paternal Great-grandmother)	**Father's Biological Grandmother (Child's Paternal Great-grandmother)**
Name (include unmarried, married, and former names or aliases):	Name (include unmarried, married, and former names or aliases):
Current address:	Current address:
Former address:	Former address:
Birth date and place:	Birth date and place:
Tribe and location:	Tribe and location:

Tribal membership or enrollment number, if known:	Tribal membership or enrollment number, if known:
If deceased, date and place of death:	If deceased, date and place of death:

Father's Biological Grandfather (Child's Paternal Great-grandfather)	**Father's Biological Grandfather (Child's Paternal Great-grandfather)**
Name (include unmarried, married, and former names or aliases):	Name (include unmarried, married, and former names or aliases):
Current address:	Current address:
Former address:	Former address:
Birth date and place:	Birth date and place:
Tribe and location:	Tribe and location:
Tribal membership or enrollment number, if known:	Tribal membership or enrollment number, if known:
If deceased, date and place of death:	If deceased, date and place of death:

INFORMATION ON THE CHILD (CONTINUED)

Indian Custodian Information	**Indian Custodian Information**
Name (include unmarried, married, and former names or aliases):	Name (include unmarried, married, and former names or aliases):
Current address:	Current address:
Former address:	Former address:
Birth date and place:	Birth date and place:
Tribe and location:	Tribe and location:
Tribal membership or enrollment number, if known:	Tribal membership or enrollment number, if known:
If deceased, date and place of death:	If deceased, date and place of death:

INFORMATION ON THE CHILD (CONTINUED)

(Answer "yes", "no", or "unknown")

a. Biological father is named on birth certificate ______________

b. Biological father has acknowledged parentage ______________

c. There has been a judicial declaration of parentage __________

d. There are other alleged fathers __ (If yes, name here: _____)

PARTIES NOTIFIED

Relationship to Child	Name	Address	Telephone Number

The following optional questions may also be helpful:

Has the child or any of the child's biological family members ever:

a. Attended an Indian school? ____________________

If so, provide details here: ____________________

b. Received medical treatment at an Indian health clinic or Health Service hospital? ____________________

If so, provide details here: ____________________

c. Lived on federal trust land, on an Indian reservation, or in an Alaska Native village? ____________________

If so, provide details here: ____________________

Other relative information (e.g., aunts, uncles, first and second cousins, stepparents)

Name/relationship to child	Current and former address	Birth date and place	Tribe and location

DECLARATION OF ACCURACY (to be completed by petitioner)
I am the petitioner. I have given all the information I have about the relatives and, if applicable, the Indian custodian, of the child who is the subject of the child-custody proceeding named on this form. I declare under penalty of perjury that the foregoing and all attachments are true and correct.

Name (printed) ______________________________

Signature ________________ Date ____________

Name (printed) ______________________________

Signature ____________ Date __________________

DECLARATION OF MAILING (to be completed by social worker)
I certify that a copy of this notice with a copy of the petition identified on page 1 of this notice was mailed as follows. Each copy was enclosed in an envelope with postage for registered or certified mail, return receipt requested, fully prepaid. The envelopes were addressed to each person, Tribe, or agency as indicated above. Each envelope was sealed and deposited with the U.S. Postal Service at [location] ______________ on [date] ___________

Name (printed) ______________________________

Title (printed) ______________________________

Signature __________________ Date ___________

ATTACHMENTS

[END OF FORM]

PARENTAL CONSENT TO [FOSTER CARE, ADOPTION, TERMINATION OF PARENTAL RIGHTS] OF AN INDIAN CHILD

In the Matter of the Petition of:

____

Petitioner

County of: __________________ State of: __________________

I, ____

Name of Parent or Indian Custodian

being the (choose one): Birth mother ___ Biological Father ____
Presumed Father ______ Other _____ Legal Parent ______
Of ____

Name of Child

(Gender: F ____ M ____) born on ______________________

Child's Birth Date

in ____

Child's Place of Birth

give my consent to the [foster care, adoption, termination of parental rights] of said child.

I desire to (place my child in foster care or terminate my rights to said child or consent to the adoption of said child) and prefer the child to be placed with _______, (name), my _______, (relationship if any), pursuant to the placement preferences of the Indian Child Welfare Act of 1978, 25 U.S.C. § 1915 (a) and (c).

I fully understand the consequences of my actions and no threats or promises have been made to me to get me to sign this consent.

I fully understand that I have the right to withdraw my consent to foster care placement at any time and regain custody of my child. I understand that I have the right to withdraw my consent to the termination of my parental rights before an order terminating my rights and/or an order of adoption has been issued at which time the child will be returned to my custody.

I wish to be notified if the final decree of adoption is set aside or vacated so that I may exercise my right to petition the Court for a return of custody and the child shall be returned if the court finds that it is in the best interests of the child to be returned to me.

This consent was not signed prior to, or within ten (10) days of the birth of the child.

I acknowledge that at the time of the execution of this consent I am not domiciled or residing on any Indian land or reservation.

I DO NOT WAIVE ANY OF MY RIGHTS UNDER THE INDIAN CHILD WELFARE ACT BY SIGNING THIS CONTRACT.

Additional Information

Name of the Indian child's Tribe: ___________________________

Tribal enrollment number for the parent (if known): __________

Tribal enrollment number for the Indian child (if known): _____

Name and address of the person or entity, if any, who arranged the placement: ___________________________________

Name and address of the prospective foster parents (if known):

____

I certify that the terms and consequences of the consent were explained on the record in detail in English (or the language of the parent or Indian custodian, if English is not the primary language) and were fully understood by the parent or Indian custodian. ______________________________ ____________ Signature of Court Official Date

PETITION REQUESTING EMERGENCY REMOVAL OF AN INDIAN CHILD

IN THE __________ COURT FOR _________
COUNTY, STATE OF __________

In the Matter of: ____________,	)	Case No.
	)	
DOB: _________,	)	PETITION
______________________________	)	REQUESTING
	)	EMERGENCY
An Indian Person Under Eighteen	)	REMOVAL OF AN
Years of Age.	)	INDIAN CHILD
______________________________	)	

COMES NOW the Petitioner, (SUPERVISING AGENCY AND EMPLOYEE NAME), the undersigned, and represents to the Court as follows:

1. The child/children's names, date(s) of birth, gender and address(s) and domicile are as follows:____________________
______________________;
2. The Tribal affiliation of the child is ___, the tribal affiliation of the mother is ______ _____________ and the tribal affiliation of the father is ___________; [alternatively, there is reason to know the child is an Indian child based upon the following facts __________________________, continuing due diligence will be used to determine if any of the potential tribes are the Indian child's tribe, and Indian Child Welfare Act will be applied to the child during that process];
3. The residence or the domicile of the Indian child is/is not believed to be on a reservation or in an Alaska Native village, the name of the Tribe affiliated with that reservation or village

is ________ (If the child is believed to reside or be domiciled on a reservation where the Tribe exercises exclusive jurisdiction over child-custody matters, a statement of efforts that have been made and are being made to contact the Tribe and transfer the child to the Tribe's jurisdiction);

4. The child/children's parents and Indian custodian(s) names, addresses, tribal affiliation and other contact information is as follows: ________________________________;
5. The following steps to provide notice to child's parents, Indian custodians, and Tribe about the emergency proceeding include the following ______________________________ ____________; (If the child's parents and Indian custodians are unknown, a detailed explanation of what efforts have been made to locate and contact them, including contact with the appropriate BIA Regional Director (see *www.bia.gov*);
6. The following efforts have been taken to assist the parents or Indian custodians so the Indian child may safely be returned to their custody: ______________________________ ____ ____; (NOTE: Per 25 C.F.R. § 23.113(e): An emergency proceeding regarding an Indian child should not be continued for more than 30 days unless the court makes the following determinations: (1) Restoring the child to the parent or Indian custodian would subject the child to imminent physical damage or harm; (2) The court has been unable to transfer the proceeding to the jurisdiction of the appropriate Indian Tribe; and (3) It has not been possible to initiate a "child-custody proceeding" as defined in 25 U.S.C. 1903(1).)

WHEREFORE, Petitioner requests the Court to make the following findings:

1. The minor child/children involved in this proceeding is/are an "Indian child(ren)" as defined by the Indian Child Welfare Act,

25 U.S.C. § 1903(4), in that the child is under eighteen years of age, unmarried date of birth ____________, and the child is a member of the Tribe or is eligible for membership in the Tribe and the biological child of a member. [or alternatively, There is reason to know the child is an Indian child and the Court will apply the Indian Child Welfare Act while the agency uses continued due diligence to determine if any of the potential tribes are the Indian child's tribe.]

2. The ______________ is an "Indian tribe" as defined by the Indian Child Welfare Act, 25 U.S.C. § 1903(8), and this fact is entitled to judicial notice by virtue of publication in the Federal Register, [list most recent publication of tribes entitled to federal services and benefits].
3. The Tribe is "the Indian child's tribe" as defined by the Indian Child Welfare Act, 25 U.S.C. § 1903(5), in that the child is a member of or eligible for membership in the Tribe.
4. This is a child custody proceeding as defined by the Indian Child Welfare Act, 25 U.S.C. § 1903(1), in that it involves a foster care placement, termination of parental rights, pre-adoptive placement or adoptive placement.
5. The emergency removal or placement is and/or continues to be necessary to prevent imminent physical damage or harm to the child based upon the following details and facts:__________
   ____
   ____; (If no emergency is found the court should order one of the following: Immediately terminate (or ensure that the agency immediately terminates) the emergency proceeding once the court or agency possesses sufficient evidence to determine that the emergency removal or placement is no longer necessary to prevent imminent physical damage or harm to the child. 25 C.F.R. § 23.113(b)(4). An emergency proceeding can be terminated by one or more of the following actions: (1) Initiation

of a child-custody proceeding subject to the provisions of ICWA; (2) Transfer of the child to the jurisdiction of the appropriate Indian Tribe; or (3) Restoring the child to the parent or Indian custodian. 25 C.F.R. § 23.113(c)).

6. The next hearing on this matter will be scheduled on __________.

IT IS SO ORDERED THIS ____ DAY OF ____, 20____.

_____________, Signature

I hereby certify that a true and correct copy of this Petition for Emergency Removal of an Indian Child was mailed to the opposing party this _____ day of ______________, 20____.

By:

WITHDRAWAL OF CONSENT TO [FOSTER CARE, ADOPTION, TERMINATION OF PARENTAL RIGHTS] OF AN INDIAN CHILD

In the Matter of the Petition of:

____

Petitioner

County of:________________ State of:________________

I, ____

Name of Parent

being the (choose one): Birth mother_____ Biological Father___ Presumed Father____ Other Legal Parent________________

Of ____________________ (Gender: F___ M___)

Name of Child

born on__________________In ______________________

Child's Birth Date Child's Place of Birth

withdraw my consent to the [foster care, adoption, termination of parental rights] of said child and understand that the child will be returned to me as soon as practicable.

______________________ ________________

Signature of Parent Date

____

Address of Parent

Selected Bibliography

Books, Articles, and Links

Adoptive Couple v. Baby Girl legal materials relating to the case found at https://sct.narf.org/caseindexes/adoptivecouplevbabygirl.html

Kirk Albertson, *Special Feature: Applying Twenty-five Years of Experience: The Iowa Indian Child Welfare Act*, 29 AM. INDIAN L. REV. 193 (2004/2005).

Diane Allbaugh, *Tribal Jurisdiction over Indian Children:* Mississippi Band of Choctaw Indians v. Holyfield, 16 AM. INDIAN L. REV. 533 (1991).

Mark Andrews, *"Active" Versus "Reasonable" Efforts: The Duties to Reunify the Family under the Indian Child Welfare Act and the Alaska Child in Need of Aid Statutes*, 19 ALASKA L. REV. 85 (2002).

David E. Arrodondo & Leonard P. Edwards, *Attachment, Bonding, and Reciprocal Connectedness.* J. CENTER FOR FAM. CHILD. & CTS. 109 (2000).

Neelum Arya & Addie C. Rolnick, "A Tangled Web of Justice: American Indian and Alaska Native Youth in Federal State, and Tribal Justice Systems," Washington, D.C.: Campaign for Youth Justice Policy Brief 1 (2008).

Barbara Ann Atwood, *Fighting over Indian Children: The Uses and Abuses of Jurisdictional Ambiguity*, 36 UCLA L. REV. 1051 (Aug. 1989).

Barbara Ann Atwood, *Flashpoints under the Indian Child Welfare Act: Toward a New Understanding of State Court Resistance*, 51 EMORY L.J. 587 (2002).

Barbara Ann Atwood, *Identity and Assimilation: Changing Definitions of Tribal Power Over Children*, 83 MINN. L. REV. 927 (1999).

Russel Lawrence Barsh, *The Indian Child Welfare Act of 1978: A Critical Analysis*, 31 HASTINGS L.J. 1287 (1980).

Elizabeth Bartholet, *Where Do Black Children Belong? The Politics of Race Matching in Adoption*, 139 U. PA. L. REV. 1163 (May 1991).

Theresa Rocha Beardall & Frank R. Edwards, *Abolition, Elimination, and Indian Child Welfare*, 11(3) COLUM. J. RACE & L. (2021).

Michelle K. Bennett, *Native American Children: Caught in the Web of the Indian Child Welfare Act*, 16 HAMLINE L. REV. 953 (Spring 1993).

Bethany R. Berger, *Race, Descent, and Tribal Citizenship*, 4 CAL. L. REV. CIR. 23 (2013).

I. N. Berlin, *Anglo Adoptions of Native Americans: Repercussions in Adolescence*, 17(2) J. AM. ACAD. CHILD PSYCHIATRY 387 (1978).

I. N. Berlin, *Suicide among American Indian Adolescents: An Overview*, 17(3) SUICIDE & LIFE-THREATENING BEHAVIOR 218 (1987).

Gretchen G. Biggs, *Is There Indian Country in Alaska? Forty-Four Million Acres in Legal Limbo*, 64 U. COLO. L. REV. 849 (1993).

Brackeen v. Haaland legal materials relating to the case found at https://turtletalk.blog/texas-v-zinke-documents-and-additional-materials/texas-v-haaland-supreme-court-documents/.

D. Marianne Brower Blair, *The New Oklahoma Adoption Code: A Quest to Accommodate Diverse Interests*, 33 TULSA L.J. 177 (1997).

Bringing our Children Home: An Introduction to the Indian Child Welfare Act found at http://www.ncjfcj.org/icwa-educational-resource-video.

Fredric Brandton, *Tradition and Judicial Review in the American Indian Tribal Court System*, 38 UCLA L. REV. 991 (Apr. 1991).

Laura Briggs, *Haaland v. Brackeen and Mancari: On History, Taking Children, and the Right-Wing Assault on Indigenous Sovereignty*, 56 CONN. L. REV. 1121 (2024).

Dusten Brown Statement in *Adoptive Couple v. Baby Girl found at* https://www.youtube.com/watch?v=Yzntaa7OZzY.

Hana E. Brown, *Who Is an Indian Child? Institutional Context, Tribal Sovereignty, and Race-Making in Fragmented States*, 85 AM. SOCIO. REV. 776 (2020).

JOHN F. BRYDE, MODERN INDIAN PSYCHOLOGY, INSTITUTE OF INDIAN STUDIES, UNIVERSITY OF SOUTH DAKOTA (1971).

BUREAU OF INDIAN AFFAIRS, FEDERAL INDIAN BOARDING SCHOOL INITIATIVE INVESTIGATIVE REPORT (May 2022), https://tinyurl.com/2s48xf95.

Margaret Burt, *How the New ICWA Regulations Impact Practice*, 36 CHILD L. PRAC. 10 (2017).

Michael J. Caduto and Joseph Bruchac, Keepers of the Animals: Native American Stories and Wildlife Activities for Children (Fulcrum Publishing, 1991).

Sen. Ben Nighthorse Campbell, *Introduction in Indian Law Symposium*, 24 N.M. L. Rev. 171 (Spring 1994).

Capacity Building Ctr. for Courts, ICWA Baseline Measures Project Findings Report (2020), https://tinyurl.com/spa68nm.

Jennifer Nutt Carleton, *The Indian Child Welfare Act: A Study in the Codification of the Ethnic Best Interests of the Child*, 81 Marq. L. Rev. 21 (1997).

Casey Family Programs, Child and Family Services Practice Model (2018), https://tinyurl.com/2p8xb4eb.

Casey Family Programs, Native American/Alaska Native Children Overview (2022), https://tinyurl.com/32aym6t4.

Robert N. Clinton, *Redressing the Legacy of Conquest: A Vision Quest for a Decolonized Federal Indian Law*, 46 Ark. L. Rev. 77 (1993).

Robert N. Clinton, *The Rights of Indigenous Peoples as Collective Group Rights*, 32 Ariz. L. Rev. 739 (1990).

Robert N. Clinton, *Tribal Courts and the Federal Union*, 26 Willamette L. Rev. 841 (Fall 1990).

Felix S. Cohen, Handbook of Federal Indian Law (1982 ed., Michie, Bobbs-Merrill).

Michael E. Connelly, *Tribal Jurisdiction under Section 1911(b) of the Indian Child Welfare Act of 1978: Are the States Respecting Indian Sovereignty?*, 23 N.M. L. Rev. 479 (Spring 1993).

Charmel L. Cross, *The Existing Indian Family Exception: Is It Appropriate to Use a Judicially Created Exception to Render the Indian Child Welfare Act of 1978 Inapplicable?*, 26 Cap. U.L. Rev. 847 (1997).

Terry L. Cross, *Child Welfare In Indian Country: A Story of Painful Removals*, 33 Health Affairs 12 (2014).

Michael J. Dale, *State Court Jurisdiction under the Indian Child Welfare Act and the Unstated Best Interest of the Child Test*, 27 Gonz. L. Rev. 353 (1991/1992).

Toni Hahn Davis, *The Existing Indian Family Exception to the Indian Child Welfare Act*, 69 N.D.L. Rev. 465 (1993).

Ella Cara Deloria, Waterlily (University of Nebraska Press, 1990).

Department of Health and Human Services, Office of Inspector General, Special Report, Opportunities for Act to Improve Child Welfare Services and Protections for Native American Children (Aug. 1994).

Brenda C. Desmond, *Montana Tribal Courts: Influencing the Development of Contemporary Indian Law*, 52 MONT. L. REV. 211 (Summer 1991).

Susanne Di Pietro, *Tribal Court Jurisdiction and Public Law 280: What Role for Tribal Courts in Alaska?*, 10 ALASKA L. REV. 335 (Dec. 1993).

US Senator Byron L. Dorgan & Joanne Shenandoah, *Attorney General's Advisory Committee on American Indian/Alaska Native Children Exposed to Violence: Ending Violence So Children Can Thrive*, United States Dept. of Justice, Office of Juvenile Justice and Delinquency Prevention (OJJDP) November 2014.

CRAIG J. DORSAY, THE INDIAN CHILD WELFARE ACT AND LAWS AFFECTING INDIAN JUVENILES, INDIAN LAW SUPPORT CENTER, NATIVE AMERICAN RIGHTS FUND (1984).

CRAIG J. DORSAY, STEVEN C. MOORE & THOMAS J. VAN NORMAN, 1992 UPDATE TO THE INDIAN CHILD WELFARE ACT AND LAWS AFFECTING INDIAN JUVENILES MANUAL, INDIAN LAW SUPPORT CENTER (1992).

Allison M. Dussias, *Geographically Based and Membership-Based Views of Indian Tribal Sovereignty: The Supreme Court's Changing Vision*, 55 U. PITT. L. REV. 1 (Fall 1993).

Kathleen A. Earle, *Child Abuse and Neglect: An Examination of American Indian Data,* Casey Family Programs; National Indian Child Welfare Association (2000).

Frank R. Edwards, Theresa Rocha Beardall & Hannah Curtis, *American Indian and Alaska Native Overexposure to Foster Care and Family Surveillance in the US: A Quantitative Overview of Contemporary System Contact*, 149 CHILD. & YOUTH SERVS. REV. 106915 (June 2023).

Robert E. Emery et al., *A Critical Assessment of Child Custody Evaluations: Limited Science and a Flawed System,* 6 PSYCHOL. SCI. PUBLIC INTEREST 1 (2005).

Jo Beth Eubanks, Comment, *Transracial Adoption in Texas: Should the Best Interests Standard Be Color-Blind?*, 24 ST. MARY'S L.J. 1225 (1993).

Executive Summary of the Preliminary Report of the Ninth Circuit Task Force on Gender Bias, 45 STAN. L. REV. 2153 (July 1993).

Susan B. Fallek, *In the Child's Best Interests: Termination of Parental Rights in Minnesota:* In re J.J.B., *390 N.W.2d 274*, 10 Hamline L. Rev. 693 (Fall 1987).

Zanita E. Fenton, *In a World Not Their Own: The Adoption of Black Children*, 10 Harv. Blackletter J. 39 (Spring 1993).

Matthew Fletcher, *Origins of the Indian Child Welfare Act: A Survey of Legislative History* (Michigan State Univ. College of Law, Indigenous Law and Policy Center 2009), http://www.law.msu.edu/indigenous/papers/2009-04.pdf.

Matthew Fletcher & Wenona Singel, ICWA and the Commerce Clause: The Indian Child Welfare at 30: Facing the Future, (Michigan State Univ. Press 2007, revised 2016).

Kim Forde-Mazrui, *Black Identity and Child Placement: The Best Interests of Black and Biracial Children*, 92 Mich. L. Rev. 925 (Feb. 1994).

Kathryn E. Fort, American Indian Children and the Law (Carolina Academic Press 2018).

Kathryn E. Fort, *The Road to Brackeen: Defending ICWA 2013–2023*, 72 Am. Univ. L. Rev. 1673 (2023).

Kathryn E. Fort & Adrian Smith, *The Indian Child Welfare Act During the Brackeen Years*, 74 Juv. & Fam. Ct. J. 9 (2023).

Kathryn E. Fort & Adrian Smith, *Indian Child Welfare Act Annual Case Law Update and Commentary 2019*, 8 Am. Indian L.J. 2 (2020).

Kathryn E. Fort & Adrian T. Smith, *Indian Child Welfare Act Annual Case Law Update and Commentary*, 7(2) Am. Indian L.J. Art. 2 (2019).

Kathryn E. Fort & Adrian T. Smith, *Indian Child Welfare Act Annual Case Law Update and Commentary 2018*, 6(2) Am. Indian L.J. Art. 2 (2018).

Phillip P. Frickey, *Congressional Intent, Practical Reasoning and the Dynamic Nature of Federal Indian Law*, 78 Cal. L. Rev. 1137 (October 1990).

Joaquin R. Gallegos & Kathryn E. Fort, *Protecting the Public Health of Indian Tribes: the Indian Child Welfare Act,* 8 Harv. Pub. Health Rev. (2018), http://harvardpublichealthreview.org/protecting-the-public-health-of-indian-tribes-the-indian-child-welfare-act/

Sophia Gatowski, Alicia Summers & Bree Bussey, *The Effectiveness of an ICWA Court at Achieving Improved ICWA Implementation and Outcomes: A Pre-Post Intervention Study*, 74 Juv. & Fam. Ct. J. 51–70 (2023), https://doi.org/10.1111/jfcj.12233.

John W. Gillingham, *Pathfinder: Tribal, Federal, and State Court Subject Matter Jurisdictional Bounds: Suits Involving Native American Interests*, 18 AM. INDIAN L. REV. 73 (1993).

Timothy P. Glynn, *The Role of Race in Adoption Proceedings: A Constitutional Critique of the Minnesota Preference Statute*, 77 MINN. L. REV. 925 (April 1993).

Carole Goldberg, *Critical Race Studies: Descent into Race*, 49 UCLA L. REV. 1373 (2002).

Donna J. Goldsmith, *Individual vs. Collective Rights: Indian Child Welfare Act*, 13 HARV. WOMEN'S L.J. 1 (Spring 1990).

JOSEPH GOLDSTEIN, ANNA FREUD & ALBERT J. SOLNIT, BEYOND THE BEST INTERESTS OF THE CHILD (New York: The Free Press, 1973).

Gover, Stetson & Williams, P.C., *Tribal-State Dispute Resolution: Recent Attempts*, 36 S.D. L. REV. 277 (1991).

Lorie Graham, *Content: Indigenous Peoples: Reparations and the Indian Child Welfare Act*, 25 LEGAL STUD. F. 619 (2001).

Lorie M. Graham, *"The Past Never Vanishes": A Contextual Critique of the Existing Indian Family Doctrine*, 23 AM. INDIAN L. REV. 1 (1998/1999).

Sandra Hansen, *Survey of Civil Jurisdiction in Indian Country*, 16 AM. INDIAN L. REV. 319 (1991).

Cynthia G. Hawkins-Leon, *The Indian Child Welfare Act and the African American Tribe: Facing the Adoption Crisis*, 36 BRANDEIS J. FAM. L. 201 (Spring 1997/1998).

The Heart of ICWA: Becky, https://www.youtube.com/watch?v=tYMG13pKq4Y.

The Heart of ICWA: Fawn, https://www.youtube.com/watch?v=VpxlN7vL_lA.

The Heart of ICWA: Lukas, https://www.youtube.com/watch?v=quYwcvZQVEM

The Heart of ICWA: Rhonda, https://www.youtube.com/watch?v=oTNNjA-

Margaret Howard, *Transracial Adoption: Analysis of the Best Interests Standard*, 59 NOTRE DAME L. REV. 503 (1984).

Mary Jo Brooks Hunter, *Special Report: Minnesota Supreme Court Foster Care and Adoption Task Force*, 19 HAMLINE J. PUB. L. & POL'Y 1 (1997).

Scott C. Idleman, *Multiculturalism and the Future of Tribal Sovereignty*, 35 COLUM. HUM. RTS. L. REV. 589 (Summer 2004).

Kristen Jones Indermark, *Permissive Intervention—Grandparents' Key to Entering Adoption Proceedings*, 26 GA. L. REV. 787 (Spring 1992).

Margaret D. Jacobs, *Remembering the "Forgotten Child": The American Indian Child Welfare Crisis of the 1960s and 1970s*, 37 AM. INDIAN Q. 136 (2013).

Cheyanna L. Jaffke, *The "Existing Indian Family" Exception to the Indian Child Welfare Act: The States' Attempt to Slaughter Tribal Interests in Indian Children*, 66 LA. L. REV. 733 (2006).

James M. Jannetta, *Reciprocity between State and Tribal Legal Systems*, 71 MICH. B. J. 400 (May 1992).

B. J. Jones, *In Their Native Lands: The Legal Status of American Indian Children in North Dakota*, 75 N.D.L. REV. 241 (1999).

B. J. Jones, *The Indian Child Welfare Act: In Search of a Federal Forum to Vindicate the Rights of Indian Tribes and Children Against the Vagaries of State Courts*, 73 N.D.L. REV. 395 (1997).

B. J. Jones, *Tribal Considerations in Comity and Full Faith and Credit Issues*, 68 N.D.L. REV. 689 (1992).

B. J. Jones, *Welcoming Tribal Courts into the Judicial Fraternity: Emerging Issues in Tribal-State and Tribal-Federal Court Relations*, 24 WM. MITCHELL L. REV. 457 (1998).

Mikayla Jones, *Heads Held High and Hands Holding Hope: The Victory and Vulnerabilities of the Indian Child Welfare Act After* Haaland v. Brackeen, 103 NEB. L. REV. 65 (2024).

Juvenile and Family Law, 16 HAMLINE L. REV. 624 (Spring 1993).

Lynn A. Kerbeshian, *Indians—Domicile: Federal Definition of Domicile Determines Jurisdiction under Indian Child Welfare Act*, 66 N.D.L. REV. 553 (1990).

Ester C. Kim, *Mississippi Band of Choctaw Indians v. Holyfield: The Contemplation of All, The Best Interests of None,* 43 RUTGERS L. REV. 761 (Spring 1991).

Rebecca L. Koch, *Transracial Adoption in Light of the Foster Care Crisis: A Horse of a Different Color*, 10 N.Y.L. SCH. J. HUM. RTS. 147 (Fall 1992).

Adrea Korthase, Sophia I. Gatowski & Mark Erickson, *Indian Child Welfare Act (ICWA) Courts: A Tool for Improving Outcomes for American Indian*

Children and Families, NAT'L COUNCIL JUV. & FAM. CT. JUDGES (2021), https://www.ncjfcj.org/wp-content/uploads/2021/04/NCJFCJ_ICWA_Tool_UMD_Final.pdf.

Rose M. Kreider, Interracial Adoptive Families and Their Children: 2008, *in* NATIONAL COUNCIL FOR ADOPTION FACTBOOK V (2011).

Patrice Kunesh-Hartman, *The Indian Child Welfare Act of 1978: Protecting Essential Tribal Interests*, 60 U. COLO. L. REV. 131 (1989).

Teresa D. LaFromboise et al., *Family, Community, and School Influences on Resilience Among American Indian Adolescents in the Upper Midwest,* 34 J. COMMUNITY PSYCHOLOGY 193 (2006).

Keri B. Lazarus, *Adoption of Native American and First Nations Children: Are The United States and Canada Recognizing the Best Interests of the Children?*, 14 ARIZ. J. INT'L & COMP. LAW 255 (1997).

Stacy L. Leeds, *Cross-Jurisdictional Recognition and Enforcement of Judgments: A Tribal Court Perspective*, 76 N.D.L. REV. 311 (2000).

Michelle L. Lehmann, *The Indian Child Welfare Act of 1978: Does It Apply to the Adoption of an Illegitimate Indian Child?*, 38 CATH. U. L. REV. 511 (Winter 1989).

Michael J. Leiber et al., *An Examination of the Factors that Influence Justice Decision Making in Anchorage and Fairbanks, Alaska, An Assessment Study, Alaska* (2006).

Wendy Lewis, *The Role of Domicile in Adopting Indian Children:* Mississippi Band of Choctaw Indians v. Holyfield, 1990 UTAH L. REV. 899 (1990).

Elizabeth Low, *Keeping Cultural Bias Out of the Courtroom: How ICWA "Qualified Expert Witnesses" Make a Difference*, 44 AM. INDIAN L. REV. 43, 61 (2019).

Joan Mahoney, *The Black Baby Doll: Transracial Adoption and Cultural Preservation,* 59 UMKC L. REV. 487 (Spring 1991).

Kevin Noble Maillard, *Parental Ratification: Legal Manifestations of Cultural Authenticity in Cross-Racial Adoption*, 28 AM. INDIAN L. REV. 107 (2003/2004).

THOMAS MAILS, FOOLS CROW: WISDOM AND POWER (Council Oak Books, 1991).

Solangel Maldonado, *Race, Culture, and Adoption: Lessons from Mississippi Band of Choctaw Indians v. Holyfield*, 17(1) COLUM. J. GENDER & L. (2008).

Richard B. Maltby, *The Indian Child Welfare Act of 1978 and the Missed Opportunity to Apply the Act in Guardianships*, 46 ST. LOUIS U. L.J. 213 (2002).

Andrea Jane Martin, *Beyond Brackeen: Active Efforts Toward Antiracist Child Welfare Policy*, 42 YALE L. & POL'Y REV. 42 (2023).

Richard McCartney, *The American Indian Child Welfare Crisis: Cultural Genocide or First Amendment Preservation?*, 7 COLUM. HUM. RTS. L. REV. 529 (1975).

Thomas P. McLish, Note, *Tribal Sovereign Immunity: Searching for Sensible Limits*, 88 COLUM. L. REV. 173 (Jan. 1988).

D. McShane, *An Analysis of Mental Health Research with American Indian Youth*, 11(2) J. ADOL. 87 (1988).

Christine Metteer, *Hard Cases Making Bad Law: The Need for Revision of the Indian Child Welfare Act*, 38 SANTA CLARA L. REV. 419 (1998).

Christine Metteer, *The Trust Doctrine, Sovereignty, and Membership: Determining Who Is Indian*, 5 RUTGERS RACE & L. REV. 53 (2003).

Christine M. Metteer, *A Law Unto Itself: The Indian Child Welfare Act as Inapplicable and Inappropriate to the Transracial/Race-Matching Adoption Controversy*, 38 BRANDEIS L.J. 47 (Fall 1999/Fall 2000).

Native American Rights Fund. *A Practical Guide to the Indian Child Welfare Act*, https://www.narf.org/nill/documents/icwa/.

Native American Rights Fund, *A Victory for Rule of Law and Tribal Children*, 48(2) NARF LEGAL REV. (2023), https://narf.org/nill/documents/nlr/nlr48-2.pdf.

Raymond Neckoway et al., *Is Attachment Theory Consistent with Aboriginal Parenting Realities?*, 3 FIRST PEOPLES CHILD & FAM. REV. 65 (2007).

Sharon O'Brien, *Tribes and Indians: With Whom Does the United States Maintain a Relationship?*, 66 NOTRE DAME L. REV. 1461 (1991).

Shannon O'Loughlin, *A Survey and Analysis of Tribal-State Indian Child Welfare Act Agreements* (Rockville MD: Association on American Indian Affairs, June 2017), https://www.indian-affairs.org/uploads/8/7/3/8/87380358/icwa_tribal-state_agreements_report.pdf.

Michelle Therese Paquin, *A Minnesota Lawyer's Guide to the Indian Child Welfare Act*, 10 LAW & INEQ. 311 (June 1992).

Elizabeth A. Pearce, *Self-Determination for Native Americans: Land Rights and the Utility of Domestic and International Law*, 22 COLUM. HUM. RTS. L. REV. 361 (Spring 1991).

Twila L. Perry, *Race and Child Placement: The Best Interests Test and the Cost of Discretion*, 29 J. FAM. L. 51 (1990/1991).

PIMA COUNTY JUVENILE CT. CENTER, INDIAN CHILD WELFARE ACT COURT DATA BRIEF (Mar. 2022).

Frank R. Pommersheim, *The Crucible of Sovereignty: Analyzing Issues of Tribal Jurisdiction*, 31 ARIZ. L. REV. 329 (Apr. 1989).

Frank R. Pommersheim, *The Reservation as Place: A South Dakota Essay*, 34 S.D. L. REV. 246 (1989).

Hon. Maurice Portley, *The Indian Child Welfare Act: A Primer*, 36 ARIZ. ATT'Y 24 (2000).

John W. Ragsdale, Jr., *Indian Reservations and the Preservation of Tribal Culture: Beyond Wardship to Stewardship*, 59 UMKC L. REV. 503 (Spring 1991).

John Robert Renner, *The Indian Child Welfare Act and Equal Protection Limitations on the Federal Power over Indian Affairs*, 17 AM. INDIAN L. REV. 129 (1992).

Rethinking the Trust Doctrine in Federal Indian Law, 98 HARV. L. REV. 422 (Dec. 1984).

Sandra C. Ruffin, *Postmodernism, Spirit Healing, and the Proposed Amendments to the Indian Child Welfare Act*, 30 MCGEORGE L. REV. 1221 (1999).

Kim Laree Schnuelle, *When the Bough Breaks: Federal and Washington State Indian Child Welfare Law and Its Applications*, 17 U. PUGET SOUND L. REV. 101 (Fall 1993).

Laura J. Schwartz, *Religious Matching for Adoption: Unraveling the Interests behind the "Best Interests" Standard,* 25 FAM. L. Q. 171 (Summer 1991).

Darla M. Silva, *Family Law,* 21 N.M. L. REV. 677 (Summer 1991).

David Simmons & Jack Trope, P.L. 105-89 Adoption and Safe Families Act of 1997: Issues for Tribes and States Serving Indian Children (The National Resource Center for Organizational Improvement, 1999).

David E. Simmons, *Improving the Well-Being of American Indian and Alaska Native Children and Families Through State-Level Efforts to Improve Indian Child Welfare Act Compliance*, Nat'l Indian Child Welfare Ass'n (Oct. 2014).

Alex Tallchief Skibine, *Applicability of Federal Laws—General Application to Indian Tribes and Reservation Indians*, 25 U. C. Davis L. Rev. 85 (Fall 1991).

Alex Tallchief Skibine, *Deference Owed Tribal Court's Jurisdictional Determinations: Towards Co-Existence, Understanding, and Respect between Different Cultural and Judicial Norms*, 24 N.M. L. Rev. 191 (Spring 1994).

Patti Slider, *Indian Tribal Law*, 63 J. Kan. B. Ass'n 20 (May 1994).

Sheldon Spotted Elk, *The Rights of Indian Children: Indian Child Welfare Act Regulations*, ABA Section of Litigation (2017), https://qa.americanbar.org/publications/litigation-committees/childrens-rights/articles/2017/rights-of-indian-children-indian-child-welfare-act-regulations.html.

A. Streissgurth, A Manual on Adolescents and Adults with Fetal Alcohol Syndrome with Special Reference to American Indians, Washington, D.C. (Indian Health Services Publication 1988).

Rennard Strickland, *Indian Law and the Miner's Canary: The Signs of Poison Gas*, 39 Clev. St. L. Rev. 483 (1991).

Alicia Summers, *Exploring Indian Child Welfare Act Implementation and Case Outcomes*, 74 Juv. & Fam. Ct. J. 37–50 (2023), https://doi.org/10.1111/jfcj.12232.

Alicia Summers, National Council of Juvenile and Family Court Judges, *Technical Assistance Bulletin: Disproportionality Rates for Children of Color* (2014).

Task Force on American Indian and Alaska Native Children Exposed to Violence, Hearings, https://www.justice.gov/archives/defendingchildhood/task-force-hearings-0.

Richard B. Taylor, *Curbing the Erosion of the Rights of Native Americans: Was the Supreme Court Successful in* Mississippi Band of Choctaw Indians v. Holyfield?, 29 J. Fam. L. 171 (1990/1991).

Roger A. Tellinghuisen, *The Indian Child Welfare Act of 1978: A Practical Guide with (Limited) Commentary*, 34 S.D. L. Rev. 660 (1988/1989).

Edward L. Thompson, *Protecting Abused Children: A Judge's Perspective on Public Law, Deprived Child Proceedings and the Impact of the Indian Child Welfare Acts*, 15 Am. Indian L. Rev. 1 (1990).

Tribal Justice, http://makepeaceproductions.com/tribaljustice/.

Tribal Law and Policy Institute Indian Child Welfare Act Resources, http://www.tribal-institute.org/lists/icwa.htm.

Jack Trope & Shannon O'Loughlin. *A Survey and Analysis of Select Title IV-E Tribal State Agreements* (Rockville, MD: Association on American Indian Affairs, March 2014) at 1 *found at* http://www.narf.org/nill/resources/title-iv-e/20140320_title_iv-e_report.pdf.

Jack Trope & Adrian Smith, *The Continued Protection of Indian Children and Families after Adoptive Couple v. Baby Girl: What the Case Means and How to Respond,* 2 Am. Indian L. Rev. 434 (2014).

Rebecca Tsosie, *Native Americans and the Constitution: Tribalism, Constitutionalism, and Cultural Pluralism: Where Do Indigenous Peoples Fit Within Civil Society?*, 5 U. Pa. J. Const. L. 357 (2003).

David M. Ujke, *Tribal Court Jurisdiction in Domestic Relations Matters Involving Indian Children: Not Just a Matter of Comity*, 66 Wis. L. Rev. 10 (Aug. 1993).

Lynn Klicker Uthe, *The Best Interests of Indian Children in Minnesota,* 17 Am. Indian L. Rev 237 (1992).

Robert M. Utley, The Lance and the Shield: The Life and Times of Sitting Bull (Henry Holt & Co. 1993).

Gloria Valencia-Weber, *Tribal Courts: Custom and Innovative Law,* 24 N.M. L. Rev. 225 (Spring 1994).

Ivy N. Voss, *In the Best Interest: The Adoption of F. H., An Indian Child*, 8 BYU J. Pub. L. 151 (Jan. 1993).

Bruce A. Wagman, *Advancing Tribal Sovereign Immunity as a Pathway to Power*, 27 U.S.F. L. Rev. 419 (Winter 1993).

Peter K. Wahl, *Children in the Law Issue: Contributors Little Power to Help Brenda? A Defense of the Indian Child Welfare Act and Its Continued Implementation in Minnesota*, 26 Wm. Mitchell L. Rev. 811 (2000).

Patricia M. Wald, *One Nation Indivisible with Liberty and Justice for All: Lessons from the American Experience for New Democracies*, 59 Fordham L. Rev. 283 (November 1990).

Andrea V. W. Wan, *The Indian Child Welfare Act and Inupiat Customs: A Case Study of Conflicting Values, with Suggestions for Change*, 21 ALASKA L. REV. 43 (2004).

Stan Watts, *Voluntary Adoptions under the Indian Child Welfare Act of 1978: Balancing the Interests of Children, Families, and Tribes*, 63 S. CAL. L. REV. 213 (Nov. 1989).

J. Westermeyer, *The Apple Syndrome in Minnesota: A Complication of Racial-Ethnic Discontinuity*, 10(2) J. OPERATIONAL PSYCHIATRY 134 (1979).

Amanda B. Westphal, *An Argument in Favor of Abrogating the Use of the Best Interests of the Child Standard to Circumvent the Jurisdictional Provisions of the Indian Child Welfare Act in South Dakota*, 49 S.D. L. REV. 107 (2003).

Maureen White Eagle et al., *Responses to the Co-Occurrence of Domestic Violence and Child Maltreatment in Indian Country: Repairing the Harm and Protecting Children and Mothers* (Tribal Law and Policy Institute, December 2011).

SANDY WHITE HAWK, A CHILD OF THE INDIAN RACE: A STORY OF RETURN (Minnesota Historical Society Press 2022).

David Williams, *Legitimation and Statutory Interpretation: Conquest, Consent, and Community in Federal Indian Law*, 80 VA. L. REV. 403 (Mar. 1994).

Jason R. Williams et al., *What Is Measured Is What Is Done: Methods to Measure Compliance with the Indian Child Welfare Act*, 4(2) AM. INDIAN L.J. Art. 8 (2016).Robert A. Williams, *Encounters on the Frontiers of International Human Rights Law: Redefining the Terms of Indigenous Peoples' Survival in the World*, 1990 DUKE L. J. 660 (Sept. 1990).

Gorden K. Wright, *Recognition of Tribal Decisions in State Courts*, 37 STAN. L. REV. 1397 (May 1985).

Marcia Yablon, *The Indian Child Welfare Act Amendments of 2003*, 38 FAM. L.Q. 689, 695 (2005).

Marlon N. Yarbrough, *Trans-Racial Adoption: The Genesis or Genocide of Minority Cultural Existence*, 15 S.U. L. REV. 353 (Fall 1988).

Soo See Yeo, *Bonding and Attachment of Australian Aboriginal Children*, 12 CHILD ABUSE REV. 292 (2003).

Alison Harvison Young, *Reconceiving the Family: Challenging the Paradigm of the Exclusive Family*, 6 AM. U. J. GENDER & L. 505 (1998).

Table of Cases

Index

V

W

Y